Ethnic Russia
in the USSR

Pergamon Policy Studies on the Soviet Union and Eastern Europe

Related Titles

PERGAMON POLICY STUDIES

ON THE SOVIET UNION AND EASTERN EUROPE

Ethnic Russia in the USSR
The Dilemma of Dominance

Edited by
Edward Allworth

Published in cooperation with the
Program on Soviet Nationality Problems,
Columbia University in the City of New York

Pergamon Press
NEW YORK • OXFORD • TORONTO • SYDNEY • FRANKFURT • PARIS

C./

Burgess
DK
33
.E83
1980

Pergamon Press Offices:

U.S.A   Pergamon Press Inc., Maxwell House, Fairview Park, Elmsford, New York 10523, U.S.A.

U.K.   Pergamon Press Ltd., Headington Hill Hall, Oxford OX3 0BW, England

CANADA   Pergamon of Canada Ltd., 150 Consumers Road, Willowdale, Ontario M2J 1P9, Canada

AUSTRALIA   Pergamon Press (Aust) Pty. Ltd., P.O. Box 544, Potts Point, NSW 2011, Australia

FRANCE   Pergamon Press SARL, 24 rue des Ecoles, 75240 Paris, Cedex 05, France

FEDERAL REPUBLIC Pergamon Press GmbH, 6242 Kronberg/Taunus,
OF GERMANY   Pferdstrasse 1, Federal Republic of Germany

C.1

Library of Congress Cataloging in Publication Data

Main entry under title:

Ethnic Russia in the USSR.

 (Pergamon policy studies)
 Bibliography: p.
 Includes index.
 1. Russia—Ethnic relations. 2. Minorities—Russia.
I. Allworth, Edward.
DK33.E83 1979 301.45'1'0947 79-22959
ISBN 0-08-023700-2

Printed in the United States of America

Contents

CONTENTS

Part VII - Shared Language/Jargonized Language:
        The Risk to Ethnic Identity

Part VIII - Blurring the Russian Demographic Profile

Part IX - Leadership Quandaries in a Multiethnic State

CONTENTS

Preface

A substantial study of contemporary Russia, distinct from the USSR, becomes more and more desirable as other ethnic groups of the Soviet Union progress and emerge in Western understanding from the generality to which they had long been consigned. An inquiry of this kind is possible today because so many scholars in North America and Europe concern themselves with Russia as such, despite continuing difficulties with distinguishing it quantitatively or qualitatively from non-Russia in Soviet sources. No standard work presently in print seems to provide such a view of ethnic Russia.

The present volume, eighth in a series about the Soviet ethnic question, fills an important part of the gap in knowledge of Russia today by focusing upon signs of modern ethnicity, recent currents in particularist Russian thought and outlook, and developments affecting them. This is a book of argument, however, rather than an encyclopedic handbook. Appendix A has been prepared from data for 1959 and 1970 expressly in order to show readers rather precisely where Russians are scattered throughout the RSFSR and the additional union republics, and to offer a detailed basis for comparing forthcoming figures promised in a year or two by the 1979 Soviet census. The central problems and propositions addressed here were put forward in this form and discussed first in the Seminar on Soviet Nationality Problems, Columbia University, six of whose members appear here as authors. The main themes were then focused during the Colloquium, "Ethnic Russia Today: Undergoing an Identity Crisis?" organized and sponsored by the Program on Soviet Nationality Problems and the Russian Institute, Columbia University, May 5-6, 1978, in New York City.

Among many others who helped bring this book into being are Professors Robert L. Belknap, William E. Harkins, Marc

Raeff, George V. Shevelov, Immanuel Wallerstein, and Dr.
Seweryn Bialer, whose early advice benefited both the
planning and execution of the effort. In the Columbia
University Libraries, Ms. Diane Goon, Ms. Eileen R. McIlvaine,
and Ms. Nina Lencek, and in the New York Public Library,
Dr. Victor Koressaar, were especially helpful in locating
needed references and sources. Mr. Christopher Brest
supplied the cartography for the map in the Introduction. Ms.
Patricia Blake, Professor John Malmsted, Dr. Gene Sosin, Ms.
Pearl Spiro, and graduate student Bruce P. Cooper aided in
tracking down elusive facts. Ms. Marjean Ebong and Ms.
Janet Allworth repeatedly with good cheer eased the
administrative path for this multiauthored manuscript.
Graduate assistants Linda Cook, Christopher Doersam, and
Kenneth E. Nyirady, with Judith Strong (who also prepared
the Index), performed heroically in checking and completing
the many, diverse footnotes and vexing bibliographical
references.

Material assistance in preparing the manuscript for this
volume came especially from the Program on Soviet Nationality
Problems. Grants from the Ford Foundation and from the
Columbia University Soviet and East European Languages and
Area Studies Center funded under the National Defense
Education Act, in support of the entire activity, are most
gratefully acknowledged.

Except in the discussions of Professor K. D. Kristof and
Mr. Leopold Labedz, where a hierarchical presentation of
"ethnic" and "national" is outlined, the term "ethnic group"
will be employed generically for Russian and non-Russian
groups of the Czarist Empire as well as the USSR. "Nation"
or "nationality" will be retained in the text in quoted material.
"Ethnocentrism," therefore, universally replaced "nationalism,"
with the few exceptions just noted. The conventional term
"minority" has also been avoided as an ethnic group
designation, again to remove ambiguity. The term "Great
Russian" has regularly been rendered as "Russian." The
disagreement between American and Soviet meanings for
"nation," "nationality," and "minority," as well as the wide
variation in application of the words among the writings of the
37 contributors to this study, necessitate a rather stringent
editorial stabilization of this essential terminology. The terms
"Russian," "Russians," or "Ethnic Russia" refer to that
distinct ethnic population alone, and exclude all other Czarist
and Soviet ethnic groups. The distinction between the
Russian attributives russkii and rossiiskii, especially important
in the pages which follow, has been rendered in English with
"Russian" and "Russia-wide," respectively. Transliteration
from Russian follows the system found in Nationalities of the
Soviet East; Publications and Writing Systems (1971), p. 387,
by Edward Allworth.

Introduction —
A Russian Dilemma:
Political Equality or
Ethnic Neutrality in the
RSFSR and USSR

Contemporary Russia is regarded in at least three general ways. It may be identified as a ruling oligarchy indiscriminately dominating 99.999 percent of the Soviet population, including Russians and other ethnic groups; a large entity virtually equivalent to the USSR; or one ethnic group among many in the Soviet Union. The first and second methods of scrutinizing today's Russia have been used the most, whereas the third is largely untried in broad investigations combining knowledge and discipline from many fields of study. Nevertheless, the ethnic approach offers insights especially appropriate to a time of group self-determination worldwide. The USSR has not escaped the common urge, but exhibits its own peculiarities. Within the USSR, ethnic Russia currently exists in an authoritarian state both socially and politically most conservative. Advancing technologically in a few areas, Russia today is also modernizing unevenly and slowly in the sphere of human and group rights. Perhaps through a feeling of inadequacy, Russians display a powerful thirst to be considered ethnically superior to others. In the 1970s, this urge continues to be expressed, for example, in an insistence upon referring to themselves, through their namesake administrative unit, the RSFSR, as "first among equals."(1) These circumstances and drives have prepared what appear to be an inescapable set of problems for the ethnic Russians.

---

*Russia-wide Soviet Federated Socialist Republic (Rossiiskaia Sovetskaia Federativnaia Sotsialisticheskaia Respublika) and Union of Soviet Socialist Republics (Soiuz Sovetskikh Sotsialis-ticheskikh Respublik).

A dilemma poses two equally undesirable choices. The ethnic question confronting the Russians of the USSR in the late 1970s and thereafter is sometimes framed in those deceptively simple terms. Presuming that the USSR will continue with approximately its present composition, the Russians will manage to abdicate the satisfactions of ruling ethnically, thus opting for genuine democracy, or, electing to dictate as before, must largely abandon survival as a unified ethnic group. The last is a course advocated by convinced Marxist-Leninist ideologists. Volatile pools of political energy, now steadily widening in the Soviet domestic arena, may force the issue very nearly in these terms. Ethnic Russians, schooled for decades running back into the previous century to live undifferentiated under and amidst a supraethnic regime and state, presently show many signs of belatedly claiming modern group ethnicity. Simultaneously, key non-Russian groups in the USSR grow to significant numbers and evidence a disinclination to accept the omnipresent Russian tutelage they have known in the past.

When populations are as large as the ethnic Russian one, relatively small statistical changes objectively mean little in the overall situation. The decline between 1959 and 1970 of the Russian percentage in the population of the RSFSR from 83.3 to 82.8 and of the entire USSR from 54.6 to 53.4 in itself signifies a minor fluctuation over a fairly short period.(2) Another type of slight alteration in the demographic equilibrium between Russians and non-Russians of the RSFSR can be detected quickly in the Soviet census material for 1959 and 1970 (reported in Appendix A). Among 55 ordinary subordinate divisions (oblasts and krais) of the RSFSR, 28 experienced noticeable declines in the percentage of Russians. In 12 of the 55, including two whose Russian proportion rose, the Russian population went down absolutely. In the RSFSR's non-Russian subunit, the Russian percentage of the population slipped in 11 out of 16 autonomous Soviet socialist republics (ASSRs) and absolute numbers fell in one. Among the 15 autonomous oblasts (AOBs) and autonomous okrugs (AOs) of the RSFSR, the Russian proportion declined in four, and absolute numbers went down in one. Thus, in more than half (45) of the ordinary or eponymous subunits among the 86 in the RSFSR, between 1959 and 1970 ethnic Russians lost ground in the population relatively, absolutely, or both. But behind those figures stand demographic facts which seem to portend continued later declines, data showing that the birthrate among Russians for the decade preceding the 1970 census ranked fourth from the bottom among the eponyms for the 15 union republics of the USSR. Also, the child-woman ratio in 1970, again fourth from the bottom, had dropped from sixth place in 1959. Soviet experts predicted that the already low birthrate among Russians would slip further in the early 1970s.(3)

Together, most of these variations form a noticeable pattern, though individually they may be inconsequential to statisticians. Russian authorities as well as demographers are aware of these gradual trends leading their group toward what will very likely become a plurality in the Soviet population rather than the present scant majority. This knowledge has alarmed some in the USSR, reflecting itself in calls for tendering increasing incentives to Russian childbearing and reducing them among the non-Slavs of Soviet Asia. There has been talk also about a "demographic trauma," which Russians are suffering because of the undermining of an important part of the group's self-confidence which heretofore rested upon an awareness of its superior numbers.

Precedents in plenty exist for the large significance sometimes given in the minds of ruling ethnic group representatives at the pinnacle of multiethnic states to small demographic changes. In the Austro-Hungarian Monarchy late in the nineteenth century, the dominant Magyars more than once reacted with consternation and culturally repressive measures to census information about the declining proportion of their own group in certain localities by comparison with Swabians (Germans), Slovaks, and perhaps others.(4)

Despite obvious concern over implications of their population changes, Russian public officials repeat that the ethnic question of the RSFSR and USSR has been resolved. Thoughtful Soviet intellectuals disagree completely. An eminent Russian scholar who visited the West for a period during the 1978-1979 academic year candidly remarked that the most crucial matter (. . . samyi ostryi vopros) facing Soviet society now is the ethnic question.(5) The Russian dilemma makes up an important portion, though by no means all, of the question. An evaluation of the Russian side of that predicament depends considerably upon the standpoint - non-Russian, Russian, foreign, scholarly, or political - from which the matter is assessed. Most aspects of the dilemma as it has already been formulated (Russian ethnic group well-being vs. political hegemony) likewise will be interpreted variably from the viewpoint of different parts and strata of ethnic Russian society. The same is true when one carefully seeks to appraise the corporate status of Russians in the RSFSR and USSR. Serious difficulty stems from the assumption that the identity of the entire ethnic Russian population may be projected appropriately onto the relative handful of unelected, generally unpopular, upper political elite of Russian extraction.

A contemplation of the ethnic condition and morale of the RSFSR's 61.1 million (1970) common laborers and farmers plus the 68.9 million outside the workforce, in contrast with the 3.6 million chiefs and managers - all but 17.2 percent of that total 130 million being Russian - will undoubtedly reveal something else. That picture is unlikely to resemble the one observed through a focus upon literary and scientific intellectuals of the union republic's population.(6) Another bias can be introduced through a preoccupation with "the top executive and administrative arm of state authority of the RSFSR," its Council of Ministers. They constitute a phalanx of ethnic Russians, yet 1976 included no names from among the most numerous, structurally "equal" eponymous groups in the RSFSR (Tatars, Bashkirs, and the like). The Council heads the multiethnic Russia-wide Federation (Rossiiskaia Federatsiia, short for RSFSR), but all is not as it seems. Identifying that ministerial circle as Russian is risky, because, though its makeup is formally approved by the RSFSR's Supreme Soviet, which is ". . .the government, the top arm of state authority of the RSFSR," the Council is in reality appointed by a party from beyond the RSFSR administration. Thus, the governors are sanctioned not by the Communist Party (CP) of Russia, for no such publicly-acknowledged division is presently known, but of the Soviet Union (CPSU), "the leading and directing force of Soviet society, the kernel of its political system," according to the 1978 Constitution of the RSFSR. Inserting Articles 6 and 7 about the CPSU and the Union-wide Leninist Communist Union of Young People (Komsomol) into the RSFSR Constitution verbatim from the USSR Constitution of 1977 makes explicit the CPSU's monopoly of partisan political power in the RSFSR, formerly unstated in the union republic constitution. The passage acts to remind Russians that this constituent republic's Council of Ministers is the creature of the Union-wide party to a greater degree than in any other union republic, for the CPSU intervenes directly in RSFSR governance without the intermediation of the regional party structure to be found in the 14 Soviet socialist (union) republics.(7) Although the arrangement undoubtedly has significance for the current exercise of power in the USSR, more to the point is the likelihood in the longer run that it would disconcert the ethnic Russian aggregate in the RSFSR.

Soviet Russians attract special attention today in ethnic study especially, but not solely, because of the role they have acquired in the USSR, officially a state assertively "internationalist" (professing ethnic neutrality). For divers reasons, Russians very likely would be worth ethnic study if they were to become sole occupants of their own "nation state." A forecast of the ethnic outlook for an unprecedented, monoethnic Russian state would, by necessity, look mainly for traces left by its nineteenth and twentieth-century experience. For at least 150 years, the numerous Russians have been the largely passive support for the Russian masters of many other ethnic groups. About a score of the non-Russian groups were and are populous, compact bodies now with the capacity, through ethnically well-identified leaders, to articulate and supervise their corporate interests. But, a Russia divested of subject groups would surely exhibit ethnic character different from the one it presents today. The Russians have been significantly conditioned by their practice of ethnic dominance over a very long period.(8) Hardly unique in its multiethnicity, the USSR falls well outside that select circle of the world's modern states counted as ethnically homogeneous: Austria, Denmark, West and East Germany, Japan, Norway, and perhaps eight others.(9) The patterns of unified ethnic life and group identity among these monoethnic states may offer models for Russia solo, but contrast remarkably with the prevailing Soviet ethnic fragmentation.

If resolution of the dilemma is not to be accomplished in the separation of ethnic Russia from the USSR, what is a probable alternative? Russian ethnic parity with other ethnic groups in the USSR, calling for an establishment of a neutral center like Washington, D.C. or possibly Vatican City, seems to imply a stronger, unified, naturally more self-satisfied Russia. Its continued dominance over the USSR, on the other hand, legitimized by Russian disavowal of ethnic motivations, eventually should weaken the already widely scattered, disunified Russians to a point of fission into several embryonic ethnic entities (see map). For the time being, the lack of strongly coherent Russian group self-awareness merely allows the entrenched political oligarchy (Politburo and Central Committee of the CPSU) to manipulate Russia and rule it and non-Russia of the USSR arbitrarily. In the practices of modernized as well as less-developed multiethnic states, there are examples in India, the United States, Yugoslavia, and elsewhere showing that a generally unmobilized ethnicity within the foundation (often called "dominant") group temporarily does not inconvenience the central authorities very much. Often, such diffuseness is helpful, even essential, to governors who would otherwise be forced to contend with unmanageable chauvinism and ethnocentrism in that principal group. That passivity in ethnic Russians would not alter the present situation, but an ethnic group normally cannot survive in a multiethnic state as a distinct body without response to a somewhat challenging environment.(10) Both the revival of Russian interest in its ethnic past during the 1960s and early 1970s and the simultaneous strengthening of neighboring non-Russians of the Soviet Union contribute, among Russians, to feelings of rivalry and insecurity. Neither is typical of a confident, ruling ethnic group standing comfortably beyond the reach of subject group psychology and pressures. These and other signs forecast progress down toward Russian consolidation in the era ahead, with the suggestion that important ethnic consequences will result.

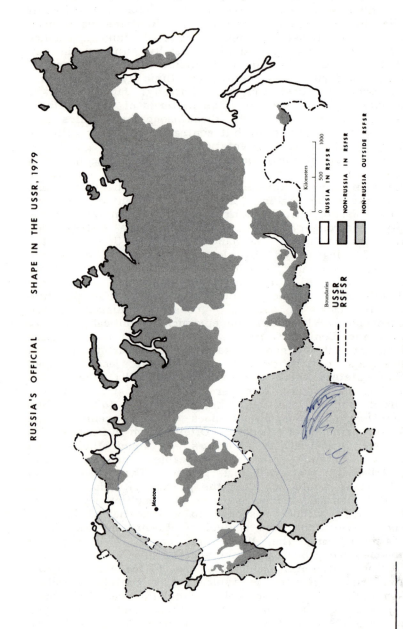

RUSSIA'S OFFICIAL   SHAPE IN THE USSR, 1979

Boundaries
USSR
RSFSR

RUSSIA IN RSFSR

NON-RUSSIA IN RSFSR

NON-RUSSIA OUTSIDE RSFSR

Kilometers

0   500   1000

MOSCOW

Source: Atlas SSSR (Moscow: Glavnoe Upravlenie Geodezii i Kartografii pri Sovete Ministrov SSSR, 1969); Edward Allworth, ed., Soviet Nationality Problems (New York: Columbia University Press, 1971), pp. xvi–xvii.

This entire inquiry into the foregoing problems, and subjects related to them, is organized generally around the following propositions which correspond to the sections of the book numbered one through nine: 1) The effect of mistiming can no more be reversed in the existence and behavior of ethnic groups than the consequences of retardation in the development of men and women. 2) The current revival of literary concern with ethnic roots, like the resurgent interest in Russian history and in earlier Russian art and artifacts among Russian writers and other intellectuals, has import for the Soviet ethnic and political situation. 3) Except for times of extreme external peril, Russian orthodoxy has not recently and cannot be expected soon to exert strong influence upon ethnic identity in the Russia-wide Soviet Federated Socialist Republic (RSFSR). Nor will it attract, even nominally, active adherence from most of Russian society, despite the church's genuine links with the homely values of old and inspiration for important artistic expressions in the past. 4) The renewed ideological emphasis placed by Soviet authorities upon the supposed unity of the "Soviet People (narod)" as a whole tends to dampen Russian self-awareness and obscure external identity politically. 5) Russians lack some of the crucial official recognition (for example, a branch of the Communist Party of the Soviet Union designated for the RSFSR, a separate union republic capital for "Russia," or a specific arm of the Academy of Sciences of the USSR) which supports the group awareness of many other Soviet ethnic groups. This deprivation may continue to deny significant support to Russian ethnic identity. 6) Neither the present RSFSR nor USSR as such provides the Russians, staunch adherents of the idea of homeland, with a symbolic territory which offers an emotional attachment precise enough for their ethnic needs today. 7) Alien usages introduced into the tongue by the widespread adoption of Russian as an intergroup language among all Soviet ethnic groups, have undermined the important role of the language as an exclusive attribute of Russian identity and, thus, removed another pillar heretofore bolstering Russian group unity. 8) As the Russian population urbanizes, grows in number but slips closer to plurality status among the people of the state, and further disperses throughout the USSR, the Russian group's basic physical outline seems to become ever less distinct. These demographic developments put pressure upon those concerned with guarding Russian values and identity to counteract or compensate for this diffusion of the ethnic group. 9) Reconciliation of the opposing Soviet drives for ethnic integration vs. self-determination in the Russian case will probably entail including one drive in the other. The second will likely camouflage the inner drive. This will produce a Russianism thinly covered by Sovietism - barely differing from the past -

until the Russian group finally becomes uncontrollably apprehensive for its survival and turns actively ethnocentric once more, destroying all pretense of "internationalism" in the RSFSR and USSR.

NOTES

(1) Edward Allworth, "Nationality Group Rights in the Soviet Union," Detente. Hearings before the Sub-Committee on Europe of the Committee on Foreign Affairs, House of Representatives. Ninety-Third Congress, Second Session (Washington, D.C.: U. S. Government Printing Office, 1974), pp. 327-38; Rossiiskaia federatsiia. Obshchii obzor. Evropeiskii sever (Moscow: Izdatel'stvo "Mysl'," 1971), p. 11; Russian Soviet Federated Socialist Republic (Moscow: Novosti Press Agency Publishing House, 1972), p. 5.

(2) Itogi vsesoiuznoi perepisi naseleniia 1970 goda. Natsional'nyi sostav naseleniia SSSR, vol. IV (Moscow: "Statistika," 1973), pp. 12, 9.

(3) Robert A. Lewis and Richard H. Rowland, "East is West is East . . . Population Redistribution in the USSR and its Impact on Society," International Migration Review, 11, no. 1 (Spring 1977): 20; Galina A. Bondarskaia, Rozhdaemost' v SSSR (Etnodemograficheskii aspekt) (Moscow: "Statistika," 1977), pp. 28, 64-65.

(4) C. A. Macartney The Hapsburg Empire 1790-1918 (New York: Macmillan Co., 1969), pp. 724-733; Thomas Spira, German-Hungarian Relations and the Swabian Problem (Boulder, Colo.: East European Quarterly, dist. by Columbia University Press, 1977), pp. 3-8, 360. Professor Joseph Rothschild kindly pointed out these references.

(5) Both the published writings of the Soviet visitor and the reliability of the Western scholar who reported the comment are known to this author, but the source must remain confidential for the present.

(6) Itogi...1970 goda..., vol. IV, p. 12; Ibid., Raspredelenie naseleniia SSSR po zaniatiiam, vol. VI (Moscow: Izdatel' stvo "Statistika," 1973), pp. 24-33.

(7) "Konstitutsiia (osnovnoi zakon) rossiiskoi sovetskoi federativnoi sotsialisticheskoi respubliki," Sovetskaia Rossiia (Apr. 13, 1978), Articles 104, 122, p.3; Directory of Soviet Officials vol. II: RSFSR (n.p.: Central Intelligence Agency, Dec. 1976), pp. 1-2; "Konstitutsiia, . . ." Articles 6, 7, p. 1; "Konstitutsiia (osnovnoi zakon) soiuza sovetskikh sotsialisticheskikh respublik," Izvestiia (Oct. 8, 1977), p. 3.

(8)   Zbigniew Brzezinski in "The World According to Brzezinski. James Reston Interviews the President's National Security Adviser, Zbigniew Brzezinski," The New York Times Magazine (Dec. 31. 1978), p. 26.

(9)   Walker Connor, "The Politics of Ethnonationalism," Journal of International Affairs no. 1 (1973), p. 1.

(10) Nationality Group Survival in Multi-Ethnic States. Shifting Support Patterns in the Soviet Baltic Region, edited by Edward Allworth (New York: Praeger Publishers, 1977), pp. 1-23.

Symbolism and Stance of a Ruling Ethnic Group

Proposition 1: The effect of mistiming can no more be reversed in the existence and behavior of ethnic groups than the consequences of retardation in the development of men and women.

1 Royal Russian Behavior, Style, and Self-Image

Edward Keenan

How is one to discuss matters of "nation" and "ethnicity" with reference to premodern society, particularly Muscovite court society, in which the first concept had little effective meaning, and the second was far less important than other types of "belonging": familial, social, functional, and the like?

The assortment of categories by which individuals choose to group themselves and identify others - language, sex, religion, tribe, family, locality, or occupation - has not changed much over recent centuries, but the relative importance of these indicators has. Moreover, the general tendency of modern society to subordinate all of these real and humanly significant distinctions to the aggregated categories of "nation" and "class" is really quite revolutionary, when viewed against the background of the whole of our history. As a result of this modern reassignment of values, ethnicity has become for the great majority of citizens of media-influenced societies a form of instant identity, avidly purveyed by governments, benign and pernicious persuaders, and T-shirt salesmen. Anyone who thinks that historical or cultural fact has anything to do with such sentiments in modern mass society is advised to test his hypothesis by announcing in a South Boston bar the "fact" that "When Irish Eyes are Smiling" was composed, for cash, by a Dutchman in Philadelphia - or in a tavern (pivnaia) in Ivanovo that certain Russian "folk songs" are translations from German. Responsibility for the result of such experiments cannot be taken lightly.

From the anthropological point of view - and the anthropologists are the custodians of definitions of "culture" - what we laymen call "ethnicity" has become essentially a statistical concept, a weighted sum, in a sense, of a half-dozen indexes related to somewhat aggregated indicators (such as the relationship of one's dialect to the dialect that

has been declared the standard literary language of a given
group, the relationship of one's religion to the dominant
orthodoxy, and so on, and in particular the combination of
these factors.) The boundaries of such statistical clusters are
necessarily rather indistinct, for they are by definition
transition areas. Moreover, an individual, in developing his
own personality, has a certain freedom in choosing just how
close to the modal center of his "nation" or "ethos" he wishes
to stand. He can, for example, suppress those features of his
mother tongue that separate it from the metropolitan norm of
the schoolmarms, or abandon his native language entirely and
join a speech community different from - even hostile to - that
of his parents. He can, in modern societies, change his
religion, occupation, locality, wife, (that is, his family), and
even his sex.

A certain mobility among social and ethnic groups existed
in Muscovite society, but the dominant cleavages were far more
rigid and permanent than those of modern society, and they
ran along lines that have in our times become not only
obscured, but even difficult for us to comprehend.

As a consequence of this major change, the great majority
of modern attempts to describe Muscovite attitudes about
"nation" and "ethos" have failed. They have failed because,
for example, they have wrongly been based on the assumption
that "nation" was as important to members of the Muscovite
court culture as was, for example, clan (rod). They have
failed because they have assumed that religion was as
important as "face" or seniority (as expressed, for example, in
the system of precedence (mestnichestvo). They have failed
because they have imagined Muscovite boyars and czars as
unwesternized Russian peasants, who ran about in rustic
holiday clothes, speaking (o-unstressed okaiushchie) dialects,
and generally behaving like nineteenth-century Old-Believer
merchants. They have failed, finally, because they have not
distinguished the court and its culture from the primarily
monastic ecclesiastical culture that produced what have
traditionally been the standard narrative bases for many of our
conceptions about Muscovite life.

From an anthropological point of view, the Muscovite
court culture was a functionally specialized, and distinct
subculture, separated - even isolated - from other parts of the
Russian speech community by, among other things, its strict
system of inheritance and the practice of seclusion of women.
The functional "assignment" of this subculture was politics and
military administration. Its members organized themselves into
strictly disciplined clans or large families whose internal
hierarchies were determined by a fixed system of "place" or
seniority, and whose interrelations came to be regulated
by precedence (mestnichestvo), a system that combined clan
seniority with the other crucial Muscovite measure of status,
proximity to the czar.

From at least the time of Ivan III (1462-1505), when the leading Muscovite families, under still fresh impressions of the chaotic civil war that had gripped Muscovy for two generations, established the practices that were to remain typical of Muscovite court politics until modern times, these leading clans formed a rather stable oligarchy. At its center was a czar who was "divinely appointed" (that is, entitled to the succession by heredity) and "out of bounds" in political terms (that is, no one could either remove him from the throne or aspire himself to the throne). The combination of this conventional arrangement with normal vagaries of health, longevity, and talent produced, of course, a system in which the czar was as often as not a mere figurehead. By and large, things ran more smoothly in the Kremlin when he <u>was</u> a figurehead, and it would appear that the system was constructed accordingly.

At the center of the political system stood the czar, whose nominal authority was not only never challenged, but also greatly hyperbolized by the powerful magnates, the heads of the several clan interests. They went out of their way, publicly at least, to humble themselves with the title of "slave," and the like. The untouchability of the czar and his crown was, in fact, the guarantee to these grandees that none of their number could ever grow too strong, that a majority of insiders acting in the name of the czar could always overpower anyone who violated the code, and that the chaotic free-for-all among clan armies that had marked the great fifteenth-century civil war could never be repeated. These wise patriarchs so badly needed a czar who was at least nominally strong that when nature provided none, as in the Time of Troubles, they invented one - or rather several.

For the majority of the period from the civil war until the time of Peter the Great, the czar was, in fact, not personally strong as a politician, and the real power lay with the oligarchs. These men typically sat in the Boyar Duma and were related by marriage to the czar in many cases, and to one another almost always. The source of their power was their position as senior members of the most cohesive and powerful political unit in Muscovy. This was the clan (<u>rod</u>), a complex patronage organization built around an extended biological family. These men - the Obolenskys, Morozovs, Shiuskys, Golitsyns, and others - were not only the leaders of Muscovite (and their own) armies, they were also the "godfathers" of tightly controlled clan organizations, organizations that carefully regulated seniority and status, inter- and intraclan marriages, the distribution of the clan property, and all other significant matters for all clan members. Power (military and political) was the family business of these clans, and for roughly three centuries after 1450 they ran that business in Muscovy extremely well, according to rules that changed very little. Over most of the period to be considered, they ran the czar, and the court. Theirs was the royal style, the royal behavior, the royal self-image.

This court culture was, in several interesting and anthropologically significant ways, quite different from the culture of the great bulk of the Russian population. The family of the Grand Prince itself practiced a peculiar kind of primogeniture - the only Slavic family in Muscovy to do so. The clans, by contrast, practiced a form of family seniority that was not unlike the common lateral seniority, but was different in that the economic and political unit was the clan, and not the otherwise almost universal household or village. Both the royal family and the oligarchy practiced seclusion of women - a necessary adjunct of marriage politics - which was utterly contrary to the patterns of Slavic agrarian society. They were preeminently nonagriculturalists, whereas ninety percent of the population were pure agriculturalists. They spoke differently (the dialect of their nursemaids from a few villages around Moscow and Riazan'), ate differently, dressed differently, and thought about themselves, about society, and about others, differently from the great bulk of Muscovite Slavs.

Unfortunately, few, if any, members of this court culture ever set to paper any such thoughts. Most discussions of the "style" of the Muscovite royal culture, whether devoted to some specific theme like the one focused upon here or to more general matters, rely heavily upon such sources as the chronicles or coronation ceremonies. Those texts are probably only obliquely related to the secular culture of the court. A significant set of barriers seems to separate the culture of the clerical, primarily monastic, writers who wrote those highly literary texts from that of the practical men who, in fact, set the stylistic tone of the court. But it should probably be agreed that many aspects of Muscovite imperial court culture are simply not captured by the classical Slavonic texts.

A part of our conceptual problem is created by the fact that most nineteenth and twentieth-century scholars have mistakenly assumed that as one moved further and further from modern times, he would become further removed from modern sensibilities - in the Muscovite case, into an increasingly ritualistic and Byzantinomorphic culture. Such seems not to have been the case.

It may be argued that the official church and "Byzantine" ideas and style played a surprisingly modest role in the culture of the Muscovite court itself, well into the reign of Ivan the Terrible (Ivan IV) - perhaps, really, into the reign of Boris Godunov. It is arguable, too, that these elements of court culture reached the level of influence and stylistic domination usually assigned to them only in the reign of

Aleksey Mikhailovich (1645-1676), shortly before lapsing again into a subsidiary position under Peter the Great.

When the written sources upon which our traditional view of a piously - even militantly - orthodox court is based are examined with modern methods, they turn out to be highly questionable from a number of points of view. The coronation ceremonies that are so often cited were, in several cases, clearly composed after the fact; the myth of the Third Rome is not only a myth, but a myth whose influence is questionable. The role of Metropolitan Makarius, Sil'vestr, and other clerics who allegedly were always at the right hand of the czars has clearly been exaggerated in the historiography.

To consult the archival records that most closely reflect the day-to-day activities and the authentic style of the Muscovite court - the diplomatic correspondence, other working documents of the court, the accounts of foreigners - is to be struck by the absence of evidence of major contact with or knowledge of the Byzantine tradition for the first and formative century of the truly Muscovite court (circa 1462). The same might be said about a lack of Greek, and of dogmatic or ideological niceties aside from those provided for the purely liturgical occasions of the ecclesiastical year. Over the same period, there is surprising evidence of some stylistic features that can be found in changed forms in the Russian courts of later centuries, such as the imitation of foreign courts, the clear separation of the court culture from Russian peasant culture, and the constant presence of non-Russians and even non-Christians in the inner circles of the court.

When, early in the reign of Ivan III, the Muscovite court, in increasing awareness of its new power and potential, began casting about for a style more appropriate to its new stature, it appears first to have effected what we might call the style of the "new Sarai." Ivan made an effort to collect the regalia of the now fallen khans; he cultivated Tatar clients and allies, many of whom were resident in his court. He styled himself according to Golden Horde tradition as the "White" or Western Khan ("Albus imperator") in his first diplomatic contacts with the Italian courts through which he was eventually to obtain his second wife, Italian-educated, Greek Sophie Paleologue. Sophie's arrival in 1472 is a convenient marker of the beginning of another stylistic period, not really Byzantine as some would have it but rather Italianate, during which Ivan rebuilt the Kremlin, ("in the Italian style," as Sigmund Herberstein noted) down to the original tiled roofs, employed Greco-Italian mint-masters and diplomats, engraved a Latin inscription over the main gates to the Kremlin, married his daughter to the son of his (also Italophile) neighbor, Sigismund, and generally followed the contemporary European vogue for things Italian.

The time of Ivan's son, Vasiliy III, is not marked by so pronounced a vogue. That may be seen - along with the beginning of Ivan the Terrible's reign - by the reemergence of the "domestic style" (see Fig. 1.1). The turning toward the West was terminated by a sharp change in relations with

Fig. 1.1.   State seal of Ivan the Terrible, Czar 1547-1584.

Source: P. P. fon-Vinkler, comp., Gerby gorodov gubernii, oblastei i posadov rossiiskoi Imperii . . . .   St.   Petersburg, Izdanie Knigoprodavtsa Iv. Iv. Ivanova, passed by censor 1899, p. VIII.

Poland, but some of its traditions continued, gradually assimilated to Russian or other previously absorbed styles. This was the period, in particular, of the building of St. Basil's Cathedral, in which Western forms and traditional oriental decorative elements are combined, and the period of the beginning of the progressive "Russification" of the buildings of the Kremlin. It was a period of turning inward as well, there being (especially in Byzantium, now occupied by the Turks) no suitable other imperial court to look to as a style setter.

Somewhat later, a truly imperial, culturally impressive court did arise, the Isfahan of the Safavids. There is quite massive evidence, not yet sufficiently appreciated, that the Muscovite court, in the latter sixteenth and early seventeenth centuries, was strongly influenced by Safavid style. The impact was felt particularly in the minor arts and crafts, such as clothing, interior decoration, especially tapestries and rugs, the design of furniture and utensils, and in the realm particularly important to Muscovite czars and boyars, of cavalry gear, sabers, saddles, and equestrian accoutrements generally. This vogue continued well into the seventeenth century, blending with the previously mentioned characteristics of the Muscovite court style, and is one of the reasons why Western travelers were so often reminded of Ottoman Constantinople (itself going through a "Persian" phase) when they visited the court.

The last important phase of the evolution of the style of the imperial court in the pre-Petrine age is a complex one. It could be called the period of Polish and East European baroque, but this would be to oversimplify and to miss an important countercurrent, because by this time the Muscovite amalgam of traditional and previously assimilated styles was stabilized and vigorous, and not easily swept aside by even so powerful a vogue. To miss an important countercurrent, because, while the court of, say, Aleksey Mikhailovich, certainly followed many "Polish" vogues, their reception was tempered by anti-Polish and particularly anti-Catholic sentiments. They arose from the Time of Troubles and particularly from the experience of Ukrainians and Belorussians who, while often the bearers of Polish culture to Moscow, were at the same time the bearers of a new "Hellenism," which they systematically counterposed to Catholic and Western influences.

The role of other Westerners (Germans, Dutchmen, Englishmen, and even Scots) was increasing throughout this latter period. That laid the groundwork for Peter's only seemingly abrupt turn to the traditions of the courts of Northern Europe. Increasing, too, was the role of Greeks who brought the fruits of the revival of Greek learning in the Balkans and Eastern Mediterranean, setting the stage for the brief struggle - particularly in the 1680s - between Latin and Greek learning.

To generalize, first, the Muscovite Royal court - as opposed to the Church which was, of course, an important style-setter for the bulk of the population - was not so insular and isolated as is commonly believed. Although its responses to the vogues already listed were clearly derivative and modest in scale, the Kremlin was, in a peculiar way, a rather cosmopolitan place. Second, it was responding to many of the same vogues that in more striking and better-documented forms were sweeping other European courts. When Italian architects were building chateaus and townhouses for French and German Dukes, Ivan III was not far behind the game. When the French and English discovered Safavid Persia, Ivan the Terrible was already in the swim. Third, in the court itself existed little of the religious and xenophobic isolationism that is so often attributed to the Muscovite culture. Godunov and Ivan the Terrible seem to have had no more qualms about sitting on thrones constructed by Muslim craftsmen than did Ivan III about going to church in a royal cathedral built by a Catholic who had just completed a Muslim mausoleum in the Crimea, or living in a house built by another Catholic. Aleksey Mikhailovich seems not to have been uneasy about having as his court poet a Belorussian of questionable orthodoxy, Semen Polotsky, who wrote poetry few could understand, according to the rules of Polish prosody. Filaret himself was happy to have, from the Shah and religious leader of the Sufi Muslims, a piece of fabric advertized as the Lord's chasuble (riza gospodnia).

Finally, it is striking that this royal style - whether the imperial style of regalia and regal symbolism or the more domestic style of the court - had so little influence upon, and was so little influenced by, the traditional culture of both the Orthodox Church and the mass of the Russian population. Outside the innermost circle of boyars, few Russians emulated the outward-looking habits of the court or the styles that were acquired. Similarly, throughout this period - and later as well - the royal style never had a period of nativism, of imitation or romanticization of peasant styles. Aside from Peter's charade in the boatyards, it is difficult to think of any czar until Nicholas II who was seen to affect the kaftan and peasant boots. This exception, if indeed it is the only one, is precisely the appropriate one to cite.

To conclude that the style of the Muscovite court had been determined by conceptual categories of ethnicity as we understand the term today is, of course, to raise a more difficult question: such cultural externalities aside, to what extent was the behavior of king and courtiers shaped by an awareness of ethnic, as opposed to other, categories?

Historians often despair of achieving any adequate understanding of the social behavior of this milieu, primarily because the explicit documentary record - particularly with regard to first-hand descriptive accounts - is so scanty. However, the incomplete assortment of sources and their "pattern" are arguably important forms of information about Muscovite behavior and social relationships. For it must be concluded that what was carefully recorded and passed down was somehow important to medieval, Muscovite court life, and what was not recorded was of lesser concern.

Three rather unusual types of sources, meticulously prepared and preserved, whose very creation tells something quite significant about Muscovite society, are the genealogical books (rodoslovnye), the muster rolls (razriady), and the particularly interesting "marriage musters" (svadebnye razriady). Their presence confirms that, in the inner circles of the court, genealogy (or clan) was important, and that politics (marriage politics in particular) and military administration were activities of primary concern to Kremlin courtiers. These crucial sources reveal some particularly interesting aspects of royal behavior and of its relation to ethnicity.

What mattered to participants in Muscovite court culture was status (chest') - the status of one's clan (rod) and one's status within that clan. The status of the clan was determined by, and in its turn determined, the rank occupied by an individual during the perennial military expeditions; status within the clan was determined by a complex calculus based upon order of birth (not age). It mattered little whether an individual or his descendants were "foreign" or "native"; Greeks, "Lithuanians" (that is, Ukrainians and Belorussians, in modern parlance), or Tatars. Once "made" as members of the court, they enjoyed full political rights and conveyed these in the customary way to their progeny.

This insensitivity to ethnic origins was behavioral and systematic, and many of the individuals thus "made" retained markers of linguistic and cultural ethnicity as we understand it. Khanlets and Lithuanian lords (pany) participated without impediment in military campaigns (to repeat, the most important activity of their class), in court ceremonies, in marriages, and in the system of precedence. They were entered in the genealogical books. They married each other and "pure" Russians; they intermarried with the family of the grand prince.

And this integration clearly occurred independently of what today would be called cultural assimilation. Elena Gliskaia, Ivan IV's wife, and her uncles probably never lost the traces of their non-Muscovite mother tongue; nor did her mother, the redoubtable Anna, eradicate the habits of her South Slavic dialect. Certainly, Ivan's second wife, Mariia Temriukovna, could have learned little Russian in the month between her arrival in Moscow and her marriage, and some form of Kipchak Turkic must have been widely used among the entourage of ladies-in-waiting, brothers, and half-brothers who accompanied her to Moscow. Moreover, other members of the court - both Muscovite and Lithuanian - hastened to intermarry with the "Cherkessian" newcomers, a sure sign of their having been "inducted" into court society.

For an individual fully to enter the life of court politics - that is, to become a part of the marriage system - he or she had to be baptized, but Paris vaut bien une messe. Even the unbaptized, however - those who were being "saved" for possible foreign-policy uses, like Shigaley and Mariia's brothers - were not actually denied entree at court. Certainly the Muslim Shigaley enjoyed greater social acceptance at court than did the good Orthodox Maksim Grek among Muscovite clerics; Maksim was rotting in prison as Shigaley drank with the grandees. The strain of xenophobia in the circumstances of Maksim's trial emphasizes the very different attitudes of the ecclesiastical culture.

Royal behavior, as it was expressed in the activities most important to the royal entourage - in war, in marriage, in precedence - recognized status as determined by genealogy and service, and cared little about ethnicity. Furthermore, it was possible for a non-Russian to "convert" his status at some foreign court into roughly comparable status in the Muscovite system, but it was impossible for a Muscovite commoner to enter that milieu (keep in mind, for example, the Suleshov family).

One aspect of the problem of self-image is what might be called the "after-image" of self-image, if the use of such a ghost figure may be permitted. By self-image is meant the perception that Grand Princes and their closest cronies had of themselves in some context with relation to other identifiable types of people, rather than simply as individuals. As for the Grand Princes themselves, because there is little evidence of any kind about them as individuals and since they were so few in number as to be by definition atypical, there is really very little to say. Certainly they felt, and were made to feel, different from all other men, but it is equally certain that their very important and intense relationships with their numerous relatives, who were also their courtiers, must have taught them that these differences were not terribly significant. And, in any case, they had few dealings with anyone but their courtiers. It can be guessed that many of them felt rather lonely and angry with their splendid isolation. In a sense, they could not take advantage of the uniqueness of their position and, aside from creature comforts, experienced probably more negative than positive feelings about it. Certainly, Mikhail Fedorovich hardly felt particularly good about being czar under the tutelage of his father, and he probably felt rather abused by fate. Ivan the Terrible, it seems, tried to feel as little as possible, and took the necessary pharmaceutical steps toward that end. Aleksey Mikhailovich, like Nicholas II, went hunting.

The leading boyars were very much a group of Brahmans, whose self-image and image about others was quite specific and different from that portrayed in most of the historical literature. The member of a boyar family thought of himself and conceived of his personal significance first of all as a member of his clan, as a person who shared in and was existentially defined by biological and historical fortunes of that clan, as a person who was responsible first of all to that clan. Modern sensibilities certainly lead to an intuitive feeling that the immediate family with its intimate personal relationships is the more natural first meaningful context beyond the individual personality. But the circumstances of Muscovite family life in this class and in this class only, with the regular participation of nursemaids in the raising of children, the participation of distant relatives in the same process, the extraordinarily high mortality of both wives and children, and the web of legal and political sanctions that gave the clan its importance, all argue that the clan was really more important in the life of a typical member of this class than was the family, as understood today.

A second observation is that the significant conceptual boundaries that separated a member of this class from other men ran along lines determined by the centrality of birth. The first significant border was a very important and delicate one. That was the line separating one's clan from other similar clans in the same Muscovite aristocracy. But while this was an important border, it was rather like a modern "national" frontier in that it could, depending upon circumstances, be open and friendly or closed and the scene of warfare. For the members of these great families, as for the Guelphs and Ghibellines or Lancasters and Yorks, feuds and making up were a part of the normal biography of a clan.

Moving outward through the concentric circles that for Muscovite courtiers separated the locus of "us" from the chaos of "other," the next most proximate category to suggest itself was composed of members of aristocratic clans of the most familiar nearby courts, those of Lithuania and the Tatar world. It has been seen that some members of these courts transferred their status to the precedence system of Muscovy. Within a generation or so, many highborn Muscovites found themselves with new cousins in Vilnius or Bakhchisarai or Kabardiia. But it is not clear that these links were perceived as more significant than the links that most important clans had with non-boyar families of nearly equal status - families of chancellery secretaries (prikaznye d'iaki) or other important court clients. They formed a kind of demiclass around the political clans and often made up the client networks - or in today's terminology, khvosty.

In the universe of self-image of the royal family and its close relations, the Russian peasant was, throughout the formative period of Muscovite political culture, conceived of as being considerably more distant and "other" than Lithuanian (that is, Belorussian or Ukrainian) or Crimean clan nobility, and perhaps than Swedish or Dutch. This is not meant to exaggerate. Russian boyars knew that their serfs were not Chinese, but for people of this class, the obvious ethnic categories that have become so important in modern societies were not yet so significant as certain social and cultural traditions that were tightly bound up with their whole functional reason for existence in public life. Of course, these two axes of discrimination were locked in a kind of intuitive tension in the self-image of this group. As the centuries passed, the strength of the ethnic or linguistic or "natural" axis began to predominate. In the seventeenth century, especially, under the influence of increased contact with non-noble foreigners, including Orthodox East Slavs, and in general of a powerful influx of foreign culture, Russians of very high status began to reconstrue these relationships. But the process was slow, and it was not until Peter the Great had broken the power of the clans and other familiar processes of the eighteenth century had run their course, that the final change took place.

To illustrate the changing but still unclear attitudes of the period as late as the mid-sixteenth century with an interesting example: In 1656, during a Muscovite occupation of Lithuanian territory around Vilnius, the new Muscovite military governor of the town wrote a report to Aleksey Mikhailovich. It included the following, "It became known to me...that Prince Andrey Kurbsky (the grandson of the famous renegade) was living with his brother Jan in his estates in the province of Volkomir, and I . . . wrote and sent Mikhail Vlasov to him, (telling him) to remember his Orthodox faith and his native kind (prirodu svoiu) . . . (and) to come over to you with his brother."

Prince Andrey was not moved by this appeal, but the choice of words is interesting. That a Muscovite trying to recruit a defector should mention Orthodoxy in Belorussian territory in 1656 is entirely expected - it was the operative distinction of the time for what the Poles called the natio of the Ruthenians or Rus'. More puzzling is the additional phrase "and his native kind" (i prirodu svoiu): not clan - even though the writer was himself a relative of Kurbsky of the clan of Yaroslav princes (rod iaroslavskikh kniazei) - perhaps because the whole clan of Kurbskys was now in Lithuania; but also not people (narod), or any term explicitly ethnic, rather native (prirodu). "Remember what kind of man you are" - in which, even allowing for semantic drift over the ages, a carefully ambiguous term can be seen, one that reflects the tension between categories considered here. Notice, by the way, that Kurbsky's grandsons, by then probably thoroughly Belorussianized and properly Polonized, did come to Moscow, and, being Catholics, were rebaptized and inducted into the Golitsyn clan, even taking the patronymics of the two Golitsyns who stood as their godfathers.

To sum up, the self-image of the Muscovite royal family and its retainers was projected through a lens whose crystalline structure had many planes, among which the ethnic plane was clearly subordinate. It was not that a sense of ethnic difference did not exist - rather, it was simply not noted as significant. In this, as the other matters discussed, the style was set by the royal family. It is worth remembering one of the few nonceremonial comments on this subject that has been preserved. Ivan the Terrible had only one Russian grandparent (his two grandmothers were Greek and Serbian, his maternal grandfather a Ukrainian of Tatar antecedents). That one grandparent is quoted by Giles Fletcher (who got the story from Herberstein) to the effect that: "I am no Russe, my ancestors were German," referring, of course, to the mythical genealogy of the house of Rurik. What is interesting here is not that both Fletcher and Ivan III had their facts garbled, but that what was significant to Ivan III, as to his descendants and most everyone he knew, was his clan (rod), and not his people (narod).

To conclude with a few words about the "after-image" of the Muscovite royal self-image. It is one of the characteristics of modern societies, in which the priorities of traditional society have been reversed, and such once-decisive categories as clan count for nothing, that any man can claim to be the descendant of Norman barons, of Miles Standish, of the chief Rabbi of Ostroh, or of legendary Irish horse-thieves. Russians do not commonly claim descent from Ivan the Terrible, but they do readily express a great affinity for this unhappy man, in whom, as he is commonly represented, they sense familiar features of "our Soviet - pah - Russian man" (nash sovetskii - t'fu - russkii chelovek). There is something to this, perhaps. But the feeling would not be mutual. And those who search for the roots of the ethnic attitudes of Russians in the culture of the Muscovite court, which in so many other ways did lay its impress upon modern political culture, are looking under the wrong stone. These are modern attitudes, whose mature development has as a prerequisite the popular assimilation and refinement of the drawing-room notion of narod, and whose most pernicious effects are, unfortunately, but a part of the price to be paid for popular sovereignty (narodnaia vlast').

READINGS

Berry, Lloyd E., and Robert O. Crummey, eds. Rude and Barbarous Kingdom. Madison: University of Wisconsin Press, 1968.

Herberstein, Sigmund Freiherr von. Notes upon Russia, trans. by R. H. Major. New York: B. Franklin, 1964. Repr. of "Hakluyt Society" ed. of 1851-52.

Keenan, Edward. "Muscovite Political Folkways." Domestic Context of Soviet Foreign Policy, edited by Seweryn Bialer (Boulder, Colo.: Westview Press, 1980 forthcoming).

ethnicity : modern phenomenon
early Muscovite loyalty | i.D. was clan, 1st & foremost

2 Ambiguities in Russian Group Identity and Leadership of the RSFSR*

Edward Allworth

The human raw material out of which to form a distinct ethnic group no doubt existed among Russians long ago. For sufficient reasons, ethnic Russia did not congeal deep in the past, nor yet during the making of Muscovy in the fifteenth and sixteenth centuries, as Professor Edward Keenan has shown in chapter 1. By the time the Czarist Empire approached its day of reckoning - March 2, 1917 - can it be said that the numerous Russians (55.7 million within czarist borders of 1897, making up just under 45 percent of the Empire's population) had turned into a coherent, self-conscious group united horizontally (socially and politically) and vertically (ethnically)? (1)

A central consideration in the answer concerns the non-Russians being rapidly accumulated in Moscow's and then St. Petersburg's expansion, especially with the onset of the nineteenth century. If a czar in one era regarded non-Russians differently than his successor saw them in another, the imperial attitude usually focused upon the method of their absorption into the Empire. Roayl regard, then, depended greatly upon the military and economic status, and sometimes religion, prevailing among the nobility or aristocrats, if any, of the alien group annexed. Actual or potential ethnic group identity of the new subjects ordinarily remained merely of peripheral, ceremonial interest. (2)

In this way, the factor of timing seemed to condition the outlook of both the governors and governed respecting the status of each non-Russian group within the state. Near

---

*Russia-wide Soviet Federated Socialist Republic (Rossiiskaia Sovetskaia Federativnaia Sotsialisticheskaia Respublika).

17

the end of the nineteenth century, it has been said, "...the apogee of empire coincided with a rising tide of...Russian nationalism...."(3)   But this was not the group ethnocentrism of today, not the concerted expression of articulate ethnic Russians.   It was a reflection shared by the czar's court, and conservative adherents, of strong apprehensions regarding the evident disconnection between the sovereign and the common people, anxieties vented in a campaign to promote an official but sterile ethnarchy.

But repeating the old theme of the supposed unity among the czar and all his people, which the last Romanov ruler undertook to do, failed to secure the result desired by the court.   The formula was pronounced on various occasions and in official documents, including Czar Nicholas II's manifesto dated Agusut 6, 1905:   "The Russia-wide (Rossiiskii) state has been created and fortified by the indissoluble oneness of the Czar and the people (narod) and the people (narod) with the Czar."(4)   No doubt this reassertion of the alleged union of monarch and populace came tardily into a situation beyond repair.   But that was not the entire explanation for its notable ineffectiveness.   In   a   time   when   so   many   neighboring countries,   along   with   the   Russian   Empire   itself,   were experiencing obvious ethnic stirrings in various subordinate bodies, the czar's messages about the union continued blandly to be misaddressed to some sort of nonexistent homogeneity (see Fig. 2.1).   That choice of words and undifferentiated target for them could scarcely sound a resonance among any non-Russian group growingly interested in self-determination.

The political style and behavior of the czarist government during this era, starting especially in the 1880s and 1890s, as well as of some political factions like the Nationalists and Monarchists   active   during   the   life   of   the   State   Dumas (1906-1917), have often been broadly and probably unaptly termed "nationalistic."   Official restrictions then placed upon the employment of Polish, Ukrainian, and other sub- ordinate languages in the Empire for schooling or publication seemed to represent a policy of Russification.   Political disenfranchisement of selected Asian ethnic groups occurred. Religious intolerance directed against Jews, Protestants, and Roman Catholics looked like the same kind of measure, though ethnic Russians who were religious dissenters from Orthodoxy also suffered severe disabilities.(5)   Besides all that, some Russian-language   newspapers,   particularly   those   aligned closely with the government and the Nationalist party in the Dumas, worked vigorously to stir up strong patriotic feelings for "Russia" during World War I.   Whatever the combination of forces lying behind these actions - even hatred, bigotry, and thoughtlessness - which wounded non-Russians' dignity and sensibilities, nothing of a negative sort could provide affirmative support or definition for ethnic Russian identity.

Fig. 2.1.   The Great Coat of Arms of Russia-wide Empire
(1882-1917) emphasizes multiethnicity by combining old Moscow
crest on Byzantine double-eagle with circle of shields bearing
arms of kingdoms and main principalities of Kazan, Astrakhan,
Poland, and five others.

Source: Polnoe sobranie zakonov rossiiskoi Imperii   sobranie
tretie, St. Petersburg, n. p., 1882, Vol. 2, part 1 (1886),
leaf 12; V. K. Lukomskii and N. A. Tipol't, Russkaia
geral'dika... Petrograd, Izdanie Imperatorskago Obshchestva
Pooshchreniia Khudozhestv, 1915, p. 38a.

Negative ethnic identity, normally a product of real or fancied oppression, characterizes many subordinate groups to some extent, but in the eyes of the dominant, at least, scarcely the image of ruling groups. The central problem here goes beyond determining responsibility for unpopular measures or public opinion formed among non-Russians, to the effect upon the main ethnic body itself. Not victims of racial discrimination, not subject to arbitrary outside authority, nor the objects of potent economic or cultural sanctions from other groups within the czarist state, the ethnic Russians hovered in a kind of limbo. For they could not, in these types of initiatives from officials and other czarist-oriented politicians, find the leadership, still less the model, to form or strengthen in them a sense of the ethnic group solidarity so lacking. And the throne refused to convert ethnic Russians truly into a ruling group.

Late in the Empire's day, certain czarist bureaucrats and personnel in the institutions close to them had recognized a peculiar disunity splitting ethnic Russians. Theirs was an unsubtle echo of ideas advanced by Konstantin N. Leont'ev, Nikolay Ia. Danilevsky, and kindred Slavophiles after the mid-1800s. But Leont'ev believed that ethnic Russia was distinguished from Europe and other Slavic groups, at least, by its "Asiatic-Turanian" nature.(6) Twentieth-century recognition was again confined to a thin, literate social stratum among which disagreement continued to be voiced over what were claimed to be native Russian forms and spirit of governance as opposed to western "borrowed" notions and institutions. Essentially, that was a repetition of old arguments for and against changes instituted in the Russian Empire at the beginning of the eighteenth century by Peter the Great. This last-minute controversy failed to penetrate the issue of positively defining ethnic Russia at large for the sake of the group's own vitality. Nor did it serve the purposes of the government in those perilous times. Among opponents of pre-1917 constitutionalism in any guise, "...creating an ethnic (natsional'nyi) type of state,..." in contrast to a cosmopolitan, western-influenced one, was an aim advanced for Russia.(7) Obscuring, rather than clarifying, the problem of distinguishing group identity, these discussions once more failed to provide adequate sustenance for a discrete ethnic Russia.

Another line of thought among supporters of czarist autocracy goes more to the ethnic point. This thinking assigns the Empire, and other contemporary states, " one road - the ethnic (natsional'nyi) one" along which they must travel in the 1900s. This means giving a Russian direction to the multiethnic czarist combination. Within it, they contend, survival and welfare depend upon success in putting the impress of "the one host ethnic group (narod - khoziain), the master ethnic group (narod-gospodin)," firmly upon the many others which populate the state:

> The ethnic group (narod) ruling in the state must conceive of total might. Therefore, a multiethnic (mnogoplemennyi) state wishing to ensure its own future must give all its attention to the physical strengthening, economic enrichment, and spiritual development precisely of the host ethnic group. A slackening of attention to this basic task must inevitably draw upon itself the downfall of the state.(8)

The motif repeated in that prescription rings a familiar note today. But the general public in czarist Russia, including ethnic Russians, saw little, if any, practical response, official or otherwise, to the announced theme.(9) The unbending style of the autocracy created periods that have since been called "long grey winter(s) of despotism" in Russia.(10) Here, too, an ability to alter the operative set of preconceptions and state symbols was literally frozen in that unimaginative regime. Men outside government circles generated insufficient heat to thaw the jam, and to say that most of them, like the ordinary person, disliked and disrespected the government would be putting it politely. The experience demonstrated that in the era of ethnic agitation an entrenched authority can yet exert great influence, in this case negative, upon the ethnic aspirations of groups, not excluding the "host ethnic group" itself, in a composite state. The latent group ethnocentrism, if any, of the czarist Russians could find no constructive form of outlet.(11)

Among ethnic Russians, the class or group which might have spoken effectively for the ethnic Russians and possibly united the general public of Russian farmers (the greatest part of the population) and the urban working people, had not formed itself by the date fatal to czarism. The commercial-industrial class that remained was so conservative that it failed to assume the leading ethnic role taken on by its counterparts in the West. Czar-oriented and backward-looking, there could be no effective alliance between Russian industrialists and liberal intellectuals searching for a base and means upon which to establish a new social and political life for ethnic Russia, as well as for non-Russians in the Empire.(12)

The consequences following from this immaturity in the ethnic Russian group, already serious in the 1800s, were to become extraordinary in the 1900s. Very likely the impasse between the czarist state and its leading group would have been avoided, and the overturn of Nicholas II and his bureaucracy would have taken quite a different course, with a strongly-identified "master ethnic group" of Russians emplaced behind the government. Furthermore, had the ethnic Russian group solidified and concentrated its outlook before the March 1917 events, subsequent "internationalization" of ethnic Russians would probably not have taken place so quickly and thoroughly. Political disorientation, in ethnic terms, partly resulted from the absence of a rallying ethnic Russian leader-hero. Then, after the brief term as head of state of Vladimir Ilyich Lenin (d. 1924), ambitious men from among the long-subordinate ethnic groups of the czarist domain acquired and vigorously exercised control as the new regime over ethnic Russians, along with the others. In his professions and conduct, Joseph V. Stalin (d. 1953) may have been more "Russian" than the czar, but people knew that ethnically he was a Georgian. A self-contained, well-formed ethnic Russia could hardly have been persuaded, even by Lenin, to submit to the imposition of a political equality that the establishment of the USSR promised to impose upon them in late 1922. Nor would the nearly three decades of Stalin's rule have been acceptable to a vital, numerous group already ethnically come of age.

The installation of an all-powerful, supraethnic political organization - until 1925 named in imitation of the czarist precedent the "Russia-wide (Vserossiiskii) Communist Party (Bolshevik)," and then the Communist Party of the Soviet Union (CPSU), - above the people of the USSR, including Russians, was the logical next step. Raised upon that structure, an oligarchy of self-appointed leaders, remote from the governed, until World War II again responded coldly to ethnic Russian yearning for group reassurance.

From the outset, Russians were enrolled in the new party in numbers always far in excess of the group's share in the overall population of the USSR. It has taken 54 years for the percentage of ethnic Russians in the total to sink from 72 (in 1922) to 60.5 (in 1977).(13) The territorial-administrative unit in the USSR named for the Russians was, from the beginning late in 1917, a federated, rather than a unitary, "national republic." Within that RSFSR, ethnic Russians comprise an overwhelming share of the CPSU membership. By conservative estimate, in the mid-1970s, some 87 percent of the CPSU members counted in the RSFSR were ethnic Russians (surpassing the 82.8 percent of the RSFSR's entire population made up of ethnic Russians in 1970).(14) (Data, often scarce, concerning distribution of the CPSU membership within union republics, have, for the RSFSR from January 1973, been paired with figures for Union-wide enrollments as of January 1976 divided according to ethnic group. This calculation supplies information about numbers of ethnic Russian members registered in their own eponymous union republic. Statistics showing the party population of non-Russians presumed located almost entirely in the RSFSR, as well as proportionate numbers of Jewish, Osset, Tatar, Armenian, Ukrainian and unidentified members present in the RSFSR, have been subtracted from the overall RSFSR membership to leave a fairly close approximation for ethnic Russians.)

Disregarding the roughly 1.4 million ethnic Russian communists located in the Soviet union republics outside the RSFSR, Russian members in the RSFSR alone constitute a preponderance throughout the USSR. The 87 percent of the CPSU membership within the RSFSR amounted to around 8.1 million individuals, whose proportion on the CPSU rolls for the whole Soviet Union stood at about 52 percent. Those 8.1 million are concentrated even more in the ethnic Russian core area - far from the Asian expanses to the East. With justification, Russia's traditional center in the territory west of the Urals and east of the Baltics, Belorussia, Ukraine, and Moldavia, has been dubbed "the 'heartland' of the CPSU."(15)

Figures revealing the obvious overproportion as well as formidable numbers of ethnic Russians in CPSU ranks are customarily cited to indicate a politically advantageous inequity for Russians in Soviet life. That reasoning may have had some validity in the short run, but over the longer term the slant of those statistics seeming to favor Russians so greatly may spell difficulty for the ethnic Russian group. In addition, the immediate command and wielding of political power by a dozen or several hundred Russians at the top of the authoritarian USSR edifice, distant and detached from the general ethnic Russian public, under Marxist circumstances, offers rather little support to a population fumbling for clearer self-realization and group identity. The party's programs nowhere claim to strive for separate ethnic Russian development or hegemony. Currently, the lack of any branch of that organization designated for Russia or Russians strikingly differentiates the RSFSR from the remaining eponymous union republics of the USSR, each of which has one. Note especially, the exclusively supraethnic (internationalist) emphasis given to party statements and policies down through 1978, at least, and the strict discipline maintained upon the subject of ethnicity throughout the CPSU. Recruiting numbers of ethnic Russians far above those justifiable on a pro-rata basis from Soviet society into a class-oriented, anti-ethnic political instrument has a numbing effect on ethnic expression. This purpose was served rather effectively when the excessive participation of Russians in the CPSU diminished and largely defused Russian group ethnocentrism for most of the five and a half decades since the USSR was founded.

While the number of ethnic Russians in the CPSU has approached closer than ever before to the Russian share in the entire Soviet population, it is auspicious that several

significant, but related, developments have occurred in the
RSFSR, if not precisely in the Russian ethnic scene. Some of
those changes have taken place directly in the political sphere.
Soviet Russia, in reality, acquired not a branch but a special
bureau of the CPSU in 1956, as Professor Michael Rywkin
shows (chap. 19). That did not create exact parallelism
between the RSFSR and its fellow union republics, but it drew
them closer in this respect. Like this undertaking, most of
those actions leading toward RSFSR parity with the remaining
eponymous constituent Soviet republics began to happen during
Nikita S. Khrushchev's leadership of the party, 1953-1964.
Two years after deposing Khrushchev, his successor disbanded
that bureau of the party's Central Committee devoted to
Russia, probably because a distinct "Russia" was so hard to
define. Nevertheless, not all other moves in a similar
direction among RSFSR institutions were reversed. Beginning
in October 1957, for the first time, the RSFSR Supreme Soviet
started to issue separate editions of its own Register of
proceedings (Vedomosti), much behind the Tajik SSR (1939-),
Ukrainian SSR (1941-), and other union republics which had
established the practice much earlier, usually in bilingual
editions.(16)

Ethnic Russians until after the mid-1950s had also been
obliged to depend upon or participate in several cultural
organizations operating Union-wide. But on July 1, 1956, the
RSFSR almost came journalistically into line with the other
union republics when a publication, Soviet Russia (Sovetskaia
Rossiia), began appearing six days a week under the auspices
of the Bureau of the Central Committee of the CPSU for the
RSFSR plus the Council of Ministers of the RSFSR, the two
highest executive bodies for that eponymous Russian
administrative unit. When the Bureau was abolished in 1966,
its sponsorship of Soviet Russia evaporated and that of the
RSFSR Council of Ministers was removed. Both were replaced
as publishers by the supraethnic Central Committee of the
CPSU until 1974. Later, the authorities of the USSR again
permitted a certain official RSFSR connection to Soviet Russia
when The Supreme Soviet of the RSFSR and, once more, the
Council of Ministers of the RSFSR, became the announced
sponsors, this time along with the Central Committee of the
CPSU. Union republic publications of this type outside the
RSFSR are each sponsored by the Central Committee of the
CPSU branch of their area plus the Supreme Soviet and
Council of Ministers of the eponymous unit. These vacillations
in assigning direct control of Soviet Russia seem to reveal
substantial indecision among central authorities. They may
doubt the wisdom of permitting an eponymous, popular press
outlet with a 2.7 million circulation (in 1975) to become rooted
firmly in the ethnic Russian life of the Soviet Union but
outside the direct, strict managerial surveillance of the
Union-wide party.(17)

Their continuing caution is shown in the circulation figures of Soviet Russia, for it is barely a token number, taking into account the ethnic Russian population alone (107.7 million in 1970) of the highly-literate RSFSR. The ratio of press run to ethnic Russian population for Soviet Russia in the RSFSR was therefore 1:40 (one copy for every 40 Russians).(18) In other union republics, the situation is very different. The main, wide-circulation publication of the Uzbek Soviet Socialist Republic (SSR) in the eponymous language, Soviet Ozbekistani, was coming out six days a week in 683,000 copies in 1975 to reach a population of 7.7 million Uzbeks (1970) within that well-educated union republic, a ratio of 1:20. The Georgian-language Kommunisti in 1972 appeared in 620,000 copies for 3.1 million Georgians in their SSR, one copy for every 5 people, and Estonia's Rahva haal in 1974 printed 148,000 copies, a ratio of 1:6.3. Furthermore, though Soviet Russia retrieved some union-republic sponsorship in 1974, it remains in the category of Union-wide rather than RSFSR press. Unlike other union republics, the RSFSR as late as 1976 possessed not a single daily (six or seven days a week) newspaper exclusively named and aimed for readers of the eponymous group throughout that constituent unit of the USSR.(19)

A publishing house especially devoted to the RSFSR's life and developments among the subunits of that union republic, was established in Moscow in May 1957. Its early books and pamphlets included several series entitled: "What's New on the Economic Map of Russia," "Individuals of Soviet Russia," "Poetic Russia," and "Writers of Soviet Russia." This publisher, too, functons under the name "Soviet Russia."(20)

In cultural fields normally fundamental to the peculiar identity of modern ethnic groups, the last of the 1950s and early 1960s saw at least three innovations for the RSFSR. After decades of being merged indiscriminately into the USSR Union of Soviet Writers, authors and poets of the RSFSR held their first separate constituent congress December 7-13, 1959. Though 36 ethnic groups were represented, the great majority of participants were ethnic Russians. Similar meetings brought together the organized music composers and fine artists of the RSFSR separately in their first congresses in April and July, 1960.(21) No doubt, similar innovations occurred in other fields in the RSFSR during that period.

Another important feature of contemporary SSR status, and a mark of most civilized, developed societies in the world today, is the preparation and issuing of one or more "national" encyclopedias. Azerbaijan, Belorussia, Estonia, Kazakhstan, Ukraine, Uzbekistan, and other SSRs some time ago began to publish such multivolume editions in their own languages. The records fail to show a comparable undertaking by the RSFSR in the Soviet period.(22)

At least equally vital to the Russians are the symbols of what is called in the USSR the "sovereignty" of the union republics. Four such symbols in particular are provided for in the 1978 Constitution of the RSFSR, in contrast to the three in the previous version.(23) The RSFSR coat of arms described there is obviously the most unadorned, severe example, exploying merely a scroll-shield in a wreath of grain, among those for all the constituent Soviet republics, none of which depicts humans, mythical creatures, or animate imagery of any visible kind (see Fig. 2.2). Without the inscription "R.S.F.S.R.," no representation links this design specifically with ethnic Russia or its eponymous union republic. In striking contrast, the circular arms of the Armenian SSR portray Mt. Ararat, use the elegant Armenian alphabet alone to spell out the union republic name, and add bunches of grapes to the heads of grain obligatory for all such union republic emblems except the arms of neighboring Georgia. That may explain why RSFSR citizens are interested in dressing up the appearance of their eponymous union republic coat of arms. Zvezdnyi Gorodok, a Soviet cosmonaut, wrote to the editor of Soviet Russia in 1978 of his "joyful response to Article 179 [of the new RSFSR Constitution] about the coat of arms of the RSFSR...," because a five-pointed red star had just then been added at the top of the symbol. That action finally conforms the RSFSR arms to those of all the union republics for the first time.(24) Even less explicit than the RSFSR arms are the great arms of the Soviet Union (Fig. 9.1). They portray a world globe showing mainly the eastern hemisphere rather plainly under the standard communist hammer and sickle, the whole encircled by sheaves of grain. No initials or wording announce the identity of this emblem. For recognition, it relies largely upon repeating, in 15 different languages and alphabets of the union republics, the Marxist slogan "proletarians of all countries, unite," to denote the fact that this is the chief state symbol of the USSR.

Differing enormously from those coats of arms is an image regularly attached to visual material including displays, banners, and printed pieces prepared for the events and activities of the CPSU. A stylized head of Vladimir Ilyich Lenin with a stern facial expression, habitually shown in left profile, appears to function tacitly as the party emblem. On the left "ear" of some SSR Komsomol dailies' front pages, the face appears sketched in a flag. Usually entirely unadorned, lacking inscription or device, the Lenin head, in a contrasting rendering has become almost fixed as an emblem on important wide-circulation publications of the Soviet communist party. Here, the CPSU's preempting the "internationalist" Lenin seems to reinforce its intent to divorce itself from any ethnic connections and emphasize its leading position in the USSR. On the front page of Pravda, outlet of the Central Committee

Fig. 2.2. Austere Russian Soviet Federated Socialist Republic
Coat of Arms avoids depicting RSFSR's multiethnicity and,
until 1978, lacked red star found on all other Union Republic
seals.

Source: Russian Soviet Federative Socialist Republic, Moscow,
Novosti Press Agency Publishing House, 1972, p. 2.

of the CPSU exclusively, the reproduction of the Order of
Lenin medal awarded that publication now appears twice in an
interlocking logo that surprisingly hints, through the
reduplication, at the old Imperial double-eagle coat of arms
(Fig. 2.1). The Order of Lenin, authorized and conferred by
the USSR Supreme Soviet's Presidium (though granted to many
others), makes an emphatic statement of identity for Pravda in
this dual form as it becomes a permanent design element
alongside that party bulletin's main heading (flag).
Particularly noticeable is the variation between this emblem and
those uniformly lifeless devices used upon the coats of arms
for the union republics, and especially the crest of the
RSFSR.(25)

A flag is the second official symbol of RSFSR
"sovereignty" designated in the constitution of that union
republic. The exact rectangular shape and proportion, red
field, small gold star outline, hammer and sickle, and narrow,
light-blue band make this banner very similar to those from a
number of other union republics.(26) Also, according to the
1978 constitution, Moscow (the capital city of the RSFSR) is
not a unique center, but the Soviet Union's central seat of
government.

The previous edition of the RSFSR constitution specified
only those three symbols of union republic status (coat of
arms, flag, and capital city).(27) The fourth and new sign of
distinctness for the RSFSR, cryptically provided for in 1978,
is a union republic anthem. Article 182 simply states that "An
official anthem of the Russian Soviet Federated Socialist
Republic is approved by the Presidium of the Supreme Soviet
of the RSFSR." Including this provision for an anthem makes
it possible to bring the RSFSR abreast with other union
republics in this respect for the first time since the period,
during and soon after World War II, when each of the others
acquired its own official song. Although published sources
maintain that the RSFSR has such an anthem, a copy of it has
not been found. A communication from the Soviet Embassy
casts further doubt upon its existence.(28)

The tendency, noticeable since the mid-1950s, toward
equipping the RSFSR drectly with more and more institutions,
symbols, and accoutrements of individuality offers ethnic
Russians in the union republic perhaps somewhat greater
opportunity than they have enjoyed since 1922 to identify
specifically with the eponymous unit. But the RSFSR is still
far from being a "Russian republic," legally or actually. Nor
is there yet a close correspondence between ethnic Russia and
the RSFSR.

The imprecision in popular as well as standard
terminology about "Russia" as a place adds perplexity as well,
and diverts attention from a stabilizing concentration upon the
RSFSR or the Russian parts of it. During an important event

specific to the RSFSR in early 1978, an unusual amount and kind of popular discourse relating appropriately to this matter of defining "Russia" took place in public. From the day the new draft Constitution for the RSFSR was promulgated, March 14, 1978, until it had been revised and adopted by the Supreme Soviet of the RSFSR on April 12, 1978, some 60,000 letters and notes are reported to have come in to newspapers, television and radio stations, union republic and local agencies, and the RSFSR's Constitutional Commission itself. Almost 40 million copies of the draft had been circulated by the press in 29 languages of the ethnic groups of the RSFSR, and more than 10,000 suggestions or revisions were offered in the course of this time, it is said.(29)   Though small, the sampling of those communications which was selected and reported in the principal eponymous daily publication serving the RSFSR, Soviet Russia, tells much about the views many ordinary people hold concerning their portion of the country, their ethnic group, and their regard for the RSFSR as an administrative reality to which they may relate.

On the second page of Soviet Russia, in 23 consecutive issues dated March 17–April 10, 1978, were printed 119 signed letters or messages originating in many parts of the RSFSR, from Kaliningrad on the Baltic Sea to Vladivostok on the Sea of Japan.   In the ethnic sphere, they referred 13 times to "Russia" as a term for the RSFSR, 13 times to "Russia-wide Federation" or to the idea of the federation, and 13 times to homeland or a home place of some specific nature (soil, factory, village, farm).   The RSFSR as part of the USSR was mentioned twice, as was the concept "Soviet People."   The topic of family, private or ethnic, repeated itself 7 times. RSFSR "sovereignty" was ignored, and equality among ethnic groups came up only three times.   The most prevalent pattern, therefore, seems to link the ideas of "Russia" and those of "family" plus multiethnicity with motherland and birthplace. Most of these subjects were written about with great feeling.

Letters from many, and speeches by deputies, define their sense of place in terms of sweep and expanse of the land, especially employing phrases like "boundless Russia" (neob"iatnaia Rossiia).(30)   The RSFSR is called "our soil," "our house," "our beloved motherland" (nasha zemlia, nash dom, nasha liubimaia rodina) by an equipment operator in Stavropol Krai and by others.   Repeatedly, correspondents and deputies refer to their "native kolkhoz," "native farmstead," "native soil," "native group of businesses," even "native Communist party" (rodnoi kolkhoz, rodnoi khutor, rodnaia zemlia, rodnaia kombinat, rodnaia kommunisticheskaia partiia) in their wish to express close connection with certain places and institutions in the RSFSR important for their lives from an early moment.(31)

Behind that language sound recurrent variations on the theme of being born to a Russian mother, of one's own birth and birthplace, and the awareness of belonging to community or family (sem'ia), in several nuances of the word. Such emphasis upon working in one's birthplace openly speaks of permanence and the desirability of remaining always close to the home village or farm. Throughout the four-week discussion, the notion of economically-motivated migration or geographic mobility is never praised as a way of life. In one instance, a major-general, the Military Commissar for Primorskii Krai in the Soviet Far East, accentuates this feeling when he writes about the importance of soldiers' settling down once their service is completed. Describing what he calls a practice (traditsiia) frequent since the 1930s among subunits stationed along the Amur and Ussuri rivers bordering China, he tells how they remain there as a group after demobilization, founding kolkhozes, and raising grain. The general lauds their staying and "sinking deep roots in far off, but nevertheless, our own soil (nashenskaia zemlia)."

Mention of "family" in these letters seems to convey a great need for assurance that Russia is not alone, that it too belongs to a group. Most often, this indicates the RSFSR "family" of ethnic groups, but several times points to the RSFSR within the USSR "family" of union republics. Politicians and officials employing this same phraseology appear to be intent upon reassuring quite another body about the unity of the larger "family" of the USSR.(32)

Those allusions to nativity are augmented by statements making a gesture toward establishing firm local identity with the yet larger place. Russia (Rossiia) itself, is often identified popularly with the entire multiethnic RSFSR. The RSFSR Constitution under discussion frequently is considered to be the Constitution of Russia.(33)

Citizens who wrote in to Soviet Russia about ethnic equality in the course of the constitutional discussion were almost invariably non-Russians in the RSFSR who seemed intent upon reminding Russians of non-Russians' legal parity and claims to a portion of that union republic. The constitutional provision (Article 69) authorizing the RSFSR to secede from the Soviet Union drew a positive comment from a correspondent with a Russian surname and none from others. General remarks specifically about Soviet ethnic policies, likewise, appeared primarily over Russian signatures, as did references to the "special characteristics" of the RSFSR or underscoring the RSFSR's being a component part of the USSR.(34) Throughout this 28-day public discussion reflected on the pages of Soviet Russia there was a sparsity of ethnic Russian correspondents or deputies who spoke of Russia in terms of "friendship between ethnic groups" (druzhba narodov) or of Russia's ethnic emancipation. Very few made any direct address at all to something ethnic about Russia, outside of those observations couched in the purely bureaucratic language imitated in speaking generally of Soviet ethnic policies. Such silence was not so much a reticence to touch upon difficult issues as a lack of practice in thinking of themselves - Russians collectively - as just one of the ethnic groups, with their typical concerns in the USSR.

In his long address about the new RSFSR Constitution to the special Seventh Session of the Supreme Soviet of the RSFSR's Ninth Convocation, April 10, 1978, the principal speaker demonstrated the peculiar restrictions governing politicians dealing with the issue of Russia's identity and function in the RSFSR and USSR. Because of the lack of a chief executive usual for a USSR union republic (in the other 14 units this is the first secretary of the communist party of the specific area), Mikhail S. Solomentsev, since July 1971 Chairman of the RSFSR Council of Ministers, took the lead here. Simultaneously Chairman of the Commission for preparing the Draft Constitution for the RSFSR, his main points touched the ethnic field and their phrasing. The RSFSR's multiethnicity is repeatedly emphasized, Russian ethnicity never hinted at. When turning to what he calls "special traits" of the RSFSR he does so only to recognize numerous eponymous subunits (autonomous Soviet socialist republics - ASSRs - and the like) to be found within the union republic. His sole mention of "Russia" as such is prefixed with "Soviet," a combination everywhere regularly avoided in the 100-plus letters printed by the editors of Soviet Russia throughout the weeks preceding Chairman Solomentsev's speech. Singling out what he calls a "socialist internationalism" said to be inherent in Soviet individuals, the speaker makes a point of linking the RSFSR to the remaining union republics. Ignoring the constitutional provision for union republic secession, he asserts that the "Russia-wide Federation" (Rossiiskaia Federatsiia) is an inseverable part of an indivisible Soviet state. Here, he stresses the theme that the RSFSR and the SSRs, in his view comprise a friendly fraternal family (sem'ia) (the standard CPSU formula). Repeating this motif, he insists that the ethnic groups within the RSFSR belong in what he calls the family of Soviet ethnic groups (narody). The address deals with the RSFSR's alleged sovereignty only indirectly by once mentioning the many ministries and departments of the union republic engaged in economic, technical, and cultural exchanges with foreign countries. Overall, Chairman Solomentsev persistently stresses similarity rather than difference between the USSR and RSFSR constitutions, declaring that the RSFSR version springs from the Union-wide edition, although the reverse was originally true. Revealing an obvious intention to identify the RSFSR as closely as possible with the USSR, he diminishes any aspect of

Russia's separateness. This obfuscation can allow Soviet leaders (and ethnic Russians) to believe that their "Russia," defined as they prefer, is the real USSR, or that the USSR is the real Russia, notwithstanding the names by which it may be designated today.

In taking this line, the speaker manipulates the theme of collectivity (family) but entirely skirts those individual group ethnic concerns most on the minds of letter writers whose comments were printed during the RSFSR's constitutional discussion. If the tiny fraction published from the thousands sent represent general attitudes toward ethnic matters at all, this political address only tangentially relates to them. Especially the powerful feeling for place of origin, for motherland, among the general public of the RSFSR, very largely ethnic Russian, escapes Chairman Solomentsev, probably because he considers himself to be a central government figure, rather than an executive representing the interests of the ethnic Russians' eponymous union republic.(35) Czarist policy of 70 years ago finds a familiar echo in that RSFSR-CPSU dogma worded recently in a six-column banner on the front page of Soviet Russia: "The people and party are one" (Narod i partiia edinyi). The czarist slogan spoke of "...the oneness of people and Czar..." (...edinenie naroda i Tsaria...).(36)

The everyday view in ethnic affairs of the RSFSR finds channels through which to enunciate such ideas publicly when official spokesmen decline the responsibility. Aside from jokes, impressive letter and prose writing (see chaps. 6, 8, and 9), and poetic composition in this very sphere,(37) there are yet other ways of accomplishing it. In one, the popular mind and bureaucratic mentality of officialdom interact symbiotically to harness what may be the strongest twin drives in ethnic Russian character. The first of the pair appears to embrace the deep need for the individual Russian to exist among family and, by extension, for his/her group to live surrounded by other groups in a kind of comforting community of familiar but distinct entities. Both the Great Arms of the Russia-wide Empire and the USSR Arms (Figs. 1.2 and 9.1) graphically illustrate this familial principle. Besides the evidence of the public discussions held in 1978, literature and nonfiction writing persistently address the theme of isolation negatively and the urge for shared effort or experience positively. This goes far beyond the reach of propaganda for "the collective" often encountered in the official language. The trait has been discovered in Russian life-style of the past as well as the present. Exclusion from family signified, in turn, ejection from home ground.(38) Attachment to native soil, to motherland, evidently forms a second, overriding feature of Russian ethnic character.

Punitive separation from family and home terrain, undergone by so many, has been denounced but romanticized, sometimes mythologized, in Russian civilization. Not only the exiles' travail, which has been participated in by Russians nearly everywhere, but exactly the "change of place...tearing up of roots...severing of links...." generally has been felt and has stimulated great empathy and understanding, but simultaneously pervasive guilt and hostility.(39) If that exile literature and personal history are not convincing enough, there is still another sort of evidence to show that family and home soil matter more than most other group nourishment for ethnic Russians.

Both the style and extent of formal punishments provided for under the laws of the RSFSR and its czarist predecessor that mete out exile and banishment are remarkable. The contemporary Code of Criminal Law for the RSFSR specifies a minimum of 35 crimes for which sentence of exile or banishment or both may be imposed. Some of these offenses are political (Articles 64-71, 74, 227), including the notorious Article 70, used against Iuli M. Daniel, Andrey Siniavsky, and other dissidents, making free speech about the USSR's negative features a crime.(40) Augmenting that list is the decree (ukaz) issued by the RSFSR Supreme Soviet and its Presidium May 4, 1961, making persons without visible means of regular support, including intellectuals free-lancing or consulting for a living, subject to exile for periods of from two to five years, the sentence authorized for most offenses calling for this punishment in the Code of Criminal Law for the RSFSR. Under this measure, the authorities exiled Amalrik and other Russians to Siberia, usually to areas of ethnically-mixed population, or to the non-Russian subunits of the RSFSR like the Mordvin and Yakut ASSRs.(41) Exiling them to an alien ethnic society on unfamiliar soil presumably fully answered the prescription for complete ejection from the Russian community. Exile (ssylka Article 25), conventionally more forbidding than banishment (vysylka Article 26), became less terrible to up-rooted Russians in the RSFSR, because exile made the victim the resident or ward of a certain settlement or place (kept him somewhat in the family). Banishment, however, prohibited the deported person from living in some restricted areas but assigned no definite community to harbor the deportee, thus depriving him or her of formal familial protections afforded by the exile system.(42) In this contradictory manner, Russian society inflicts upon its members the devastating separation from home, hearth, and kin which it loathes the most.

Consequences of these life patterns are rife with omens for the USSR and the world. Such an alienated ethnic Russian population will likely panic without a firm, arbitrary hand at the top to dictate its behavior. Nor can that population survive comfortably on its own. Article 69 in the new RSFSR

Constitution legalizing union-republic secession is meaningless
not so much because Soviet authorities would never permit the
largely Russian constituent republic to secede from the USSR,
but because Russians could not tolerate the international
isolation and exposure to which that secession would subject
them. The eponymous union republics that cushion the core of
the Russia-wide Federation to the west, south, and southeast,
rather than protecting the Russian heartland from foreign
marauders, are performing a singularly domestic function.
Without them, ethnic Russians could, as they did in 1917-1921
in their distress over ethnic nakedness, devour each other in
an orgy of self-destruction. Reassured by the enclosing circle
of non-Russian ethnic groups subject to the common Russian
center for guidance and control, a kind of equilibrium is
sustained within the explosive Russian population itself. It is,
therefore, an ethnic group mainly unified in outline, and that
outward profile along land frontiers is defined almost everywhere by the ethnic groups which range around Russia,
except along the Chinese border (about which Russians feel
acute discomfort), both inside the RSFSR and well along the
periphery of the remaining USSR (see Fig. 1.1).

This feeling of resentful dependence upon alien subordinate groups held within the USSR, and fear of the outside
world that would confront Russians if the larger of those
internal buffers escaped domination, contributes to Russian
group behavior and persona. Suspiciousness of outsiders,
envy, parochialism, intolerance, and, above all, unthinking,
blind patriotism, grow in such a climate. That patriotism by
default attaches itself to place, and is said, for these and
similar reasons, to have "become a substitute for all other
forms of belief," according to a young Russian scientist in the
1970s.(43) Thus, Russians remain an ethnically underdeveloped people late in the twentieth century. The gradual
transformation suggested by revivals of interest in monuments
of the past or in the central Russian countryside, perhaps
augmented by official concessions to RSFSR institutional
structure and union-republic parity within the USSR, can
scarcely move expeditiously to overcome that handicap.

NOTES*

(1) Vsesoiuznaia perepis' naseleniia 17 dekabria 1926 g. Kratkie svodki, vol. 4 (Moscow: Izdanie TsSU SSSR, 1928), p. XXIV.

(2) Marc Raeff, "Patterns of Russian Imperial Policy Toward the Nationalities," Soviet Nationality Problems, edited by Edward Allworth (New York: Columbia University Press, 1971), pp. 36-39.

(3) Violet Conolly, "The 'nationalities question' in the last phase of tsardom," Russia Enters the Twentieth Century, 1894-1917, edited by Erwin Oberlander (New York: Schocken Books, 1971), p. 152-53.

(4) Polnoe sobranie zakonov rossiiskoi imperii, 3d compilation, vol. XXV (1905), Section I Supplement (St. Petersburg: n.p., 1908), p. 637, entry no. 26656; P. E. Kazanskii, Vlast' vserossiiskago Imperatora. Ocherki dieistvuiushchago russkago prava (Odessa: Tipografiia "Tekhnik," 1913), p. 688.

(5) Michael T. Florinsky, Russia: A History and an Interpretation, vol. II (New York: The MacMillan Company, 1953), pp. 1116-19.

(6) Ladis K. D. Kristof, "The Russian Image of Russia: An Applied Study in Geopolitical Methodology," Essays in Political Geography, edited by C. A. Fisher (London: Methuen & Co., 1968), pp. 367-372, citing N. Ia. Danilevskii, Rossiia i Evropa... (St. Petersburg: 1889), 4th ed., p. 531f; K. Leont'ev, Vostok, Rossiia i Slavianstvo: Sbornik statei, 2 vols., (Moscow: 1885-6), vol. I, p. 285.

(7) N. A. Zakharov, Sistema russkoi gosudarstevennoi vlasti (Novocherkassk: n.p., 1912), p. 60, cited in Kazanskii, pp. XX-XXI.

(8) Kazanskii, pp. VI-VII.

(9) Kristof, p. 352.

(10) Robert C. Tucker, "The Image of Dual Russia," The Transformation of Russian Society, edited by Cyril E. Black (Cambridge, Mass.: Harvard University Press, 1967, 2d printing), p. 588.

(11) Hans Rogger, "Nationalism and the State: A Russian Dilemma," Comparative Studies in Society and History, vol. IV (The Hague: Mouton & Co., 1962), pp. 262-63.

---

*Two abbreviations repeatedly used in the footnotes for this article are BSE for Bol'shaia sovetskaia entsiklopediia, and SR for Sovetskaia Rossiia.

(12) Leopold Haimson, "Russian Culture and Western Lib-
      eralism," Seminar Reports, Program of General Education
      in the Humanities, Columbia University, 5, no. 2 (Fall
      1976): 116, 119-21.
(13) T. H. Rigby, Communist Party Membership in the USSR
      (Princeton, N.J.: Princeton University Press, 1968), p.
      366; Spravochnik partiinogo rabotnika. Vyp. 18 for 1978
      (Moscow: Izdatel'stvo Politicheskoi Literatury, 1978), p.
      382; Partiinoe stroitel'stvo. Uchebnoe sposobie (Moscow:
      Izdatel'stvo Politcheskoi Literatury, 1970), p. 65.
(14) "KPSS v tsifrakh," Partiinaia zhizn' no. 10 (1976), p.
      16; "KPSS v tsifrakh (K 70-letiiu II s"ezda RSDRP,"
      Partiinaia zhizn', no. 14 (July 1973), p. 11; Itogi
      vsesoiuznoi perepisi naseleniia 1970 goda. Natsional'nyi
      sostav naseleniia SSSR, vol. IV (Moscow: "Statistika,"
      1973), p. 12.
(15) Rigby, p. 509.
(16) Letopis' periodicheskikh izdanii SSSR, 1955-1960 godov
      Part I "Journals" (Moscow: Izdatel'stvo Vsesoiuznoi
      Knizhnoi Palaty, 1963), pp. 62-65.
(17) "Sovetskaia Rossiia," BSE, 24 (Moscow: Izdatel'stvo
      "Sovetskaia Entsiklopediia," 1976): 23; Gazety SSSR
      1917-1960 (Moscow: Izdatel'stvo "Kniga," 1970), entry
      no. 396.
(18) Itogi...1970 goda, vol. IV, p. 12
(19) Pechat' SSSR v 1976 godu. Statisticheskii sbornik
      (Moscow: "Statistika," 1977), pp. 191-194; "Sovet
      Ozbekistani," BSE, vol. 24, book 1, 3d ed. (Moscow:
      Izdatel'stvo "Sovetskaia Entsiklopediia," 1976), p. 19;
      "Kommunisti," BSE, vol. 12, 3d ed. (Moscow:
      Izdatel'stvo "Sovetskaia Entsiklopediia," 1973), p. 604;
      "Rahva haal," BSE, vol. 21, 3d ed. (Moscow:
      Izdatel'stvo "Sovetskaia Entsiklopediia," 1975), p. 508;
      Itogi...1970 goda, vol. IV, pp. 13, 15.
(20) "Sovetskaia Rossiia," BSE, vol. 24 (Moscow: Izdatel'stvo
      "Sovetskaia Entsiklopediia," 1976), p. 23.
(21) Ezhegodnik. Bol'shaia sovetskaia entsiklopediia (Moscow:
      Gosudarstvennoe Nauchnoe Izdatel'stvo "Sovetskaia
      Entsiklopediia," 1959), p. 147; Ezhegodnik. Bol'shaia
      sovetskaia entsiklopediia (Moscow: Gosudarstvennoe
      Nauchnoe Izdatel'stvo "Sovetskaia Entsiklopediia," 1967),
      p. 126.
(22) Ukrainsk'ka radians'ka entsiklopediia 16 vols. (Kiev:
      Golovna Redaktsiia Ukrains'koi Radians'koi Entsiklopedii,
      1959-1968).
(23) "Konstitutsiia (Osnovnoi Zakon) rossiiskoi sovetskoi
      federativnoi sotsialisticheskoi respubliki," SR (Apr. 13,
      1978), p. 4.
(24) P. Klimuk, "Samaia blizkaia zvezda," SR (Apr. 9, 1978),
      p. 2; "Gosudarstvennye gerby Soiuza SSR i sovetskikh

sotsialisticheskikh respublik," BSE, vol. 6, 3d ed. (Moscow: Izdatel'stvo "Sovetskaia Entsiklopediia," 1973), between pp. 352 and 353.

(25) "Ordena SSSR," BSE vol. 18, 3d ed. (Moscow: Izdatel'stvo "Sovetskaia Entsiklopediia, 1974), pp. 492, and illustrations between pp. 496 and 497.

(26) Whitney Smith, Flags Through the Ages and Across the World (New York: McGraw Hill, 1975), pp. 282-83.

(27) Konstitutsiia (osnovnoi zakon) rossiiskoi sovetskoi federativnoi sotsialisticheskoi respubliki, chapter XIII, articles 148, 149, and 150 (Moscow: "Iuridicheskaia Literatura," 1969), p. 29.

(28) "Konstitutsiia (osnovnoi zakon) rossiiskoi sovetskoi federativnoi respubliki," (1978), p. 4; "Gosudarstvennye gimny soiuznykh respublik," Muzykal'naia entsiklopediia, vol. 2 (Moscow: Izdatel'stvo "Sovetskaia Entsiklopediia," 1974), p. 22; "Gimn," Muzykal'naia entsiklopediia, vol. I (Moscow: Izdatel'stvo "Sovetskaia Entsiklopediia," 1973), p. 983; A letter to the author dated April 27, 1979, from the Information Department, Embassy of the USSR, Washington, D. C., states: "But, as far as we know, there is no official anthem of the Russian Soviet Federated Socialist Republic (RSFSR)."

(29) "Sila nashei demokratii," SR (Apr. 10, 1978), p. 1; "Doklad M. S. Solomentseva na sessii verkhovnogo soveta RSFSR 10 aprelia 1978 g.," SR (Apr. 11, 1978), p. 3.

(30) Irina Arkhipova, "Pesn' o Rossii. Odobriaem," SR (Apr. 6, 1978), p. 2; "V bratskoi sem'e narodov," Apr. 12, 1978), pp. 1 and 3.

(31) D. Lesniak, "Istochnik vsekh bogatsv," SR (Mar. 21, 1978), p. 2; K. Drozdov, "O zemle za domom," SR (Mar. 25, 1978), p. 2; V. Kokoreva, "Schastlivy svoei sud'boi," SR (Mar. 28, 1978), p. 2; V. Volkov, "Ot imeni rabochei semi,'" SR (Apr. 9, 1978), p. 2; V. Stenkovoi, "Radost' truda," SR (Apr. 10, 1978), p. 2; "V bratskoi sem'e narodov," SR (Apr. 12, 1978), p. 3.

(32) V. Plechistov, "Prazdnik truda," SR (Mar. 17, 1978), p. 2; I. Prokop'ev, "Podlinno ravnye; v bol'shoi sem'e rossiiskoi," SR (Mar. 22, 1978), p. 2; Iu. Riurikov, "Chto zavisit ot sem'i," SR (Mar. 30, 1978), p. 2; G. Eremin, "S dumoi o rodine. Odobriaem," SR (Apr. 7, 1978), p. 2; Oleg Shestinskii, "Russkoe pole," [extract from a long poem] SR (Apr. 9, 1978), p. 3; "Partiia vedet k kommunizmu," SR (Apr. 11, 1978), p. 3; "V bratskoi sem'e narodov," SR (Apr. 12, 1978), pp. 1-3; and V. Strukov, "Sviashchennyi dolg," SR (Apr. 10, 1978), p. 2.

(33) D. Ochirov, "Trud v radost'," SR (Mar. 29, 1978), p. 2; Igor Isaev, "Zemlia zemel'--Rossiia. Odobriaem," SR (Mar. 31, 1978), p. 2; Suleiman Rabadanov, "Novye pesni

gor," SR (Apr. 9, 1978), p. 2; V. Stenkovoi, p. 2; V. Selemenev, "Tvoi vklad," SR (Apr. 10, 1978), p. 2.

(34) B. Toporin, "Na velikoi osnove," SR (Mar. 17, 1978), p. 2; V. Aizenshtein, "Vnoshu predlozhenie," SR (Mar. 18, 1978), p. 2; V. Verkin, "Vnoshu predlozhenie. Splochennost'," SR (Mar. 23, 1978), p. 2; I. Prokop'ev, p. 2; A. Ovchinnikova, "Vlast' na mestakh; v bol'shoi sem'e rossiiskoi," SR (Mar. 26, 1978), p. 2; "Nakaz naroda," SR (Apr. 9, 1978), p. 1; "Partiia vedet k kommunizm," p. 1; "V bratskoi sem'e narodov," pp. 1-2.

(35) "Solomentsev, Mikhail Sergeevich," BSE, vol. 24, book 1 (Moscow: Izdatel'stvo "Sovetskaia Entsiklopediia," 1976), p. 160; "Zasedanie Prezidiuma verkhovnogo Soveta RSFSR," SR (Mar. 15, 1978), p. 1; "Doklad tovarishcha M. S. Solomentseva na sessii verkhovnogo Soveta RSFSR 10 aprelia 1978 g.," pp. 2-3.

(36) "Narod i partiia edinyi," SR (Dec. 28, 1978), p. 1; Polnoe sobranie zakonov... (1905), p. 637.

(37) O russkoi zemle! Sbornik stikhov russkikh poetov (Moscow: "Molodaia Gvardiia," 1971); Moskva lyricheskaia. Antologiia odnogo stikhotvoreniia (Moscow: Moskovskii Rabochii, 1976).

(38) Henry V. Dicks, "Some Notes on Russian National Character," The Transformation of Russian Society, ed. Cyril E. Black (Cambridge, Mass.: Harvard University Press, 1967), pp. 640-641.

(39) Aleksandr I. Solzhenitsyn, The Gulag Archipelago 1918-1956: An Experiment in Literary Investigation Parts V-VII (New York: Harper & Row, 1978), pp. 339-40, 349, 408.

(40) Ugolovnyi kodeks RSFSR. Ofitsial'nyi tekst s izmeneniami na 16 sentiabria 1966 g.... (Moscow: Izdatel'stvo "Iuridicheskaia Literatura," 1966), pp. 39-79; George Kennan, Siberia and the Exile System, (London: James R. Osgood, McIlvaine & Co., 1891, repr. New York: Praeger Publishers, 1970), vol. 1, pp. 242-77; vol. 2, pp. 430-71.

(41) "Ob usilenii bor'by s litsami ukloniaiushchimisia ot obshchestvenno poleznogo truda i vedushchimi antiobshchestvennyi paraziticheskii obraz zhizni," SR (May 5, 1961), p. 3; Vedomosti verkhovnogo Soveta RSFSR no. 18 (May 4, 1961), Item 273; Andrei Amalrik, Involuntary Journey to Siberia (New York: Harcourt Brace Jovanovich, Inc., 1970), pp. 10, 30-113, 156-65.

(42) Ugolovnyi kodeks RSFSR, p. 13; Aleksandr I. Solzhenitsyn, pp. 450-467.

(43) Hedrick Smith, The Russians (New York: Quadrangle Books, 1976), p. 304.

II

The Implications of Group Literature and History for Ethnic Politics

Proposition 2: The current revival of literary concern with ethnic roots, like the resurgent interest in Russian history and in earlier Russian art and artifacts among Russian writers and other intellectuals, has import for the Soviet ethnic and political situation.

3 History and Russian Ethnocentrism

Roman Szporluk

Russian ethnocentrism is concerned with two basic issues: first, the relationship between the Russian ethnic group and the Soviet regime, and, second, the position of the Russians among the other ethnic groups of the USSR. On both these issues, Russian ethnic thinking has been developing its point of view by reference to history.(1)

Although such distinctions involve an oversimplification of individual positions, Russian ethnocentrist opinion, insofar as it is concerned with historical problems, may be grouped under two broad headings. One current conceives Russian ethnicity as basically cultural or spiritual in nature. It attaches fundamental importance to the language, literature, ancestral homelands (soil), and religion as markers of Russian identity, and it tends to judge politics (the state) in terms of its conformity to these nonpolitical dimensions of Russian ethnicity. Some, but by no means all, conceptions of Russian history inspired by this proposition result in a political challenge to the Soviet system, indeed, in a denial of its legitimacy. To some, the Soviet regime, because it is based on Marxism-Leninism, is "un-Russian."

The second current in Russian ethnocentrist thought views Russian history as an essentially political process, as the history of the Russian state, which it views as the most genuine expression of the Russian ethnic group. On the whole, those who share this position treat the Soviet regime as a continuation of the old Russian state, including its immediate predecessor, the Romanov Empire, and they believe that the uniquely Russian genius has created a political form of government that is opposed to western liberal and democratic political systems. They are less interested in ideologies as such, which they judge by their usefulness to the state. Because their approval of the Soviet regime is based on their recognition of it as a Russian institution, the challenge which this current of ethnocentrism poses today is directed against the federal structure of the USSR - the principle of equality of the ethnic groups of the USSR, not the party in power. While the former current attacks the regime as un-Russian, this one directs its attack against non-Russian groups, and in this attack it seeks the support of the regime.

To understand these two challenges to official ideology it is necessary to place them in historical perspective, against the background of Soviet history since 1917. So viewed, they appear to be critiques of the Stalinist historical ideology which was consolidated in the 1930s and has been retained in its essentials to the present time.

Karl Deutsch, writes: "Where all memory is lost, where all past information and preferences have ceased to be effective, we are no longer dealing with a self-determining individual or social group, but with a self-steering automation."(2) Aleksandr I. Solzhenitsyn speaks about literature, but it is clear that his words also apply to historical writing:

> There is one...invaluable direction in which literature transmits incontrovertible condensed experience; from generation to generation. In this way literature becomes the living memory of a nation [ethnic group] woe to the nation whose literature is cut short by the intrusion of force. This is not merely interference with "freedom of the press" but the sealing up of a nation's heart, the excision of its memory.(3)

The emergence of unorthodox historical ideas in post-Stalinist USSR is viewed in this essay as one of the aspects of a broader process of the rise of social and political thought, the formation of ideas expressing the point of view of diverse social, including ethnic, groups in that country. The development of separate memories and memory facilities (for this is what the emergence of uncontrolled historical views is) "may represent aspects of the process of secession."(4) In this case, it is a "secession" from Stalinism. The discussion will consider new history after 1917, the Stalinist synthesis of Marxism and Russian ethnocentrism, history after Joseph V. Stalin's death in 1953, the "culturalist" current, "statism," historical ideas of the Young Guard, and an imperialist utopia.

The Stalinist historical conception was imposed on historians in the Soviet Union after a period which may be described as "internationalist" or, perhaps more accurately, "anti-nationalist." Although Marxism considers class, not ethnicity, the primary form of social tie, its followers did not develop a conception of history as a history of classes and class struggles; such a history, one would have thought, would treat ethnic groups and states as important but subordinate phenomena in a class history; naturally, it would be a history transcending narrow geographic and ethnic boundaries. The Bolsheviks took power in Russia in the name of the world proletariat, claiming to be only its advance guard. It would have made sense from their point of view to develop an appropriate large-scale view of history. In such a history, the "precursors" of modern socialism, especially its Bolshevik incarnation, would be Spartacus, Wat Tyler, Jan Hus, Thomas Munzer, various radical religious reformers, peasant rebels, and so on. They would also be Russian revolutionaries, but the history which the first socialist state on earth would regard as it own would not be any one ethnic group's history.(5)

Immediately after 1917, universalism was in vogue, and Spartacus and the Communards, Rosa Luxemburg or Karl Liebknecht, became household names. No new history was formed, however; in place of "Russian history," a "history of the peoples of the USSR" was introduced.(6) In practice, in the largest and most powerful of constituent Soviet republics, the Russia-wide Soviet Federated Socialist Republic (RSFSR), a new name covered the same old subject, a history of Russia. (In the other union republics, but not in Russia, separate histories, besides a common history of the Soviet peoples, were written.) It became, however, an "antihistory" in relation to what it replaced: the heroes of czarist textbooks (czars, general, saints) were its villains; the outcasts of old (the Pugachevs, the Razins, the Shamils) were now transformed into heroes. This antihistory pictured the czarist state as a class exploiter and as a conqueror and oppressor of non-Russian groups. Implicit in the conception of a "history of the people of the USSR" was the idea that before 1917 they were united by common oppression; no positive value was attached to any ethnic group's inclusion under czarist rule. The Soviet Union as a multiethnic state was seen as a product of the 1917 revolution and its aftermath – not in any way as a continuation of a "unity" that had been formed earlier, in however rudimentary a form. A new opening, an initial step toward a wider international community, not a Russian Empire transformed into the USSR. Politically, this historical conception corresponded to the structure of the federal Soviet state. If the USSR consisted of various ethnic groups building "socialism in one country," history of the people of the USSR was its "history in one country."

As long as one could plausibly argue that the USSR would expand, and convincingly claim that the post-1917 system provided the formerly oppressed ethnic groups with freedom they lacked under the czars, this conception represented a tolerable framework for the study of prerevolutionary history. In the early 1930s, the prospects of a European revolution that would lift the Soviet Union's isolation were dim. About that time, the situation of the non-Russian ethnic groups began to deteriorate, the central government in Moscow began to restrict the autonomy of constituent republics, and the Russians were openly regaining a dominant position in the Soviet "federation." Those changed perceptions and realities, external and internal, provided the background for formulation of a new view of history.(7) Soviet patriotism reflected attachment to an ideology, not only to a particular portion of the earth.

The new historical conception reexamined the historical record of czarist Russia in order to declare that apart from being a class exploiter of the working people, and an oppressor of non-Russian ethnic groups, the Russian state had also played a "progressive" role; its foreign wars had been just, defensive measures aimed at saving the ethnic groups under Russia from a "foreign yoke." Thus, indirectly, an idea was suggested that Russian domination had not been foreign - not, at any rate, as foreign as Turkish, Polish, or Persian rule would have been, for the Empire's non-Russians.

More positive yet was the new official perception of Russian culture of the past: writers, painters, composers, even if they had been associated with the "ruling classes," were accorded public honor as prominent Russian figures. At the same time, Soviet ideology, including historical ideology, continued to consider itself Marxist. In reality, Marxism-Leninism in the USSR was localized. To become an ethnocentric communism, though, it managed to appear abroad, among the followers of foreign communist parties, as a force committed to internationalism. Some anticommunist Russians, in exile or at home, claimed in the early 1920s to have detected signs of a localization of the October 1917 revolutionary movement. "Nationalization of October" was the title of an article published in 1925. They were accordingly prepared to support the Soviet Union as a Russian state - the name "USSR" they regarded as a temporary expedient - even though they did not approve of its economic and social policies and goals. What they valued most in the Soviet system was its capacity to maintain the territorial integrity, with some exceptions, of the old imperial Russia. The author of that article welcomed the emergence of what he called the new "Soviet state nation," under which he understood the multiethnic population of the USSR's being politically integrated in the Soviet system, but "in a Russian national [ethnic] form." He was not concerned about the rights of non-Russian languages in education and culture; what mattered was the Russian character of the state.(8)

Certain Russian chauvinists accepted the USSR for this reason, but an overwhelming majority of Russian emigrants refused to do so. They objected to Stalinism on political, cultural, and religious grounds. Some of them correctly perceived that Stalinism was not a return to an unqualified Russian orientation. Soviet ethnocentrism, Frederick C. Barghoorn noted two decades ago, was not "a purely 'Russian' product." Rather, it was an ideology of a new ruling class which manipulated both Russian symbols and those of Marxism. This combination of a parochial Russian culture with the universalist ideology of Marxism contained an element of contradiction. Besides, the commitment on the part of the regime to Russian ethnocentrism was not fully "sincere." It did not accept such elements of traditional Russian culture as the Orthodox religion. Barghoorn argued that tension between government and people would exist as long as the Soviet system remained totalitarian, and that the Soviet population felt that "the government and the people do not really speak the same language." Soviet patriotism helped to conceal the internal contradictions of Soviet society under "familiar, vague and emotionally moving" words.(9) Writing in 1955, he speculated about the "nonofficial thought" which existed in Russia, although one could only guess its content.

Among the many and diverse currents of thought to have emerged in the USSR after Stalin's death, one has concerned Russian ethnocentrism. Stalin granted the Russians a privileged position in the country, bestowing on the Russian ethnic group the title of "elder brother," identifying the USSR with pre-1917 Russia, and making liberal use of Russian ethnic symbols. Nevertheless, the country formally remained a multiethnic state in which "Russia" was but one of many component units. Russian culture was subjected to ideological and political censorship, and the use of prerevolutionary culture remained selective. Stalin's method of promoting Russification of the non-Russians was not one of publicly affirming the Russian character of the country; rather, he promoted actual Russification while virtually obliterating the separate identity of the Russia-wide Soviet Federated Socialist Republic (RSFSR). Formally it was the eponymous republic of the Russians, within the broader concepts (but not expressly defined as Russian) of the Soviet Union, Soviet People, or Soviet Patriotism.

In those circumstances, the first post-Stalinist concessions specifically to Russian feeling expressed themselves in measures such as the revival of governmental and other public institutions of the RSFSR which had been submerged within the Union-wide framework under Stalin (ministries and voluntary associations, such as the writers union), and the greater use of the name "Russia" itself. Thus, in 1956, a newspaper called Sovetskaia Rossiia, outlet of the Central Committee, Communist Party of the Soviet Union (CC, CPSU) Bureau for the RSFSR, was founded. This may have been the first paper in several decades to carry the word "Russia" in its name. Stalin had promoted Russification - but he suppressed the words "Russia" and "Russian."

Russian ethnocentric thought seems to be concerned with two issues.(10) Russian ethnocentrism is not a homogeneous manifestation, and, moreover, Russian dissident opinion includes also explicitly nonethnocentric elements.(11) One broad current, within which further subdivisions could be made, is concerned with Russian history as the history of the Russian ethnic group which it defines in cultural terms. The history of Russia is the history of its art, architecture, literature, ideas, church, and religious thought. Its territorial core is located where the Russian ethnic group was formed. Relatively less importance is attached to the political organization of society, although such institutions as monarchy are recognized by at least some "culturalists" as part of the Russian heritage. The monarchy itself is seen as a religious institution to some extent: "the Orthodox czar." From a conception of history like this, a variety of political conclusions may be drawn that are of import today. Some people express concern about the state of preservation of Russian historical monuments. Others believe that the works of Russian Orthodox theology should be made available, and that the Church should enjoy greater freedom.

Yet others view the peasants of central Russian provinces as the most authentic representatives of Russian ethnicity and demand that various social, economic, and cultural measures be taken to help it and the region they live in. Still others question the ideological foundations of the Soviet state by arguing that Marxism-Leninism is a foreign, thus non-Russian, scheme that should be replaced by an ideology that is "truly Russian." Finally, there are those who are prepared to go one step further and advocate violent overthrow of the Soviet regime and its replacement by an ethnocentric regime.(12)

The culturalist position in its most extreme political form may be found in Solzhenitsyn. Among his many statements to this effect, the following might be considered representative: "...the transition from pre-1917 Russia to the USSR is not a continuation but a mortal fracture of the spine, which almost destroyed Russia as a nation."(13) While Solzhenitsyn has been engaged in intellectual struggle with the Soviet regime and its ideology, in Russia there existed, from 1964 to 1967, a secret organization which sought, as its ultimate goal, to overthrow communist rule and replace it by a system based on "Social-Christian" ideology. This organization called itself the Russia-wide Social-Christian Union for the Liberation of the People.(14)

The conception of Russian identity upheld by the Union was cultural-ideological, not political or ethnic in the narrower (linguistic) sense. It conceived of Russia as an Orthodox Christian ethnic unit, and it viewed this spiritual or cultural

identity of the Russian people as something taking precedence
over their political organization. The legitimacy of the
government, in this view, depended on the government's
conformity to the spiritual character of the ethnic group.
Although the program of the Union promised that other
religions would be allowed, in the future Russia, to preach
and worship without hindrance, the Russia it hoped to
establish was not going to be a secular state. It would be a
country with an official ideology, and the leaders of the
Orthodox Church would enjoy a political function in the
state.(15)   At least some of the ideologists of the Union appear
to think that a real Russian cannot be a religious person.
Evgeniy Vagin is reported to have said: "Yes, in this sense I
share Dostoevsky's belief that to be a Russian is to be
Orthodox, and that religion is certainly the profound nature of
the Russian person."(16)

Article 83 in the program offered Russian help to those
ethnic groups located where Soviet troops are now stationed
"to initiate their own ethnic self-determination on the basis of
Social-Christianity." Is one to conclude that if those ethnic
groups chose to determine their fate in some other form, they
would not be helped? Insofar as Soviet internal ethnic
problems were concerned, the Union claimed to speak for
Russia and all of the USSR when it declared itself "a patriotic
organization consisting of selfless representatives of all the
nationalities of Great Russia." (Article 73) The Union
rejected the right to independence for the Ukraine, Belorussia,
and the smaller ethnic groups of the USSR; and one of its
publicists maintains that Russia is by nature a multiethnic
state.(17)   (The Buddhist Kalmyks, accordingly, would be
given the benefit of living in an Orthodox, even though social,
state.)

Although the Russia-wide Social-Christian Union of the
People was suppressed by the authorities, Professor John
Dunlop considers its ideas to pose the most serious challenge
to the regime. He believes they will gain in influence in the
future. Among the reasons for the appeal of the Union's
ideology, according to him, are the comprehensiveness of its
program as an alternative to the Soviet system, its preference
for a "maximally bloodless coup d'etat" as a means of winning
power, and, finally, the personal heroism of its leader, Igor
Ogurtsov.(18)   In fact, ideas close to those of the Union have
been presented in such samizdat publications as Veche, Zemlia,
and Moskovskii sbornik.   They are not as uncompromisingly
hostile to the government, but they base their conception of
Russian ethnic unity on cultural (religious, spiritual) features,
and they judge political problems through an ideological,
culturalist prism.(19)

The other major grouping within Russian dissent may be
given the name of "statism." Culturalism's concern with

Russian historical identity implies that Marxist-Leninist doctrine is an inadequate tool for comprehending the richness of Russian culture. Culturalism in any form contains within itself an element of ideological dissent, but "statism" views ideology, Marxist or any other, instrumentally. Its classic spokesman in the 1920s, N. V. Ustrialov, was not in the least disturbed by Moscow's being the seat of the world communist movement. On the contrary, he regarded this internationalist, universal ideology and movement as an instrument in the policies of the Russian state. An identical sentiment was expressed by another anticommunist Russian in the 1920s: "The International will pass, but the boundaries will remain," wrote emigrant Vasiliy V. Shulgin in 1922, and he expressed essentially the same view in the 1950s and 1960s, when he was in the Soviet Union. A Ukrainian dissident has complained that "today even the enemy of communism V. V. Shulgin is welcomed among us, because he has expressed his Great-Power sympathies for the existing boundaries" (a typical statist position which cares about power, not ideology).(20)

Like the culturalists, statists represent more than a single current. One point of view within the statist orientation is represented by the authors of a document entitled "A Word of the Ethnic Group" or "An Ethnic Group Speaks" (Slovo natsii). According to Professor Dimitry V. Pospielovsky, the authors of that manifesto "may be much more interested in a revitalized national centralized dictatorship, a sort of national Bolshevism of the N. V. Ustrialov type, than in Christianity, per se. Their view of it as an institution being of the [Konstantin P.] Pobedonostsev type."(21) Pospielovsky further argues: "Their insistence on the necessity of a strong centralized government, their acceptance of dictatorship as a system of government, their elitism, are such that it becomes difficult to see in what essentials they oppose the Soviet system."(22) The document is racist and anti-Semitic. Egalitarianism and cosmopolitanism are called "an ideology of the Jewish diaspora." It demands that Russians play the dominant role in the multiethnic state in which they live. It definitely rejects federalism.(23) The statist school, then, sees the essence of Russian ethnic unity in the state as it developed in the course of Russian history; that is, a centralized, absolutist, multiethnic empire, opposed to Western style liberal and democratic societies and dominated by the Russians. Who are the contemporary "statists" in the USSR? What do they criticize, and what do they want to get?

The monthly journal Molodaia gvardiia (Young Guard), outlet of the youth organization Komsomol, served as a vehicle for statist historical ideas in the years 1968 to 1970. One specialist has devoted a special chapter to the ideology of Young Guardism in his book about the Russian "New Right." He concludes that the journal, through the contributions of its leading authors Mikhail Petrovich, Lobanov, Viktor Chalmaev, and Sergey S. Semanov, replaced the Marxist analysis of modern problems of the world in terms of classes and class conflicts with a juxtaposition of "Russia" and "Russianness" to "Americanism." Lobanov's program was to give the regime and its policies a more pronounced Russian character. For Chalmaev, "there is no gulf between Soviet and Czarist Russia....From his point of view, the October Revolution was only a stage in the maturing of the 'Russian spirit,' and by no means the epochal date of the birth of socialism....The actions of Ivan the Terrible...are just as important as those of Lenin - all of them led the 'national spirit' on behalf of the state." (24)

The same specialist believes that the ideologists of the Young Guard enjoyed considerable official support until the publication of the article by Semanov entitled "On Relative and Eternal Values." In that article Semanov not only described the revolution of November 1917 as the "Great Russian Revolution" and called it "our national achievement," but he unconditionally praised the Stalin constitution of 1936 which, according to Semanov, introduced complete unity and equality among the Soviet people. The period of the late 1930s, moreover, was especially favorable to the development of culture, Semanov said. In the earlier specialist's view, this was such an open refutation of the line of the Twentieth CPSU Congress that the regime had to intervene. The editor of Molodaia gvardiia was transferred to another post, and the theoretical journal of the Party, Kommunist, criticized the errors of the youth magazine. (25) Among the most significant articles published in Molodaia gvardiia, in addition to those by Lobanov, Chalmaev, and Semanov, might be included a "Letter by a Historian to a Writer"; one of its themes, "country No. 1" (strana No. 1) in "the world camp of socialism," another, the argument that Russia's particular claim to greatness lies in its having skipped through the historical stage of "bourgeois democracy" and in its immunity to democratic socialism (sotsial demokratism), the latter vice afflicting countries such as Czechoslovakia. (26)

Thus, it is not just any state that Molodaia gvardiia writers approved of. They had good things to say about Ivan the Terrible, Peter the Great, Nicholas I, but they were proud that Russia had managed to avoid the experience of Western-style, constitutional government. To their credit, both Andrey Sakharov and Semanov quite explicitly stated that they viewed critiques of the czars, of Russia's past persecutions of the individual, absolutist abuse, terror, and so forth as indirect forms of criticizing the Soviet system. They diligently registered such camouflaged critiques, which had been published in Novyi mir and other less ethnocentric periodicals. They were thus providing independent confirmation of the argument that interest in Russian history

has import for the Soviet political and ethnic situation.(27)
Statist ideas produced critical reactions not only in official
circles, but also among nonethnocentric dissidents, one of
whom published a scathing attack on Semanov. Her article,
entitled "A Treatise on the Charms of the Knout"
(Traktat o prelestiakh knuta) appeared first in the samizdat
journal Politicheskii dnevnik, and was then reprinted in the
West. She pointed out that Semanov, despite his words about
the Russian people and Russian culture, did not care about
either. What he did care for, however, was the idea of
Russian great power (velikoderzhavnost'), and he praised
Stalin because Stalin, while pretending to glorify the Russian
people, had, in fact, rehabilitated Russian czarism. Classifying
the ideas of Semanov as chauvinist, she warned that great
power chauvinism provokes among smaller ethnic groups a
negative reaction toward that group on whose behalf "the
Semanovs" presume to speak.(28) A similar warning, more
camouflaged in form, appeared in the legal press in an article
by Igor Kon, the distinguished Soviet philosopher and
sociologist of liberal persuasion.(29) Semanov's and other
Young Guardist's ideas were noted in at least one communist
country in Eastern Europe.(30)

A stimulating work about the new right in Russia has
devoted a chapter to the thought of Gennadiy Shimanov.
Shimanov is another representative of Statist ethnocentrism.
He argues that Russians are God's chosen people. Because of
this, God has sent great calamities to the Russians (the
reforms of Peter, the November 1917 revolution, the Gulag,
concentration camps), but this was done in order to test and
purify Russia.(31) In his political program, Shimanov
advocates an "ideocratic state," the ideology being a mixture
of Russian Orthodoxy and Leninism, but the accent is on the
state, not the specific content of ideas. He attacks
Solzhenitsyn for supporting "the free flow of ideas" in the
future Russia. He is opposed in principle to freedom of
thought and creative freedom.(32) Consistently, he condemns
democracy. Shimanov's conception of the good state,
summarized: "a state which is not absolute, not autocratic,
which does not possess a highly developed nervous system in
the form of a Party which embraces the entire organism of
society almost down to its smallest cell is not a state at all!"
Although Shimanov considers Russia God's chosen group, and
although he advocates ethnic isolationism - ethnic groups must
not "have communion with foreigners when there is no need" -
he upholds the idea of a Russian multiethnic empire.(33) In
Shimanov's words, "The Soviet Union is not a mechanical
conglomeration of nations of different kinds...but a MYSTICAL
ORGANISM, composed of nations mutually supplementing each
other and making up, under the leadership of the Russian
people, a LITTLE MANKIND - the beginning and the spiritual

detonator for the great mankind."(34) It has been concluded
from this that, in terms of practical politics, "the Russian
people is the only one which is permitted to have an empire."
This empire would be closed and isolated from other nations
(ethnic groups) until they, in turn, were ready to "speak with
it in its own language."(35)

In conclusion, culturalism in its extreme political form,
whether as an ideological current represented by Solzhenitsyn
or as an incipient political movement represented by the
Russia-wide Social-Christian Union of the People, poses a most
serious danger to the Soviet regime because it denies it
legitimacy and aims at its overthrow. What support this
current enjoys among the Russian population is another
question. (Professor Dunlop thinks that it has the greatest
potential among the various currents of dissent.) On the
other hand, statism, as such, is not dangerous to the regime's
security, even though some of its implications may be disturbing to those in the establishment who have retained faith
in a universal meaning of Marxism-Leninism. Thus, some
found it offensive that statists have reduced the meaning of
the November 1917 revolution to the status of a Russian ethnic
revolution.(36) But this "ranking" legitimizes Bolshevism in
Russian ethnocentrist terms. It, thus, helps to support the
Soviet regime, while culturalist ethnocentrism, viewing 1917 as
an anti-Russian event, opposes Lenin and the revolution.
What it proposes is to deideologize the system by making it
less internationalist in outlook and more firmly committed to
Russian ethnic goals. In this respect, the thrust of statism is
directed against non-Russian ethnic groups of the USSR,
rather than against the regime in Moscow, the principal target
of culturalism. At least some culturalists can face the
prospect of secession by the non-Russians; not so the statists,
who believe in Russian empire.

NOTES

(1) This writer's thinking about the subject owes a good
deal to two seminal Polish works: Nina Assorodobraj,
"Zywa historia. Swiadomosc historyczna: symptomy i
propozycje badawcze," Studia Socjologiczne No. 2 (9),
(1963), pp. 5-45; and Roman Zimand, "Uwagi o teorii
narodu na marginesie analizy nacjonalistycznej teorii
narodu," Studia Filozoficzne No. 4 (51), (1967), pp.
3-39. Relevant works in English include David C.
Gordon, Self-Determination and History in the Third
World (Princeton, N.J.: Princeton University Press,
1971); Stanley Mellon, The Political Uses of History: A
Study of Historians in the French Revolution (Stanford.

Calif.: Stanford University Press, 1958); Donald Denoon and Adam Kuper, "Nationalist Historians in Search of a Nation: The 'New Historiography' in Dar Es Salaam," African Affairs, 69, No. 277 (October 1970): pp. 329-49; Frank Hearn, "Remembrance and Critique: The Uses of the Past for Discrediting the Present and Anticipating the Future," Politics and Society, 5, no. 2 (1975) 201-27; and David Thomson, "Must History Stay Nationalist?" Encounter, 30 no. 6 (June 1968): pp. 22-28.

(2)   Karl W. Deutsch, The Nerves Of Government (New York and London: The Free Press and Collier-Macmillan, 1966), pp. 128-29, 206-07.

(3)   Aleksandr Solzhenitsyn, The Nobel Lecture, trans. by Alexis Klimoff (New York: Ad Hoc Committee for Intellectual Freedom, 1973), pp. 14-15.

(4)   Deutsch, p. 207

(5)   The problem of antecedents of socialism interested Marx and Engels, and Karl Kautsky wrote a number of works about it, including one entitled "The Predecessors of Modern Socialism." See Assorodobraj, p. 19.

(6)   Historiography after 1917 is reviewed in Anatole G. Mazour, Modern Russian Historiography (Princeton, N.J.: Van Nostrand, 1958); Mazour, The Writing of History in the Soviet Union (Stanford, Calif.: Hoover Institution Press, 1971); Konstantin F. Shteppa, Russian Historians and the Soviet State (New Brunswick, N. J.: Rutgers University Press, 1962); Cyril E. Black, ed., Rewriting Russian History (New York: Vintage Books, 1962); Lowell Tillett, The Great Friendship: Soviet Historians on the Non-Russian Nationalities (Chapel Hill: University of North Carolina Press, 1969); Walter Kolarz, Stalin and Eternal Russia (London: Lindsay Drummond, 1944); and Klaus Mehnert, Stalin versus Marx (London: George Allen and Unwin, 1952). Historical problems in a wider context of Soviet ideological development are examined by Frederick C. Barghoorn, Soviet Russian Nationalism (New York: Oxford University Press, 1956) and Elliot R. Goodman, The Soviet Design for a World State (New York: Columbia University Press, 1960).

(7)   For the ideology of Stalinism in relation to Russian ethnocentrism, see Barghoorn, passim. See also Richard Pipes, The Formation of the Soviet Union (New York: Atheneum, 1968 2d ed.); and Richard V. Burks, The Dynamics of Communism in Eastern Europe (Princeton, N.J.: Princeton University Press, 1961).

(8)   N. V. Ustrialov, "Natsionalizatsiia Oktiabria" Novosti zhizni (Nov. 7, 1925), reprinted in Pod znakom revoliutsii (Kharbin 1927), pp. 212-18.

(9)   Barghoorn, pp. 25, 148-52, 182, 233-37, and 260.

(10) See   Rudolf   L.   Tokes,   ed.,   Dissent in the USSR:
      Politics, Ideology, and People   (Baltimore and London:
      The   Johns   Hopkins   University   Press,   1975);   Peter
      Reddaway,   "The Development of Dissent and Opposition,"
      in The Soviet Union since the Fall of Khruschchev, edited
      by Archie Brown and Michael Kaser (New York: The Free
      Press, 1976), pp. 121-56; F. M. Feldgrugge, Samizdat
      and Political Dissent in the Soviet Union (Leyden: A. W.
      Sijthoff, 1975) on the first issue and Frederick C.
      Barghoorn,   Detente and the Democratic Movement in
      the USSR (New York: The Free Press, 1976); Dimitry
      Pospielovsky,   "The Resurgence of Russian Nationalism in
      Samizdat," Survey, 19, no. 1 (1973): 51-74; Roman
      Szporluk, "Nationalities and the Russian Problem in the
      U.S.S.R.: Historical Outline," Journal of International
      Affairs 27, no. 1 (1973): 22-40 on the second.
(11) Andrei Amalrik, "Ideologies in Soviet Society," Survey
      no. 2 (1976), pp. 1-11; Alexander Yanov, The Russian
      New Right: Right-Wing Ideologies in the Contemporary
      USSR   (Berkeley,   Calif.:   Institute   of   International
      Studies, 1978).
(12) For the less anti-Soviet trends, for example, Deming
      Brown,   "Nationalism   and   Ruralism   in   Recent   Soviet
      Russian Literature,"   Review of National Literatures,   3,
      no. 1 (1972), 183-209, and Jack V. Haney, "The Revival
      of Interest in the Russian Past in the Soviet Union,"
      (from whom we have borrowed the term "culturalism"),
      and comments by Thomas E. Bird and George L. Kline in
      Slavic 32, no. 1, (March 1973): 1-44.
(13) Solzhenitsyn's speech at Stanford University.   Russian
      text in Vestnik RKhd, No. 118, p. 170, here quoted from
      Boris Shragin,   The Challenge of the Spirit (New York:
      Knopf, 1978), p. xiii.   The representative text of the
      political culturalist position is found in From under the
      Rubble,   edited   by   Aleksandr   Solzhenitsyn,   et   al.
      (Boston: Little, Brown, 1975), especially the contribu-
      tions of Solzhenitsyn, Igor Shafarevich, and Vadim
      Borisov.
(14) John B. Dunlop, The New Russian Revolutionaries
      (Belmont, Mass.: Nordland, 1976), is a study of the
      origins, ideas, and suppression of the union.
(15) Ibid., pp. 290 and 287.
(16) Yanov, pp. 33-35; Dunlop, p. 293.
(17) Dunlop, pp. 214-17.
(18) Ibid., pp. 225-27.
(19) Ibid., pp. 199 ff.; and Yanov, pp. 62-84.
(20) Ivan   Dzyuba,   Internationalism or Russification?   (New
      York: Monad Press, 1974), pp. 66, 57.
(21) Dimitry V. Pospielovsky, "The Resurgence," Survey 19,
      no. 1 (1973): 56.

(22) Ibid., p. 62.

(23) Ibid., pp. 60-61.

(24) Yanov, p. 45.

(25) Yanov, pp. 53-55.

(26) M. Alpatov, "Pis'mo istorika pisateliu," Molodaia gvardiia No. 9, (1969) pp. 306, 310-11, 312-15.

(27) Ibid., p. 318; A. N. Sakharov, "Istoriia istinnaia i mnimaia," Molodaia gvardiia No. 3, (1970) p. 320, and Sergei S. Semanov, "O tsennostiakh otnositel'nykh i vechnykh," Molodaia gvardiia No. 8, (1970) pp. 312-13.

(28) Rissa B. Lert, "Traktat o prelestiakh knuta," Novyi kolokol (London, 1972), pp. 62, 68-69, and 71. See also Politicheskii dnevnik 1965-1970, Vol. II (Amsterdam: Herzen Foundation, 1975), pp. 711 ff.

(29) Igor Kon, "Dialektika razvitiia natsii," Novyi mir No. 3, (1970) p. 141.

(30) W. [sic], "Polemiki literackie," Polityka (September 27, 1969), pp. 8-9.

(31) Yanov, p. 117.

(32) Ibid., p. 120.

(33) Ibid., p. 122.

(34) Ibid., p. 123. Shimanov's work is titled "Kak ponimat' nashu istoriiu," a samizdat text.

(35) Yanov.

(36) A. N. Iakovlev, "Protiv antiistorizma," Literaturnaia gazeta (November 15, 1972), pp. 4-5: Yanov, p. 59.

4 Four Faces of Soviet Russian Ethnocentrism

Frederick C. Barghoorn

Findings from the following inquiry are strongly in agreement with the proposition that the current revival of literary concern with Russian roots has import for the Soviet ethnic and political situation. The word "current" requires clarification. Most, perhaps all, the manifestations of "interest" in the Russian past which were permitted expression in the censored Soviet official media, are compatible with themes that Joseph V. Stalin caused to be expressed, especially during the last fifteen or twenty years of his dictatorship (1939-1953). Moreover, to the extent that such "interest" took forms incompatible with official ideological and cultural policy in the early post-Khrushchev years (1965-) when the above-mentioned literary "revival" was at its height, its exponents were repressed as objectionable dissidents. Also, the muzzling hit regime propagandists as well, such as Viktor Chalmaev, who too flamboyantly pushed a "pseudo-Slavophile" line in the late 1960s. This may have happened because, among other things, they had already sufficiently served the regime's purpose of whipping up hatred for Peking when Sino-Soviet tensions were at their height and of helping to complete the rout of the Novyi mir (the relatively less conservative Russian literary periodical) liberals in the late 1960s, and were beginning to be viewed as doing more harm than good. Finally, the ethnic and political situation of Russia must be regarded not so much as influenced by the revival of interest in the past but, on the contrary, as the independent variable which influenced the form that this revival took, at least in the official press. However, it should also be stressed that there has been a complex process of interaction between ethnic and political factors on the one hand and the expression of interest in Russian history, art (including religious art), and the like, on the other. Let us now turn to an excellent, highly relevant definition of patriotism and "nationalism."

Patriotism and "nationalism" have been defined as follows:

Patriotism: the more or less conscious conviction of a person that his own welfare and that of the significant groups to which he belongs are dependent upon the preservation or expansion (or both) of the power and culture of his society.

Nationalism [ethnocentrism]: the set of more or less uniform demands 1) which people in a society share, 2) which arise from their patriotism, 3) for which justifications exist, 4) which incline them to make personal sacrifices in behalf of their government's aims, and 5) which may or may not lead to appropriate action.(1)

These definitions and emphasis on the ability of political leaders to inculcate ethnocentrist sentiments and on links between them and perceived threats to the external or domestic security of ethnic groups are useful. Some difficulties arise in applying them to the USSR. The Soviet leaders still believe that the legitimacy of the Soviet regime and justification of their power and that of their junior partners who rule other East European "socialist" states require incessant affirmation of their devotion to Marxist revolutionary "internationalism." They are right. Having rejected traditional justifications for political power, and lacking the legitimacy conferred on democratic governments by competitive political parties and elections, they cling to Marxism-Leninism as the only legitimizing ideology available to them.

Unfortunately for the Soviet people, and the world in general, the authoritarian political culture inherited by the Bolsheviks from the Russian past has played a far more influential role in shaping Soviet political culture and behavior than have the elements in Marxist thought of genuine internationalism and of Western democracy to which Vladimir Ilyich Lenin, Leon Trotsky, and Nikolay Bukharin at least paid lip service. Lenin substituted Marxist internationalism for particularistic Russian messianism, and he was apparently a sincere opponent of Russian chauvinism. However, he was responsible for an "infusion of csarist patterns of authority into the theory and practice" of the Soviet political system. This was probably inevitable, in view of the dominant role of Russians and Russianized non-Russians in the Soviet Union.

Motivated by political pragmatism and personal preference,(2) Stalin abandoned Lenin's contained authoritarianism in favor of an amalgam of despotism, ethnocentrism, and coercive modernization. His new Soviet

Russian ethnocentrism was central to the "socialist patriotism" to which he required unconditional commitment from Soviet citizens. While he never abandoned Marxist symbols, his assertion that Leninism was the highest achievement of Russian and world culture can be interpreted as indicative of priority of Russian over Marxist values in his thinking.

Stalin "fanned the flames of the fires of nationalism...." The ethnocentristic-expansionist essence of Stalinism was symbolized by the erection in 1947 in Moscow of a gigantic statue of the twelfth-century Muscovite prince, Iuri Dolgoruky, at a time when there were no statues of Marx, Engels or Lenin in the Soviet Union.(3)

Stalin must have realized that his overt assignment to the Russians of the leading role in the Soviet "family of peoples" was offensive to many non-Russians, but he apparently calculated that eventually, by means of indoctrination and coercion, he could create a homogeneous Soviet Russian socialist "nation." Today, however, Stalin's dream seems as far from realization as ever. There is much evidence of ethnic tension between Russians and non-Russians regarding the meaning of Russian historical experience and culture. There are four subtypes of Russian ethnocentrism which will be discussed briefly in the remainder of this analysis: "neo-Stalinist," "pseudo-Slavophile," "Black hundred" (super-conservative), and "neo-Slavophile." There is much more overlap among the first three categories than between them, lumped together, and the fourth. That fact helps to explain the much higher probability that men like Aleksandr I. Solzhenitsyn, or Vladimir Osipov, both of whom are included in the neo-Slavophile group, would be subjected to severe repression than is likely to befall representatives of the other subcurrents - provided they exercise a measure of political prudence.

Neo-Stalinist ethnocentrism is familiar to every reader of the Soviet press. Perhaps its most salient feature is the demand that Soviet citizens and "progressive mankind" support the policies of the leaders of the Communist Party of the Soviet Union (CPSU) and the assumption that opponents and critics of these policies are knaves or fools. While, formally and quantitatively, priority is assigned in the propaganda of neo-Stalinist Soviet Russian ethnocentrism to "Soviet" as against "Russian" symbols, from time to time the "special historical role" of the Russians is acclaimed, as in Leonid I. Brezhnev's very important speech on December 21, 1972, in celebration of the fiftieth anniversary of the Soviet Union. In this and other major speeches, Brezhnev also emphasized the growing importance of the Russian language for Soviet society. Probably, Brezhnev's most important contribution to the continuation of Stalin's effort to construct a Soviet Russian ethnic group was his assertion that a "new historical community of people, the Soviet people, took shape in our country during the years of socialist construction." Note that, at the Twenty-fifth Congress of the CPSU, tributes to the Russians (unprecedented in their fulsomeness in the post-Stalin period) were accorded by leaders of party delegations to the congress representing non-Russian constituent Soviet republics.(4)

Brezhnev is a Russifier and exponent of neo-Stalinist Russian ethnocentrism, but, probably in part because of constraints imposed by his top leadership position and partly because he is a cautious man, he has exercised considerable circumspection in expressing his views about ethnic problems - as, indeed, on political issues generally. Less inhibited were certain Soviet publicists such as Sergey Semanov, Chalmaev, and Vladimir Soloukhin. These men and a number of others, especially in the late 1960s, published numerous articles, some of them written in angry, emotional language, designed to appeal to and inculcate authoritarian, xenophobic and, particularly, antiliberal and anti-Western attitudes. Also, the ethnocentrists often exalted Russian military and state-building traditions, as did Stalin, and in some cases they, or at least some of them, sang the praises of industrial, rural life and its surviving remnants. Soloukhin, the most sophisticated and talented of all of these writers, and also the most moderate and tactful, is widely known in the West for such works, translated into Western languages, as A Walk in Rural Russia. Chalmaev and Semanov are probably well known in the West to only a few specialists on Soviet affairs, but their articles, published in Molodaia gvardiia, and elsewhere, were probably seen by millions of Soviet readers. Semanov seems to be a more "Stalinist" author than Chalmaev or Soloukhin, and he alone of the trio still publishes "nationalist" tracts. Therefore, he is dealt with in this section, with comment on Chalmaev and Soloukhin in the one that follows.

Semanov's most famous - or infamous - publication, so far, was undoubtedly his August, 1970 Molodaia gvardiia article entitled (in translation), "On Values, Relative and Eternal." It, together with two articles by Chalmaev (to be discussed later) and two by Iuri D. Ivanov (passed over here) led, according to a samizdat item dated January, 1971, to the dismissal and replacement of the editor of Molodaia gvardiia in November, 1971. Semanov's piece was certainly Stalinist in style, tone, and content, although, in keeping with post-Stalin standards, it did not mention the dictator's name. Semanov reaffirmed most of the main themes in Stalinist military-patriotic-historical propaganda. He referred to the USSR as a "united and monolithic whole" - a formula akin to the czarist conception "Russia, one and indivisible." He devoted more than a page to dancing on the grave of Lenin's friend, the Marxist historian Mikhail Pokrovsky, condemned posthumously by Stalin for his negative attitude toward czarist imperialism and its harsh treatment of the conquered people of Central Asia and the Caucasus. Semanov also praised the successful "struggle against wreckers and nihilists" in the years of Stalin's great purges.(5)

The publication in 1977 of a 200 page collection of Semanov's articles - not, however, including the one just discussed - indicated the continued vitality of neo-Stalinist Soviet Russian ethnocentrism. Entitled The Heart of the Motherland, obviously a reference to Moscow, the volume contains a long piece, with the same title as the booklet itself, which asserts, among other things, that the ringing of the Kremlin chimes symbolizes "the pulse of the heart of our power." And, says Semanov, the significance of Moscow "as the center of our state" represents something which has no equal anywhere else. It is not surprising that he praises the service of the Soviet Border Guards against foreign threats. He commends the writer Mikhail A. Sholokhov, notorious for his broad hint, given at the Twenty-third Congress of the CPSU, that his fellow writers, Andrey Siniavsky, and Iuli M. Daniel, should have been shot for allegedly "slandering" the USSR. Semanov asserts - unsupported by reference to evidence - that Lenin once said "we are believers in the state (gosudarstvenniki) and not homeless cosmopolitans." This indicates, in its use of the sinister, anti-Semitic code word "homeless cosmopolitan," an affinity for perhaps the worst aspect of the Stalin tradition.(6)

Those Soviet publicists characterized here as pseudo-Slavophiles are also often referred to as "Russites," "Russophiles" or, probably correctly, as "neo-Slavophiles." The pseudo-Slavophiles share with the neo-Stalinists a contempt for Western "bourgeois" culture. They differ from the neo-Stalinists, however, in their positive evaluation of features of the pre-Soviet past toward which neo-Stalinists, such as Semanov or the late "dogmatist" writer Vsevolod Kochetov, are indifferent or hostile.

Soloukhin and Chalmaev - here they have something in common with Solzhenitsyn and Osipov - have written very sympathetically about ancient Russian wooden architecture, and Soloukhin is famous for his interest in icons. However, unlike Solzhenitsyn and his friends, the pseudo-Slavophiles are careful not to exalt publicly the contribution of Christianity to Russian life. Moreover, they conspicuously refrain from criticizing any major feature of Soviet official doctrine or policy. For example, they do not attack censorship or persecution of dissidents. However, they have but in a much more restrained fashion than Osipov, expressed indignation regarding the destruction of old churches and other monuments of prerevolutionary Russian architecture.

Chalmaev, in two sensational articles published in Molodaia gvardiia in 1968, the titles of which translate as "Great Aspirations" and "Inevitability," called for a revival of Russian ethnic pride, based on appreciation of ostensibly superior - in comparison with the West - "spiritual" values of the Russian people, manifested, he averred, in Russian history and literature.(7) He expressed satisfaction with the burgeoning output of historical novels in the USSR, featuring, among other characters, czars and patriarchs. He praised Konstantin N. Leontev, Vasiliy Rozanov and other nineteenth century Russian conservative thinkers. He chided "ruralist" writers, to whom in some degree Solzhenitsyn might be said to belong, for alleged "idealization of the Russian peasant [muzhik]." To the extent that Chalmaev's often vague, pathetic, but sometimes eloquent meanderings conveyed an implicit ideological program, it was, perhaps, best expressed in a passage in "Inevitability": "There will be a people's and not merely an intelligentsia stage in the rebirth of the best national [ethnic] traditions. That is the inevitability of the age."

Although Chalmaev aspired to be a leading propagandist for the regime rather than one of its critics, his sometimes flamboyant articulation of themes, usually muted in offical propaganda, made him vulnerable to attacks both by liberals within the system from the Novyi mir group and by orthodox ideological bureaucrats. By way of contrast, the elegant stylist, Soloukhin, in his Letters from the Russian Museum, like Chalmaev, did his best to arm Soviet readers against the insidious seductiveness of Western culture. But Soloukhin escaped public criticism, probably because he did not lay himself open to the charge, leveled against Chalmaev and other rather brash neo-Slavophiles, of seeming to treat the Bolshevik revolution as a primarily Russian and ethnic, rather than an international and proletarian, movement.

There is massive evidence of the existence in the USSR, both in certain elite circles and at lower levels of society, of currents of chauvinistic, anti-Semitic ethnocentrism. It is partially inspired by the very same myths and deliberately concocted fictions that charged "world Jewry" with striving for world rule, which, in the declining years of the Russian Empire, helped to trigger savage pogroms against Jews. The same myths, exported from Russia to Germany, played a baneful role in the development of Hitler's National Socialist ideology. The samizdat data about this topic are scattered and couched in language so outlandish that they have, perhaps, not been taken as seriously by Western scholars as they should have been. That part of the pertinent evidence about the subject contained in official Soviet publications presents difficulties of interpretation because of its often somewhat covert and masked style of articulation. To the extent that anti-Semitic propaganda has been discussed by

Soviet citizens, both in the USSR and in emigration, its treatment - not surprisingly - has tended to be more polemical than analytical.

But, the concern expressed with regard to Russian "fascists" and "neo-Nazis" by such present and former residents of the USSR as Grigori Pomerants, Grigori Svirsky, Mikhail Argursky, and Aleksandr Yanov, seems to be justified. Svirsky and Yanov, for example, point to the impunity with which notorious anti-Semites (such as Vasiliy Smirnov, editor, ironically, of a journal entitled Druzhba narodov, or Ivan Shevtsov, author of the anti-Zionist, anti-Trotsky and, in essence, anti-Semitic novel, In the Name of the Father and the Son) have been able to conduct hate-inspiring activities. These would have been severely punishable had not their protectors in high places seen to it that encouragement, rather than the penalties seemingly called for by Soviet law, was forthcoming. Pomerants appears to regard Soloukhin, Chalmaev and the well-known painter Ilia Glazunov as masked agents of highly placed anti-Semitic Soviet politicians. According to Julia Vishnevskaia, some Soviet dissidents have accused even Solzhenitsyn of anti-Semitism. Yanov argues that Solzhenitsyn's ethnocentrist, authoritarian outlook has the potential for conferring legitimacy on forces that might eventually install in Russia a regime with an ideology based on a synthesis of Marxism and Christianity, which would be more anti-Semitic and repressive than the present Soviet one.

Argursky, however, takes a very different view of the matter. He contributed a chapter to the well-known collection of essays published in English as From Under the Rubble. Solzhenitsyn, who was editor and the most important co-author, has expressed the opinion that only a "Christian revival" in the USSR can save Soviet Jews from Nazi-style racism. Argursky also has praised Vladimir Osipov as a leader of the "healthy forces" in the Russian ethnic movement, which the KGB sought to crush by arresting Osipov and closing down his journal, Veche.(8)

The views of those exponents of this current of thought associated with Solzhenitsyn are well known to Western readers from Solzhenitsyn's Nobel lecture, his famous Letter to the Soviet Leaders, and, in more detail, from the symposium From Under the Rubble. The latter includes three essays by Solzhenitsyn, and three by the famous algebraist, Igor Shafarevich, as well as contributions by five other authors. In their interpretation of Russian history and the Russian cultural heritage, Solzhenitsyn and his collaborators differ drastically from men like Semanov, Chalmaev, and Soloukhin. There is nothing in the writings of the pseudo-Slavophiles, let alone in those of the even more chauvinistic neo-Stalinists and anti-Semites, even remotely comparable to Solzhenitsyn's summons to the Russian people to

strive to regain what he called in one of his most famous
essays "the gift of repentance." If the ethical-religious
patriotism of Solzhenitsyn is a form of ethnocentrism, it
probably is as Andrey Sakharov (who criticized it on the
grounds that the Russian people were already ethnocentric
enough without needing reinforcement from Solzhenitsyn)
suggested, "defensive" in character. A certain touchiness is,
indeed, indicated by Solzhenitsyn's somewhat heated reaction
to Sakharov's characteristically mild criticism and his angry
rejoinder to samizdat articles published in the Paris-based
journal, Vestnik RSKhD, which saw in Russian ethnocentrism
and "messianism" the greatest threat to a humane and
enlightened future for Russia.

There is no doubt that the critics of Solzhenitsyn's
Russian-centeredness were on firm ground - from the point of
view of believers in Western democratic and "internationalist"
principles - but it is only fair to recognize the relative
mildness of Solzhenitsyn's ethnocentrism in the Soviet context.

Thus, in contrast to the pseudo-Slavophiles' and
neo-Stalinists' exaltation of Peter the Great, Solzhenitsyn,
following the early Slavophile tradition, characterizes Peter's
reforms as "soulless" and takes a rather positive view of the
pre-Petrine period of Russian history. He has argued that a
limited authoritarianism is more in keeping with Russian
tradition than Western democracy. This incurred criticism
from Sakharov and others. But Solzhenitsyn has sharply
criticized individual and group tyranny and what he sees as a
pernicious Soviet habit of blaming, for political and social
evils, not the Soviet leaders and people but "Zionists,
imperialists, even moderates," indeed, "anyone and everyone
except you and me."(9) Solzhenitsyn also is one of the
sharpest critics of the Kremlin's expansionist foreign policy.
Moreover, in his Letter to the Soviet Leaders, he went so far
as to express the opinion that, if non-Russian border ethnic
groups wished to secede from the Soviet Russian state, they
should not be held within it against their will. Surely, these
views and his interpretation of Christianity, which emphasizes
individual moral responsibility as well as self-criticism,
repentance, and mercy, distinguish Solzhenitsyn's outlook from
that of most contemporary Soviet thinkers to whom the term
"ethnocentric" may with any precision be applied.

On balance, it seems the Russian patriotic sentiments
expressed in Osipov's journal, Veche, were relatively moderate
and tolerant. Like a good many other Soviet dissenters,
Osipov turned to Christianity and a neo-Slavophile approach to
Russian history and ethnic values in a labor camp. He had
been sentenced in 1961 for "anti-Soviet agitation," after
exuberant participation in the cultural ferment with which some
Moscow youths responded to Khrushchev's exposure of some of
Stalin's misdeeds. Between January 1971 and his arrest late in

1974, Osipov, notwithstanding KGB harassment - which occurred in spite of the fact that he published Veche completely openly and not, he insisted, as a samizdat journal (the same was true of his other journal, Zemlia) - provided Soviet readers with by far the fullest access that they had ever enjoyed to the Slavophile heritage. This came in the form of both interpretations by Osipov and his collaborators and a great deal of original source material. These journals also provided considerable factual material about Dostoevski, Nikolay Ia. Danilevsky, Leont'ev, and other conservative and ethnocentrist Russian thinkers. Also, Osipov made available to his readers a good deal of information about developments in the Russian Orthodox church. He acquainted them with the views of such critics of the Soviet-dominated official church as Anatoliy Levitin-Krasnov.

Like Solzhenitsyn, whom he admired and whose side he took in the Solzhenitsyn-Sahgarov dispute, Osipov propagated an ethical-religious patriotism, stressing the right of every ethnic group to cultivate and express its own distinctive values and identity. He frequently asserted that such a stance in no way involved animosity toward any ethnic group, although, of course, the special object of his affectation was his own Russian ethnic group, which he felt was threatened by moral and cultural decay, and even by biological destruction owing to demographic and ecological factors. His fairly frequent criticism of "cosmopolitanism" doubtless aroused alarm in some quarters, but the fact that such leading participants in the Soviet civil rights movement as Andrey Tverdokhlebov eloquently protested against his 1974 arrest is among many indications of Osipov's sincere devotion to democratic principles. Although his letter to U.S. Senator Henry M. Jackson, requesting assistance in his effort to emigrate, may have helped trigger his arrest, it resulted, more fundamentally no doubt, from his resistance to KGB efforts to "tame" him and force him to become a mouthpiece of regime propaganda.(10) Osipov's fate - like Solzhenitsyn's - provides impressive evidence that the Soviet rulers are as intolerant of unauthorized, independent thinking about ethnic identity as they are of all other aspirations for individuality, personal or group autonomy, or unfettered exercise of creative imagination. "Don't think, obey!" seems to be the motto of Soviet authorities, in this as in other fields.

The dissemination, in samizdat, and in censored Soviet media, of expressions of Russian ethnic consciousness that must be regarded as dysfunctional in a "socialist" multiethnic political community, obviously reflects the impact of processes too numerous to list here. During the 1968 to 1970 period, tension on the Soviet-Chinese border was probably an important spur to whipping up chauvinistic moods. The rulers' desire to combat Western ideological influence is certainly an important factor. However, the most important source of both independent and official Russian ethnocentrism was - and still is - the continuing decline in the capability of official Marxism-Leninism to generate support for the Soviet system.(11)   There is considerable evidence that Stalin's death and the limited success and quiet burial of Khrushchev's reforms were followed by widespread strivings, especially among Soviet youths, for new values and satisfactions. Many settled for materialism, alcoholism, or the fascination of the occult.   Some of the best Soviet people found an outlet for their idealism in the struggle, led by Sakharov and others, to "democratize" Soviet society.   Others, both Russians and non-Russians, turned to ethnic values.   The political leadership responded - among other ways - by attempting to graft onto the increasingly irrelevant official political culture selected elements of Russian tradition, in hopes of turning to its advantage ethnocentric and chauvinist sentiments widely held among the Russian people. Among the disadvantages of this superficially rational strategy of symbolically indulging the still dominant Russian element in the Soviet population is the, perhaps unintended, legitimation it may have seemed to offer to open articulation of images of Russia that the Soviet leaders were bound to find unacceptable.

Thus far, there have been no clear "winners" or "losers" in the struggle over the proper weight to be accorded in Soviet indoctrination to "traditional" and "revolutionary," or to "Russian" versus "Soviet" themes.   It seems unlikely that any will emerge in the foreseeable future. However, for the next few years, assuming the continued existence of the USSR, it seems more probable that the present blend of pseudo-Marxist and pseudo-Slavophile messianism will persist - given a more or less rational leadership in Moscow - than that Solzhenitsyn's isolationist ethnocentrism, Sakharov's liberalism, or (and this would be the worst variant now conceivable) that the neo-Nazism feared by Argursky will triumph.

NOTES

(1)   Leonard   W.   Doob,   Patriotism and Nationalism   (New Haven: Yale University Press, 1964), p. 6.
(2)   Teresa   Rakowska-Harmstone,   in   Dynamics of Soviet Politics edited by Paul Cocks et al. (Cambridge, Mass.: Harvard Univ. Press, 1976), p. 54; Robert C. Tucker, Stalin as Revolutionary (New   York: W.   W.   Norton, 1973).
(3)   Grigory Svirsky, Hostages (London: Bodley-Head, 1976), p. 268.

(4) For details see Boris Meissner, "The Soviet Concept of Nation and the Right of Nations to Self-Determination," International Journal, XXXII, no. 1 (Winter, 1976-77): 71-73; and George W. Breslauer, "The Twenty-fifth Congress: Domestic Issues," in The Twenty-fifth Congress of the CPSU edited by Alexander Dallin (Stanford, Cal.: Hoover Institution Press, 1977), pp. 20-25.

(5) Sergei Semanov's article was in Molodaia gvardiia, no. 4 (1968), pp. 308-20; Raissa Lert blasted Semanov's article as an attack on Lenin in Politicheskii dnevnik 1965-1970, Vol. II (Amsterdam: Herzen Foundation, 1975), pp. 713-738; Arkhiv samizdata, no. 1013 reported on a Komsomol Secretariat meeting which condemned the offending articles mentioned above; according to Politicheskii dnevnik, Vol. II, p. 702, Brezhnev spoke at a Politburo meeting on the same subject.

(6) Sergei Semanov's reference to "homeless cosmopolitans" appears in Serdtse rodiny (Moscow: "Moskovskii Rabochii," 1977), p. 63. In the same neo-Stalinist vein as Semanov's writings, was a full page article by L. Larionov entitled "Nasledie narodnogo geniia," in Sovetskaia Rossiia (September 15, 1976), p. 3. Larionov's piece was subtitled: "Sokhranit' na veka pamiatniki istorii i kul'tury severa."

(7) Chalmaev's "Great Aspirations" ("Velikie iskaniia") and "Inevitability" ("Neizbezhnost'") appeared in Molodaia gvardiia, nos. 3 and 9, respectively (1968). Soloukhin's Pisma iz russkogo muzeia (Letters from the Russian Museum), published in the same journal in 1966, later appeared in book form in Moscow and in French translation in Paris.

(8) A well-known, virulent racist samizdat document is "A Word to the Nation" ("Slovo natsii," AS 590). Similar, are documents published by Argursky as appendixes to his article, "Neonatsistskaia opasnost' v sovetskom soiuze," Novy zhurnal, (1975) pp. 118, 198-205. Appendixes, pp. 205-227. The first of these ferocious documents accuses Solzhenitsyn of Zionist sympathies. Pomerants accuses the pseudo-Slavophiles of covert anti-Semitism in Neopublikovannoe (Frankfurt, Main: Posev Verlag, 1972), p. 165. See also Alexander Yanov, Detente After Brezhnev (Berkeley, Cal.: Institute of International Studies, 1977), pp. 45-55; and Yanov's chapter in Vadim Belotserkovski, comp.), SSSR: demokraticheskie alternativy (Achberg, West Germany: Achberger Verlags anstalt, 1976); and Julia Vishnevskaia's chapter in the same volume.

(9)   From Under the Rubble (Boston: Little Brown, 1975).
      All the quotations from Solzhenitsyn are in his chapter,
      "Repentance and Self-limitation in the Life of Nations,"
      From Under the Rubble, pp. 105-43. See also The Nobel
      Lecture, trans. by F. D. Reeve (New York, 1973); and
      Pis'mo vozhdiam sovetskogo soiuza (Paris: YMCA Press,
      1974).   Sakharov's criticism of Solzhenitsyn's ethno-
      centrism is most fully expressed in "O pisme Aleksandra
      Solzhenitsyna,"   (New   York: Chronicle   Press,   1974).
(10) Remarks about Osipov are based mainly on reading
      Veche, Nos. 1-2, 4-6, as well as the text of American
      correspondent Stevens Browning's interview with him,
      published in Vestnik RSKhD, 106 (1972), pp. 296-303.
      See Arkhiv samizdata nos. 1013, 1020, 1140, 1230, 1596,
      1599, 1787, 1790, 1791 for works by Osipov and other
      contributors to Veche, and AS195 for Tverdokhlebov's
      protest against Osipov's arrest.   Some valuable source
      material in English translation, including an essay by
      Osipov and background data on the "national renaissance
      in Russia," appears in Michael Meerson-Aksenov and
      Boris Shragin, eds., The Political, Social, and Religious
      Thought of Russian Samizdat - An Anthology   (Belmont,
      Mass.: Nordland, 1977), pp. 345-450.
(11) See AS1009; Roy Medvedev, On Socialist Democracy (New
      York: Knopf, 1975), pp. 88-89.

5 Comment -- Russophilism: No Reflection of Popular Grievances

Sheila Fitzpatrick

As Professor Frederick Barghoorn reminds us (Chapter 4), the recent revival of Russian ethnocentrism is not the first such phenomenon in the Soviet period. By the mid-1930s, the Bolsheviks' original proletarian internationalism had been much diluted. Socialism was to be built in one country - the Soviet Union - and the center of that country was Russia. A new spirit of Soviet patriotism was officially encouraged, and it appears to have gained wide popular acceptance. Like all patriotisms, this was a hybrid, combining pride in the Russian past and respect for traditional culture with celebration of the party's leadership, the achievements of Soviet industrialization, and the doctrines of Marxism-Leninism. It was not a high-brow ideology, in contrast to the Bolshevik Marxism of the 1920s; and it was as unsuitable for intellectual debate as the complex of right-thinking attitudes which in this country are commonly attributed to "Middle America." As far as we can tell, this type of Soviet patriotism - including a considerable dose of Russian ethnocentrism - remains alive and well in Middletown, USSR to the present day.

The recent revival of Russian ethnocentrism falls into a quite different category, not so much because it is "unorthodox" as because it is high-brow - essentially a movement of part of the Russian literary intelligentsia to upgrade one element of the old hybrid Soviet patriotism. There are other competing trends within the contemporary intelligentsia, ranging from the Westernizing-technocratic to the deStalinizing Marxist-Leninist, which stand in a similar relationship to the eclectic middle-brow orthodoxy of the Stalin era. This fact in itself has political significance. It is always possible that one intellectual trend might develop a big following among youth, find a broad popular constituency, or develop strong antiregime overtones; and it is clear that the

present Soviet leadership continues to keep this possibility
firmly in mind.

But is the Russian-ethnocentrist revival within the
intelligentsia likely to be perceived by the political leadership
as peculiarly threatening? As Professor Roman Szporluk
indicates in Chapter 3, the Russophile trend suffered an
official rebuff in the early 1970s. However, similar rebuffs
have been administered to other intellectual trends, for
example that associated with editor Tvardovsky's journal Novyi
mir in the 1960s. And the domestic policies most closely
related to Russophile sentiments, like the restoration of
churches as historical monuments and the encouragement of
internal cultural tourism, seem to have been unaffected.
Szporluk's conclusion that there is no room within the Soviet
system for self-conscious Russian ethnocentrism may perhaps
be premature or overly schematic. In principle, to use a
favorite Soviet phrase, neither the collection of Russian icons
nor (on the Westernizing side) the wearing of blue jeans is a
particularly desirable activity. In practice, as recent visitors
to the Soviet Union are aware, both are still extremely
fashionable among the intelligentsia.

The most sensitive political aspect of Russian
ethnocentrist sentiment must surely be the possible offense
caused to non-Russian ethnic groups. So far, this seems to
be a potential problem rather than an actual one, though the
situation may change as the weight of non-Russians in the
total Soviet population increases. At present, Russophilism
among the intelligentsia seems the least serious of the regime's
nationality or ethnic problems since, unlike the non-Russian
ethnocentrisms, it has no obvious links with deep-seated
popular grievances. The Russian peasantry, whose numbers
continue to decline, are almost certainly more interested in
television sets and urban employment opportunities for their
children than in the true Russian tradition which intellectuals
suppose them to represent. Their response to the ruralists
[derevenshchiki], like that of stalwart English yeomen to the
Chesterbellocian vision of Merrie Englande, is likely to be nil.

Perhaps the Russian population, or at least the Russian
intelligentsia, has a psychological need for an ethnic identity
separate from the Soviet one, despite the strong Russian
component of traditional Soviet patriotism. But this must be a
marginal need, comparable at best with that of English-
speaking Canadians, where, in political terms, the threat
comes from the underdog nationalism of the Quebecois in
Canada, not from the traditionally dominant English-speaking
group. In the Soviet Union, similarly, the politically
significant -isms (ethnocentrism or nationalism) will almost
inevitably be non-Russian for the foreseeable future.

6 The Consequences of Seeking Roots

Jack V. Haney

Five years ago, one could argue without hesitation that there had been a revival of literary concern with Russian roots.(1) It was claimed that this was part of a much larger concern with the relationship between Russia and the Soviet Union, past and present. In reference to the 1960s, it was evident that "in nearly every field of endeavor, in every branch of culture, there have been noticeable efforts to rediscover the past and to elucidate the essence of the 'Russian soul'."(2) It is now appropriate to examine this question anew and to look once again at the "revival of interest in the Russian past," but this time with reference solely to literature and literary criticism.

Literature is different in several ways that are obvious but perhaps worth restating, for they directly affect this discussion about whether the current revival of literary concern with Russian roots has import for the Soviet ethnic and political situation. At its base, literature remains an individual effort aimed at speaking through an externally imposed screen at the writer's "people," his audience. It is this screen that distinguishes literature from, say, criticism, where the product is, in fact, the screen. This screen may be purely an economic one - a publisher for financial reasons will not support the printing of a work, or perhaps paper is scarce and the 13 volumes of Dostoevski's letters, notes, sketches, essays, and tracts will not be published. This last is scarcely to be distinguished from the political screen, but the political screen may, in addition, be sinister in that it denies access to the writer's people.

It is the thesis here that the revival of interest in Russia's past on the part of writers and critics, though certainly not ended, is nonetheless muted now, and that it is muted precisely because there no longer exists an open forum for its discussion. On the other hand, its role has been usurped by those whose primary concern is not literary but political, thus forcing honest writers to abandon this particular topic in their writing.

A second thesis is that, given the innocuous nature of most contemporary, approved Russian writing about Russia in the USSR, one can only conclude that the movement has had less impact on the Russian ethnic movement than expected, and is of little import except - and this is a big exception, in a negative way - it provided a model which non-Russians may well choose to follow, citing in particular no less an authority than the journal of the Union-Wide (not just Russian) Komsomol, Molodaia gvardiia, as its example.

An attack on the patriotism of the editorial board of Novyi Mir printed in the July 26, 1969, issue of Ogonek signaled a shift in the most recent attempt of the Russians to examine in their literature their relationship to their past. From that date onward, the Russians' examination of their roots in their literature, a process that seems to have been initiated in the eleventh century and continued intermittently ever since, has generally taken a more benign, less nationalist tone. It has tended quite obviously to accommodate itself to the reality of the multinationalist Soviet state and to the dictates of the ruling party. In the 1960s a number of factors had aroused this interest in the Russian past. In part, it may have been simply the novelty of it all - the quaint, provincial, and colorful arts and crafts attracted a bored and frustrated urban population. In part, one can attribute it to the scholarly work of researchers in the universities and institutes and to their attempts to publicize the results of their often quite remarkable research.

The sterility of official dogma was a major factor in turning Russians to their past. Certainly, the search for an alternative to Marxist-Leninist doctrine, even in its Brezhnev form, played a role in the creation of this movement, which was not - at least in its inception - so much a movement as a spontaneous phenomenon.

A more obvious source of this interest is to be found in nonliterary popularizations of prerevolutionary works and subjects. Such a film as Andrey Tarkovsky's Andrey Rublev (1964), with its fascinating debates about God, good and evil between the monk-painter Rublev and his Greek teacher, Feofan, provided much of the stimulus. But arts and crafts, artistic films, and scholarly works certainly did not provide more than a tiny bit of the impulse that led to the debates about Russians and their view of their past which were carried on in literature and in the literary journals. It was when the attention shifted from tourists [turisty] collecting icons and wooden spoons in the Pri-Onezhie (and, to the disgust of some, leaving their intitials carved into the white stone walls of Solovetskii Monastery) to alternatives to the Soviet vision and version of modern society that the debate began over the goals of those whose interest in pre-October was not strictly academic.

Now it seems possible to discern a fifth, perhaps official and more sinister, force behind this movement: the ethnocentric, chauvinist writings centered on the journal Molodaia gvardiia. In a reply to discussions about them, Professor George Kline suggested that this searching for the Russian past - in rural Russia, in the Church, this recent version of going to the people - was not entirely honest and not without ulterior motivation.(3) At the time, it appeared that there was insufficient evidence to establish this point, and, indeed, many of the ruralists [derevenshchiki], as some of these writers came to be called, were entirely honest in their treatment of the theme. They were addressing a theme long absent from all but official prose. Though some, no doubt, romanticized the past, they sought to recapture values they believed were worth preserving. For many of these, however, this fascination with the past proved to be short-lived. And even Vladimir Soloukhin, whose motives were far from clear five years ago, has turned away from this theme in recent years, so much so that one author, writing in the journal of the USSR Writer's Union in December 1977, found reason to complain somewhat of Soloukhin's new direction:

> The circle of literary scholars who...have continued working with great artistic effort the theme of the Motherland-Russia, with which Soloukhin began, becomes stronger and expands, but in critical reviews one encounters his name more and more rarely...for unfortunately this theme in his creative work turns out to have been completely exhausted.(4)

But of others one may have more serious doubts. There is some evidence that the most shrill of the chauvinist voices raised in this debate were quite aware that raising the cry of "motherland" [Mat' - rodina] and for purity of the Russian Language" [Za chistotu russkogo - iazyka] could well be directed at some writers of the "other" camp. (The language of those others fell below "accepted" standards and their themes unquestionably reflected Western and the young Soviet reader's taste.) The prose of Vasiliy Aksenov, Bulat Okudzhava, the poetry of Andrey Voznesensky and Evgeny Evtushenko were derisively referred to by some of the more virulent critics as "zhidovskaia" (Jewish [pejor.]), precisely because of the experimental (!) nature of their work. Whether or not this term was widely used is unclear, but it is indicative of the nastiest strain in the movement. This

extreme chauvinism, as perhaps best exemplified in the articles
of Viktor Chalmaev in Molodaia gvardiia (1968), finally brought
about the end to whatever official support the seekers for
Russia's roots may have had in the literary journals.

In the 1970s, Molodaia gvardiia has undergone a marked
change. Though Vasiliy Belov, Sergey Vikulov and the late
Vasiliy Shukshin continued to publish more or less regularly,
their themes rather quickly evolved away from the
countryside. Although poetry dealing with such well-tried
themes as motherland and patriotism continue to be published,
the religious overtones are more difficult to discern, the tone
less strident. The uniqueness of the historical phenomenon
"Russia" "Rus" is no longer obvious. What did appear in
Molodaia gvardiia was a long series of patriotic, Soviet articles
by various marshals, generals, and commanders of the Soviet
Armed Forces exhorting young people to the usual patriotic
deeds and preparations to defend the motherland - but largely
missing were ethnocentrist references to Borodino, Poltava, or
the Russian as opposed to Soviet people. More obvious were
references to the sacrifices made during the last war by all
true Soviet people. Chalmaev wrote more or less innocuous
literary reviews to honor the 100th birthday of X, the 50th
anniversary of Y's appearing in print, but no more polemics.
His place was taken, after the generals, by reports and
speeches from a seemingly random assortment of non-Russian
functionaries calling for dedication to Leninist principles, and
the like, those very elements in Soviet culture that Molodaia
gvardiia had suggested, though never stated, were passe, not
to say dead, just months before.

In 1975 and 1976 a few articles of interest to the theme of
this discussion appeared, all of them in Molodaia gvardiia.
One, hardly objective, was an essay highly critical of
Voznesensky and Evtushenko, for Voznesensky's vulgarization
of Michelangelo's poetry and for Evtushenko's "modernism."(5)
On the other hand, a well-established poet in 1975 published a
long poem, "Evpatii Kolvrat," about the freedom-loving, Tatar-
slaying hero of the razing of Riazan' in 1237, a theme that
could not but evoke memories of various Oriental despotisms
in the mind of the most casual reader.(6)

All this is really to say that what a Russian critic wrote
in her review of a work about the art of Rus' concerning the
attraction of icons for Soviet people in 1975 is applicable to
our discussion of the theme of ethnocentrist nationalist
searching in Russian literature: "In our time, a fashion for the
icon has arisen, in part dictated by an honest and deep
interest in the past, in the history of our country, in the
history of art; in part, alas, by a desire to demonstrate a
refinement of taste."(7)

Those literary aspects of the search for identity which
were characterized by a virulent chauvinist and ethnocentric

bent no longer typify the Russian literary scene, in part perhaps, because the topic is exhausted (as is claimed to be the case with Soloukhin) or, more likely, because it is no longer useful or productive in the struggle to maintain ideological and cultural purity.

But, then, it may all depend on whose ox is being gored. There are topics for discussion and topics for disagreement in literature. There are also taboos. One of these taboos seems to illustrate the extreme sensitivity of Russians to attacks on their cultural heritage as they choose to interpret it. It also illustrates the most important fact to emerge from this study of the search for Old Russian literary roots - the example provided to subordinate Soviet ethnic groups by the treatment given to the "Song of Igor's Host" (Slovo o polku Igoreve). Nearly every journal in the USSR celebrated the 175th anniversary of the first edition of "Song...": a new ballet appeared (by a Ukrainian), there were new editions issued, Borodin's Prince-Igor was sung and resung, postage stamps were issued, the usual symposia organized, and even a pilgrimage to Chernigov, to the battle sites themselves, was organized. In Alma Ata, a Kazakh publishing house released a book by the poet, Olzhas Suleimenov, whose verse has appeared in Molodaia gvardiia and elsewhere. This book was entitled Az i ia. Kniga blagonamerennogo chitatelia.(8) Suleimenov obviously considered himself "the well-intentioned reader," although his critics soon challenged that opinion, and the first part of his title, which when read as one word becomes "Asia," contained a further reference to himself - the Ia. The first word "Az" was, of course the first letter of the old Slavic alphabet. It, too, means "I" but Suleimenov's none-too-subtle juxtaposition of the Old Slavic word to himself, a Kazakh poet, was quick to attract the attention of Russians. Though reviews have appeared in several leading, scholarly and popular journals, Suleimenov's book was not for sale in the book stores. As a case study in miniature, this incident is not only revealing of some of the most obvious tensions existing between the various ethnic groups and the Russians. The Russians' response seems to indicate that a certain part of them suffer from what Suleimenov calls "an inferiority complex [kompleks nepolnotsennosti, vyzvannyi Igom]."(9) In Zvezda (June 1976) D. S. Likhachev, the leading Soviet specialist on the "The Song" and author of numerous articles and books dedicated in part or whole to its study, wrote a highly critical, but largely scholarly review of Az i ia. It serves as a healthy balance to an article which appeared in Molodaia gvardiia, December 1975.

The Molodaia gvardiia article was set in type October 2, 1975, a scant two to three months after the appearance of Suleimenov's book in Alma Ata. It apparently assumes a wide acquaintanceship on the part of his Komsomol readers with the

book, for the critique nowhere states Suleimenov's theses. Its
approach is rather more polemical. It scores the Kazakh poet
for referring to Jews as "the chief people" [glavnyi narod],
for saying that the Russians have been racists since the
eighteenth century (and presumedly still are, in his view),
for reference to Astrakhan as a colony, to its governor
V. N. Tatishchev (the father of modern Russian historiography) as a falsifier, for claiming that all Russian
historians since him have suffered from an inferiority complex,
and so on. The critic is particularly incensed by Suleimenov's
references to blood, race, and racism, and particularly to the
Jews as "the chief people." After all, it notes, Lenin himself
had indicated that the notion of a Jewish people which has
existed since Biblical times is a reactionary idea - obviously
this critic believes in no such thing. His objections to any
kind of distinction based on biological race ring hollow in the
light of recent history: "It has already been established by
Marxist science that the progressive development of various
ethnic unities is connected with the rupture of biological and
strengthening of social-economic and spiritual ties (!). Etnos
is first of all a social and not a biological category."(10)

Likhachev is much more fair and thus more convincing in
his review of Suleimenov's book. He points to a whole series
of errors, misconceptions, and distortions that abound in
Az i ia. Likhachev's review reflects the great scholar he is,
and he does not hesitate to state Suleimenov's notion, but, in
particular, he notes and attacks Suleimenov's notion that the
reason why nothing of lasting value has been discovered about
"The Song..." is the "patriotism of the defenders of [its]
authenticity... overwhelming the initiative of the skeptics.
Over two centuries of oratory in the bibliography of The
Song... have accumulated several hundred titles in which, as
in a swamp, the same arguments, not always scientific but
always patriotic, spar."(11)

These attacks on the patriotism of "The Song's..."
defenders, who include the overwhelming majority of Russian
scholars, Likhachev does not leave unanswered, and his view
is interesting in that it defines the borders between
ethnocentrism and chauvinism on the one hand, and patriotism
on the other.

> True patriotism cannot commit violence and go
> against the truth. Only chauvinism, crude nation-
> alism [ethnocentrism] conceals truth, attempts to
> embellish reality. Only nationalists [ethnocentrists],
> who in the depth of their soul do not believe in
> their people and its culture, artificially exaggerate
> the contribution of their people, ascribe to it
> dubious qualities and merits.(12)

These two articles, read in their entirety, like those in the journal Voprosy istorii and elsewhere, may simply be a case of overkill, for, after all, the book was all but supressed in the USSR. Suleimenov's attempts to show that "The song..." is a thirteenth century dual-language text are preposterous; his attempt to trace his Turkic roots to Sumer, taking in "The Song..." along the way, emphasizing the distinct (as he sees it) racial and cultural characteristics of Turkic people, stands squarely at variance with the idea of Soviet man, expressed above in Molodaia gvardiia. It also points up the dangers to the Soviet state of permitting local chauvinism to develop to the point where it might pose, however remotely, a threat to the multiethnic state, and, more important, a threat to the authorities' power to decide the boundaries between patriotism and ethnocentrism. Thus, although the Russian people may be permitted a certain pride in their leading role in the Soviet-style federation, and they may be encouraged to maintain the purity of their language as a defense against the onslaught of Western ideas and fashions, the same is not permitted other people of the USSR. For there, the real danger is that the ethnocentrism will be directed against Russians, to the obvious detriment of the entire system. Suleimenov may, indeed, recall that Russian Prince Igor's hapless foray against the Turkic Polovetsians in 1185 was unprovoked and imperialist in design. And, by linking it, however indirectly, to the colony of Astrakhan and Russian racism which he continues to find, apparently, in the modern USSR, he seems to wish to show the present situation to be in some way analogous to the Steppe-Rus' relations of the twelfth century. In doing so, he has transgressed not only the boundaries of historical accuracy, but also of good Soviet taste and, more important, he has laid himself open to a charge of "nationalism."

The chief importance of reviving concern over Russian roots for the Soviet ethnic and political situation, if it has any at all, is that it has provided a model for writers in other languages and of other cultures. And this, as in the extreme case of Olzhas Suleimenov, is not something that can be tolerated, let alone encouraged, by Russian authorities.

NOTES

(1) See the articles by Jack V. Haney, Thomas E. Bird, and George L. Kline in the Discussion section of the Slavic Review (March 1973) "The Revival of Interest in the Russian Past in the Soviet Union," pp. 1-44.

(2) Ibid., p. 1.

(3) Ibid., pp. 36-38.

(4)   Georgii Tsvetov, "Neobratimost' evoliutsii," Zvezda, No.
      12 (1977), pp. 196-99.
(5)   Vadim Nazarenko, "O provintsialisme dukha," Molodaia
      gvardiia, 3 (1976): 259-78.
(6)   Valentin Sorokin, "Evpatii Kolovrat," Molodaia gvardiia,
      10 (1975): 29-48.
(7)   Iskra Mikhailova, "U istokov russkogo iskusstva,"
      Zvezda, 7 (1975): 219.
(8)   Olzhas Suleimenov, Az i Ia.   Kniga blagonamerennogo
      chitatel'ia. (Alma Ata: Izdatel'stvo "Zhazushi," 1975).
      303 pp.
(9)   Quoted by D. S. Likhachev in "Gipotezy ili fantazii v
      istolkovanii tëmnykh mest 'Slova o polku Igoreve',"
      Zvezda, 6 (June, 1976): 210, quoting p. 187 of
      Suleimenov's book.
(10) A. Kuz'min, "'Tochka v kruge', iz kotoroi vyrastaet
      repei," Molodaia gvardiia, 12 (1975): 276.
(11) D. S. Likhachev, p. 203, quoting from p. 17 of
      Suleimenov's book.
(12) Ibid., p. 204.

7 Comment — The Uses of History

Robert A. Maguire

Russians share in the sickness of spirit that infects all twentieth century industrial societies. Among its symptoms are a sense of fragmentation, isolation, and dislocation in time and space. Among the remedies that have been tried is a "quest for roots." The Russian version of this quest is intimately bound up with the whole problem of the past.

For one thing, Marxism-Leninism is profoundly historical in concept. It reinforces the deep-rooted Russian tendency to think historically. For another, it professes views of man and the world which find striking parallels in the past, if by "past" we mean, as Professor Jack Haney usually does, the period stretching from Kievan Rus' to the rise of Muscovy. Also, the tendency to view the individual almost entirely in terms of his social function, clear-cut standards of good and evil, and interest in the universal qualities of the human condition rather than in particular manifestations of it. These are but a few of the parallels that a casual observer might find. An awareness of the aesthetics of socialist realism might stimulate a greater receptiveness to the esthetics of Old Russian Literature. These aesthetic values on the surface have much in common. They could take on greater validity and reality in the chronicles and saints' lives of that far earlier period. That could occur once the socialist version of them is perceived, as it is by so many of today's intellectuals, as being incompetent, because it favors only a selective study of the past, or ineffectual insofar as Soviet society is deemed subject to the same kinds of disorientation as Western industrial societies. An appreciation of the Russian past undoubtedly fosters a sense of wholeness, completeness, and stability that people find lacking in contemporary Soviet life. It also helps provide an ethical, and moral dimension for an existence that otherwise may seem shallow and drab.

Given the preeminence of the written word throughout the centuries of Russian culture, most expressions of interest in the past inevitably involve literature. Here, Professor Haney shows that in recent years there is less and less evidence of such interest, at least in published form. But he does not, it seems, really address himself to two questions which arise inescapably from this fact: 1) why has such a decline of interest occurred; and 2) are the manifestations of interest in the literature of the past the most important ones?

To take the second question first, in the last ten years or so, there has been an enormous preoccupation, among Russian scholars and amateurs alike, in nonliterary remnants of the past, such as icons, architecture, and furnishings. One reason may be that such artifacts are less subject to the kinds of manipulation that Soviet ideologists practice upon the verbal evidence of history and, therefore, inspire more confidence in those who view, study, or possess them. Any serious consideration of interest in the Russian past should make a clear distinction between written evidence of that past, and various nonverbal artifacts.

The first question is pricklier. Professor Haney suggests that official apprehension about rampant Russian ethnocentrism (and, by extension, about any other ethnocentrism in the USSR) is one reason why fewer overt expressions of interest in the Russian past are being seen. But, surely, other factors would come into play in any deeper study of the problem. There are very real dangers that any modern industrial society must face as a consequence of intellectual and emotional attachments to a nonindustrial past. It has often been suggested that the Soviet obsession with nineteenth century Russian literature is a way of trying to borrow and utilize a set of values - esthetic, moral, and ethical - that are perceived to be lacking in contemporary society. Similar motives may underlie the turn to a still older period; and the consequences are potentially even greater, not only because that earlier period is more remote, but particularly because Christianity was then professed and practiced far more actively and vigorously than the nineteenth century. It is no coincidence that the recent "quest for roots" has more or less paralleled a revival of active interest in the ideology and practice of Russian Orthodoxy. Icons and church buildings may be appreciated simply as works of art. But, as any believer knows and many a former nonbeliever has discovered, artifacts that were created as expressions of a religious impulse are capable of quickening that same impulse centuries later. Because they are visible signs of larger historical and spiritual realities, and since those realities were actively Christian, the artifacts do not always remain merely aesthetic for any reasonably well-educated observer. This may go far to explain the discomfort felt by Soviet authorities at the

spectacle of intense curiosity about the past, whether or not
that curiosity is labeled "aesthetic," "cultural," or "historical."
The relevance of the Old Russian past to the New Russian
present is also vitally at issue. Marxist-Leninist aestheticians
have never satisfactorily confronted or resolved the question
of why the culture of the past continues to appeal so strongly
to a society which supposedly stands at great remove from it
in all respects.

8 Ruralist Prose Writers in the Russian Ethnic Movement

John B. Dunlop

In a speech delivered during the Sixth Congress of Soviet Writers in 1976, Fedor Abramov, a leading representative of the so-called "ruralist" [derevenshchik] school of prose, offered some tongue-in-cheek comments about the state of contemporary Russian letters:

> Around us a scientific and technical revolution is taking place, it is the era of sputniks, but our writers (including some who are well-known) have gotten hopelessly bogged down in village back-roads. What has happened to the avant-garde role of literature?...So what is this? Perhaps our literature is, to put it mildly, not exactly marching in step with the times? Perhaps it is lagging behind, suffering from provincialism?(1)

Abramov went on to explain why it was appropriate, indeed necessary, for Russian writers to concern themselves with the fate of the Russian village. "The question," he underlined, "concerns not simply the root reconstruction of village productivity and the whole structure of village life. It also concerns the alteration of Russian geography and the changing of the face of the Russian land....To put it briefly, the old village and its thousand-year history are vanishing today into nonexistence."(2)

Why should this matter? Because, Abramov believes, the contribution of the village and its dwellers has been undervalued during the Soviet period. "In our expectation of a new, beautiful man, in our avid reaching out toward the new promised land of socialism, we often looked down on them [village folk] as an inferior breed of men....Yet the edifice of our entire contemporary life stands on the shoulders of these

80

nameless laborers and soldiers."(3) Moreover, when contemplating Russia's future, her young people, one all too frequently observes the following: "overweening egocentrism and individualism, parasitical and acquisitive inclinations, the loss of a careful and loving attitude toward the land and toward nature, and a cold rationalism."(4) Perhaps, Abramov suggests, today's youth could learn something from the disappearing Russian village.

"What does it mean," Abramov asks, "that the old village is departing forever? It means that the age-old pillars are giving way, that the soil [pochva] of many centuries in which our entire ethnic culture has been rooted - its ethics and aesthetics, its folklore and literature, its miraculous language - is disappearing. Because, to paraphrase Fedor M. Dostoevski, all of us have come out of the village. The village represents our primal source [istoki] and our roots [korni]."(5)

It is appropriate to begin with these lengthy quotations from Abramov, because his comments aptly and provocatively summarize the major concerns of what is probably the leading school of Soviet letters today. They also provide a clue to the reasons for that school's popularity and longevity (Vladimir Soloukhin's seminal Vladimir Back-Roads [Vladimirskie prosëlki] appeared in 1957).

Over the past two decades, the ruralists have attempted, consciously or unconsciously, to carry out a quiet revolution aimed at changing the minds and hearts of the Russian reading public. The implicit negative goal of this "revolution" has been to challenge a number of Marxist-Leninist teachings and assumptions. Like Boris Pasternak and Aleksandr I. Solzhenitsyn, but in more muted fashion, the ruralists have contested Soviet Prometheanism and titanism, that traditional Soviet commitment to unrestricted industrial growth and the accompanying lack of concern for the effect of such growth on the environment or on Russians themselves. The cult of the so-called "scientific and technical revolution" (NTR) [nauchno-teknicheskaia revoliutsiia], which is almost an article of faith to an orthodox Marxist-Leninist, is challenged at every step by the ruralists. One should stress, incidentally, that the ruralists are not denying the importance of the NTR; it is the evaluation of the phenomenon that is at issue. Abramov refers to the NTR as "the Babylonian tower of the age," whose "three magical and hypnotic letters" are everywhere venerated.(6) And a critic points out that "...our era is not only the epoch of the NTR, above all, it is a great period of self-determination - ideological, social, and moral-spiritual self-determination."(7) And he asks: "What about those who do not poeticize the NTR but reveal, for example, the poetry of the human soul, the feeling of love for one's homeland, for its nature and people?"(8) The NTR, the ruralists suggest, has nothing to offer with which to fill the spiritual vacuum in the souls of modern men; in fact, it may even help cause that vacuum.

A related aim of the ruralists has been to explore the psychological and spiritual costs of the immense migration from the country to the city which has been taking place since World War II. According to a Soviet sociologist, 84 percent of the populace lived in the village in 1920; in 1939, this percentage was still very high – 76 percent. By 1959, however, it had dropped radically to 51 percent, and by 1970 it stood at 44 percent.(9) These statistics prompt the comment:

> Having ceased to be a peasant country according to the basic means of production of material values and according to the class affiliation of the basic mass of the populace, spiritually and, as it were, by the memory of the heart our country is still not very far from its peasant past: it is close enough to feel a need...to cast a common glance over this past, to evaluate morally and aesthetically that from which it has moved away and from which it continues to depart in headlong fashion.(10)

Ruralist writers such as Vasiliy Shukshin (d. 1974) have investigated the costs of such vast social and demographic dislocation. Furthermore, because it has now become evident that much of the migration is to the detriment of the country (because workers are urgently needed back on the farm), ruralist publicists feel all the more justified in questioning the direction given to today's young people. "Many of the most varied reasons," writes Sergey Vikulov, editor of the journal Nash sovremennik, "have been advanced for this migration, including an absence of love for the land and of an attachment to it..."(11)

The positive mission of the "quiet revolution" has been to resurrect values and moral reflexes from near-extinction – indeed subjected to persecution and derision – during the Soviet period. "Ethics and aesthetics" is how many ruralists choose to sum up this cluster of desired qualities.(12) One writer believes that the yearning of the ruralists is "not simply for the village, but for lofty moral achievements, for humaneness, for spiritual perfection. And this is not elicited at all by a striving to preserve the past but by a thirst to find the true path and by anxiety for the future."(13) Vikulov writes: "...the village is closest to those wellsprings [istoki] which in many ways determine our national [ethnic] character...character which includes not only customs and clothing, but also moral norms, songs, traditions, and, most important, the language."(14) And Fedor Abramov provides

the following list of virtues which he believes flow to
contemporary man from the Russian village: "Boundless
self-sacrifice, an alert Russian conscience and sense of duty,
the capacity to practice self-limitation and compassion, love of
labor, love of the earth and of everything living...."(15) The
ruralists make no attempt to conceal that they are doing battle
for the allegiance of Russia's young people, upon whom, of
course, the fate of the country depends. In the writings of
the ruralists, Soviet youths are depicted as rootless and
confused but not depraved, capable of being educated and
returning to the path of their fathers, a path which is
brightly illumined by the "sun" of nineteenth century Russian
classical literature.(16)

The message of the ruralists does not, predictably, sit
well with those purporting to be orthodox Marxist-Leninists.
An attack made in 1973 may be taken as representative:
"...the spiritual, moral, and everyday structure of the old
Russian village," it reminds the ruralists, "did not fall from
the skies but was the result of the economic structure of
peasant life...."(17) These structures have now been
rendered obsolete by the NTR, whose glories are often sung.
Technology, machines, electricity, chemistry, radio,
newspapers, books, television, the cinema, compulsory
education - a critic ticks off achievements of the Soviet period
and concludes: "Let us pose the question bluntly, is [all]
this a boon or a misfortune? The question, of course, is a
rhetorical one."(18) To add punch to the argument, the critic
recalls that Vladimir Ilyich Lenin himself (as well as Aleksandr
Herzen and Nikolay Chernyshevsky) was wont to caution
against the danger of the "sentimental romantics."(19)
Another doctrinaire commentator would have the ruralists
understand that "the Revolution changed not only the economic
structure and external form of life but also the entire moral
order of peasant existence."(20)

It is a measure of the shifting political forces in today's
Soviet Russia that such critics can do little more than stick
pins into the ruralists. For their part, the ruralists are
permitted to strike back, and do. It would seem that the
ruling gerontocracy's strategy is to keep both Marxist-Leninist
purists and Russian ethnocentrists from gaining a decisive
upper hand, although the influence of the latter is clearly
growing. That the successors of the present leadership will
be able or even willing to continue this balancing act is
probably doubtful.

To demonstrate the present strength and influence of
the ruralists, consider briefly Valentin G. Rasputin (b. 1937),
a relatively young son of a Siberian lumberjack who is
deservedly gaining a reputation as a major contemporary prosaist. He and Vladimir Voinovich seem the two
most promising Russian prose writers currently living in the

USSR.(21)   In 1977, Rasputin was awarded the prestigious
State   Prize   for   his tale Live and Remember [Zhivi i pomni],
which treats the unorthodox theme of the tribulations of a
Soviet deserter and his devoted wife during World War II.
The deserter is shown in a far from negative light, and his
wife, Nastena, will be recognized by every reader of Turgenev
and Tolstoi.   In a February 4, 1978, interview,(22) Rasputin
asserted, "It [Live and Remember] is not a book about a deserter.   It is a book about a woman, about a Russian
character, ready to sacrifice anything, possessing all the best
features of Russian character.   At present this traditional
character is subjected, if not to doubts, then to changes."
While Rasputin does not have any irrational attachment to the
old forms of life - he recognizes that in the past "people very
often lived in primitive conditions" - he laments that "alongside
the   old   style   of   life,   the   old,   everlasting   values   are
disappearing."   "People are nostalgic," he explains, "not for
the villages themselves but for the old morality that existed in
the villages, the style of living there, the good neighbors."
    Rasputin is surprisingly outspoken about some of the
more sensitive issues of Soviet policy.   He does not conceal his
aversion to the Soviet Union's war against religion and the
concommitant destruction of so many churches, and he terms
the   policy   of   forced   collectivization   "an   unnatural   radical
thing."   And he does not hide his admiration for Aleksandr I.
Solzhenitsyn as an artist.   "I think it is unjust that his
[Solzhenitsyn's] real literary work is not published.   It has a
right to be published here in its own time."
    Like other ruralist writers, Rasputin has his differences
with enthusiasts of the NTR.   In an interview which appeared
in 1976, he emphasized his keen concern for the future of the
Siberian environment.   Siberia, he stressed, represents not
just "a gigantic construction site" for him but also a homeland,
the land on which his fathers lived and on which his children
and grandchildren will live.(23)   He has singled out three
specific environmental concerns for particular emphasis: the
fate of Lake Baikal, the Angara River, and the Siberian
forest.(24)
    In   late   1976,   the   publishing   house   of   the   Young
Communist League issued 200,000 copies of an important (656
page) collection of Rasputin's tales.   Included in this volume is
Rasputin's latest work, "Farewell to Matera" [Proshchanie s
Materoi], which had been serialized in 1976.(25)   An ambitious, highly symbolic work, "Farewell" tells the story of the
inhabitants of a large island in the middle of the Angara River
which is due shortly to be flooded as a result of the construction of a huge dam downriver.   Those who dwell on the
island are mostly older people, and Rasputin scrutinizes them
closely in the period preceding their evacuation.   One of the
purposes of the tale is to contrast the balanced way of life of

those on the island to the roar and cacophony of the workers' settlements on the mainland; the author also compares the younger and older generations. "If you only knew, grand-mother, what machines they've built," an uprooted grandson exclaims to his grandmother. She replies that the machines have ceased working for man, and that it is now man who works for his machines.(26)

Finally, it is worth stressing that the ruralists should be seen as part and parcel of a larger phenomenon - the Russian ethnic movement.(27) Several illustrations show this to be true. The ruralists have affinities to two important Russian, patriotic, voluntary societies - the Russia-wide Society for the Preservation of Historical and Cultural Monuments (member-ship: 12.5 million(28)) and the Russia-wide Society for the Preservation of Nature (an ecological organization, reported to have had 19 million members in 1971(29)). In their striving for ethical and spiritual values, as well as in their concern for the fate of ancient Russian churches and icons, the ruralists also have obvious links to the Russian Orthodox Church(30) and its 50 million members. The similarity of many views articulated by the ruralists to those appearing in the Russian ethnocentric samizdat journal, Veche, in the collection From Under the Rubble, and in the "Program" of the Russia-wide Social-Christian Union for the Liberation of the People, is equally clear.(31) The writings of the Russian ruralists rest on a mass base.

From the above, it should be clear that evidence is in full agreement with the proposition that the recent revival of concern among Russian writers for matters traditionally Russian has serious implications for the Soviet ethnic question and the Russian ethnocentrism which affects it so greatly.

NOTES

(1) Fedor Abramov, "O khlebe nasushchnom i khlebe dukhovnom: Vystuplenie na VI s"ezde pisatelei SSSR," Nash sovremennik, No. 9 (1976), p. 170.

(2) Ibid., p. 171.

(3) Ibid.

(4) Ibid., p. 172.

(5) Ibid., p. 171.

(6) Ibid.

(7) Iurii Seleznev, Vechnoe dvizhenie: Iskanniia sovremen-noi prozy 60-x nachala 70-x godov (Moscow: "Sovremen-nik," 1976), p. 7.

(8) Ibid., p. 13.

(9) E. Starikova, "Sotsiologicheskii aspekt sovremennoi 'derevenskoi prozy'," Voprosy literatury, No. 7 (1972),

p. 15. See the collection of reactions to Starikova's article in Voprosy literatury, No. 3 (1973), pp. 45-78. See also Viktor Perevedentsev, "Iz derevni v gorod," Nash sovremennik, No. 11 (1972), pp. 100-10, and J. A. Newth, "Demographic Developments," in The Soviet Union Since the Fall of Khrushchev edited by Archie Brown and Michael Kaser, (New York: The Free Press, 1975), pp. 76-95.

(10) Starikova, p. 21.

(11) Sergei Vikulov, "O derevne i 'derevenshchikakh'," Molodaia gvardiia, No. 6 (1971), p. 277.

(12) See, for example, M. Lobanov, "Uroki 'derevenskoi prozy'," in the collection of his essays Vnutrennee i vneshnee (Moscow: "Sovetskii Pisatel'," 1976), p. 156.

(13) Sh. Galimov, "Khudozhestvennost', sotsiologiia, zhizn'," Voprosy literatury, No. 3 (1973), p. 55.

(14) Vikulov, p. 277.

(15) Abramov, p. 172. His reference to "self-limitation" might be an allusion to Solzhenitsyn's essay "Raskaianie i samoogranichenie" in Iz-pod glyb (Paris: YMCA-Press, 1974), pp. 115-50.

(16) Seleznev, p. 235.

(17) Feliks Kuznetsov, "Sud'by derevni v proze i kritike," Novyi mir, No. 6 (1973), p. 247. For an overview of recent Soviet responses to the derevenshchiki, see V. I. Protchenko, "Sovremennaia derevenskaia proza' v literaturnoi kritike," Russkaia literatura, No. 2 (1977), pp. 54-66.

(18) Kuznetsov, p. 248.

(19) Ibid., p. 249-50.

(20) Iu. Galkin, "Derevnia-literaturnaia i podlinnaia," Voprosy literatury, No. 3 (1973), p. 57.

(21) During his visit to Oberlin College in the fall of 1977, Iurii Trifonov told me that he considers Rasputin to be probably the most talented of the ruralist writers.

(22) "Valentin Rasputin: The Soviet Faulkner from Siberia" (Interview with Peggy Polk of UPI). Dispatch of February 4, 1978. From a copy of the text of the interview which, presumably, appeared in various American newspapers.

(23) Valentin Rasputin, "Byt' samin soboi" (Interview with Evg. Osetrov), Voprosy literatury, No. 9 (1976), p. 150.

(24) Ibid., p. 149.

(25) Valentin Rasputin, "Povesti" (Moscow: "Molodaia Gvardiia," 1976), 656 pp.; "Proshchanie s Materoi" appeared in Nash sovremennik (1976), nos. 10 and 11.

(26) Rasputin, "Povesti," pp. 117-18.

(27) About this movement, see John B. Dunlop, "The Eleventh Hour," Frontier, 18, no. 2 (1975): 71-82. About the relationship of the movement to Soviet literature, see

Dunlop's review of the collection Nash sovremennik: Izbrannaia proza zhurnala, 1964-1974 in The Times Literary Supplement (Nov. 19, 1976) p. 1447, and his forthcoming piece, in the same publication, about Soviet writer Vasiliy Shukshin.

(28)   Membership as of the summer of 1977. The figure was quoted to Dr. Arcadi Nebolsine, formerly of the University of Pittsburgh, when he visited with leaders of the society in Moscow at that time.

(29)   Figure cited by Petr Dudochkin in "Kak chelovek sdaet ekzamen prirode?" Veche, No. 4 (January 31, 1972): Arkhiv samizdata 1140, p. 115.

(30)   Barbara Wolfe Jancar, "Religious Dissent in the Soviet Union" Dissent in the USSR ed. Rudolf L. Tokes, (Baltimore: Johns Hopkins University Press, 1975), p. 197. The same estimate of 50 million members has been made by Anatoliy Levitin-Krasnov, a well-informed church activist who recently emigrated from the Soviet Union.

(31)   Veche's ten issues are available from the Radio Liberty Samizdat Archive. The Russian original of From Under the Rubble was Iz-pod glyb; the English tranlation was published by Little, Brown and Company (Boston and Toronto) in 1975. About the Social-Christian Union, see the collection VSKhSON: Sbornik materialov (Paris: YMCA-Press, 1975) and John B. Dunlop, The New Russian Revolutionaries (Belmont, Mass.: Nordland, 1976).

9 The Search for Russian Identity in Contemporary Soviet Russian Literature

Catharine Theimer Nepomnyashchy

Joseph V. Stalin's death in 1953 set in motion the process of liberating Soviet literature from the strictures of "socialist realism." During that period, the more liberal forces in Soviet literature raised profound questions about the quality of life in Soviet society. Many writers, especially during the early 1960s, were content merely to pose the problem, portraying rootless and alienated individuals unable to find happiness and fulfillment in a society shaped by communist ideology. Another group of writers, however, has attempted to fill the spiritual vacuum which has become increasingly evident in Soviet society during the past 25 years by positing an alternative source of values. These writers, the ruralists or rural prose writers [derevenshchiki], began to emerge shortly after Stalin's death and have come to be a dominant force in Soviet Russian literature during this decade. They have turned from the urban, industrial environment - favored under socialist realism and by many of the writers of the late 1950s and early 1960s - to the countryside in search of enduring values rooted in the Russian historical and cultural experience.

Although the ruralists are hardly a homogeneous group, they are united by their common concern with life in the Russian countryside and by their persistent efforts to assert the need for historical continuity despite the upheavals of revolution, collectivization, and war which have shaken the Russian countryside during the 60 years of Soviet rule. Their organic vision of history - especially the history of the Russian people - demands that the life of the future be built on the best that may be salvaged of the rapidly disappearing Russian past. During the Sixth Congress of Soviet Writers in June 1976, Fedor Abramov, one of the leading exponents of rural prose, eloquently defended its basic tenets. Condemning the indiscriminate belief in progress, Abramov pleaded the cause of

88

the dying Russian village and of "the type of person created
by it...our mothers and fathers, grandfathers and grandmothers" whose "moral forces...did not allow Russia to perish
in the years of its hardest trials":

> Yes, they are semiliterate and much too credulous,
> at times politically ignorant, but what treasures of
> the soul, what spiritual light! Endless self-
> sacrifice, the sharpened Russian conscience, love
> of work, of the land, of all that lives - there is
> no way to count it all....In short, it is impossible
> to plough the Russian field anew without ploughing
> up human souls, without mobilizing all the spiritu-
> al resources of the people [narod], of the nation
> [natsiia].(1)

The evident Russian ethnocentricity of Abramov's
pronouncements is a common, implicit and sometimes explicit
feature of many rural prose works. The ruralists turn to the
past, trying to capture the values of a way of life now rapidly
becoming extinct. Their explorations into the past appear to
be a search for self-identity outside the conventional values
actively advocated in Soviet society. The efforts of these
writers are inextricably tied to an awareness of, and a desire
to define, their own Russian ethnic roots.

The ruralist prose writers' search for Russian roots has
unleashed a storm of debate in the Soviet press, and this
debate has become even more crucial since the Soviet
government's announcement in 1974 of an extensive project to
transform Russia's non-black earth region (nechernozem'e), the
setting for the majority of rural prose works. The ruralists
are now being enjoined with increasing frequency to turn their
attention from the past to the future, to abandon their
self-imposed historical, documentary function. They are being
encouraged to embrace the official vision of the future
countryside, consolidated into agricultural centers on a par
with urban areas in material goods and services, educational
and job opportunities, and cultural offerings.

Because of the project in the non-black earth region, the
ruralists stand at a crucial point in the development of their
vision of Russian self-image. On the one hand, most of these
writers are themselves from peasant backgrounds and grew to
maturity in villages of the non-black earth region impoverished
by war, collectivization, and inefficient management. Their
literary works contain eloquent pleas for economic rehabilitation
of the Russian village and material improvement of life in the
countryside. From this point of view, the ruralists can feel
only sympathy for the economic goals of the project of the
non-black earth region. On the other hand, the project
threatens to destroy those vestiges of the past left in the

central Russian countryside and, along with them, the remnants of the historical bases of Russian ethnic self-identification. The project represents the great leveling force of Soviet modernization, the goal of which is the destruction of the traditional division between city and country. The situation appears even more poignant in the light of Russia's peculiar stance as the leading union republic in a multiethnic state, the existence of which is based on communist "internationalism." As the forces of modernization and "internationalism" increasingly pressure the rural prose writers to abandon their idealization of the Russian past and of the Russian peasant, these writers and their sympathizers will be forced either to turn from their quest for ethnic self-identification or to retrench into a more militantly chauvinistic stance. The hypothesis that this paper will address is that this aspect of the trend toward growing Russian ethnocentricity represents a threat to the authorities' ability to control the Soviet ethnic question in the future.(2)

In their self-imposed role as chroniclers of the dying Russian village and guardians of the Russian cultural heritage, the ruralists have shown a marked preference for nonfictional narrative forms, and, in general, there is a thin line dividing fiction from nonfiction in rural prose. There is a strong documentary, often journalistic, element in their writings, and it is no accident that one of their favorite genres is the semi-journalistic sketch [ocherk] and that many of their works are clearly autobiographical. These efforts to authenticate the realism of their works reflect the concern of the ruralists with preserving the texture of life in the disappearing Russian countryside in its minutest detail. Even in patently fictional works, these writers often painstakingly reproduce the customs, traditions, and the language of the village, all of which are recognized as essential components in the formation of Russian character. This attention to detail - and especially to details deriving from the ethnic cultural heritage - sharply distinguishes rural prose works from traditional "socialist realism." The "positive hero" of "socialist realism" was drawn in broad, generalizing strokes. Raised to superhuman proportions by his devotion to the communist ideal, he was as devoid of particularized characteristics as a propaganda poster and was thus robbed of all traces of ethnic origin. In reducing their characters to life-size, the ruralists have also given them back their ethnic identity.

There is another side to the works of the ruralists which coexists with and complements the documentary realism of their works. A Russian critic wrote about the ruralists in the mid-1960s: "One of the new tendencies is the striving of writers to capture traits of national character in images."(3) Aside from their concern with recording anthropological data, the ruralists also work in images. Their vision of Russian character is created largely of the stuff of literature, drawing heavily on myth and potent archetypal symbolism. In fact, it may be argued that with the disappearance of the tangible manifestations of the Russian cultural heritage, myth takes on an ever greater role in the definition of Russian character.

Of all the symbols which the ruralists use to create their highly mythical vision of what it means to be Russian, the central one is unquestionably the land: the land in its archetypal role as the source of life, the land as a manifestation of natural beauty, and, above all, the land as the "little motherland" ("malaia rodina").

The "little motherland," in concrete terms, is the writer's native village and the natural landscape which surrounds it. Since by far the majority of the ruralists come from the north central non-black earth region of Russia, their "little motherlands" are the small villages in the historical core of Russia. In a more abstract sense, the "little motherland" is the symbolic focus for the Russian ethnocentricity of the ruralists; it is their tie to the past and to the eternal continuity of life, and, ultimately, it is a synecdochic image for all Russia. One Russian critic, trying to define the concept of the "little motherland," recently suggested that it provides these writers with a necessary grasp on life, that in writing about the "little motherland" they are reaffirming "their ties with the fundamental life of the people":

> Is it as if they want to make sure that they have not been torn away from the continent, that they have not lost their way, that they have not gotten lost in the boundless sea of life?
> Or is it perhaps better to equate this feeling of the fundamental principle to the feeling of a supporting center, of a magnetic pole, the attraction of which is life-saving? Isn't this what the lines of Nikolay Rubtsov are about: 'And around the unconquerable love for the villages, the pines, the berries of Rus' my life invisibly rotates like the earth around its axis.'(4)

The critic then continues: "Today the feeling for the little motherland, for its locality, for its ties with the life of the people is especially sharp, because the lively sensation of Home, of Motherland helps every day to oppose the cosmopolitan pressure of fashion, the magnetism of the consumer ideal."(5)

The native villages of these writers, to which they continually return to explore and record, and, above all, to reaffirm their generic and ethnic roots, are their own personal havens of safety from the leveling forces of "cosmopolitan uni-fication" and "standardization of personality." The ruralists' fear of standardization is the link between their hostility to modernization and to "internationalism"; both threaten to destroy the differences among people which have traditionally served as bases for self definition. In this context, the "little motherland," with its ties to the family and remembrances of childhood and its associations with the continuity of the Russian cultural heritage, becomes a powerful image in the understanding of personal identity.

In some rural prose works the return to the "little motherland" takes on the emotional coloring of what may almost be termed a religious pilgrimage. In one such story, the main character returns to his native village after 40 years of wandering throughout the Soviet Union. By chance, he comes across a distant relative, and he manages to visit the house where he grew up, where his senses call up the texture of the country life of the not so far distant past. At the end of the story, he goes to the local cemetery to look for the grave of his grandfather. He does not find it, and this leads him to meditations on Russia:

> Why only after forty years did I remember my motherland? Where was I earlier? I even lost track of the graves of my ancestors!...And for the first time in this bitter hour I took the time to think about the motherland, about Russia: and do I understand Russia as I should understand her, and do I understand her in general?...In deep thought I came out on the bank of the Obnora. Quietly and unbrokenly she carried her waters into the blue distance....And thoughtfully I imagined how long she will run along the ravine among fields and meadows until merging with the River Kostroma and together with her rushing farther...entering as a large river into the mighty Volga, in order to add to her strength, in order that she should not grow weak, the great river of Russia.(6)

The efforts of the ruralists to delineate the Russian self-image have precipitated a lively debate among Soviet critics. This debate centers around the problem of the role of ethnicity in the multiethnic literature of the Soviet Union. The old Stalinist formula "socialist in content and national in form" has been largely discredited, but the assumption remains in Soviet criticism that any work of Soviet literature must be partly socialist and partly ethnic, or, as one Soviet commentator put it: "It's bad if national narrow-mindedness is in the nature of a writer, but it's just as bad if he has no national aspect."(7) The critic's task is further complicated by the need to make judgments about life as well as literature. The ruralists' search for spiritual values in the Russian ethnic

heritage raises the question of the interaction of what is
socialist and what is ethnic in the formation of character.
Thus, one critic, in speaking of the ethnicity [narodnost'] of
contemporary, Soviet multiethnic literature, pointed out the
need "to show the effect of socialist principles on national
character, which is in constant movement and growth, not
losing, however, during all of these changes, its national
[ethnic] definition and originality."(8)   In dealing with the
ruralists' preoccupation with the past, critics have once again
stressed the need to find a "golden mean":

> Criticism must see two extremes, two dangers: the
> danger of negativism in relation to the past of the
> fatherland, and, on the other hand, the danger of a
> supra-social, supra-class approach to the history of
> one's native country, which leads to the idealization
> of the past, to anti-historicism in one's approach to
> it.(9)

The ambiguity of programmatic statements such as these
leaves the door open for relative freedom of discussion about
the contrast between the role of ethnicity and communist
"internationalism" in contemporary Soviet literature. This
freedom, however, is confined primarily to Russian writers,
while tighter controls are kept on discussions relating to the
literature of other Soviet ethnic groups. This suggests
strongly that sympathy for the ruralists Russian
ethnocentricity thrives among Soviet officials.
    The existence of Russian chauvinism within the central
government of the Soviet Union may well have been a factor in
the creation of the project to rehabilitate the non-black earth
region. Certainly, there is an unmistakable Russian ethnic
bias in the propaganda released to the public about the
project. Statements in the press often revolve around
emotional appeals to Russian chauvinism: "The non-black earth
region is the authentic, deep Russia. Native, because
historically the Urals, Siberia and many other areas were
'added' later, but the root, the beginning of the Russia in
which we now live is here, in her so-called central zone."(10)
    But the project has as its ultimate goal the destruction of
what many regard as the traditional bases of Russian
ethnicity. The plan to abandon hundreds of small villages and
resettle their inhabitants - over half the population of central
Russia - in rural centers spells the end of the Russian
countryside as it has existed for centuries and the final
disappearance of the ruralists' treasured "little motherlands."
    Strong protests and words of caution directed at the
resettlement project have appeared in the Soviet press. In
1976, one article carried an emotional attack against the
project. It was cast as a poignant account of the effect of the

project on one couple whose village has been marked for resettlement. Crushed by the need to abandon his home, yet unable to bear the psychological strain of life in the slowly dying village, the husband must decide whether he and his wife should move to the box-like apartment offered to them in the regional center:

> It's easy to say: think, decide. But for him it meant giving up his native home, into which he had poured all his soul and hopes of prosperity; it meant abandoning accustomed comfort, leaving the village with the graveyard on the hill. He wasn't a boy – to begin life all over again, in an alien place where it would be necessary to get used to the people, to everything around him....And his brother will not come to visit all the time. What does he care for a new place? There will be no motherland.(11)

This man's dilemma vividly illustrates the threat to the ruralists' vision of life inherent in the resettlement project. It means not only depriving people of their homes, but, more important, destroying the continuity of life, severing the deep ties to the past which are, to these writers, an essential factor in man's understanding of himself and of his place in the world around him.

While such open questioning of the project continues to appear in the Soviet press, the ruralists are being called upon with greater and greater frequency to abandon their "patriarchal," "idealized" portrayals of the village, to turn from the past to the future, and to mobilize their forces in support of this ambitious plan to alter the face of the traditional Russian countryside: "In the great transformation of the non-black earth region, literature has a great role....The irresistible influence of ideas and images, expressed by the power of the writer's talent, sets it still more firmly in the first rank of the most powerful means of communist education."(12)

There has been a call for a "new literature" to deal with the problems of the non-black earth region: "The breadth and scale of problems standing before the non-black earth region are calling to life new, great, many-faceted literature. It is destined to become the accelerator of socioeconomic transformations in the non-black earth region."(13) Such statements have the ominous ring of a call for a new rural "socialist realism," for a literature praising the economic achievements of the countryside in a spirit of uncritical optimism about the prospects for future progress. A steady stream of publicistic, economically- and technically-oriented literature about the non-black earth region, in fact, appeared in the Soviet Union between 1974 and 1976.(14) However, so far, the main body of ruralists' work appears to have been left untouched by this trend, and it is doubtful that these writers will ever be willing to give up the relative freedom in dealing with real life problems which Soviet literature has acquired in the years since Stalin's death for a return to the largely discredited doctrine of "socialist realism." Yet, at the same time, the discrepancy between these two visions of rural literature - one future-oriented and concerned primarily with economic questions, the other focused on the spiritual values of the past - represents the dilemma in which the ruralists find themselves today. They are caught between their love for the Russian past with its cultural heritage and their desire for material improvement of life in the Russian countryside. Thus far, an uneasy compromise appears to have been established between the two factions, with the militant supporters of the regional project manipulating the ruralists to gain their own ends. However, ultimately, as the project progresses in transforming the Russian countryside, the ruralists will have to make a choice between the official model for the modernization of the non-black earth region and the nostalgic vision of the countryside as it is now portrayed in their works. The decision that the ruralists come to in dealing with this dilemma will shape the course of Soviet Russian rural literature in the future, as well as determine the future relationship between these writers and the Soviet government. The insistence of these writers on their identification with the continuity of the Russian ethnic group could ultimately prove to be an embarrassment to the Soviet government in its dealings with the other ethnic groups in the Soviet Union.

The real political importance of the Russian ruralists, however, lies in their role as a "mouthpiece" for the ethnic awareness growing among larger segments of the Russian population of the Soviet Union. While it appears that in response to the disappearance of traditional bases for the definition of Russian ethnic identity many Russians are losing a sense of their identification with the Russian ethnic group, there seems to be a growing concern with the Russian ethnic heritage. This new movement toward growing Russian ethnocentricity has manifested itself in a variety of forms, from the faddish collecting of icons and folk implements or Komsomol projects to restore old churches to the declarations of the ultra-conservative group: "A Word of the Ethnic Group" (Slovo natsii). The ruralists represent a fairly moderate element in this spectrum of Russian ethnocentricity. As "peasant writers," they are connected both with the life of the countryside and with the urban intelligentsia, and their views may be assumed to reflect to a certain extent the ideas and values of both. The attitudes of the ruralists also appear to reflect those of the older generation, of people who have lived through war and collectivization. One of the greatest concerns touched upon in their works is the degeneration of values among the younger generation that grew up after World War II, its preoccupation with the accoutrements of modern society, and its lack of loyalty to the continuity of life in the countryside. Certainly, the magnitude of the response, both positive and negative, to the works of this relatively small group of writers would suggest that they are dealing with problems that are of the utmost concern in literary and government circles in the Soviet Union today.

The resettlement project represents the inevitable victory of the modern world over the backwardness of the Russian countryside. However, for the ruralists the passing of the old order of things also means the end of values they have idealized as the source of Russian ethnic identity. For the time being, they have devoted themselves to saving what may still be salvaged of the dying past, a mission which Abramov forcefully reaffirmed in the speech mentioned earlier:

> And one of the greatest tasks of contemporary literature is to warn young people of the danger of spiritual staleness, to help them become familiar with and enrich the spiritual baggage accumulated by preceding generations.... In the final analysis, the rise of the Russian non-black earth region must rest on it.(15)

The ruralists are evidently among the most vocal, if moderate, indicators of a problem which penetrates deep into Soviet Russian society today. This problem - the search for ethnic self-identity in an increasingly standardized society - may ultimately grow into a serious threat to Soviet internationalism, if the Russian ethnic group, deprived of the traditional bases for the definition of Russian ethnicity, falls back into militant Russian chauvinism and corresponding hostility to the other ethnic groups in the Soviet Union.

NOTES

(1) [Fedor Abramov], "Vystuplenie uchastnikov s"ezda... Fedor Abramov (Leningrad)," Literaturnaia gazeta, No. 26 (June 30, 1976), p. 11.

(2) The material upon which this inquiry is principally based was gleaned from surveys of relevant Soviet and Western publications. Nash sovremennik, Molodaia gvardiia, Novyi mir, and Literaturnaia gazeta were surveyed for varying lengths of time during the period 1974-1976, and Current Digest of the Soviet Press, Slavic Review, The

Slavonic and East European Review, The Salvic and East European Journal, The Russian Review, and Survey during the period 1965-1976. Further, I am greatly indebted to the Russian writer Abramov for having discussed with me at some length his views about matters dealt with in this paper.

(3) Pavel Glinkin, "Zemlia i asfal't," Molodaia gvardiia, No. 9 (1967), pp. 253-254.

(4) Igor Dedkov, "Vozvrashchenie k sebe," Nash sovremennik, No. 7 (1975), p. 176.

(5) Ibid.

(6) Sergei Voronin, "Istoriya odnoi poezdki," in his Derevenskie povesti i rasskazy (Leningrad: Isdatel'stvo "Sovetskii Pisatel'," 1974), p. 515.

(7) Akram Ailisli, "Vyrazhat' glubiny natsional'nogo," in "Zemlia. Liudi. Literatura," Druzhba narodov, No. 9 (1970), p. 262.

(8) Aleksandr Khvatov, "Cherty narodnosti," Nash sovremennik, No. 1 (1973), p. 182.

(9) Feliks Kuznetsov, "S vekom naravne," Novyi mir, No. 2 (1975), p. 235.

(10) Semen Shurtakov, "Moe nechernozem'e," Literaturnaia gazeta, No. 1 (Jan. 1, 1976), p. 3.

(11) Ivan Filonenko, "Berezy," Nash sovremennik, No. 5 (1976), p. 153.

(12) N. V. Sviridov, "Nechernozem'e: problemy i knigi," Molodaia gvardiia, No. 4 (1976), p. 18.

(13) Ibid., p. 12.

(14) Ibid., See pp. 10-30, for a detailed discussion of recent Soviet publications concerning the non-black earth region.

(15) Abramov, p. 11.

10 Comment — Beyond Soviet Categories of Literary Ethnocentrism

George Gibian

Professor John Dunlop and Catharine Nepomnyashchy, in Chapters 8 and 9, present an excellent picture of the views of Russia expressed or implied in the works of the "ruralists" [derevenshchiki]. There is little to be added to these surveys. Particularly those who have read Professor Dunlop's long review of the anthology of stories from Nash sovremennik have only admiration for his rich, cogent analysis of the ruralist movement.(1) These are convincing statements that offer nothing to be disagreed with, as far as they go. However, do they go far enough? What is there beyond the limits of their scope?

Two additional avenues of investigation could be pursued. First, staying within their definition of the topic of ethnocentrism in literature: has there not been any significant shift within village prose in the last decade? Is village prose really basically one continuous movement, from 1967 (or earlier) to the present? Should we not attempt to articulate various phases or stages? Is this really a homogeneous, unchanging school?

There are people who would go so far as to say the movement has now been shattered, and others who believe it is declining. If we feel that, indeed, there has not been any considerable articulation in rural literature, and that it would be wrong . to speak of various wings or subcategories or periods, then this should be openly affirmed. If that is so, then it is something to marvel at, and the reasons for it to be commented upon - for such a lack of development is a very rare thing in the history of literature, at least in the modern Western world.

There is a second, still broader question. Are the claims of the ruralists themselves and the assumptions of both their theoretical apologists and their ideological opponents -

Viktor Chalmaev, Mikhail P. Lobanov and others - to be accepted? Is rural prose the sole or chief expression of Russian ethnocentrism today? It is hard to agree with any claim to its uniqueness. While Russian ethnocentrism is rooted in, and derives its tenets from, the soil of the countryside and the simple rural population, in addition, it is also rooted in, and derives tenets from, the soil and the buildings and other artifacts and social creations of Russian cities, as well as from the values, conventions, genres, and codes of the urban, literary, educated, intellectual tradition.

Not only villages with ancient, pure Russian names like Chisto Pole, Khakhily, Visuchii Bor, but also Stara Rusa, Moscow, and Petersburg play an important part in present-day Russian literary expressions of ethnocentrism. Surely, it is not necessary to review the tremendous importance which both capitals have had in shaping the feelings of Russians about who they are, how they differ from other ethnic groups, and what their virtues, strengths, and missions are? Moreover, is it not true that the literary peculiarities and achievements of the works of Russian writers, which grew into a characteristically ethnic literary tradition - consciously or unconsciously - also form part and parcel of what constitutes Russian ethnocentric pride? To give just a few examples, think of the character type of the urban dreamer [mechtatel'] in Fedor M. Dostoevsky, the spiritual searching of Leo Tolstoy's Pierre Bezukhov, the society splendor of Tatiana Larina once she has "arrived" in Petersburg, the savage indignation of Aleksandr Griboedov's Chatsky, the various "underground men."

When Aleksandr Pushkin, Ivan Turgenev, or Tolstoy speculated on what ethnicity [narodnost'] was, they took it to be an amalgam of spiritual and social attitudes of literary, technical features and devices, and of psychological emphasis - not merely rural subject matter.

Soviet essayists and the ruralists themselves concentrate not on literary features so much as on abstractable themes, ideas to be deduced from the content of literary works. But do we need to follow them?

In a recent work, Daniil Granin has his narrator make the following dig at rural prose: "Don't you have a fresher theme? Let literary lions [molodtsy] who don't have anything left to say write about that.... They cherish nostalgia for the countryside because they have gotten themselves snazzy [shikarnuiu] apartments and now have to ride in elevators and take baths in bathtubs."(2) Granin's works supplement the ruralist's ethnocentrism with probings of Russian traditions of somewhat different kinds already discussed elsewhere.(3) Granin presents a sophisticated mingling of attitudes toward historical and intellectual Russian legacies as something to be treasured and used in the moral shaping of future generations.

He is just one example of a writer whose ethnocentrism, while implicit and covert, is complex and deep, and exemplifies an important current within present-day Russian consciousness.

Neither he nor his narrator talks about ethnocentrism. He does not call himself a "nationalist," nor do his critics attack or praise anything in his works as being ethnocentric. Nevertheless, the attitudes and feelings of his works may constitute something which we ought to call ethnocentric, even if it is not called by any such name by anyone in Soviet print.

Granin's works deal with urban situations. He presents perennial emotions in a new, Soviet, urban, yet very Russian, incarnation. Other writers (Vasiliy Aksenov, Anatoliy T. Gladilin, Grigoriy M. Trifonov, Andrey G. Bitov, Natalia V. Baranskaia) have also, each in a different manner, drawn on traditional Russian literary ways of conceiving of contemporary models of the Russian ethnic past.

Boris Pasternak's Zhivago wrote in his notebooks about his return to Moscow in 1922: "Cities are the only source of inspiration for a new, truly modern art....Pastoral simplicity does not exist in these conditions....The living language of our time...is the language of urbanism. The city, incessantly moving and roaring outside our doors and windows, is an immense introduction to the life of each of us."(4)

The rural ethnocentrism displayed by Vasiliy Shukshin, Valentin G. Rasputin, and others is an important phenomenon; their works at times are fine works of art. Yet, an immensely significant part of Russian ethnocentrism would be missed if it were thought that ruralists expressed all there was. Nostalgia for the past, indignation over the cruelties wreaked in the Russian countryside by the Soviet regime and by modern technological society, admiration for the strengths of the simple, rural population - all of these must be fully appreciated and analyzed. But other writers, also, present us with descendants or cousins of rural inhabitants now transported into an urban setting, in the modern world of research institutes or factories (e.g., Baranskaia's Week Like Any Other Week). Basing themselves on Dostoevskian-Turgenevan-Tolstoyan traditions, they express a Russian ethnocentrism which is, perhaps, more complex, and it might be said, in the Russian sense of sereznyi, more serious, more complex and weightier than the ruralist.

There are other forms of ethnocentrism in Russian literature than ruralism: that concentrating on the concepts of human psychology derived from the Russian literary tradition - Pushkin, Tolstoy, Dostoevksi, Chekhov; that alluding to literary, artistic conventions of nineteenth-century Russian traditions; and that dealing with urban, middle, and high educated culture, rather than the simple ethnic group [narod] and the countryside.

NOTES

(1) John Dunlop, "Reclaiming the Russian Past," (London) Times Literary Supplement (Nov. 19, 1976), p. 1447.

(2) Daniil Granin, "Obratnyi bilet," Novyi Mir No. 8 (Aug. 1976), pp. 5-6.

(3) George Gibian, "The Urban Theme in Recent Soviet Prose: Notes Toward a Typology," Slavic Review, 37, no. 1 (March 1978), pp. 40-50; "Forward Movement through Backward Glances: Hrabal, Syomin, Granin," Fiction and Drama in Eastern Europe edited by T. Eekman and H. Birnbaum (Slavica: Columbua, Ohio, 1979).

(4) Boris Pasternak, Doctor Zhivago (New York: Signet Books, 1960), pp. 406-07. (Translation slightly revised by G. Gibian.)

III

Religion and
Ethnic Cohesion

Proposition 3:   Except for times of extreme
external peril, Russian orthodoxy has not
recently and cannot be expected soon to
exert strong influence upon ethnic identity
in the Russia-wide Soviet Federated Socialist
Republic (RSFSR).   Nor will it attract, even
nominally, active adherence from most of
Russian society, despite the church's
genuine links with the homely values of old
and inspiration for important artistic
expressions in the past.

11 The Influence of the Orthodox Church on Russian Ethnic Identity

Michael Aksenov Meerson

This chapter deals with the problems of the influence of the Church on Soviet society; the place that the Church occupies in the formative history of Russian ethnic identity; and the future perspective for the influence of the Church on Russian self-awareness. Church influence is determined by the regime's attitude toward the Church, the attitude of the public toward the Church, and the ability of the Church to fulfill its mission in given circumstances. Let us deal with each of those factors separately. Soviet society is not simply secular, characterized by separation between Church and state. It is an ideocratic regime that demands, for the whole population, a total ideological identification.(1) Leninist ideology has been defined as a new form of gnosticism, and Soviet communism is considered to be an embodiment of gnosticism in a politico-bureaucratic structure - the first gnostic empire in history.(2)

Such a perception might explain the invariably hostile, antireligious character of the Soviet regime throughout its 60 years. The regime is deliberately atheistic and antichurch oriented, claiming that religion is a "bourgeois vestige," a "weapon of the class enemy," "opium for the people," allowing for no possible reconciliation. Therefore, the regime's invariable goal is to "uproot religious prejudices."

From the outset, the Soviet regime started a war against religious communities, particularly against the Orthodox Church, the prevailing religious denomination in pre-Soviet Russia. The regime's war manifested itself in legislative discrimination against the Church in denying her civil rights; physical extermination of the clergy; a split within the Church's unity by provoking schisms; and unswerving attempts to subject the Church to government control.(3)

As a result, the Church acknowledged the government's right to draw up her canon law and to determine her internal and external policies.(4) However, despite exercising total control, the regime is afraid of the Church, seeing it as a potentially oppositional organization. (Within an ideocratic society, where no distinct boundaries exist between government and party, religious organizations enjoy relative freedom and autonomy in view of the fact that they maintain their own hierarchy, and - most important - propound their own ideological message.) This phobia forces the regime to view the Church with the greatest suspicion, immediately suppressing the smallest movement arising within its sphere. Maintaining complete control over the Church, the regime continues its unceasing battle with it by means of administrative coercion, which openly contradicts Soviet law.

The ideocratic nature of Soviet society also determines the relations between the Church and the population.(5) In Russia, secularism is not merely a fad, but the policy of a totalitarian state which has imposed an obligatory secular culture and a conformist type of secular man. Within the framework of a totalitarian ideological education, religion has no means of social expression, surviving merely as a cult, forever removed from Soviet culture and easily displaced to the very peripheries of social life. As an ideocratic community, Soviet society is monistic and simplistic. It allows for no ideological pluralism. Thus, the very adherence to an ideocratic structure excludes any religious tendencies. The entire Soviet population is subject to communist indoctrination, with total control over each individual through employment and place of residence. From childhood, the working portion of the population is incorporated into the ideocratic structure, either through membership in the party or Young Communist League, or in being called upon to perform various "official social duties" in addition to working in their own professions. Participation in a collective, secular ideology automatically generates a hostile or indifferent attitude toward religion. The more active the participation, the greater the hostility. The higher and stronger an individual rises in the ideocratic structure, ever obliging him to be a follower of the communist gnosis, the more inaccessible he is to religion.

Thus, open confession of any religion becomes an act of dissidence. It sets a believer in juxtaposition to society, making him an outcast and "social emigrant." It is by no means fortuitous that, during the past decades, the main body of believers has consisted of elderly women of the lower social strata. Within the social framework, Orthodox believers comprise the peripheries of Soviet society.

At the very best, an average Soviet citizen becomes involved with the Church at two points in his life - birth and death. The Church baptizes him and holds a funeral service.

Such an involvement can hardly leave any notable impression on a person's consciousness. Legally, the Church is deprived of educational activity, charitable work, preaching, or religious education of the faithful. Furthermore, as a hierarchic, centralized institution neither can it perform this work on an illegal basis. This is due to the regime's total control over the episcopate, the faculty in theological schools (of which there are only three for the entire Russian Orthodox Church), over the student body, and all individuals holding key positions within the Church. The regime further exerts pressure upon parish clergy through local administrative bodies.

Moreover, throughout the period of the battle against religion, in proportion to population growth, the number of churches has decreased to almost one-tenth of the original number. Through intensive urbanization, the rural populations have, over the past decades, become city dwellers. Mass migration to cities was not accompanied by corresponding church construction in new population centers. In spite of the lack of churches in villages and the fact that many faithful there have never even seen a priest, there exists a tremendous disproportion between the number of city and rural churches. In older cities, churches have been closed and torn down, in new cities they were never built. In cities with a population numbering over a million, there remain only two or three active churches. Several generations of Russians have been born who never saw a cross and do not know what a church looks like. As a result, a young Russian knows more about Indian Yoga - information which is available to him from the press - than about Orthodox monasteries.

Legally, the Church's activity is limited to holding services in churches registered with the state. The priest is called the "officiator of a cult," which best reflects the reality of the Church's standing. Owing to the lack of churches, it is impossible to discuss a parish even in its traditional sense. A single priest in a city comes into contact with thousands of strangers and becomes a mere appendage of ritual, absorbed into an endless chain of church services. Frightened, he is locked into a specific church environment. There is a wall of incomprehension between him and the average Soviet citizen. For the layman, a priest is most definitely a "vestige of the past."

The Orthodox Church found itself unprepared both for the secular revolution and its new status under an atheistic government. The Church carries the canonical and psychological burden of 15 centuries of the Orthodox Empire. Much too late, only 15 years before the 1917 Revolution, a movement toward reforms began within the Church, aimed at updating Church life in accordance with contemporary needs. However, the reformist movement had no time to develop, strengthen, and acquire form. It was curtailed by the revolution. The Bolshevik regime rechanneled reformist efforts into schismatic movements, creating a destructive force within the Church.(6) By its own efforts, the Church was unable to accomplish an internal reorganization which would permit it to stand up to the new governmental regime and allow a continuance of the mission under the new circumstances. As a result, a conservative trend has taken over within the leadership of the present hierarchy (the Moscow patriarchate). This trend combines theological and cultural conservatism with a traditional servility toward authorities.

Having outlined the basic problems of the Church's influence upon Soviet society, we shall turn to the question of its influence on Russian ethnic identity. Orthodoxy, existing in the form of regional Churches, easily adapts itself to local conditions and becomes a constituent element of a specific ethnic culture. From the Byzantine period, Orthodoxy has served as the imperial ideology. However, Christianity itself was adopted within Byzantium by a pagan empire, which left Christianity with an indelible mark under the name of Caesaropapism.

In Russia, this process was quite different. Orthodoxy had brought to Russia a well-formulated imperial ideology, provided the young Russian state with a set political identity, and placed its own universalistic goals before her. Byzantium had no knowledge of messianism; it was an empire from its origin. Orthodox messianism developed in Russia in the country's desire to become a worldwide, universal empire by right of dogmatic succession. From there came the idea of the only Orthodox Empire, heir to Byzantium, which supposedly was destroyed in the fall of Constantinople (1453) by way of punishment for its apostasy (union of Florence - 1439). It was this which gave birth to the messianic vision of Moscow as the third and the last Rome, the mystical center of the world, where the true, "orthodox" faith would be preserved until the second coming of Christ. The Church provided the centralist and authoritarian policy of the czars with a messianic ideology, and thus, through political means, assisted in the creation and expansion of a Russian state.

After the reforms of Peter the Great, which had introduced Western values to the educated strata of Russian society and weakened their ties with Orthodoxy, Russian ethnic identity was restored by the Slavophiles in the nineteenth century on the basis that Orthodoxy was a specifically Russian faith. Through Iuri Samarin and Ivan Aksakov, the romantic liberal ethnocentrism of the early Slavophiles grew into the imperial state chauvinism of the reactionary neo-Slavophiles (N. Ia. Danilevsky and Konstantin N. Leontev) and justified the great-power policies of the last Russian czars, which plunged Russia into the 1917 revolution.

The revolutionary movement was antiimperial, and the fall of the old regime was, at the same time, a breakdown of the Russian Empire. Utilizing military force, the Soviet regime reinstated the old empire under the new symbol of proletarian internationalism. Therefore, in terms of its ethnic history, Russian communism can be regarded as the new ideological and political form of survival of the Russian Empire. The Orthodox messianism of Moscow - as the third Rome - was revived in the form of communist internationalism with its seat of power in the Kremlin. Maiakovsky wrote: "As is well known, the world begins in the Kremlin. Across the land, beyond the sea the communists are obeyed."(7) The red star had replaced the Orthodox cross as the symbol of unification for all the oppressed ethnic groups around Moscow. Orthodox Marxism had replaced Orthodox Christianity. As a successor to Orthodox Christian ideology, communism launched a campaign of brutal persecutions against the Church and destroyed its independence through almost total physical extermination. At the beginning of World War II, only about 300 active churches and four ruling, unjailed bishops remained on USSR territory.

Joseph V. Stalin's postwar empire, surpassing even the wildest dreams of the Slavophiles, afforded the "newly tamed" Orthodoxy its own place (as an element of ethnic antiquity in the grand style of the Soviet empire). However, throngs of Russian people surged to the churches, monasteries, and seminaries which had been reopened after the war. The new wave of Nikita S. Khrushchev's persecutions, shutting down more than half of them, was motivated by two factors: the regime's fear of Orthodoxy's increasing influence on the peasant and working-class population; and neocommunist romanticism, which attempted to revive the ideology and style of the postrevolutionary 1920s.

The Church's identity during this period is characterized by a loyal patriotism aimed at attracting government recognition and consequent permission for the Church to minister freely to the new society. The Church stresses its role in the building of the Russian state and its faithful service to Russia. It is as if the Church overlooks the ideocratic nature of Soviet society and its own hopeless position in it. It continues to identify Soviet society with the Russian state, as if saying: "My ethnic conscience is clear, I have been true to the interests of the Russian state as they are interpreted by its contemporary leaders." It is precisely here that Orthodox political consciousness exhibits its backwardness. The Church does not conceive itself other than being under state tutelage. As in former times, it wants to be useful to the Russian "state" in exchange for the latter's patronage. But the Russian state has no further need of her. On the contrary, in order to survive as an empire, the state must totally reject Christian morality. The Empire now requires brutal ideology, which styles it a self-made god and permits it to answer to no one. The Church is suspended in nonfunction, not because it is a "vestige" within a secularized world, but because the state has turned into an antichurch, usurping that area of activity which belongs to the Church. Thus, in the light of the inner logic of this situation, the regime makes the Church a potential ally of antiimperial forces.

Within a totalitarian, ideocratic empire, all forms of nonconformist thinking are labeled dissident. Any form of dissidence is considered destructive for the empire which exists by virtue of ideological uniformity and conformance. The 1960s and 1970s are characterized by a rapid disintegration of communist ideological identity among intellectuals, giving way to an ideological pluralism and a search for an alternative world outlook. Among the various dissident trends, there are two related directly to our topic: The ethnocentrist patriotic movement and the democratic, or human rights, movement.

Both trends emerged within the communist intellectual elite as certain amendments to state policy: one trend takes a stand on cultural and ethnic self-preservation, the other on the human rights issue. At the outset, both movements considered themselves to be reformist and stressed their complete loyalty to the regime. However, the regime forced them out, into the "ranks of the enemy."

Briefly review the history of the Russian ethnocentrist patriotic movement. In its origins, this movement sprang up within the ranks of Molodaia gvardiia an official, government magazine. It took a stand in opposition to the Western and "cosmopolitan" democratic movement. Despite support by some Komsomol and party factions, the ethnocentrist group of Molodaia gvardiia was suppressed by orders from the top. The movement was now forced underground. Its first samizdat publication, Veche, "the journal of Russian patriots," proclaimed its loyalty to and support of the "great Soviet power" and reaffirmed its stand in opposition to the "cosmopolitan" human rights movement. This, however, did not help the journal survive. Its popularity as an independent Russian periodical began to grow very quickly, resulting in a sweep of political persecution and harassment. This literally forced Vladimir Osipov, chief editor of Veche, to join forces with the human rights movement. In 1972, Osipov had already declared: "Our relations with the democratic movement are most favorable. Without a doubt, no cultural renaissance is possible in the absence of a guarantee of constitutional rights and freedom. Veche and the 'democrats' are a joint embodiment of the Slavophile political principle, that is simultaneously both national [ethnic] and liberal."(8) The closing down of Veche was followed by an alliance between the ethnic patriotic and human rights movements. Through Aleksandr I. Solzhenitsyn and Igor Shafarevich, both prominent dissidents within the Soviet intellectual community, the patriotic movement linked itself to the dissidents and Orthodoxy.(9) It was, by no means, fortuitous that the movement turned to Orthodoxy. Russia knows of only two long-standing and steadfast traditions: the religious tradition of Orthodoxy and that of an expansionist authoritarian statehood. The continuity of Russian culture, curtailed by Soviet cultural policy, is interconnected with Orthodoxy. No ethnocentrist Russian movement can bypass Orthodoxy, for only there can it acquire historical roots. Any other possible basis such as, for example, the traditional peasantry, has already disappeared. The Church has preserved an ethnic identity and, in a sense, carries Russia's past within itself. For instance, five centuries of Turkish occupation could not force the Greek Church to forget Byzantium. For five centuries now, the Greek Orthodox Community in Istanbul has called itself the "Oecumenical Constantinople Patriarchate."

Russian ethnocentrist patriotism wants to preserve the imperial quality of the USSR. Having now rejected its international ideology, it is inclined to blame "the Marxism brought from the West" for all of Russia's troubles. It idealizes Russia's past and regards pre-Soviet Russian history as the Russian "Golden Age." On the basis of a traditional, Russian Orthodox identity, it seeks the restoration of pre-Soviet Russia, and the preservation of an empire devoid of any communist ideology. In essence, Russian patriotism's demands are the same as those of other ethnocentric movements in the USSR: a free ethnic and cultural life along with historical continuity. As in the case of the other movements, the psychology of a small, colonized ethnic group is characteristic of Russian ethnocentrist patriotism. It is preservationist patriotism, suffering from an anticolonial complex directed against a certain form of cosmopolitan danger - Marxism.

The emergence of Russian ethnocentrist patriotism, an ethnocentric movement within the empire's dominant ethnic group, testifies to the fact that the burden of the empire is becoming unbearable for the Russian people, crushing them under its weight. The sacrifice at which the empire had been achieved cost the Russian people their freedom, their faith, their culture, and, finally, their personal material welfare. From the Veche group to Solzhenitsyn, all laments of Russian patriots - about the ethnocentric humiliation of an ethnic group inhabiting the world's largest state territory and dominating the sphere of international politics - could appear to be those of the insane. Yet these laments merely attest to the profoundest crisis in the ethnic existence of the Russian people. Russian patriotism is a very deeply pathetic phenomenon. It is not the identity of a great people, responsible for their history, but rather the stifled identity of a subordinate ethnic group oppressed under the yoke of its conqueror and powerless to liberate itself.

Among the other ethnic liberation movements emerging to tear apart the body of the Soviet empire, Russian patriotism stands apart for, whereas other ethnocentrists oppose Russification, it fights for "genuine" Russification, devoid of any Soviet concepts. Owing, therefore, to the force of circumstances, the Russian Patriotic Movement, by virtue of the domestically operative logistics, is subject to persecution by the great-power politics of the state. This was evidenced with particular clarity and symbolism in the case of Solzhenitsyn. He addressed the Soviet leaders as "Russian patriots,"(10) and was, in turn, exiled as a "betrayer of the fatherland" and "traitor to the native land."

Soviet power is imperial power in which communist ideology and an imperial nature have become inseparably fused. It understands patriotism as inherent to its empire, an empire doomed to collapse at the dissipation of the communist ideocracy. The merest whiff of freedom and the slightest trace of pluralism within the framework of communist doctrine, not to speak of an alternate ideology, would be disastrous for the regime. Therefore, notwithstanding all its pretenses to loyalty, Russian ethnocentrist patriotism emerges as a powerful antiimperial force. Moreover, in view of the increasing disappointment in Leninism, large portions of the Russian population are ready to embrace the ethnocentrist patriotic identity. Yet, if not all the USSR's non-Russian ethnocentric movements are able to emerge under the banner of Marxist ideology, Russian patriotism forfeits this possibility. Its protests are aimed at the very Marxist mode within Russia. In its search for an ideological ally, it first confronts Russian Orthodoxy.

The religious and ethnocentrist movements are united by virtue of their fidelity to the religious and ethnocultural interests of the Russian ethnic group. This fidelity places them in irreconcilable contradiction to Russia's suicidal, imperial form of existence as the Soviet Union. This brings both movements - which are, as a matter of principle, conservative, preservationist, and isolationist - into alliance with the human rights, democratic, and Western movement. This alliance, in turn, is further promoted by the Christianization of the human rights movement among Russians.

The human rights movement has no ethnocentrist ideology. It could rather be called a Westernizing trend, insofar as it is rooted in the age-old Western values of justice, democracy, and humanitarianism. Originating within a Marxist-oriented milieu, the ideology of the human rights movement began to evolve in the direction of existentialism and

Christianity. It was through its members, converted to Orthodoxy, that the movement came into contact with the Church. And it was in the Church that the meeting occurred with the representatives of ethnocentrist patriotism, who have also become converts to Orthodoxy. Thus, the Church became the meeting place of indigenous, alien, dissident movements and the common territory for the alliance.

The Church, in light of being discriminated against, should be in the front ranks of the battle for civil rights and the liberalization of Soviet society. However, as a result of long-term repression and the constant destruction of its active members, a spirit of passive submission has pervaded the Church. In every way possible, the regime, on the one hand, encourages quietism within the Church, and, on the other, severely suppresses the slightest breath of initiative on its part. At the same time, the regime extensively exploits the Church's prestige to its advantage in foreign policy. A further obstacle to the Church's activity and participation in the civil rights movement lies in its centralized organizational structure. Through this, the regime succeeds in snuffing out any Church dissent by operating through its own hierarchy.

Nonetheless, the general trend of thought, the discontent of the intellectuals, the domestic processes of emancipation from ideology, and the fight for liberalization have penetrated the Church. Paradoxically, the era of Nikita S. Khrushchev, which brought unheard of freedom to the Soviet regime, by releasing millions of political prisoners, subjected the Church to severe persecutions, demonstrating that the Church can expect nothing for itself, even from a relatively permissive Soviet government. The inner logic of an ideocratic regime remains unchangeable.

For this reason, the movement for religious freedom and revival of the Church began within Russian Orthodoxy simultaneously with the origin of the human rights movement, despite their obviously independent sources. The human rights movement was born on December 5, 1965, with the first demonstration on Pushkin Square in Moscow, bearing the slogans of "Free [Andrey] Sinyavsky and [Iuli M.] Daniel" and "respect your own constitution." The religious freedom movement was born on December 15, 1965, in the form of two letters written by the Russian Orthodox priests, Nikolay Eshliman and Gleb Iakunin, addressed to the Patriarch Aleksey and Nikolay Podgorny, President of the USSR, accusing the state of infringement upon Church canon law and violation of the state's own constitution. Quite characteristic is the fact that these letters were written by a pair of Russian ethnocentrists and Orthodox romanticists. This constituted the earliest awakening of the Church's movement for human rights in parallel with religious revival (that is, religious conversion of young people and intellectuals brought up in Soviet society).(11)

In December 1976, Father Gleb Iakunin, one of the authors of the letter to the Patriarch, with two other Orthodox Christians, Deacon Varsonofiy Khaibulin and layman Viktor Kapitanchuk, founded the Christian Committee for the Defense of Believers' Rights in the USSR. As a Church organization, they now joined the human rights movement. It is significant that this move, as well, was made under the initiative of ethnocentrists and romanticists. Both Khaibulin and Kapitanchuk were supporters and participants of Veche. But the movement to free the Church, originally a movement of ethnic and religious romanticism, seeks contact with the West, with worldwide Christianity, and with those forces in the USSR which are fighting for human rights.

The founding of the Christian Committee, and its fight, in the name of Orthodoxy, for freedom for all faiths (Jewish, Protestant, and others) previously persecuted by the same Orthodox Church, is symptomatic in character. It reflects the tendency of a Church deprived of all rights to form alliances with all forces fighting for rights, including those of small ethnic and religious groups.

In conclusion, we can only add that Orthodoxy is beginning to exert ever-increasing influence on the overall development of the dissident movement. One of the channels for this influence is Orthodoxy's attractiveness to Russian ethnocentrist patriots.

NOTES

(1)   D. Nelidov, "Ideocratic Consciousness and Personality," The Political, Social and Religious Though of Russian 'Samizdat' An Anthology, edited by Michael Aksenov Meerson and Boris Shragin, (Belmont, Mass.: Nordland, 1977), pp. 256, 287.

(2)   Alain Besancon, Les Origines Intellectuelles du Leninism (Paris: Calmann-Levy, 1977), p. 287.

(3)   For communist policy toward the Church: A. Bogolepov, Tserkov pod vlastu Rommunisma (Munich: Institut po Izucheniiu SSSR, TZOPE 1958); Nikita Struve, Les chretiens en URSS (Paris: Ed. du Seuil, 1963), pp. 31-49.

(4)   The surrender of the Russian Church is described by samizdat author Lev Regel'son, Tragediia russkoi tserkvi, 1917-1945 (Paris: YMCA Press, 1977), pp. 103-97.

(5)   M. Aksenov Meerson, "L'Eglise en URSS," in Etude (June 1973), pp. 917-34.

(6)   A. Levitin and B. Shavrov, "Ocherki po istorii russkoi tserkovnoi smuty 20-30kh godov XX veka; Istoriia obnovlenchestva," (Moscow: samizdat, 1962) and

A. A. Shishkin, Suchnost' i kriticheskaia otsenka obnovlencheskogo raskola russkoi pravoslavnoi tserkvi (Kazan: Kazanskii Universitet, 1970).

(7) "Nachinaetsia zemlia, kak izvestno, ot Kremlia; za morem, za susheiu kommunistov slushaiut; Okna satiry Rosta." Cited in Samosoznanie (A Collection of Articles), edited by P. Litvinov, M. Meerson, B. Skragin (New York: Chronika, 1976), p. 103.

(8) The political...thought of Russian "Samizdat," p. 350.

(9) Aleksandr I. Solzhenitsyn, ed., Iz-pod glyb (Paris: YMCA Press, 1974), pp. 7, 29, 97, 115, 217, 261.

(10) Aleksandr I. Solzhenitsyn, Pis'mo vozhdiam Sovetskogo Soiuza (Paris: YMCA Press, 1974), p. 7.

(11) Michael Bourdeaux, Patriarch and Prophets (London: Macmillan, 1969), p. 189.

12 Russian Orthodoxy and Ethnic Identity Today

Marina Ledkovsky

Can Russian Orthodoxy be expected to exert a strong influence upon ethnic self-awareness in the Russia-wide Soviet Federated Socialist Republic (RSFSR)? The proposition posed is a serious one, possibly the most crucial one in the light of current events and prospective developments.

It has been noted before "that the reemergence of vigorous Russian nationalism [ethnocentrism] has gone hand in hand with an increasing interest in religion"(1) (Russian Orthodoxy). This spiritual awakening seems to be acquiring increased strength and importance among members of the Russian ethnic group. More recently, Aleksandr I. Solzhenitsyn has stated that religion is the major form, an organizing pivot, of the Russian people's spiritual renaissance.(2) This fact, of course, is well-founded in the history of Russian culture. Very far back can be detected a powerful religious idealism penetrating all spheres of life and well attested in the earliest records available since the Christianization of Rus'. The highly significant self-definition of Russians as Holy Russia (Sviataia Rus') seems to have imposed a historical task on the Russian people. The awareness of this ever present goal of an ideal Christian existence has determined the ethnic consciousness of Russians for centuries. And precisely this awareness seems to have survived throughout all the recent decades of terror and persecution. Russian Orthodoxy has continued to exist as an institution in the officially established Patriarchate in spite of repression and humiliation. But, more important, it has lived on in the hearts of people, in the clandestine catacomb church or, as it also is called, the Truly Orthodox Church (Istinno-Pravoslvnaia Tserkov').(3) In a recently published book, an enormous amount of factual material has been adduced pointing to the ceaseless religious resistance of Russians to the

totalitarian, atheist ideology enforced during the years 1917 to
1945.(4)   The steadfastness of the Russian people's living faith
became strikingly evident when, during World War II, masses
of believers flocked to the churches newly opened on one side
of the front by the Germans in the occupied territories, or, on
the other side, by Stalin under the pressure of Hitler's
advancing armies.

Beginning with the famous "Open Letter to the Moscow
Patriarch Aleksey" in 1965 by two Orthodox priests - Nikolay
Eshliman and Gleb Iakunin - an enormous number of
documents, letters, and articles has appeared bearing witness
to the revival of the consciousness of a religious missionary
purpose for the Russian people.   All of this literature basically
represents an appeal to drop materialistic, hackneyed, and
worn criteria for the evaluation of human existence and to turn
to the fundamental eternal values of good and evil as they are
found in the teaching of the Orthodox Church.   Priests,
writers, scholars, and scientists (some already emigrants by
now) proceed from a moral religious point of view and envisage
the possibility of a new "Holy Russia" in religious ethnic
terms.   Their ideas in many respects fermented in the
nineteenth century Slavophile movement and were only
"enriched" by the experience of life in "the most progressive
country of the world," as the USSR has been called.   In the
words of Soviet dissident Igor Shafarevich, "Russia passed
through death and [now] can hear the voice of God."(5)

The orthodoxy of many of those diverse groupings of the
religious, of intellectual societies, and ordinary parishioners
bears a pronounced ethnocentrist tinge; "Russia and
Orthodoxy are synonyms" and "Orthodoxy has its center in
Moscow" are phrases encountered frequently in recent
unofficial writings.   Some newly-arrived emigrants from the
USSR affirm that the most important movement among the
religious dissidents and samizdat is "certainly the movement
that represents the Russian people as such, that expressly
stands for the Orthodox and national [ethnocentric] ideas of
the Russian people."(6)   The samizdat journals Veche and
Zemlia, founded in 1971 and suppressed in 1974, devoted most
of their pages to urging the necessity for a strong revival of
Russian Orthodoxy as a means of preserving and continuing
life as an ethnic entity.   The appeals of Solzhenitsyn,
Maksimov, Aleksandr A. Galich, and many others, along with
Father Dimitriy Dudko's sermons and Talks point to the same
awareness of the connection between Russian Orthodoxy and
ethnic identity.

Probably, few Western observers will know of and
attribute significance to an eminently Russian Orthodox
ethnocentric movement which existed in the underground as
a full-fledged organization with an elaborate program for
more than three years (1964-1967).   Igor Ogurtsov, founder,

leader, and principal ideologist of the "All-Russia Social-Christian Union for the Liberation of the People [Vserossiiskii Sotsial Khristianskii Soiuz Osvobozhdeniia Naroda--"VSKhSON"] was arrested in 1967 and given a 15 year prison sentence, to be followed by five years of exile. The program of VSKhSON calls for a Christianization of politics, economy, culture, and of society as a whole because, it claims, "if the Russian people have learned anything at all in these sixty years of useless pain and deprivation, they have learned to be forced to live in the reality of a civilization without God and its inevitable consequences."(7) Yet, the leaders of VSKhSON as well as Solzhenitsyn, Shafarevich, even Osipov (the editor-in-chief) and other contributors to Veche make it clear that, although they maintain Russian Orthodoxy as the central tradition of Russian culture, they also insist on religious freedom and respect for other ethnic traditions in the future pluralistic "Sacred Society" of Russia.(8) The ideas of the defunct organization, VSKhSON, have reached many corners of Russia, especially through the activity of prisoners released from forced labor camps. If no immediate result can be detected on the surface, more and more noticeable is a general alertness to those ideas in recent literature, correspondence, and mainly in the severe reaction of the Soviet regime.

The formation of various religiophilosophical circles and seminars in recent years in most major cities inhabited by Russians, particularly Moscow, Leningrad, and Kiev, is of considerable significance. In 1974 a study group for Orthodox religious and ethnic topics was founded in Moscow by a young student at the Union-Wide Institute of Cinematography, Aleksandr Ogorodnikov. A similar religiophilosophical seminar was organized in the fall of 1975 in Leningrad. The samizdat journal "37" is published by members of this group. It provides interesting articles written at a respectable intellectual level. There are discussions, for example, of "Dostoevsky and Kierkegaard," "Christian and Social Life," and "Anonymous Christianity in Philosophy." The focus, again, seems to be on the Russian Orthodox Christian's search for his place in the world. Those study groups eventually may be broken up by the authorities (this has already happened to the Moscow Seminar). But their very emergence proves that the spiritual restlessness of the Russian intellectual elite is assuming a creative aspect which may reach unexpected proportions.

The language and the topics of many unoffical works testify that the great tradition of Russian Orthodox thought has not been curbed and that it seems to increase in importance, depth, and breadth. The major concern of those anonymous correspondents, also, is the fate of Russia, in light of its Orthodox tradition and ethnic identity. Their views coincide in general with those of Solzhenitsyn, Ogurtsov, or Osipov and seem to be shared by a considerable number of supporters and sympathizers. Recent documents published by the Christian Committee for the Defense of Believers' Rights in the USSR point to a widespread range of partisans.

This committee was founded in late 1976 by the prominent religious activists Father Gleb Iakunin, Hierodeacon Varsonofiy Khaibulin, and Viktor Kapitanchuk. The last two are Russian ethnocentrists with links to the journal, Veche. The goal of the committee is to aid believers in the realization of their right to live in accord with their convictions. To accomplish this goal, the committee intends:

1) to collect, study, and distribute information about the situation of believers in the USSR.
2) to render advisory assistance to believers in instances when their rights have been violated;
3) to appeal to government institutions about questions of the defense of believers' rights;
4) to carry on all feasible research for clarification of the legal and actual position of religion in the USSR; and
5) to aid in perfecting Soviet legislation regarding religion.

The committee pursues no political goals and is loyal to Soviet laws. The committee is prepared to cooperate with community and government organizations to the extent that such cooperation will help to improve the situation of believers in the USSR.(9)

The existence of this committee may be one of the most remarkable phenomena in the movement of spiritual awakening in the Soviet Union. Its bold aim to ascertain the reality of the regime's claim of religious freedom for all must be quite alarming to the authorities. Ever since December 1977, the founders and members of this Committee have been harassed by agencies of the Committee for State Security (KGB). Some of the papers published by this religious committee attest the farreaching revival of ethnic consciousness. One document, for example, contains an appeal by the "Christian Committee" to support a petition to the authorities by monks and a group of Orthodox young men and women. They requested that the Kievan Cave Monastery be reopened and returned to the Church. In this petition, special mention is made of the important year 1988, when Russians will celebrate the thousandth anniversary of their Christianization in Kiev. That city is labeled "the cradle of Russia's religious, cultural, and national [ethnic] life."(10) Similar petitions addressed to the Patriarch, to Leonid I. Brezhnev, and to local, state, or church authorities betray deep concern for the deplorable condition of some monasteries (especially the Pochaev Monastery) and churches. They request their reopening as well as better care for the existing "working" church buildings and monasteries.

In many respects, the concerns of the "Christian Committee" coincide with those of the official, voluntary Russia-wide Society for the Preservation of Historical and Cultural Monuments (which was founded in 1965 and by the summer of 1977 had 12.5 million active members), and also with those of the leading school of contemporary Soviet literature - the ruralists (derevenshchiki). Those concerns are tinged with anxiety over the loss of the ethnic heritage and contain appeals to return to the group's roots, to cherish the legacy of its ancestors. All these quests, in turn, explain the widespread interest in the philosophy of Nikolay Fedorovich Fedorov (1825-1903) among intellectuals and writers of the USSR. Fedorov was a highly original nineteenth-century Russian thinker, and his major work Philosophy of the Common Task, (Filosofiia obshchego diela), with the appeal for true Christian love leading to universal brotherhood and for a philosophy of "activity," has prompted numerous discussions in recent official and unofficial publications.

The genuine worry over a possible disappearance of the "ethnic countenance" (national'nogo oblika) is, likewise, clearly reflected in the breadth and variety of Soviet official and unofficial writing. Works on ideological and historical themes show an ever growing concern with ethnic awareness and self-assertion. Within this concern, a neo-Slavophile school of thinking manifests itself prominently with as many factions and differences of emphasis in attitudes toward other ethnic groups and religions as there were among the original Slavophiles themselves. Variations are even more evident between them and Dostoevsky's "soilrooted" school (pochvennichestvo) and various types of ethnocentrists. An obvious positive idea binds them together like it did Slavophilism in the nineteenth century. It is a deep reverence for the Orthodox Church, and the open (unofficial) or silent (official and most of the time hostile) recognition that a moral and cultural survival of the Russian ethnic group is directly related to emphasis on the vitality of the Orthodox Church and revival of Russian Orthodox traditions in the USSR today.

Those neo-Slavophile trends are present in the works of both the most prominent and less known contemporary Soviet writers in the officially sanctioned journals Molodaia gvardiia, Moskva, Novyi mir, Literaturnaia Rossia, Nash sovremennik, and Kontekst which appeared during the past 15 to 20 years. But again the bulk of neo-Slavophile literature is to be found in samizdat journals such as Veche (significantly, the name of the earliest Russian citizens' assemblies in the first centuries of the formation of the Russian state), Zemlia, or,

more recently, the journal "37". In those clandestine journals,
neo-Slavophiles of all shades are trying to fill the spiritual
vacuum of Soviet reality in various ways. Sometimes they look
for solutions in the main Russian cultural legacy, the Russian
Orthodox tradition; sometimes they revive the roots inevitably
linked to the Orthodox Church and Russian religiophilosophic
thought as developed by Aleksey S. Khomiakov, the brothers
Ivan V. and Petr V. Kireevsky, and further by Fedor M.
Dostoevsky, Vladimir S. Solov'ev, Nikolay F. Fedorov, Pavel
A. Florensky, Nikolay A. Berdiaev, and many others.

The religious commitment to the Russian Orthodox Church
in this "rediscovery of Russian roots" seems to be quite strong
and to prevail over aesthetic and "antiquarian" motives which
have been suggested by several Western scholars.(11)
According to an American authority "one emigre specialist
recently calculated that 115 million Soviet citizens remain at
least passively attached to Orthodoxy."(12) Many reports from
visitors to the Soviet Union as well as the testimonies
presented in this inquiry support that assumption. A western
scholar, necessarily anonymous, who was in Russia in
February 1978, writes in a private letter:

> We...attended the divine liturgy in the [suburban]
> church....It was particularly gratifying to witness
> the many private services that were held after the
> end of the liturgy. In one place they were
> baptizing babies, in another they had requiem
> services, in still another special thanksgiving or
> petition offices were conducted. All of this is a
> strong indication that the life of the church has not
> died away, that the Russian people have kept the
> Orthodox faith in spite of all persecutions and
> humiliations, and presently they yearn for prayer
> and ritual.
>
> It is a joy to witness that steadfastness of
> belief in Russia. The Russians have suffered for the
> right to be real people: Good for them!

The universalist vision of Russian ethnocentrism rooted in
the teachings of the Orthodox Church and in accordance with
the concepts of Khomiakov, Dostoevsky, Berdiaev, and many
others seems to form the basis of modern Russia's renewed
spiritual quest. Yet, only the future will show whether there
has been an unbroken continuity of the high quality of
intellectual culture and pre-revolutionary breadth of thinking,
and how much of the true Orthodox tradition has been
preserved on the surface and in the underground.

The testament of Father Mikhail Ershov,(13) a priest of
the Truly Orthodox Church, is imbued with that magnanimous

messianic spirit characteristic of some great Russian Orthodox thinkers:

> Love one another, brethern....Preserve all traditions of Russia, teach one another. If a stranger comes to learn from you - teach him and explain to him simply and lovingly....Do not look to the ends of the earth, your mother is Holy Rus'. We, we, will accept in Russia all pilgrims into life eternal. They will come to us to learn from us, [because] we possess Christ's Church....In our Russia lies the mystery of events, in our Russia is the legacy of life eternal....Do not fear a small flock, you wretched ones [ubogie], we are the chosen ones, God is with us!(14)

Father Ershov's "testament" echoes Father Dimitriy Dudko's lines from his "Poems about Russia" (Stikhi o Rossii): "And from Russia, Christ will appear to resurrect your [the West's] corpses."(15)

All of the evidence presented prompts an affirmative answer to the question raised at the beginning. Russian Orthodoxy is an all-important element in Russian self-awareness and, indeed, can be expected to exert influence strongly and widely upon ethnic group identity in the RSFSR.

NOTES

(1) Jack V. Haney, "The Revival of Interest in the Russian Past in the Soviet Union," Slavic Review, no. 1 (1973), p. 14.

(2) Aleksandr I. Solzhenitsyn, "O rabote russkoi sektsii BBC," Kontinent, no. 9 (1976), p. 218.

(3) Samizdat originated well before World War II as religious underground literature distributed in handwritten or typed form among the members of the Truly Orthodox Church. Information about this unofficial, severely-persecuted branch of the Russian Orthodox Church reaches the West quite regularly through samizdat publications; see recent copies of Russkaia mysl' (Paris) (August 25, 1977) p. 5; (April 20, 1978, p.5), and other current emigrant periodicals.

(4) Lev Regel'son, Tragediia russkoi tserkvi 1917-1945 (Paris YMCA Press, 1977).

(5) Igor' Shafarevich, "Est' li u Rossii budushchee?," Iz pod glyb (Paris: YMCA Press, 1974), p. 276.

(6) Alexander Udodov, currently in Rome, Italy, unpublished interview with the author.

(7)   Ibid.
(8)   <u>Vestnik</u> (Paris), No. 123, publication of the Russian Christian Movement.
(9)   Documents of the Christian Committee for the Defense of Believers' Rights in the USSR, Moscow 1977 (San Francisco: Washington Street Research Center, 1977), p. 36.
(10) Ibid., p. 46.
(11) Jack V. Haney, "The Revival . . . ;" and "Reply;" and George L. Kline, "Religion, National Character, and the 'Rediscovery of Russian Roots,'" <u>Slavic Review</u>, no. 1 (1973), pp. 1-16; 29-44.
(12) John B. Dunlop, <u>The New Russian Revolutionaries</u> (Belmont, Mass.: Nordland, 1976), pp. 204; 329.
(13) Father Mikhail Ershov has been imprisoned for the past thirty-five years. A long <u>samizdat</u> report, reprinted in <u>Russkaia mysl' (Russian Thought)</u> (Paris (May 11, 1978), No. 3203 p. 5, tells of Father Ershov's great popularity among the Truly Orthodox Christians.
(14) Father Mikhail Ershov, "Zaveshchanie katakombnogo sviashchenno-sluzhitelia, <u>Pravoslavnaia Rus'</u>, no. 18 (Sept. 28, 1977), p. 2.
(15) Dimitriy Dudko, "Preodolenie soblaznov," <u>Russkoe vozrozhdenie</u>, no. 1 (Paris-Moscow-New York, 1978) p. 101.

13 Ethnocentrism, Ethnic Tensions, and Marxism/Leninism

Dimitry V. Pospielovsky

"Nationalism" is a relatively recent concept; in Russia, the term was first used in print as late as the first decade of the twentieth century. In contrast, the earliest use of the term in French belongs to 1812, and in English to 1836.(1) This does not mean that by then the concept had penetrated to the public. The Russian peasant at the time identified himself as Orthodox (pravoslavnyi) rather than as Russian. When a Russian peasant or worker used the word native land (rodina) he meant the province, town, or village where he was born, rather than Russia as a whole. What existed as a meaningful term for centuries was the Russian soil and Holy Russia (Zemlia russkaia and Sviataia Rus', respectively) which for him embraced all orthodox Christian eastern Slavs and was more of a spiritual than ethnic concept. One of the peculiarities of Russia was that ethnocentric movements with some popular following had appeared among a number of non-Russian groups within the empire long before the appearance of ethnic consciousness among Russians. The imperial government itself was not sure about what should replace the defunct notions of dynastic loyalty, for no other notions could satisfy all of its diverse ethnic groups. Consequently, the concept of "Russianness" remained undefined. Prior to Alexander III (r.1881-1894) Russian tended to mean a subject of the Russian Emperor of whatever ethnic group, creed (except Judaic), language or race, with, however, preference for Orthodoxy as the state religion. Adoption of the Russian language, and with it culture, became a necessary ingredient of the concept from the late nineteenth century.

The ethnic consciousness of such people as the Poles, Finns, Georgians, and Armenians, and a type of pan-Turkic consciousness of the Tatars, preceded that of the Russians, and growing groups of Ukrainophile intelligentsia in the

Ukraine were disgruntled by the czarist government's prohibition of Ukrainian as a legal language. Naturally, antagonisms against the Russians preceded the latter's self-recognition as an ethnic group. An obstacle on the road to Russians' ethnic self-recognition was their role in the empire: were they a separate local ethnic group or an imperial catalyst for forming a multifaceted supraethnic entity?

It was in this state of the country's insecurity and confusion that extremist proto-Nazi and proto-Fascist theories and groups, from the milder and tolerant corporativist ideas of Lev K. Tikhomirov and Sergey V. Zubatov to the pogromist Black Hundred, began to appear in Russia in the early twentieth century.(2) Not accidentally (as in most later Nazi and Fascist movements of Europe), many leaders of these movements were representatives of the Russianized non-Russians: Vladimir M. Purishkevich was a Bessarabian; Vasiliy V. Shulgin, a Ukrainian; Gringmut a Jew; and the list could be continued.

Despite the many predictions of revolutionaries that Russia as an empire would disintegrate at the first shot of a major war because of the disgruntled non-Russian ethnic groups, this did not happen until after the 1917 revolution, which began in Petrograd and not in any of the non-Russian territories. Probably the miscalculations of the revolutionaries, including Lenin, were caused by their inability to appreciate the force of nonmaterial culture. According to an outstanding contemporary Russian philosopher, Evgeniy Barabanov, the imperial concept of Russia was broader than its ethnic borders. To identify oneself with Russia at the time meant to adopt a universalist culture (although rooted in the localized version of the Orthodox-Christian spiritual tradition), in which merged all the component parts of the empire.(3) The only alternative was to revert to the local ethnic, mostly ruralist, provincialism of any of these component parts, whether the ruralist culture of the Russian or Ukrainian "tribe," or much more ancient but still provincial cultures of Georgia or Armenia. These invisible, spiritual ties to the Russian culture of the empire attracted the upper intellectual and cultural strata of the empire's component groups. Along with the attractions of prestigious imperial service for their aristocracies, they probably held the empire together and continued the assimilationist, Russianizing trend beyond and despite the irritating Russificatory policies of the last two Russian emperors. (The term "Russianization" is used here in the sense of a natural process of voluntary assimilation, and "Russification" as a state policy with at least some forms of coercion.)

Much of the Empire collapsed in the course of the two revolutions of 1917 and the subsequent civil war, in the classical pattern of provinces devouring the empire. This was a product of the rise of the ordinary provincial population and semiintelligentsia with their localist rather than universalist outlook. External manifestations of this included the reversion to Cossack costumes and haircuts in the Ukraine, and adoption of the early Muscovite militiamen's (strel'tsy) uniforms for the first internationalist (!) Red Army by the Jewish commissar of war, Leon Trotsky. In the latter case, of course, ethnocentrism could not go further or deeper, because it would contradict the worldwide communist aims of the revolution. The slogans, after all, continued to be: "world international brotherhood," "end to all wars and secret diplomacy," and the like. The disproportionate large contingents of non-Russians in the Soviet communist administration on all levels was too obvious to make it pass for an ethnic Russian government. It has been argued that precisely the lack of any deep sense of ethnocentrism among the Russians, Ukrainians, or Belorussians allowed the first, avowedly cosmopolitan, internationalist, communist state to assert itself on the ruins of the Russian Empire. Moreover, at the time, its internationalism and its ideological promises of eventual achievement of a materialist paradise on earth probably were responsible for the reconsolidation of an empire,(4) federal in form, centralized in content.

But how were the communists prepared to treat ethnic issues theoretically? In Karl Marx's writings there is no theory of ethnicity. He brushed it aside as a bourgeois class invention which would disappear in a classless society. The concept of ethnocentrism was supposed to be totally foreign to the working class, which in case of international war would refuse to fight for their exploiters and would turn the war into an international civil war bringing about world communism. Lenin had counted precisely on this. Failure of this doctrine, as well as the failure to export communism from the Soviet Union after the October 1917 revolution and the civil war, forced Lenin to adopt and Stalin to formulate the policy of "socialism in one country."

As contrasted to Marx and Frederick Engels, Lenin did pay more attention to the realities of growing popular ethnocentrism; and in 1913, Joseph V. Stalin, under Lenin's supervision, devised the Bolshevik platform in ethnic matters defining "nation" as: "A historically formed, permanent community of men, unified by a common language, common territory, common economic ties, and common psychic cast realized in a common culture."(5)

This definition is obviously not applicable either to such ethnic groups lacking common territory, and the like, as Jews, Gypsies and others, or to the appearance of new ethnic groups and development of ethnic consciousnesses in groups of people where formerly there were just vague tribal units or ethnic subgroups. The definition, which remains the official one, speaks of _permanent_ communities, not dynamic phenomena. Neither is there any room for an ethnic diaspora, in terms of large fragments of ethnic groups living outside their ethnic territories and yet desiring some cultural autonomy, for example, Ukrainian schools for the Ukrainians in Siberia, Kazakhstan, or the North Caucasus.

Socialism in one country is the result of a failure of the world proletariat to behave in the way Marx had expected it to behave. It is a failure of one of the basic precepts of Marxist ideology. Only two conclusions can be drawn from this lesson. Either Marx was wrong about this issue, and, therefore, Marxism is not an infallible science and can be critically approached on all other issues as well, or Marxism remains true but the working class is no good. This premise is not unlike Hitler's at the end of the war when he asserted that the German nation was not worthy of him. Moreover, in this thinking, the proletariat in the noncommunist states is now under the rule of those bourgeois regimes which form the enemy encirclement around the socialist Soviet Union. Gradually, a logical displacement begins to take its course. The world working class, as the Marxian chosen people, begins to be replaced by the first people who embraced the Marxist-Leninist system, the Soviet people. They become, willingly or not, the "chosen people." But to make this socialist state work, in conditions of extreme centralization of the economy and of all other spheres of social, cultural, and political life, there must be maximum uniformity: one language, and, if possible, one culture, one law, unified customs, and the like. The Russian language, being the language spoken by the largest number of people in the unit, performs this role. Thus, artificial state Russification, or rather, Sovietization in the Russian language, began roughly in 1934.(6) To justify this, to rationalize it in conditions of the withering away of faith in the ideology and its promises, the Russian ethnic group had to be boosted into position of first among equals, as the great people, the greatest ethnic group in the Soviet state. Some Russian ethnic slogans and historical heroes were pulled out of the archives. This happened during World War II, but unevenly and semiofficially continues to the present day.

How about the brotherhood of ethnic groups in a communist or socialist commonwealth? It appears that as long as there was sufficient enthusiasm generated for the attractive promises of communism, the ideology helped to keep the ethnic groups together for their new Soviet intelligentsia, and kept Komsomol members busy building "the new society." In this process, the Russian ethnic group - Russian language being at the core of the state - appeared to generate continuing attraction for assimilation. This is the most logical explanation for the disproportionate increase in the Russian population during the first thirty years of the Soviet regime, despite the fact that Stalinist terror took at least as heavy a toll of Russians as of any other Soviet ethnic group.

World War II convinced Stalin that communist ideological appeals were a dead letter, at least for the general public. He switched to ethnic appeals. This included such appeals to the ethnocentrism of the non-Russian union republics as the creation of some ethnic army divisions. This was followed by the law of February 1, 1944, permitting the union republics to form local armed forces and ministries of external affairs. But the emphasis was clearly placed on the Russian group and Russian patriotism exemplified, for instance, by the words of the Soviet anthem: "Great Russia has molded together forever / Th'indestructible union of free republics."(7)

This emphasis on things Russian was, in the face of the Nazi invasion, apparently less irritating for non-Russian Soviet citizens than communist internationalism.(8) This is a fact that should instill at least a little more caution in "diagnoses" of anti-Russian feelings and of the centrifugal force of ethnic self-awareness in the USSR.

So far as the relegitimized Russian ethnocentrism of the war years was concerned, it was apparently clear, even to Stalin, that, in the Russian historical tradition, ethnic awareness would be meaningless without its spiritual side. Stalin's flirtation with the Church during the war, in an atheistic, communist state, could be neither consistent, sincere, nor long-lasting. Soon after the war, those policies began to give way to measures against the Church. They were followed by Nikita S. Khrushchev's severe antireligious persecutions of 1959 to 1964 in the name of the advent of communism promised for the immediate future. But "the core of Russian cultural life," Nikolay Berdiaev said, "is religious."(9) Therefore, a consistent "...Russian nationalism [ethnocentrism] is in principle impossible in the framework of the existing communist regime, be it in external or internal policies."

The main centrifugal agent in the Soviet state is the ideological underpinning of the system itself: "Militant class internationalism...being organically tied with the idea of class struggle and with civil war moods,"(10) would lead to the perpetuation of a civil war atmosphere. Where ethnocentric wars unify ethnic groups, civil wars split and disunite them. An ideology that builds upon class antagonism, therefore, atomizes and disintegrates the ethnic group and/or the state from within.(11)

The Soviet leadership's maneuvers in using ethnocentrism to mobilize the ethnic group could not be complete and consistent in view of that ideological duality. On the other hand, their materialist, ideological platform, as well as the totalitarian nature of the regime, precludes any long-lasting absorption of the spiritual, cultural, and historical values of the given ethnic group into their forms of ethnocentrism. What attraction does Soviet Russian ethnocentrism have, as a force for assimilation, for ethnic groups, or even for the Russian group itself? This must be asked when the Orthodox Church is persecuted, when ancient churches and monasteries, even if appreciated only as architectural monuments, are razed to the ground, when Russian history is being presented in predominantly negative tones, when Russia's best writers, poets, and artists are either destroyed in prisons and concentration camps, silenced, or expelled abroad, and her thinkers and philosophers suppressed and concealed from the ethnic group. The type of Russification that is one way or another affected by the Soviet system attracts recruits only out of career considerations. On a deeper, more sincere, emotional level it breeds centrifugal forces among the non-Russians of the Soviet Union, stimulates antagonism and hatred for the Russian group, while making the latter feel that as a group it is being insulted by this type of administrative Russification of other ethnic groups.(12) Moreover, the continued use by the regime of the Russians as a physical assimilation medium, by economically encouraging them to move out of the Russian Soviet Federated Socialist Republic (RSFSR) to other union republics in conditions of the currently catastrophically declining Russian birth rates, forces Russian patriots to fear that their ethnic group is under threat of racial disintegration and biological extinction. These fears are reinforced by the factor of unprecedented rates of growth of alcoholism among the Russians, as well, it seems, as among other Soviet Slavs, which is probably at least one of the factors in the fall of birth rates and certainly a leading factor in the moral disintegration of the ethnic group.(13)

This has led to the development among the Russians of a vocal tendency "to pull the RSFSR out of the USSR." Let those willing to lead an existence independent from Russians do so, they say. Let the Russians reconverge on their native land, becoming a much more compact group there, developing at last a self-consciousness as an ethnic group instead of being pawns in the hands of empire-building governments, under whatever ideological pretext.(14)

This Russian nativist or soil-bound (pochvennaia) orientation claims that, in addition, such facts as lack of a Russian party organization deprive the Russians of a separate identity in the USSR, making them ethnically underprivileged in comparison with the Ukrainians and other Soviet groups.(15) Russia has, thus, no ethnic pressure group in all-important party hierarchy, no one to plead for her particular interest, including even the defenses of a Russian cultural identity. It has been argued that were Aleksandr I. Solzhenitsyn a Georgian or Uzbek writer, the local party authorities would be so proud of him that he would not have been suppressed as he was in the 1960s, nor subsequently expelled abroad.(16)   In Soviet Russia there was simply no ethnic party body in which pressure could have been brought by an ethnocentric intelligentsia.

The discussion so far points to the following tentative conclusions: The degenerated, Nazified, form of Marxism necessarily resulting from the failure of the world revolution breeds a chauvinistic, racist ethnocentrism devoid of all spiritual values, therefore, extreme and intolerant, being the product of a totalitarian ideology and system.   Elements and rationalizations of the original materialist, class ideology remain and cause a schizoid, dualistic oscillation between the original ideology and the product of its degeneration.   Loss of faith in the ideology, together with the above processes, leads to its becoming not a unifying but an ethnically antagonizing and centrifugal factor in society.   The inadequately formulated, original ethnic doctrine of the party precludes its application to changing conditions, to appearances of new ethnic identities, and to groups whose destinies failed to follow theoretical prescriptions of the Marxist pillars.   The general petrification of all ideological creativity in the USSR, fear of changing a word in that legacy which had the approval of Lenin, seen as infallible, as well as the limits created by materialistic dogmatism, has precluded any change in the ethnic doctrine or a more pragmatic practical approach to the issues.   Refusal of the totalitarian system to allow any expression of ethnic, cultural, and spiritual autonomy, refusal to give any spiritual content and meaning to the Russian and other ethnocentrisms occasionally experimented with, lead to further interethnic antagonisms within the Soviet Union and fail to satisfy the sincerely patriotic and ethnocentrist factions, particularly the Russian ones.

Elsewhere, various aspects of the evolution in post-Stalin Russian thought, from Marxist-revisionism to liberalism and ethnocentrism, have been dealt with.(17)

Except for a chauvinistic, racist, neo-Nazi wing within the Komsomol and some sections of the party bureaucracy, secular Russian ethnocentrism, with which those party and Komsomol members had played for a while, failed to satisfy anyone.   Under the guise of a seemingly atheistic ethnocentrism tolerated by the regime for a while on the pages of such Soviet publications as Molodaia gvardiia and Voprosy literatury, a search for Russian spirituality went on.   A genuine interest in Russian religious philosophy was being asserted as a need to fill in the ideological vacuum produced by the death of Marxism.(18)   The ideology is still the reason for the system's existence, an umbrella to rationalize the policies and actions of the regime.   It is in this sense that Solzhenitsyn's argument (that it is the source of evil and petrification of the Soviet system) remains correct despite the death of the ideology as a popularly-held faith. It is probably the recognition of what went on beneath semiofficial Russian ethnocentrism that forced the party to attack the ethnocentrists in the early 1970s, beginning with a purge of Molodaia gvardiia and ending with the heinous prison term of eight years for Vladimir Osipov.(19)

The considerable religious revival and large-scale conversions of young intellectuals to the Orthodox faith during the last decade and a half, especially among the patriotically and ethnocentrically oriented factions, further demonstrated to the Soviet authorities as well as to foreigners the intricate connection between ethnic orientation and the Church of Russia. This was probably another decisive factor in the regime's refusal to build on Russian ethnocentrism, or any other for that matter, although it has not heart to replace it again with a full return to the communist ideological orthodoxy. The dualism remains. But the toughening of antireligious policies since 1971 gives further indication of the rise of religion in society and, indirectly, of its organic ties with patriotic and ethnic orientations.

In the early stages of the existence of Veche, the most significant neo-Slavophile samizdat journal in the USSR, its editor Osipov wrote: "I am a religious believer....I prefer Christ and His teaching to nationalism [ethnocentrism]. But I know the soul of the contemporary Russian; his ethnic feeling is more dynamic and clearer at the present time than the religious principle. Therefore, patriotism, ethnic consciousness, self-respect are at the moment the only reliable bridge to a moral, cultural, and biological salvation."(20)

Another author in the same journal contradicted Osipov somewhat:

> Ethnic feelings of the Russians...have been more undermined than those of the other groups; therefore, it is hardly possible to unite Russians under the colors of patriotism. But, because there is simply no other way out, we must continue to appeal to this and act as energetically in this direction as possible, appealing to God for help. If the Russian people want to regenerate as a great ethnic group once again, they must...purge themselves of their ignorance of ethnocentrism, [and] return...to the Orthodox Church and its ethnic culture....(21)

Identity of Russians as ethnic Russians and as Christian Orthodox is here practically merged.

And when Veche died under the dual attack of the Committee for State Security (KGB) and the racist, secular chauvinists of the ethnocentric Bolshevik and neo-Nazi brands, in its place Osipov began the publication of a much more moderate and Christian-nativist oriented journal, Zemlia. Its first programmatic editorial stated that in isolation from Christianity, ethnocentrism is satanic and will throw the group once again into an abyss; Zemlia's main aim is the regeneration of ethics, morality, and the ethnic culture; and these ethnic aims cannot be achieved without constitutional guarantees of human rights and without freedom of expression.(22)

All the evidence discussed, as well as complaints by Soviet military leaders about a lack of patriotism among the general public, throws doubt on the existence of a widespread ethnocentric or patriotic base among the Russians. The same appears to be true in the Ukraine, and to an even greater extent in Belorussia. However, the reality is that there are at least 30 million practicing Orthodox Christians in the USSR, in addition to all the other religions and the rapidly rising Christian sects (such as Baptists, Pentecostal, or Jehovah's Witnesses), and the numbers are rising. If this figure were to be translated into political terms, one could probably call Soviet Orthodox Christians the biggest "party" of the Soviet Union. It looms much larger than the formal relationship would indicate between 14 million members of the communist party and 30 to 50 million members of the Orthodox Church. Most people join the communist party for career considerations and under pressure, whereas Christians are in the churches against career considerations and despite the pressure against joining them. In comparison with these very real figures, the potential size of a Russian ethnic "party" is still problematic.

During World War II, "at a time of great peril," Stalin found it necessary to give in to both sentiments, the Church and ethnocentric patriotism, simultaneously in order to raise morale. He saw the two forces as interconnected. Several contemporary Russian Orthodox Christian neophytes have stated that through the Orthodox Church one embraces the depths of Russian culture, organically begins to appreciate its Christian character, and begins to feel oneself a part of it. Often the process is reversed. Those turning to Russian history and culture in search of identity discover the Church. Whatever comes first, it cannot be denied that the soil-bound or nativist-oriented intelligentsia is more likely to establish contact with the general public via the Church than by a direct appeal to ethnocentrism and patriotism via small-circulation samizdat publications.(23) The Moscow priest Fr. Dimitriy Dudko baptizes several hundred adults, mostly young intellectuals, per year. According to Andrey Grigorenko, a son of Petr Grigorenko and an adult convert to Christianity, Fr. Dudko's figures are not exceptional (cited at a Russian Student Christian Movement meeting at Our Lady of Kazan' Church, Sea Cliff, N.Y., April 1977).

To conclude, one analyst sees only a negative progression of Russian ethnocentrist and patriotic trends ranging from the liberal version of Osipov and Solzhenitsyn to the ethnocentric Bolshevism of Gennadiy Shimanov, and neo-racism. The analyst bases his argument on the historical parallel of devolution of the original liberal Slavophile opposition into the reactionary ethnocentrist alliance with the state.(24) But the parallel is hardly historically valid. The early Slavophiles ideologically opposed not the principles on which the Russian nineteenth century state was based, but its "betrayal" of their idealized version of Orthodox monarchy. The contemporary soil-bound and neo-Slavophile orientations oppose the very ideological foundations of the Soviet state. They have attacked the ethnocentric Bolsheviks for their deification of Russian history generally and of the Soviet state particularly.(25)

If anything, the trend appears to be moving not from liberal ethnocentrists to ethnocentric Bolsheviks, as the same analyst claims, but just the other way. Soviet persecutions of the ethnocentrists and patriots only help this process, which is not at all unlike the progressive alienation of the Democratic Movement from Marxism in the late 1960s. The analysis emphasizes every case of contact, kinship, or coincidence between the establishment and the dissident ethnocentrists. But it completely overlooks much more intimate ideological contacts and kinship between the Democratic Movement and the establishment in the 1960s, especially the Marxist wing of the former. Solzhenitsyn critically defined ethnocentric Bolsheviks as those who "try to save dying communism by fusing it with Russian ethnocentrism....This movement recognizes neither communist nor ethnic blemishes. And bad things for which our country is responsible are characterized as good. . . ."(26) The movement among Russian ethnocentrists heads away from a purely secularist ethnocentrism to a soil-bound, Christian orientation, away from the establishment, at least from any of its forms in the last 60 years. This is a trend which one specialist observes with hope, another with fear. Yet both agree that "'young Russia'...disposed toward nationalism [ethnocentrism]...may one day find itself at the head of the masses."(27) In contrast to the analyst's apprehensive remarks about the Christian orientation of Russian ethnocentrist and patriotic thought, a specialist writes: "Christianity in the Russian national [ethnic] movement has already turned out to be a powerful obstacle for Neo-Nazism." It is worth looking quickly at replacements for the Russian leadership.

If the changeover takes place in the early 1980s, the leadership will come from the age group recruited into the party during World War II, when all usual formalities and ideological preparation requirements were waived.(28) By the end of the war, almost 60 percent of all party members were members of the Soviet armed forces. Their main criteria for joining the party at the battle front was ethnopatriotic, not Marxist-ideological. It was also the period of religious revival, when many soldiers facing death turned to God while fighting under the re-created images of Russia's past, her saints and heroes. Those of the generation who managed to evade the battlefield and join the party in the rear did so purely out of career considerations. [That makes it the least ideological party membership group of the whole Soviet period. Numerically, it is also the smallest such generation, having lost most of its male population as war casualties. In respect to age, the party leadership will have to depend to a greater extent than any of its predecessors on the generation who were of student age at the time of Stalin's death and began their careers at the height of de-Stalinization. That is a generation which evolved from Stalinism-Marxism-Leninism to any of the brands of Russian ethnocentric orientation discussed already, or to cosmopolitan liberalism in a minority of cases. Again, search for a wider popular base of support would probably involve additional combinations of appeals to ethnocentrism and/or religion in one form or another.

The alternatives for the future appear to revolve around what kind of ethnocentrism, not ethnocentrism vs. antiethnocentrism. In this situation, supporters should opt for the soil-bound or neo-Slavophile Christians and show sympathy and understanding toward them and their search. Otherwise, antagonism toward all aspects of Russian ethnocentric orientation will only push the most enlightened and liberal of them into xenophobic isolationism and effect their merger with the ethnocentrist extremists.

NOTES

(1) Peter Christoff, The Third Heart (The Hague: Mouton, 1970), p. 23.
(2) For the ideas of Tikhomirov and Zubatov see Dimitry V. Pospielovsky, Russian Police Trade Unionism (London: Weidenfeld and Nicolson, 1971), pp. 35-46, 81-83, 91-92.
(3) P. Derzhavin (Evgeniy Barabanov), "Zametki o natsional'nom vozrozhdenii," Vestnik russkogo studentcheskogo khristianskogo dvizheniia (henceforth: Vestnik RKhD), No. 106 (Paris 1972), pp. 259-74.
(4) Ibid., pp. 271-73.
(5) "Natsional'nyi vopros i sotsial-demokratiia," Prosveshchenie, No. 3 (1913), p. 54.
(6) Derzhavin, p. 267; Mikhail Agursky, "The Russian Nationalism - Dissent or Legitimacy?" paper delivered at

the 9th Annual Convention, American Association for the Advancement of Slavic Studies, Washington, D.C., Oct. 12, 1977; "Ia--natsionalist!," Kontinent No. 13 (Paris 1977), pp. 235-52; additional information supplied by recent Soviet emigrants, including Mikhail Popov, an architect from Alma Ata.

(7)   Martin Shaw and Henry Coleman, eds., National Anthems of the World (London: Blanford Press, 1963, 2d rev. ed.), pp. 362-63.

(8)   D. A. Chugaev, ed., Istoriia natsional'no-gosudarstven-nogo stroitel'stva v SSSR, Vol. 2 (Moscow: Akademiia Nauk SSSR, 1972), pp. 81-101.

(9)   Alexei Stepanovich Khomiakov (Moscow: "Put'," 1912), p. 4.

(10) Derzhavin, p. 271.

(11) Petr Struve, De Profundis (Moscow, 1918-21), pp. 302-03; Derzhavin, p. 265.

(12) Vladimir Osipov, "Piat' vozrazhenii Sakharovu" (samizdat, April 1974), AS 1696; N. V., "Otryvki iz dnevnika," Veche, No. 4 (samizdat, Jan. 31, 1972), AS 1140, pp. 40-43; "Russkoe reshenie natsional'nogo voprosa," Veche, No. 6 (Oct. 19, 1972), AS 1599, pp. 7-10.

(13) Mikhail Agursky, "Otvet zhurnalu Veche," Vol'noe slovo (Samizdat selections series) (Frankfurt/M.: Possev, 1975), No. 17-18, pp. 151-52; and his "Mezhdunarodnoe znachenie 'Pis'ma k vozhdiam'," Vestnik RKhD, No. 112-113 (1974), pp. 218-21; also Osipov, "Pis'mo v redaktsiiu zhurnala" and his "Beseda...s korrespondentom Associated Press...," both in Vestnik RKhD, No. 106, pp. 294-303.

(14) Aleksandr I. Solzhenitsyn, Pis'mo vozhdiam sovetskogo soiuza (Paris: YMCA Press, 1974), pp. 23-35f.

(15) Slovo natsii (samizdat, 1970), AS 590, pp. 14-15.

(16) Naum Korzhavin, a recent emigrant from the USSR, an outstanding contemporary Russian Jewish poet and cultural philosopher. (A conversation with this author, March 1978).

(17) Dimitry V. Pospielovsky, Uncensored Thought of the Soviet Union (Belmont, Mass.: Nordland, forthcoming), chapter 10. Also, Dimitry V. Pospielovsky, "Zwanzig Jahre Dissens in der UdSSR," Osteuropa, No. 6 (June 1975), pp. 407-19.

(18) "Na seminare literaturnykh kritikov" (held in Central House of Writers, Moscow, April 25, 1969), Politicheskii dnevnik, No. 1 (Amsterdam, 1972), pp. 502-08. The only exceptions in samizdat known to this author are two violently anti-Christian, racist neo-Nazi documents reproduced by Mikhail Agursky in The Political, Social and Religious Thought of Russian "Samizdat" - an

Anthology, edited by Michael Aksenov Meerson and Boris Shragin, (Belmont, Mass.: Nordland, 1977), pp. 420-50.

(19) In an editorial article by B. Solov'ev, "Nashe kul'turnoe nasledie: velikii narodnyi poet," Kommunist, No. 17 (1970), pp. 97-99, Kommunist attacks Russian ethnocentrism in an editorial. See also: Alexander Yanov, The Russian New Right (Berkeley: Institute of International Studies, 1978), pp. 57-60.

(20) Osipov, "Pis'mo...," p. 295.

(21) N. V., "Otryvki iz dnevnika," Veche No. 4 (samizdat January 31, 1972; Arkhiv Samizdata 1140), p. 43.

(22) Zemlia, No. 1 (Aug. 1, 1974), Vol'noe slovo, no. 20 (1975), pp. 5-6.

(23) I. Denisov, "Slovo otstupnikov," Vestnik RKhD, no. 99 (1971) pp. 112-13; K. Vol'nyi, Intelligentsiia i demokraticheskoe dvizhenie (samizdat), AS 607; E. Vagin (formerly one of the leading members of the Leningrad-based Russian-wide Social-Christian Union for the Liberation of Peoples) in: "Seminar 'Budushchaia Rossiia'" (Rome Nov. 15, 1976), Nasha strana (Buenos Aires), no. 1410-1412, p. 3; Dimitriy Dudko, "Kreshchenie na Rusi," Vestnik RKhD, no. 117 (1976), pp. 188-208.

(24) Yanov, pp. 1-20.

(25) Osipov, "Otkrytoe pis'mo Gennadiiu Shimanovu," Vol'noe slovo, no. 17-18 (selections from Veche), pp. 13-19; Dve presskonferentsii (Paris: YMCA Press, 1975), p. 49.

(26) Meerson and Shragin, p. 418.

(27) Yanov, pp. 17, 21-38, 44-47; Meerson and Shragin, p. 418.

(28) "Postanovlenie TsKVKP (b). 19 avgusta 1941 g.," Kommunisticheskaia partiia v velikoi otechestvennoi voine. Dokumenty i materialy (Moscow: Politicheskoe Izdatel'stvo, 1970), p. 55; Chugaev, p. 88.

14 Comment — Ethnicity, Orthodoxy, and the Return to the Russian Past
George L. Kline

The substance of the proposition that Russian Orthodoxy can no longer strongly or widely influence ethnic group identity in RSFSR rings true, provided that the adverbs "strongly" and "widely" are given their full force. And this despite the fact - recognized and welcomed by some - that several tens of millions of Soviet citizens, most but not all of whom are ethnic Russians, remain Russian Orthodox believers, and with an awareness that in recent years there has, indeed, been a modest revival of Orthodox religiousness and a concomitant revival of interest in Russian religious thought in the Soviet Union. The turn to the Russian past is a second clear development of the last 12 or 15 years. However, contrary to what most of the authors who have addressed this proposition seem to have assumed, the primary motivation for this turn seems not religious but secular. It is analyzable into at least five motives: aesthetic-cultural and antiquarian; military-ideological and ethnocentric; demographic-statistical; philosophical-methodological; and anti-Promethean and anti-future-oriented.

Joseph Brodsky has testified that in prison existence an acute shortage of space is compensated for by an overabundance of time.(1) Something like this might be said about the cultural and aesthetic imprisonment of cultivated Soviet citizens in general, and of ethnic Russians in particular. The vast majority of them have been poignantly aware for some decades now that the great works of the plastic arts in the world outside Soviet geographical space are permanently cut off from them. Thus, to compensate for a culturally intolerable constriction of their aesthetic space they attempt to stretch their aesthetic and cultural time in the only available direction - into the historical past, as a realm of achieved cultural and aesthetic values. This primarily aesthetic quest takes on a secondary religious coloring as a result of the fact that in Russia, as in Western Europe, until quite recently the products of high culture were all religiously inspired - integrally involved with Christian (and in Russia with Orthodox) symbolism and doctrine. But the searching out and celebrating of wooden churches, onion-dome cathedrals, and Andrey Rublev's incandescent icons is a result of aesthetic, and to some extent antiquarian, considerations, rather than strictly religious ones. For the Soviet authorities the motives for parallel activities may be even more remote from religion. For example, the regilding and remounting of crosses on Orthodox churches is partly to impress tourists and thus to increase earnings of foreign currency as well as to gain international goodwill.

That the turn to the Russian past and commitment to Russian Orthodoxy are, to a significant extent, independent variables is evidenced by the fact that Vladimir Soloukhin remains Orthodox despite the fact that over the past six years his writings have managed to avoid the topic of his earlier, apparently deep and permanent, literary passion: the saving of ancient Russian churches and the collecting, restoring, and admiring of ancient Russian icons.

Professor Ledkovsky sees the growth of the All Russia Society for the Preservation of Historical and Cultural Monuments (Vserossiiskoe obshchestvo okhrany pamiatnikov istorii i kul'tury, VOOPIK) to 12.5 million members in its first 12 years (1966-1977) as evidence of growing Russian Orthodox commitment. But if this were the case, the growth of the latter, over the same period, should have been comparably rapid. In fact, it was much more modest. The dramatic increase in religious commitment - Professor Pospielovsky noted this (chap. 13) - has been limited to Protestant and Fundamentalist denominations - Evangelical Baptists, Pentecostals, Jehovah's Witnesses, and others - few if any of which have any special interest in Russian ethnicity or the recovery of the Russian past.

Why was VOOPIK founded in the mid-1960s rather than, say, the mid-1950s or the mid-1970s? As Professor Barghoorn observed (chap. 4) with respect to a parallel phenomenon (the spate of ethnocentrist-chauvinist and anti-Western articles by Viktor Chalmaev, Soloukhin, and others, in Molodaia gvardiia (1968-69) the towering new factor was the Chinese military-ideological threat, which had been growing since 1960 and had "peaked" by 1966. The official encouragement of VOOPIK by the Soviet authorities, and its military-ideological motivation, has been clear from the beginning. It was simply given its final public stamp in 1976 with the inclusion of VOOPIK, pre-viously a voluntary "public" organization, under the Ministry of Culture. From the start, VOOPIK's honorary chair-man, was, and evidently still is, Marshal Vasiliy I. Chuikov, hero of Stalingrad. Molodaia gvardiia, over the past decade and a half, has featured a series of memoirs of Soviet generals, including those of Chuikov himself. And Chalmaev is the author of several popular panegyrics to the exploits of Soviet arms.

The motives of individual Soviet citizens, most of them ethnic Russians, for collaborating with VOOPIK were and are cultural, aesthetic, antiquarian, ecological, and, in only a few cases, genuinely religious. The motives of the authorities for permitting and supporting VOOPIK's work are primarily military and ideological. They are a response to the Chinese threat of the 1960s(2) which, of course, continues and, in some respects, increases in the 1970s. It is VOOPIK's mission, according to the highest authority, "to collaborate with the state agencies in the preservation of monuments [of history and culture] and the utilization of [such] monuments in the task of the communist upbringing of the people." The danger that the Russian ethnocentrism sponsored by the "Establishment Right" as a replacement for discredited Marxism-Leninism will merge into chauvinistic xenophobia and anti-Semitism was eloquently described by Grigoriy Pomerants in the mid-1960s and is chillingly documented in a new study.(3)

A technical account of the recent past and projected future shrinkage of the ethnic-Russian slice of the Soviet demographic pie has been ably provided by the specialists in this volume (see also Appendix A). In nontechnical terms, it seems clear that the prospect of a further decline, not only of their numbers but, ultimately, of their prestige and power, has been one of the motives for the recent withdrawal of ethnic Russians into a historical past in which they enjoyed an overwhelming pride of numbers as well as of prestige and power.

Professor Maguire has mentioned (chap. 7) something that is often forgotten, especially by such non-Marxists as most of the contributors to this volume. Marxist theory is itself historically oriented and thus predisposes Soviet citizens who have been brought up on it - university graduates, in particular - to focus upon the historical past in order to understand the present. Only one qualification: this applies to the Hegelian strand in Marxism which, indeed, stresses the importance, for the understanding of any economic, social, political, or cultural phenomenon, of studying its origin and growth. But there is another central strand in Marxism - the strong orientation toward the "world-historical" future, asserted by Karl Marx himself, and reinforced by G. V. Plekhanov, Vladimir Ilyich Lenin, and Joseph V. Stalin, which contrasts sharply with Georg W. F. Hegel's insistence that the philosopher can exhibit the rational pattern of development of a cultural phenomenon or historical epoch only after it has reached its culmination, and that it is not a philosopher's business to predict, to advocate, or to struggle for, what the future shall become.

The turn to the past is, in part, a reaction to the pervasive future-orientedness - scientific, technological, political, and ideological - of the Soviet system and ideology. Professor Ledkovsky mentions (chap. 12) the widespread interest, in the Soviet Union, in the thought of N. F. Fedorov (1828-1903). But Fedorov is sometimes seen as a precursor of future-oriented totalitarianism - for example by Boris Paramonov, a recent emigrant from Leningrad, in an unpublished paper presented before the 1978 Conference of the American Association for the Advancement of Slavic Studies. It is, therefore, essential to distinguish between what might be called the "theurgically Promethean" future-oriented, scientific-technological means which Fedorov proposes - ranging from climate control to the physical reconstitution and raising of the dead - and the moral-religious end or value which these means are intended to serve. It is the preserving of the achieved values of the present and the past, including the protecting of the lives of the living and the restoring of the lives of the dead. The end served by Fedorov's "common task" arguably involves a repudiation of Soviet-style historical future-orientedness and a return to the past, to roots, to the soil. Compare Fedorov's praise of agriculture and his characterization of museums and libraries as "holy places" which preserve the achieved cultural values of the historical past. Soviet ideology today is no less Promethean than the Russian Marxism of the 1890s, which Plekhanov praised for setting itself "just such a task as the Greeks ascribed to Prometheus," that is to say, the subjugation of the natural and social worlds through a future-oriented science and technology. Rev. Michael A. Meerson has, in another place, put the point lucidly:

> The Soviet people is uprooted from the soil to the greatest possible degree (maksimal'no bespochven), . . .It has been torn by the Revolution out of its customary culture-historical soil - Orthodoxy and the cultivation of the land - and launched into eschatological orbit through the communist utopia toward a material-technological civilization. [Soviet] society is future-oriented (futuristichno). . . . Nobody knows what happened yesterday, but everybody knows that tomorrow men will fly to the moon.(4)

It was Plekhanov, again, who defined the Marxist ideal as "the reality [or 'actuality'= deistvitel'nost'] of the future."(5) Thus, he concisely expressed the assumption, which Marxist-Leninists hold in common with other utopian theorists, that their projected historical future is in some queer sense "already there" - that future entities, including living human individuals, are just as actual, determinate, and valuable as past or present entities. This assumption has two related components, elsewhere labeled "the fallacy of the 'actual future',"(6) which infect the Marxist theory of being and the "fallacy of deferred, or historically displaced, value," and, in turn, infect the Marxist value-theory.

The turn to the Russian past by ethnic Russians as well as a return to their own heritage by other Soviet citizens is in part a protest, both natural and commendable, against the Soviet tendency to sacrifice particular achieved values, and particular values in the process of being achieved, to the generalized value-ideals of a remote world-historical future.

NOTES

(1) Joseph Brodsky, "Resisting the Machine," New Leader, no. 11 (May 26, 1979), p. 17, reviewing Alexander Dolgun with Patrick Watson, An American in the Gulag (New York: Knopf, 1975).

(2) Alexander Yanov, The Russian New Right: Right-Wing Ideologies in the Contemporary USSR (Berkeley, Calif.: Institute of International Studies, 1978), esp. pp. 1-3; Bol'shaia sovetskaia entsiklopediia, (Moscow: "Sovetskaia Entsiklopediia," 1971, 3rd ed.) V, p. 458.

(3) Yanov, esp. pp. 13-20, 39-61, and Appendixes 3-7 (pp. 173-85).

(4) M. Aksenov Meerson, "Rozhdenie novoi intelligentsii," in Samosoznanie: Sbornik statei edited by Pavel Litvinov, Mikhail Aksenov, and Boris Shragin, (New York: "Khronika," 1976), p. 111; italics added.

(5) G. V. Plekhanov, Izbrannye filosofskie sochineniia (Moscow: Izdatel'stvo Sotsial'no-Economicheskoi Literatury, 1956), II, p. 621.

(6) George L. Kline, "Was Marx an Ethical Humanist?" Studies in Soviet Thought, 9 (1969), especially p. 101.

15 Comment — The Dynamics of Orthodoxy in Russian Identity
Paul R. Valliere

The three articles addressing the proposition that Russian Orthodoxy can no longer influence Russian ethnic group identity strongly or widely supply evidence that would seem to document a connection between Russian ethnic identity and identification with Russian Orthodoxy in the Soviet Union today. How deep or extensive this connection is, of course, is debatable. But given the frequency with which it is encountered in samizdat and other sources, the burden of proof lies on those who would deny that such a connection exists to any appreciable degree. Nevertheless, the evidence supplied by our authors must be qualified in two ways. It must be qualified by an honest admission of how much is not known about either the Russian ethnic revival or the religious revival in the Soviet Union today, particularly outside of the urban intelligentsia. Second, the meaning of the evidence as a source of generalizations depends on how it is interpreted.

The distinction that gives shape to Professor Pospielovsky's discussion (chap. 13) seems acceptable. It is a distinction between a Russian ethnic consciousness based upon the spiritual concept of the unity of Orthodox Christian eastern Slavs and a Russian ethnocentrism based upon modern concepts of language and race. A distinction of this sort is indispensable in the history of religions as applied to historic collectivities. Without it an observer is almost sure to read into the history of traditions dynamics of ethnic group and race that are quite out of place there. Also, Professor Pospielovsky is right that the modern ethnocentrist concept of identity developed relatively late among the ethnic Russians, who in this respect resemble the Turks and the Chinese. They are the ones who each developed a strong sense of identity as the leading group within an imperial structure for which the reason for existence was provided by a classical

religious tradition. Finally, it is true that the spiritual
concept of Russian identity has content mainly to the extent
that this is provided by Orthodox Christianity.

Is Professor Pospielovsky's basic distinction relevant to
the Russian ethnic group in the Soviet Union today? The
sources quoted suggest that the relationship between the two
concepts of identity is by no means clear to the Russians
themselves. Moreover, assertions of "the Orthodox connection"
in contemporary Russian sources, while often passionate, are
generally vague with respect to details, particularly
institutional details. This creates a problem, for a church,
after all, is more than "the masses of believers" to whom an
ideological party might choose to issue an appeal or propose a
compact. The only conceivable vehicles of the spiritual
concept of ethnic unity and vocation are historic institutions
of religious practice that have legitimacy, autonomy, and
continuity at the grassroots level and so evoke loyalty, as it
were, effortlessly. Or, to say this in theological language, a
church is an institution that has charisma and canonicity. The
question is whether such historic structures exist or are
recoverable on a large scale in the Soviet Union today, or
whether the radical discontinuity with the Russian past
imposed by the Marxist regime has destroyed them or ruined
their coherence. What can be said about the canonicity of
church institutions in Russia today? How legitimate are the
parish and eparchial structures considered to be? How
charismatic is the clergy? How sacrosanct is the Patriarchal
institution? How much knowledge is there in Russia of the
Orthodox tradition itself? There is not enough discussion of
questions of this sort in the articles at hand or among
observers of the Russian spiritual scene generally.

A better grasp of the details and grassroots mystique of
Orthodox institutions is important to any projections that we
might be tempted to make about the role of the church in the
ethnic Russian future. It is an open question whether
Orthodox institutions can bear the weight of social action and
responsibility imposed by the sentiments of the proponents of
"the Orthodox connection." Would these structures themselves
not be profoundly reworked - or new ones created or old ones
revived - in any period of genuine institutional fluidity in the
Soviet Union? The latter possibility implies limits on the
church's potential as an independent framework of action. It
presents the church as only one element in a larger
framework, but what framework?

In this regard, consider the fundamental tension that
runs through Professor Ledkovsky's discussion (chap. 12)
between particularistic and universalistic approaches to
Orthodoxy. The Christian Committee for the Defense of
Believers' Rights in the USSR about which she reports is a
good example of the tension. This group consists, in part, of

Orthodox activists who a few years ago took a very ethnocentrist and populist approach to Orthodoxy as the religion of the "Russian Christ." But they now self-consciously are adopting the organizing style and some of the values of the international human rights movement. One way to understand this development is to see it as evidence of the limits of Orthodoxy as an independent framework for action in contemporary Russia. This, of course, is not necessarily bad for Orthodoxy in its own right. It may be very good, as Professor Ledkovsky seems to think. Beyond being the repository of the "Russian Christ," Orthodox Christianity is also a tradition that seeks, and at its best has approached, universality. In modern times, the universality of Orthodoxy may be a theme that cannot be expressed except as it is reconceived through a creative interrelationship with the modern universalism of human rights and human dignity. Evgeniy Barabanov has been making this point with much depth and clarity for a number of years, as have a few other contemporary Russian Orthodox thinkers including Rev. Michael A. Meerson.(1) But the work of reconception still has a long way to go in the Russian Orthodox tradition at large.

To conclude, in calling for a closer look at the structures and sentiments of Russian Orthodoxy at the grassroots it is not implied that what will be learned thereby will discourage scholars about the potentiality, or even actuality, of social creativity on the part of Orthodoxy in contemporary Russia. Such an investigation would, in addition to bringing a sense of realism to the subject, have to be careful not to be deceived by appearances and would be sensitive to the phenomenon with which it is dealing. Inquirers should not set out to find in Russian Orthodoxy something analogous to, say, Polish Catholicism, and then judge it negatively when they do not find it. This procedure ignores the unique modes of charisma and canonicity proper to Orthodoxy as such. It can hardly be doubted that the Church of Poland is more powerful in its social and ethnic context today than the Russian Church in Russia, but the significance of this observation should not be exaggerated. The Orthodox tradition always has aimed at a decentralized rather than centralized episcopate, resisted the development of a monarchical and bureaucratic patriarchate, and always has placed more trust in an invisible and weakly institutionalized "Orthodox consensus" than in positive, legal structures of authority. Even if the Russian Church should be as strong in Russia some day as the Polish Church is in Poland, it would be strong in a very different way – and that would be part of its strength. A closer look at Orthodox structures in Russia today hopefully will encourage observers to develop a keener appreciation of the dynamics of Orthodoxy itself.

NOTES

(1) See Evgeniy Barabanov, "Raskol Tserkvi i mira," Iz-pod
     glyb: Sbornik statei (Paris: YMCA Press, 1974), pp.
     177-97. English tran.: "The Schism Between the Church
     and the World," From Under the Rubble, edited by
     Aleksandr Solzhenitsyn et al. trans. under the direction
     of Michael Scammell (Boston and Toronto: Little, Brown
     1975), pp. 172-93.   See also Barabanov, "Sud'ba
     khristianskoi   kul'tury,"   Kontinent: Literaturnyi,
     obshchestvenno-politicheskii i religioznyi zhurnal, No. 6
     (1976), pp. 293-328; and "Pravda gumanizma," Samosoz-
     nanie: Sbornik statei, edited by P. Litvinov, M. Aksenov
     Meerson and B.   Shragin (New York: Izdatel'stvo
     "Khronika," 1976), pp. 11-26.

IV

The "Integration" of the Soviet People

Proposition 4: The renewed ideological emphasis placed by Soviet authorities upon the supposed unity of the "Soviet People (narod)" as a whole tends to dampen Russian self-awareness and obscure external identity politically.

16 The Role of Russians Among the New, Unified "Soviet People"*

Oleh S. Fedyshyn

Oh, how fine that Iu. Gagar (in),
Is neither Tungus nor Tatar;
Not from Khokhol land or Uzbekistan,
But our truly Soviet man!(1)

It may be risky to ascribe too much importance now to the simple Soviet ditty quoted above, especially because it was composed some twenty years ago. But it comes closer than any official statement from Moscow to expressing a view rather widely held among Russians in the USSR that the difference between the terms Soviet and Russian is not so very extensive. The central thesis of this essay is, in fact, that Russians, numerically the largest and politically the dominant group of the USSR, are quite comfortable with the official promotion of the concept of a unified Soviet People.* Such a promotion evidently does little "to dampen Russian self-awareness and obscure external identity politically," as the proposition goes. The author of this essay, therefore, does not accept the assertion that the continued ideological emphasis placed by Soviet authorities upon the supposed unity of "The Soviet People (narod)" as a whole tends to dampen Russian self-awareness and obscure the group's external political identity.

why not liudi (люди)

---

*Background material for this study was collected by the author during his association in 1975 with the Research Institute on International Change, the Russian Institute, and the Program on Soviet Nationality Problems, all of Columbia University. Their assistance is herewith gratefully acknowledged.

149

Putting the subject in its historical perspective, there are certain basic similarities between the old imperial term "Russian-state-wide" (rossiiskii) and its contemporary counterpart, the designation "Soviet" (sovetskii). In pre-1917 Russia, the idea of a rossiiskii, as opposed to ethnic Russian (russkii) outlook, practice, attitude, and so on, was never promoted officially with any degree of consistency or determination. And, in many instances, this tendency to develop a Russian-state-wide view, movement, or organization did not inhibit the development of specific regional, ethnic, or cultural traditions and activities. Also, often there was little governmental interference with such local particularization, especially if it did not assume a radical political color and had no direct tie with or support from a foreign power.

Still, Russia's stateness (rossiiskost') gained quite a few non-Russian adherents and supporters, and there is no doubt that it tended to weaken various non-Russian ethnic groups and to hamper their political development. The White Russian armies of the civil war period were full of these groups, and this has lingered on at home and abroad until the present day. A look through the obituaries printed in the Russian newspaper (Novoe russkoe slovo) of New York will reveal an amazing number of Ukrainian, Belorussian, Georgian, and other non-Russian names.

The promotion of this nonethnic rossiiskost' under the czars, as has been the case with the Soviet Union stateness (sovetskost') of recent years, in no way weakened the Russian ethnic group. On the contrary, it strengthened its culture, literature, science, and many other areas by giving the Russian ethnic group its Nikolay Gogols, Ilia E. Repins, Vladimir G. Korolenkos, Anna Akhmatovas, Petr Kapitsas, and many, many others.

Following the November 1917 revolution, a person of the Russian-wide state (rossiiskii chelovek) was replaced by a person of the entire Soviet state (sovetskii chelovek), but the two were not viewed as being very different, especially by the Russians. And somehow, even in Vladimir Ilyich Lenin's days, that sovetskii chelovek was regarded as a better individual if he spoke Russian and, in general, resembled the northern brand of this new Soviet breed. The popular Soviet song of the 1930s entitled "Simple Soviet person" ("Sovetskii prostoi chelovek"), an official glorification of all sorts of great accomplishments of individual Soviet citizens of that period, was composed in Russian, and the song made quite clear who this "Simple Soviet Person" really was.

In the 1920s, the term peoples of the Soviet Union (narody Sovetskogo Soiuza) was employed rather consistently. Then, in the next decade, the Soviet people (sovetskii narod) came more and more into use, but it was not yet presented as a new and distinct entity. In either case, however, one had to single out the great Russian people (velikii russkii narod) "who gave us Lenin," for special praise. And this was especially obligatory for non-Russian speakers and writers. This was matched by the clearly privileged position that Russians enjoyed in virtually all fields, not only politics, throughout the USSR.

Following Stalin's death in March 1953, there was a gradual abandonment of this practice, and the term "Soviet people" made its slow but unmistakable return to respectability. Then, toward the end of Khrushchev's rule, sovetskii narod came to mean united (and in many ways new and superior) Soviet people, with some of the characteristics of a "nation," and was viewed as a new development. And this trend in Soviet ethnic relations was given further impetus in the Communist Party Program of 1961 and the subsequent promotion of the fusion of ethnic groups plan.(2)

Not until the early 1970s was the program of systematic and vigorous promotion of the "The Soviet People - New Historic Community of Persons" (sovetskii narod--novaia istoricheskaia obshchnost' liudei) launched in highly publicized, well-orchestrated campaigns led by Leonid I. Brezhnev, the General Secretary of the CPSU. This was a new, distinct phase in Soviet ethnic policy, an integral part of the larger program of communist construction, as well as an important element in Soviet views about proletarian internationalism. It had farreaching implications for the Kremlin's position in the communist international movement as a whole.(3)

In a most condensed form, the idea of The Soviet People, presented in authoritative Soviet statements and writings, is the result of many years of successful programs and policies in Soviet ethnic relations. This united, multiethnic Soviet people (edinyi mnogonatsional'nyi sovetskii narod) is called the first interethnic, that is multiethnic, socialist community of persons in mankind's history. Consequently, The Soviet People (sovetskii narod) is presented, on the one hand, as an already accomplished fact.

Admittedly, not yet a fully developed new political entity, The Soviet People is a union (ob"edinenie) of the ethnic groups of the USSR. It is said to possess certain well-defined characteristics, such as a common territory (the USSR); a common world view and ideology of Marxism-Leninism, which gave rise to Soviet patriotism and proletarian internationalism; a common socialist experience and a common goal of communist development. All these, in turn, according to official Soviet claims, produced a common, highly-developed economic system based on centralized planning, a common culture and educational system, and even common psychology and "national" character. Moreover, this entire Soviet People, or, more precisely, its non-Russian components (who constitute less than half of the USSR's population) according to these Soviet sources, rapidly adopts the "great Russian language" (velikii Russkii iazyk) as their new mother tongue or second native language. (This second term reminds one of the born-again religious concept of the West.) In Soviet writings, The Soviet People is yet neither a new "nation" nor a supraethnic (nadnatsional'nyi) political entity.(4)   On the other hand, this "Soviet People" is viewed as the ultimate aim of Soviet ethnic policy, a goal to be achieved through the fusion (sliianie) of all Soviet ethnic groups, and that will take place under communism.

Thus, this new Soviet People is to be viewed partly as an accomplished fact and partly as a transitional form of multiethnic organization.   Consequently, throughout the 1970s, Soviet authors spoke mostly of flowering (rastsvet) and being drawn closer together (sblizhenie) of Soviet ethnic groups - two simultaneous and dialectically compatible processes which produced unity (edinstvo), though oneness may perhaps be an even more accurate term here, of the multiethnic Soviet people.

The emphasis on unity of the Soviet people was accompanied with renewed stress on Soviet patriotism and a somewhat novel use of the term motherland (rodina).   The new, recommended usage was in reference to Russia or the USSR as a whole, but not to one of the non-Russian Soviet Union republics.(5)

Russian expectations of playing a decisive role in this process coincided by and large with the view of Soviet leaders, especially General Secretary Brezhnev, about the desirability of giving a decidedly Russian color and form to the basic elements of which the Soviet People was to be made up. At the same time this new Soviet People formula left little doubt that the non-Russian ethnic ingredients in it were not going to be very important.   Careful reading of authoritative Soviet writings about the subject makes clear that non-Russian ethnic values and traditions have no future.   They could actually be termed osbolete or even harmful, and would be tolerated only as a necessary and temporary evil.   As such, they are destined to be replaced by the more "progressive" outlook and institutions embodied in Soviet People.(6)

In spite of this uncertain future, the new Soviet People formula still leaves some room for non-Russian Soviet ethnic groups.   Non-Russian critics of The Soviet People program both at home and abroad like to remind all that these are merely ideas and "trial balloons" and that their implementation, in spite of some real gains, is yet to be achieved.(7) However, no one should underestimate the resources and capabilities of the Soviet state.   It has wealth and a vast bureaucracy, its socialist federalism, and the Soviet legal system as a whole, its economic and educational institutions, and finally the power of the multiethnic communist party with its special instruments of control and coercion (including army, secret police, Komsomol, trade unions, and many similar institutions) have all been mobilized for the task of completing communist "development," for which the making of a Soviet man and the development of a new Soviet People are the most fundamental prerequisites.(8)

Some specific integrative measures involved what might be called statistical tampering and demographic manipulation in the 1970 census. For example, 18 groups listed in the 1959 census were dropped in 1970,(9) and the Ukrainians of the Kuban region of the RSFSR, (once a majority in that area) were arbitrarily listed as Russians. (Based upon directives given to census takers, according to private informants who recently left the Soviet Union.) And this was not the only case of a sudden and complete disappearance of a substantial ethnic group on the basis of administrative order.

Next should be noted greatly intensified teaching of the Russian language; virtually everybody has to take it now, and simply cannot advance a career without it. This was accompanied with an equally intensive cultural indoctrination drive, and an attempt was made to produce a bandwagon effect among non-Russians by claiming a more impressive and widespread adoption of Russian as the second language, and reading more into it than the bare figures warrant.(10)

Finally, the Soviet authorities actively promoted the "mixing of ethnic groups," especially the encouragement and facilitation of a heavy influx of Russians into the non-Russian union republics and non-Russian territories of the RSFSR. This last device in the Soviet integration program may have been the key to its ultimate success. Western demographers tend to view the population changes in the USSR, especially the migratory processes, as having their basis primarily in economic factors. Ukrainians and other non-Russians abroad usually think otherwise. Ukrainian dissident writers, who expressed their views anonymously and published them clandestinely, strongly condemned this "Russian mixing of ethnic groups" as aiming at harming and weakening non-Russian ethnic groups.(11) Professor Roman Szporluk, who studied this problem closely, stressed the significance of "terror and deportations" in Soviet population policies.(12)

Now to turn to the central question - the role and place of the Russian ethnic group in the larger context of the Soviet People idea. A number of further specific questions may be raised. How do the Russians themselves feel about this program? How has it affected them? What influence did they exert in the past, and what has been their input more recently into the process of creating a new Soviet People?

In the official Soviet view of these important questions, first, and perhaps most important, Russians were to play the key role in this process. They were to provide the core around which the new Soviet People was to develop, and the Russian parts in the plan for the Soviet People were to become increasingly dominant. Ultimately, cultures, languages, and traditions of other groups were to yield to new forms which, in practice, were to be 95 percent Russian.(13) Official Soviet writings never spelled this out in so many words, but it has been clearly implied in them and well understood by those who read this literature. This was the feeling of most non-Russian dissidents as well as the non-Russian political emigrants living in the West. It was acknowledged by certain Russian dissident groups as well,(14) though most of them expressed little interest in this question one way or another.

It is not easy to evaluate popular Russian feeling about the Soviet People idea. Because Russians control the party and government in all its forms, not only at the center but in the peripheral regions as well, it would be impossible for the Soviet leadership to promote such a plan without considerable, widespread support from Russians themselves. By now, there is a rather impressive volume of Russian dissident writings of all sorts prepared and published independently of any governmental control and interference. They deal mostly with subjects which, in the writers' views, were important and had to be treated critically and freely. The questions of non-Russian ethnic groups and The Soviet People idea were not considered to be among these important subjects. Samizdat publications dealt with them only on rare occasions.

True, there were courageous individuals such as Andrey Amalrik and Vladimir Bukovsky who tried, often at great peril to themselves, to expose the hypocrisy and destructiveness of Soviet ethnic policy. Bukovsky, while still in the Soviet Union, went so far as to declare publicly:

> I am Russian, and I grieve for my country, in which public figures openly propagate chauvinism and where Russification is raised to the status of governmental policy....I grieve further over the fact that Russia is a prison of nationalities [ethnic groups] on a scale greater than sixty years ago.(15)

But these were, and still are, rather lonely voices in the large crowd of Russian writers. It is, perhaps, most revealing that, though scores of Russian dissident writers and activists have been permitted to settle in the West in recent years - where they have been free to say and publish whatever they like - they have devoted almost as little attention to the Soviet ethnic question as they used to in the past.

On the other hand, the Soviet Union had such superethnocentrist Russian groups as the publishers of Veche, an illegal samizdat journal, tolerated by the Soviet authorities over a surprisingly long period of time. This group of "Russia firsters" repeatedly expressed concern over the possible dilution of the Russian spirit among Russians. The following brief quotations from Veche not only reveal the nature of this publication but also explain the reluctance with which Soviet authorities moved against it. For example, a 1973 issue of Veche contains an article about "a voluntary joining of nationalities [ethnic groups] to Russia." Elsewhere, it points out that there never was any "interference in the ethnic community life of the groups inhabiting Russia," and in still another, that the genius of the Russian state always aimed at a "friendly, centralized union of peoples."(16) The same issue of Veche, however, carries a considerably more ominous denunciation of the "zoological nationalisms [ethnocentrisms] of the borderlands," said to be endangering the unity of the USSR.(17) To put such views in perspective, such ideas were as isolated as was Bukovsky's criticism of government-sponsored Russification policies.

There are many indications that in the party, the army, within governmental agencies, and in the professions, as well as among most workers and peasants, the overwhelming majority of Russians has been quite comfortable with The Soviet People idea. No doubt, for most of them, terminology does not really matter very much. They can easily equate the term "Soviet" with "Russian." Motherland (rodina) is used in reference to both Russia and the USSR, and not only careless Western scholars and journalists, but more and more frequently well-informed Russian writers and other professionals have used the two terms interchangeably. This writer has noticed this tendency on many occasions among recent Russian emigrants in the United States of America.

In 1978, a certain deemphasis of The Soviet People program seems to have taken place. Perhaps the most important sign of the slowing down, or at least more cautious promotion, of this program has been the new (1977) Soviet constitution. It contains virtually nothing new. In spite of earlier indications that it would offer a number of novel features, the new Soviet constitution turns out to be a rather tame animal, proclaiming, in fact, that no drastic changes or new approaches are to be expected in Soviet policies at least in the near future.

It may be too early to discern the real reasons behind the impasse or slowdown in this vital area, but it is certain that the cause has not been a widespread Russian unhappiness with the Kremlin's ethnic policy of the 1970s, including its Soviet People formula. It has not been suggested, so far, that a new, truly supraethnic Soviet language be developed to replace Russian rather than expecting the entire Soviet population to adopt Lenin's tongue, as at present. No one has encouraged

Russians to give up their Russian ethnicity and adopt a new designation - "Soviet Nationality" (sovetskaia natsional'nost') - the way some ethnically-mixed or neutral Yugoslavs prefer to be listed in the official census (see chapter 37 by Bogdan Denitch). No one has suggested the creation of new supra-ethnic Soviet cities or regions in order to replace the old ethnic eponymous territorial units, though not all of them remain as ethnodemographically stable as they used to be. And these would be the minimal initial steps toward implementation of the Soviet People program.

To equate the Soviet People formula with Russification of non-Russians is an obvious oversimplification, although Russification may be promoted by it. To hail it as a great, progressive, new historical achievement of Moscow is to echo a grossly exaggerated claim which the Soviet leaders themselves seem to be on the verge of abandoning.

NOTES

(1) The Russian original of the ditty about the Soviet cosmonaut:

> Kak khorosho chto Iu. Gagarin
> Ne Tungus i ne tatarin,
> On ne khokhol i ne usbek,
> A nash sovetskii chelovek.

One printed version of it appears in Nepodtsenzurnaia russkaia chastushka (New York: Russica, 1978) p. 129.

(2) The Third Party Program adopted at the XXII Party Congress in 1961 was published in Pravda and Izvestiia (Nov. 2, 1961), pp. 1-9; also, Charlotte Saikowski and Leo Gruliow, eds., Current Soviet Policies, IV. The Documentary Record of the 22nd Congress of the Communist Party of the Soviet Union (New York: Columbia University Press, 1962), pp. 1-32. For a concise analysis of Khrushchev's nationality policies of that period see Olen S. Fedyshyn, "Khrushchev's 'Leap Forward,'" The Southwestern Social Science Quarterly (June 1967), pp. 34-43.

(3) Examples of Brezhnev's most important statements about the subject include "Delo Lenina zhivet i pobezhdaet," Kommunist, no. 7 (May 1970), pp. 3-38; and his "Otchetnyi doklad tsentral'nogo komiteta KPSS XXIV s"ezdu kommunisticheskoi Partii sovetskogo soiuza: Doklad general'nogo seckretaria TsK tovarishcha L. I. Brezhneva, 30 Marta 1971" Kommunist, no. 5 (March 1971), pp. 3-83; as well as his "O piatidesiatiletii Soiuza Sovetskikh Sotsialisticheskikh Respublik," Kommunist, no. 18, (Dec. 1972), pp. 14-18; see also "K narodam mira,"

Kommunist, no. 18 (Dec. 1972), pp. 43-46. The most authoritative recent work about The Soviet People concept is Sovetskii narod--novaia istoricheskaia obshchnost' liudei edited by M. P. Kim et al. (Moscow: Izdatel'stvo "Nauka," 1975) which contains one of the most comprehensive bibliographies for the subject, pp. 483-517.

(4) Kim, passim. Among earlier works may be mentioned Leninizm i natsional'ny vopros v sovremennykh usloviakh, edited by P. N. Fedseev et al. (Moscow: Izdatel'stvo Politicheskoi Literatury, 1972); M.I. Kulichenko, Natsional'nye otnosheniia v SSSR (Moscow: Izdetal'stvo "Mysil'," 1972); and Sovetskii narod i dialektika natsional'nogo razvitiia edited by F.K. Kocharli and A.F. Dashdamirov (Baku: Izdatel'stvo "Elm" 1972).

(5) N. N. Arisov and V. G. Strekozov, "Sovetskii patriotizm - patriotizm novoi istoricheskoi obshchnosti liudei," Sovetskoe gosudarstvo i pravo, no. 7 (July 1972), pp. 70-79; an editorial, "Obshchenatsional'naia gordost' sovetskogo cheloveka," Voprosy filosofii, no. 4 (1973), pp. 3-9; and an editorial entitled "Internatio-natsionalizm sovetskogo naroda," Kommunist, no. 13 (September 1973), pp. 8 and passim.

(6) For Brezhnev's special recognition of the "great Russian people's" contribution to the development of the USSR, see Kommunist, no. 5 (March 1971), p. 60; and the editorial about the fiftieth anniversary of the USSR in Sovetskoe gosudarstvo i pravo, no. 1, (Jan. 1972), pp. 7-8.

(7) The views of Ukrainian dissidents about this are available in Ukraiins'ky visnyk (Ukranian Herald), a collection of Ukranian samizdat writings published by the Smoloskyp Publishing House of Baltimore, Maryland. So far, eight volumes of this journal have been issued.

(8) The close relationship between communist development and the rise of a new Soviet People has been stressed especially in discussions during the Twenty-Fifth Party Congress. See Dokumenty i resoliutsii XXVs"esd KPSS (Moscow: Izdatel'stvo Politicheskoi Literatury, 1976).

(9) 1972 Yearbook on International Communist Affairs (Stanford, Cal.: Hoover Institution, 1972), p. 85.

(10) See, for example, Sh. Rashidov, "Moguchee sredstvo obshcheniia i international'nogo vospitaniia," Kommunist, no. 7 (May 1972), pp. 13-28; and P. Masherov, "O nekotorykh chertakh i osobennostiakh natsional'nykh otnoshenii v usloviakh razvitogo sotsializma," Kommunist, no. 15, (October 1972), pp. 15-33. More recent views and sources about this problem are available in Kim, part II, chap. 9.

(11) Such accusations have been voiced repeatedly on the pages of Ukraiins'ky visnyk.

(12) Roman Szporluk, "Russians in Ukraine and Problems of Ukrainian Identity in the USSR," in Ukraine in the Seventies, edited by Peter J. Potichnyj (Oakville, Ont.: Mosaic Press, 1975), pp. 199-201; and Szporluk's "The Nations of the USSR in 1970," Survey, no. 4 (1971), passim.

(13) Kim, and, indeed, most other Soviet writers about the subject, suggest this very clearly; Masherov, p. 28, went so far in his discussion of the new psychological traits of the Soviet people as to refer to them as "sovetskii kharakter."

(14) For the attitudes of Ukrainian dissidents about this, see Ukraiins'ky visnyk (note 7 above). Such views, as far as Russian dissidents are concerned, have most often been voiced by Andrey D. Sakharov. A samizdat proclamation, entitled Programma demokratischeskogo dvizheniia Sovetskogo Soiuza (Amsterdam: Fond imeni Gertsena, 1970), is one of the most liberal documents issued by Russian democratic forces in recent years; also see Arkhiv samizdata, no. 340 (1969), p. 39.

(15) Vladimir Bukovsky, "Eshche raz o rusifikatsii i natsionalizme," (an open letter to A. N. Kosygin) Arkhiv samizdata, No. 2364 (June-July 1975), 2 pp.

(16) "Bor'ba s tak nazyvaemym 'rusofil'stvom' ili put' gosudarstennogo samoubiistva," Veche, no. 7, Arkhiv samizdata, No. 1775 (Feb. 1973), pp. 2-8.

(17) Ibid., p. 2.

17 "The Soviet People": Multiethnic Alternative or Ruse?

Ruslan O. Rasiak

In the Tourist age, on foreign journeys
Be they Kazakh, Yakut or Estonian,
Around the globe, in all the world's countries
Soviet citizens are called simply "Russian."(1)

During the Twenty-Fourth Congress of the Communist Party of the Soviet Union (CPSU) in March 1971, General Secretary Leonid I. Brezhnev affirmed the emergence in the USSR of "a new historical community of people - The Soviet People (Sovetskii narod)."(2)   The idea and expression itself was not a new one.   The molding of a "new man" and the advent of a "Soviet People" united by a communist ideology, common culture, spiritual make-up, and way of life was confidently announced ten years earlier in the Third CPSU program.(3)   It is well known that Nikita S. Khrushchev had embarked upon a seemingly endless series of reforms and reorganizations that were ostensibly intended to launch Soviet society into a more advanced stage of development of the communist society envisioned in the Program.   With Khrushchev's ouster in 1964, however, the new regime under Brezhnev and Aleksey N. Kosygin quickly set about undoing the results of what some regime spokesmen termed Khrushchev's "hare-brained schemes."   The Program was quietly forgotten and the regime seemed determined to carry on without resort to the "campaigns" and bombast characteristics of the Khrushchev period.

Thus, the revival of the grandiose idea of the Soviet People offers a marked contrast to the more "businesslike," conservative tenor of the Brezhnev regime.   Soviet scholars and ideologists have once again been called upon to deal with a highly sensitive subject, and to provide a convincing theoretical formulation for the concept of the Soviet People.(4)

Perhaps not accidently, the renewed promotion of the idea of a unified, increasingly homogeneous Soviet People has coincided with a sharp rise in the sensitivities and aspirations of major Soviet ethnic groups, including the Russians. The Soviet authorities have responded to expressions of ethnic group unrest and assertiveness with intensified repression and calls for increased ideological vigilance.(5)

Still, evidence suggests that there are potent forces in Soviet society, both within and without the Soviet leadership hierarchy, seeking to ensure Russian group supremacy by regenerating in the Russians a sense of distinctiveness, cohesion, and purpose. Whatever special problems this may pose to the leadership's management of a vast multiethnic state, the strategic position and strength of the Russians is such that their demands and aspirations cannot be ignored or easily contained. It seems likely that the Soviet leadership will attempt to reconcile the drive for open Russian group supremacy with that of forging a "Soviet People" by creating a symbiotic relationship between the two. This will be no easy task, for non-Russians will also have to be convinced of the beneficence of this arrangement. All this suggests that, despite Brezhnev's assurances to the contrary,(6) the "ethnic question" in the Soviet Union is far from resolved.

The hypothesis advanced here is that the continued ideological emphasis by Soviet authorities upon the supposed unity of The Soviet People as a whole tends to dampen Russian self-awareness and obscure external identity. Russian self-awareness is dampened in the sense that the idea of a Soviet People puts certain limits on those kinds of public expressions and appeals that would encourage sober introspection and mobilize and focus Russian energies and resources on distinctly Russian concerns and problems. Instead, Russians are called upon to ensure the stability and welfare of the entire multiethnic country - where they are bound to collide head on with the non-Russians. Moreover, Soviet ethnic groups continue to maneuver within restricted limits to maintain their separate group identities and advance their own different interests. Under the circumstances, the much celebrated, yet elusive, Soviet People concept will probably show itself less and less capable of serving as an effective inspirational symbol around and within which Russian group identity, cohesion, and self-esteem may be regenerated in a creative, constructive manner.

Because the terms "Soviet" and "Russian" are very often casually interutilized in Western publications and media, a short summary of the current official interpretation of the Soviet People idea is useful here. Sovetskii narod, according to Soviet theoretical writings, is the world's first interethnic socialist community of people. Its emergence ostensibly initiates the beginning of a new era in the history of ethnic relations. Soviet theoreticians of ethnic policy assert that the Soviet People can be characterized by the following principal features: a single common territory (the USSR), a single ideology and world view (Marxism-Leninism), a common purpose and goal (the building of a communist society), proletarian internationalism and Soviet patriotism, and peaceful and harmonious relations between classes and ethnic groups. In addition, the Soviet People aggregate is said to be characterized by unity of class and ethnic interests, a high and growing degree of socioeconomic homogeneity, a single common multiethnic culture, common features of spiritual make-up and psychology, bilingualism and widespread, increasing use of Russian as the language of interethnic communication, and the preeminence of the working class and its vanguard - the communist party.(7)

Despite the presence of these seemingly comprehensive features, the Soviet People, according to Soviet scholars, remains a multiethnic community, an interethnic union (ob"edinenie) of people of the USSR. Such scholars point out further that the Soviet People does not constitute a "single Soviet nation," a supraethnic (nadnatsional'nyi) formation, nor a special form of ethnic community.(8) The Soviet People is not even held to be an intermediate formation between an ethnic (natsional'nyi) and a nonethnic (beznatsional'nyi) community.(9)

Nevertheless, the Soviet People is considered to be a transitional form of multiethnic entity whose ultimate end is the fusion of all its component ethnic groups. Although the tenet of fusion of ethnic groups now receives less emphasis than other canons of the concept, it has not been openly questioned or renounced. Soviet ethnic groups today are said to be in a period of intensified "flourishing" and "drawing together" which will progressively lead to a more perfect "unity" of all ethnic groups in the Soviet Union.(10) During this period, it is said, all ethnic groups will flourish by developing politically, economically, and culturally. At the same time, all ethnic groups are expected to draw closer together by assimilating the best features of each component ethnic group. Soviet ideologists say this entire process, described essentially as one of mutual aid, cooperation, and enrichment, will be a long, gradual one.(11)

A careful examination of the individual elements in the above picture of the Soviet People reveals that there are many problems - only a few of which can be touched upon here - which seriously undermine the credibility and utility of the concept. Perhaps the single most striking, uncertain aspect for advocates of ethnic group regeneration and separateness is the narrow ideological framework into which it has been cast and within which it is elaborated. The fundamental tension between the ultimate goal of fusion of ethnic groups and their continued existence remains as unresolved as ever. Most of the propositions upon which the idea of the Soviet People rests are simply dogmatic assertions strung together to furnish a semblance of substance to the alleged "new historical community" celebrated by the Soviet leaders. In effect, the whole idea takes on the character of an all-or-nothing proposition, and from this stem many of the obstacles to its gaining general voluntary acceptance.

The close connection of the Soviet People with a waning ideology may be its greatest liability.(12)   The idea of a unified, increasingly homogeneous Soviet People, as elaborated in the theoretical literature, can begin to make sense only if the whole of official ideology can be accepted.   Many of the assertions made in support of the Soviet People idea (for example, that all Soviet ethnic groups enjoy equal rights and privileges, or that ethnic identities and loyalties are essentially parochial, transitory phenomena destined to disappear altogether at some future date) are either demonstratively false or empirically unverifiable.   There is little reason to assume that Soviet citizens are less aware of these facts than are Western observers of the Soviet scene.   As with so many ideological systems, when fundamental principles are seen to conflict with actuality or are discovered to be uncertain or false, the whole system sooner or later loses its explicatory and inspirational power.   At the very least, many of the demands which assertive ethnic groups tend to perceive as inimical, such as the intermixing of ethnic groups or the generalization of a single common language, can no longer be justified on ideological grounds alone.   An added nuisance in this instance is the party's position as the sole authority on what constitutes ideological orthodoxy in general and correct ethnic policy in particular.   As has happened so often in the past, today's ideological orthodoxy may become tomorrow's heresy.   There is no assurance, for example, that a change in leadership might not also bring with it a new interpretation of what the Soviet People is all about.   This very real possibility is hardly likely to induce in Soviet ethnic groups enthusiasm for what must by now appear as yet another party-sponsored folly.

On the practical level, severe ideological rigidities stand in the way of the flexibility and sobriety required for the development of healthy, secure ethnic group identities and harmonious interethnic relations.   The demand by Soviet authorities for allegiance to the collective Soviet entity is not qualitatively different from those pleas made by the authorities of many Western multiethnic states.   Rather, the difference is in the latitude permitted the expression and exercise of ethnic group identity and allegiance below the state-wide level.   In the Soviet Union, relatively innocuous expressions of ethnic allegiance and grievances become suspect and very often evoke harsh repressive measures. The unwillingness of Soviet authorities to make even moderate but genuine concessions to increasingly self-conscious or recalcitrant ethnic groups leaves them no option but to engage in "subversive" behavior. As ideology continues to wane, and as the cycle of repression and opposition intensifies, the allegiance of some powerful group within the state becomes more urgent for the authorities. The only way in which this allegiance can be gained in the USSR today is by according some ethnic group special recognition and prerogatives, thereby violating the principles and guidelines embodied in the Sovietskii narod concept.

Finally, the full realization of the Soviet People idea requires the voluntary, earnest compliance of all major ethnic groups. Because Soviet ethnic groups are compelled to interact with one another to an ever greater extent, adherence to the alleged ethnic neutrality of the concept is essential. No large, self-conscious ethnic group is likely to sublimate its identity and interests to an idea which it perceives as being distorted and manipulated for purposes inimical to its own well-being. If we agree with the proposition that self-conscious, assertive ethnic groups in multiethnic states today are not easily persuaded to accept undifferentiated and subordinate sociopolitical roles, then gaining general, practical acceptance for the idea of a single Soviet People presents the Soviet leaders with a tall order indeed.

The manner in which Soviet ethnic groups respond to the Soviet People idea is of central importance to the future of interethnic relations in the Soviet Union. Official Soviet writings on the subject would have us believe that the Soviet People is a reality and that in the USSR ethnic identity and allegiance is already of secondary importance. Unofficial, samizdat writings emanating from ethnic groups, however, suggest that such claims are premature at best. One non-Russian samizdat source specifically labels the Soviet People a "myth," a "fable created by the Kremlin," and denounces it as an "abstract veil under which the Russian chauvinist backbone conceals itself."(13) Such a skeptical, pugnacious response is perhaps not surprising on the part of a subordinate ethnic group with a long history of competition and conflict with the dominant group. But what of the dominant Russian group itself? Are Russian aspirations and perceptions of their own interests necessarily identical to those of Soviet leadership? It is certainly not unheedful of the Russian group, but is faced with the imperative of holding togther a vast agglomeration of racially, linguistically, and culturally diverse ethnic groups. Is the Russian group immune to doubts concerning its ability to absorb other groups and survive homogenization pressures with its basic ethnic characteristics intact?

One "Russite" samizdat writing asserts that Russians play a disproportionately small role in the life of the country, complains that Russians have become "foreigners on their own soil," and warns against the "threat of biological degeneration."(14) As a solution to the ills now besetting the country this manifesto demands an end to "random hybridization" and advocates the creation of a "powerful ethnic state" where total freedom of development for all ethnic groups will be tolerated, but also where the Russian people will truly constitute the ruling group.(15) The "Russites" are an amorphous group of Russians concerned with the preservation of traditional Russian culture and values. They believe in the uniqueness and special mission of the Russian people. The "Russites" apparently range from the mildly liberal and neo-Slavophile to the extremely authoritarian and chauvinistic. In place of the Marxist doctrine of class antagonism and the primacy of socioeconomic relations in the evolution of mankind, these "Russites" assert the primacy of the ethnic group: "For us the ethnic group is primordial, and everything else derives from it. For us the ethnic group is not only a biologically differentiated [entity] but a special spiritual community whose originality contains a profound mystical meaning."(16) It is clear that for this group of militant "Russites," the Soviet People can hardly appear a worthy symbol for the Russian group.

The writings of what might be considered less militant "Russite" or neo-Slavophile groups also show little zeal for ethnically neutral, class-based formulas. The manifesto of the Russia-wide Social-Christian Union for the Liberation of the People, for example, considers Bolshevism a tragic period in the country's development. It advocates a "complete and uncompromising break with all known possible variants of communist and social-democratic ideas, schemes, and illusions."(17) The samizdat journal Veche deplores the Russian people's loss of dignity, self-respect, and greatness - qualities they once possessed, it is claimed - and the low esteem in which Russians are held by other ethnic groups in their own native territories.(18) "We want only one thing," declares Vladimir Osipov, the one-time editor of Veche and Zemlia, "the strengthening of Russian ethnic culture and traditions in the spirit of the Slavophiles and Dostoevski, and the assertion of Russia's originality and greatness."(19) Though Osipov's position toward the Soviet regime is not unequivocal, he feels that Soviet patriotism alone is "inadequate" for effecting the moral or cultural regeneration of the Russian people.(20) Says Osipov, "Times change, authorities are fleeting, but the PEOPLE are eternal."(21) Another contributor to Veche dismisses the idea of "universal man" as an "invention."(22) Still elsewhere, the idea of a proletarian or socialist culture is called absurd; culture can only be ethnic, it is asserted.(23)

These and other samizdat writings confirm that the Russians also constitute an ethnic group with separate interests and aspirations which may or may not conflict with those of the CPSU leadership, as well as with those of the non-Russians. Whatever differences may exist among these Russians with respect to questions of the political, social, and economic organization of the country, there is evident an overriding concern with the status, image, and future of the Russian group. From the standpoint of maintaining healthy ethnic group identity, cohesion, and preeminence, the idea of a Soviet People is not necessarily one that concerned spokesmen for the Russian ethnic group find desirable or acceptable, especially if they believe that Russians no longer command the esteem and deference they feel should be forthcoming from subordinate ethnic groups. These samizdat writings, both Russian and non-Russian, also suggest that few, if any, of the major Soviet ethnic groups are comfortable with the Soviet People concept, and even less happy with the prospect of ultimate fusion into some, as yet undefined and elusive, nonethnic and nonnational community.

On the other hand, in some Russian samizdat writings "Russian" solutions to problems of interethnic relations are sought. Also, a certain astonishment and indignation at others' grievances, and, at the same time, a marked unwillingness merely to contemplate the political separation of the non-Russians - as a possible solution to the ethnic malaise in the country - permeates the thinking of some Russians. These attitudes are most obvious in the Russite tract,(24) but they can also be detected in Veche. One contributor to Veche, for example, holds that all propositions regarding the evolution of "Russia" fall into two distinct categories, Russian and non-Russian. The Russian category, which includes Slavophilism, Russian populism (narodnichestvo), and Leninism, is considered sufficiently broad to express the uniqueness of "Russia." But there will be no non-Russian variants in "Russia" as far as this contributor to Veche is concerned.(25) Another article in Veche strongly denies the existence of any threat from "Russian great-power chauvinism." It considers the establishment of the Soviet federation a genuinely "Russian" form of organization and a wise move which preserved a great state.(26) Russification is defended as a progressive phenomenon when it accompanies industrialization and the influx of Russians into non-Russian areas. The Baltic ethnic groups, the Georgians, Ukrainians, and Kazakhs, however, are described as "hotheaded" and unjustified in venting their anger on the Russians.(27) In still another article in Veche, the Russian people are described as a "gatherer people" (narod sobiratel') whose psychological make-up has prepared them as no other ethnic group for becoming the center of a "voluntary" union of ethnic groups.(28)

Such attitudes and thinking are significant, considering that Russians constitute a little more than half the total population of the Soviet Union. This seeming indifference to other groups' sensitivities evidenced in the literature is underscored by the fact that only 3.0 percent of the Russians living in non-Russian units (22.9 percent of such dispersed population) has acquired knowledge of some non-Russian Soviet language.(29) The apparent obsession with maintaining the circle of ethnic groups centered on the Russians leaves the impression that many Russians (or at least Russites) feel that Russian identity, image, and greatness would somehow be damaged or diminished if other groups were to opt for separation from the Soviet Union. Despite repeatedly expressed commitments to the freedom, equality, and dignity of all Soviet ethnic groups, an "imperial temperament" of sorts shows through in some of these writings.

This seeming dependence of Russian self-esteem and prestige upon subordination and obeisance of non-Russians is clearly reflected in the more strident, popular, political literature.(30) In the theoretical literature dealing with the Soviet People idea, Russians receive slightly more recognition than do other ethnic groups. But in these writings the Russian group is sharply defined and elevated far above non-Russians. The idea of a Soviet People here places a poor second in comparison to the praise and homage accorded the Russians. Emphasis is clearly placed on the primacy of the Russians and the alleged superiority of all things Russian in the Soviet Union. Implicit also is the notion of the inferiority of non-Russians, in the sense that the "liberty and prosperity" which they enjoy is possible only with the "unselfish assistance" of the Russian people. Russians as a group are portrayed as possessing an abundance of practically every noble trait: unselfishness, magnanimity, industriousness, valor, honesty, humanity, generosity of spirit, faithfulness in friendship, irreconcilability to evil, ethnic pride, love of liberty, and so on.(31) It is difficult to determine from these writings just exactly where the boundaries of the Russian ethnic group end and those of the Soviet People begin. The ethnic neutrality of the Soviet People is discarded and a very strong Russian ethnic coloration is substituted.

The damage done to the credibility and utility of the Soviet People idea by the glorification of Russians in the political literature is magnified by the many practical realities which serve to make Russians, perhaps, the least willing or able to adhere to a requirement of ethnic neutrality. Russians are the politically and culturally dominant group in the Soviet Union; they have historically constituted the imperial ruling group; they possess strength of numbers with respect to other individual ethnic groups. They are among the most advanced of ethnic groups in terms of modernization indicators. Russians are the most intimately linked with the Soviet regime in the eyes of the other ethnic groups, and Russians seem to enjoy greater latitude in indulging ethnic pride than they do. Yet, for these very same reasons, the burden of demonstrating and ensuring the ethnic neutrality of the Soviet People concept falls most upon them.

Would the Russians then be willing or able to surrender their ruling group status and the prerogatives and benefits that derive from it in order to make a "success" of a unified Soviet People? Short of some internal crisis or catastrophe in the Soviet system, such a course seems unlikely for at least two important reasons. First, confident ruling groups do not normally surrender status without some real compensation in return. Though Russians are probably not unperturbed by homogenization pressures and the increasing indocility of some major non-Russian groups, there is no firm evidence, yet, of a general crisis of confidence in the Russian group. And, in the already tight Soviet economy, Russians could hardly expect to maintain or improve their economic position by relinquishing some of their prerogatives to the others. Second, and more important, given the nature of the Soviet system, the realization of a more equitable distribution of power, status, and wealth among ethnic groups would require a fundamental restructuring of the entire system. The present Soviet leadership could not survive this. In fact, the Soviet leadership, for its own survival, must ensure that Russian attention and energies are kept focused on the Union-wide level and that Russian ethnic identity and pride find satisfaction in the role of being "first among equals." So the Russian consciousness of and interest in this role will not weaken and stray, and partly in response to the resurgence of concern with ethnicity in the Russian group, the more strident political literature often infuses the Soviet People concept with Russian ethnic symbols and content.

Soviet ethnic groups seem increasingly concerned with marking ethnic boundaries and cultivating those ethnic specificities which strengthen identity and cohesion. Symbols and forms become important here. The Soviet People concept, as explicated in the theoretical literature, is too vague and lacking in credibility to constitute an effective, emotionally satisfying symbol either for advocates of Russian ethnic group regeneration and separateness or for those espousing open Russian group supremacy. It minimizes the Russian ethnic component in Soviet society at a time when Russians seem anxious to define it.

On the other hand, the reinforced, "Russianized" version of the Soviet People propagated in the political writings is unlikely to moderate what one Russian advocate of reconciliation among Soviet ethnic groups terms a "typically Russian vice: the inability to see the line that divides us from

other nations [ethnic groups], the lack of inner conviction in
their right to exist within their own national [ethnic] identity."(32)   If   this   "Russianized"   version   gains   general
acceptance   in   the   Russian   group,   many   Russians   may   be
expected   to   question   the   necessity   for   any   supraethnic
"camouflage."   Why should that which in their own minds
already appears implicit and clearly understood by all (Russian
group ascendancy) not be made finally explicit?

NOTES

(1) Vladimir   Gordeichev,   "V   sem'e   velikoi,"   Molodaia
     gvardiia, no. 5, (May 1973), p. 124.
(2) "Otchetnyi doklad Tsentral'nogo Komiteta KPSS XXIV
     S"ezdu   Kommunisticheskoi   partii   Sovetskogo   Soiuza.
     Doklad General'nogo sekretaria TsK tovarishcha L. I.
     Brezhneva, 30 marta 1971," Kommunist, no. 5 (March
     1971), p. 61.
(3) Programme of the Communist Party of the Soviet Union
     (Moscow: Foreign   Language   Publishing   House,   1961),
     especially pp. 102-19.
(4) For an interpretation of The Soviet People idea, the
     following works have been consulted: Bratstvo narodov
     i internatsional'noe vospitanie edited by G.A. Abdurakh-
     manov et al. (Tashkent: Tashkentskii ordena Trudovogo
     Krasnogo Znameni Gosudarstvennyi Universitet im. V. I.
     Lenina,   1974);   V druzhbe - nasha sila, nashe schast'e,
     edited by K. F. Fazylkhodzhaev (Tashkent: Izdatel'stvo
     "Uzbekistan,"   1974);   Leninizm i natsional'nyi vopros v
     sovremennykh usloviiakh edited by P. N. Fedoseev et al.
     (Moscow: Izdatel'stvo   Politicheskoi   Literatury,   1972);
     Internatsional'ne   i   natsional'ne   v   sotsialistychnomu
     suspil'stvi,   edited   by   I. P.   Holovakha   and   A. I.
     Dorochenkov   (Kiev: Vydavnytstvo   "Naukova   Dumka,"
     1972);   A. I.   Kholmogorov,   Internatsional'nye cherty
     sovetskikh natsii (Moscow: Izdatel'stvo "Mysl'," 1970);
     Maxim   P.   Kim,   Sovetskii narod - novaia istoricheskaia
     obshchnost' (Moscow: Izdatel'stvo Politicheskoi Literatury,
     1972);   Sovetskii narod - novaia istoricheskaia obshchnost'
     liudei,   edited by Maxim P. Kim et al. (Moscow: Iz-
     datel'stvo "Nauka," 1975); SSSR - velikoe sodruzhestvo
     naradov-brat'ev, edited by Maxim P. Kim (Moscow: Iz-
     datel'stvo   "Nauka,"   1972);   Sovetskii narod i dialektika
     natsional'nogo razvitiia, edited by F. K. Kocharli and A.
     F. Dashdamirov (Baku: Izdatel'stvo "Elm," 1972); Mnogo-
     natsional'noe sovetskoe gosudarstvo,   edited   by   M. I.
     Kulichenko   et   al.   (Moscow: Izdatel'stvo   Politicheskoi
     Literatury, 1972); M. I. Kulichenko, Natsional'nye otno-

sheniia v SSSR i tendentsii ikh razvitiia (Moscow: Izdatel'stvo "Mysl'," 1972); Sotsializm i natsii, edited by M.
I. Kulichenko et al. (Moscow: Izdatel'stvo "Mysl'," 1975);
Nikolai I. Matiushkin, Patriotizm i internatsionalizm sovetskogo naroda (Moscow: Izdatel'stvo Moskovskogo Universiteta, 1975); V. I. Naulko, Razvitie mezhetnicheskikh
sviazei na Ukraine (Izdatel'stvo "Naukova Dumka," 1975);
Sovremennoe revoliutsionnoe dvizhenie i natsionalizm,
edited by V. V. Zagladina and F. D. Ryzhenko (Moscow:
Izdatel'stvo Politicheskoi Literatury, 1973). For an
indication of how The Soviet People idea fares in the
popular political literature the following Russian language
journals have been surveyed for the periods indicated:
Kommunist (CC/CPSU), January 1971–July 1977; Kommunist (Estonia, Latvia, and Lithuania), January 1971–
May 1977; Molodaia gvardiia (official journal of the
Komsomol), January 1971–June 1977. The Ukrainian
language Kommunist Ukrainy has been surveyed for the
period January 1971–June 1977.

(5) Although the exact extent of these repressions is difficult to ascertain, the non-Russians generally seem to
bear the brunt of the authorities' displeasure. See
Frederick C. Barghoorn, "The Post-Khrushchev Campaign
to Suppress Dissent: Perspectives, Strategies and Tech-
niques of Repression," in Dissent in the USSR: Politics,
Ideology and People, edited by Rudolf L. Tökes (Balti-
more: Johns Hopkins, 1975), pp. 76–79; Rudolf L.
Tökes, "Dissent: The Politics for Change in the USSR,"
in Soviet Politics and Society in the Seventies, edited by
Henry W. Morton and Rudolf L. Tökes (New York: Free
Press, 1974), pp. 24–29; and Richard Pipes, "Reflections
on the Nationality Problems in the Soviet Union," in
Ethnicity: Theory and Experience, edited by Nathan
Glazer and Daniel P. Moynihan (Cambridge, Mass.:
Harvard University Press, 1975), pp. 461, 464.

(6) "O piatidesiatiletii Soiuza Sovetskikh Sotsialisticheskikh
Respublik. Doklad General'nogo sekretaria TsK KPSS
tovarishcha L. I. Brezhneva," Kommunist, no. 18 (December 1972), pp. 17–18.

(7) Fedoseev et al., pp. 225–32, 300–24; Holovakha and
Dorochenkov, pp. 10–15, 77–83; Kholmogorov, pp. 9–10,
155–67; Kim, Sovetskii narod (1972), pp. 34–44; Kim et
al., Sovetskii narod (1975), pp. 716; Kocharli and
Dashdimirov, pp. 49–109; Kulichenko, Natsional'nye otnosheniia, pp. 387–90; Kulichenko et al., Mnogonatsional'noe sovetskoe gosudarstvo, pp. 329–87; and
Matiushkin, pp. 240–45.

(8) Fedoseev et al., p. 227; Kholmogorov, p. 205; Kocharli
and Dashdimirov, p. 11; Kulichenko, Natsional'nye
otnosheniia, p. 425; Matiushkin, pp. 243–44.

(9)   Kulichenko, Natsional'nye otnosheniia, p. 525.
(10)   Fedoseev et al., pp. 208-58, 300-24; Holovakha and
       Dorochenko, pp. 75-133; Kholmogorov, pp. 104-56; Kim,
       Sovetskii narod (1972), pp. 22-33, 205-37; Kocharli and
       Dashdimirov, pp. 32-48; Kulichenko, Natsional'nye otno-
       sheniia, pp. 425-508.
(11)   Fedoseev et al., pp. 559-563; Kholmogorov, pp. 24, 98,
       106, 199-205; Kim, Sovetskii narod (1972), pp. 206-7,
       237; Kocharli and Dashdimirov, p. 321; Kulichenko,
       Natsional'nye otnosheniia, pp. 445, 526, 542, 552-56;
       Matiushkin, p. 410.
(12)   The weakening of official ideology has been remarked
       upon by both Western observers and Soviet dissidents,
       among them: Daniel Bell, "Ethnicity and Social Change,"
       in Glazer and Moynihan, p. 150; Pipes, p. 465; Tökes in
       Morton and Tökes, p. 7; Hedrick Smith, The Russians
       (New York: Quadrangle/The New York Times Book Com-
       pany, 1976), pp. 279-88; Andrei Amalrik, "Ideologii v
       sovetskom obshchestve," Arkhiv samizdata, No. 2536
       (February 7, 1976); Valentyn Moroz, "A Report From the
       Beria Reservation," in Boomerang: The Works of Valentyn
       Moroz, edited by Yaroslav Bihun (Baltimore: Smoloskyp
       Publishers, 1974), p. 43; Aleksandr I. Solzhenitsyn,
       Letter to the Soviet Leaders (New York: Harper & Row,
       1974), pp. 15, 17, 43, 47.
(13)   Ukrains'kyi visnyk, VII-VIII edited by Maksym Sahaydak
       (Baltimore: Smoloskyp Publishers, 1975), pp. 25, 67, 112.
(14)   "Slovo natsii," December 31, 1970, Arkhiv Samizdata
       (hereafter AS), No. 590, pp. 17-23.
(15)   Ibid., p. 23.
(16)   Ibid., p. 7.
(17)   "Vserossiiskii sotsial-khristianskii soiuz osvobozhdeniia
       naroda," 1969, AS, No. 525, p. 2.
(18)   Veche, no. 1 (January 1971), AS, no. 1013, p. 2;
       Veche, no. 6 (October 19, 1972), AS, no. 1599, p. 10;
       Veche, no. 7 (February 19, 1973), AS, no. 1775, pp.
       12-13; Veche, no. 8 (July 19, 1973), AS, no. 1665, p.
       210.
(19)   Veche, no. 2 (May 19, 1971), AS, no. 1020, p. 2.
(20)   Veche, no. 9 (December 19, 1973), AS, no. 2040, p.
       192.
(21)   Zemlia, no. 1 (August 1, 1974), AS, no. 1909, p. 2.
(22)   Veche, no. 2, p. 32.
(23)   "Bor'ba s tak nazyvaemym 'russofil'stvom' ili put' gosu-
       darstvennogo samoubiistva," Veche, no. 7, p. 9.
(24)   See for example the aspersions cast at several non-
       Russian groups on pp. 16-18 of "Slovo natsii".
(25)   Veche, no. 8, pp. 220-21.
(26)   "Russkoe reshenie natsional'nogo voprosa," Veche, no.
       6, pp. 7-8.

(27) Ibid., pp. 9-10.

(28) "Bor'ba s tak nazyvaemym 'russofil'stvom' ili put' gosudarstvennogo samoubiistva," pp. 4-5, 9.

(29) Calculated from data in Itogi vsesoiuznoi perepisi naseleniia 1970 goda. Natsional'nyi sostav naseleniia SSSR (Moscow: Statistika, 1973), vol. IV, Table 1, pp. 9-19.

(30) Sharaf Rashidov, "Moguchee sredstvo obshcheniia i internatsional'nogo vospitaniia," Kommunist, no 7 (May 1972), pp. 13-28; and "Iazyk bratstva i druzhby narodov," Kommunist, no. 3 (February 1976), pp. 15-26; Iurii Zbanats'kyi, "Slovo pro velykyi rossiis'kyi narod," Komunist Ukrainy, no 5 (May 1975), pp. 35-40.

(31) Rashidov, "Iazyk bratstva i druzhby narodov," pp. 18-19; Zbanats'kyi, pp. 36-37.

(32) Igor Shafarevich, "Reconciliation or Separation," in Aleksandr Solzhenitsyn, ed., From Under the Ruble edited by Alexander Solzhenitsyn (New York: Bantam Books, 1976), pp. 100-101.

18 Comment—The Concept of "The Soviet People" and the Disintegration of the Leninist Synthesis

Joseph Rothschild

The chapters by Professor Oleh S. Fedyshyn (chap. 16) and Ruslan O. Rasiak (Chap. 7) indicate that the great Leninist synthesis in the Soviet Union is disintegrating-- perhaps, has already disintegrated. That Leninist (or Leninist-Stalinist) synthesis consisted, of course, of many components. The components that are particularly relevant for our particular proposition in this volume are: the synthesis of the Westernizer versus Slavophile-Populist controversy in the form of industrializing, "national," inward-facing, etatist Bolshevism; and the synthesis between Russian hegemonial centralism and non-Russian centrifugal propensities in the form of Soviet federalism.

Interpolating here, the survival for a long interval of the supposedly dissident Russian underground periodical, Veche, (cited in both the Fedyshyn and Rasiak articles) seemingly indicates that the disintegration of the Leninist synthesis proceeds not only across Soviet society but also within the regime itself. Veche could not have survived for as long as it did without the collusion, connivance, and protection of some officials.

When two binary variables that are not direct causal functions, one of the other, break up and recombine, four possible combinations may then emerge in the realm of logically feasible, theoretical possibilities, though, of course, they are not all equally probable in the real world of historical and political contingencies. Historians and political analysts of the Soviet Union will have to inform us about which of the four hypothetically possible recombinations depicted in figure 18.1 are most and least likely.

Solution A is probably the one that most moderately well-informed, but nonspecialist, American laymen would predict as most likely to emerge from the current and coming

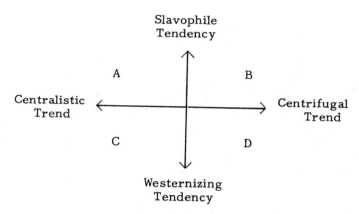

Fig. 18.1. Four possible reolutions for the Russian crisis.

crisis in the Soviet system. It is the pessimistic "worse-case" scenario, combining the reflexive traits of Russian xenophobia, autocracy, imperialism, and repressiveness.

Solution B suggests an even more radical inward-turning of Slavophile xenophobia: this time, however, so extreme as to write off and release at least some non-Russian ethnic groups of the USSR - who would then, of course, be the beneficiaries of the resultant green light to their centrifugal aspirations. Occasional passages in Aleksandr I. Solzhenitsyn's writings indicate that he is reconciled to such a scenario. Also, in Leo Tolstoy's War and Peace, General Kutuzov is depicted as a moral sage (and a specifically Russian moral sage) in part precisely because he, too, subscribes to this scenario - despising, as he does in Tolstoy's pages, the czar's acquisition of Finland, Poland, and other countries that will seduce and deflect Russia away from her proper heritage and destiny and her own culture. To what extent Tolstoy's Kutuzov replicates or distorts the historical Mikhail I. Kutuzov the historians must judge.

Solution C is, in a sense, a restatement of the classic "white man's burden" defense of imperialism. It predicts a westernized, modern, liberal Russia, nevertheless, cleaving to her non-Russian territorial acquisitions, partly for strategic reasons and partly to bring to them the supposed benefits of Western civilization - on the assumption that all except the Baltic groups lag behind the Russians in their several levels of modernity.

Solution D stipulates a logical correspondence between a possible triumph of a westernizing, cosmopolitan option for Russia with the recognition by such a Russia that the non-Russian ethnic groups must, at a minimum, be granted greater pluralistic autonomy for their own aspirations and

possibly even independence.   Several of these scenarios were
once vigorously debated within the Decembrist movement in the
1820s.

   At the present time, the Soviet regime seeks to deny,
smother, and counteract the accelerating disintegration of the
Leninist synthesis with the rhetoric and pseudo-ideology of a
Soviet, rather than a Russian, ethnicity (narodnost'). In their
respective judgments of this phenomenon, our two authors
appear to disagree with each other.   Professor Fedyshyn
regards Soviet narodnost' as a categorical fraud, a mere
screen - and a transparent screen, at that - for great Russian
chauvinism, and, therefore, as representing no threat of
offense or embarrassment to Russians, who correctly
understand and assess it to be a mere veil for their own
ongoing hegemonialism. Fedyshyn's analysis and judgment are
reminiscent of Ivan Dzyuba's devastating dismissal that "the
[so-called] friendship of [Soviet] nations [ethnic groups] is
synonymous with Russification."(1)

   Mr. Rasiak, on the other hand, judges the doctrine of a
Soviet People (sovetskii narod) to be not so much spurious as
counterproductive. It aleniates the Russians, who feel that it
profanes their Holy Russia on behalf of a cold, abstract,
nonemotive, and unsatisfying formula, as well as offending the
non-Russians whose autonomist grievances and pride it also
repudiates.   Rasiak implicitly suggests that the regime's
relations with the Russian people are those of the proverbial
lady riding a tiger.   She can neither stay on nor get off
without incurring prohibitive risks.   Ideological imperatives
preclude the Soviet regime from openly repudiating Marxism
and explicitly embracing Russian ethnocentrism.   But neither
can the regime spurn Russian ethnocentrism lest the
non-Russians perceive such a gesture as a sign of weakness
and the Russians themselves then disown the regime.   Nor,
finally, can the regime realistically hope to revitalize
Marxism-Leninism, for that ideology no longer confers
authentic legitimacy.   The attempted resolution of these
dilemmas is the rhetoric of the Soviet People and the real
policy of flattering the Russians as the supposedly most
progressive, productive, and leading component of the Soviet
People.   But this hybrid stance only irritates the non-Russians
and does not really satisfy Russian ethnocentrism.   Hence, the
degenerative cycle persists.   Rasiak is somewhat more
persuasive than Fedyshyn in suggesting that the Soviet People
formula is even more counterproductive than it is spurious or,
rather, that it is counterproductive precisely because it is
spurious in several directions, not only in the one direction
stressed by Fedyshyn.

   In conclusion, allow me to be playfully serious and
seriously playful in the manner that professors should be when
they assess ideas and trends in history. Toutes proportions

gardees, mutatis mutandis, and with all other appropriate caveats, for your entertainment and consideration is submitted the proposition that the political reaction of Russians to current trends in the USSR bears certain analogies to the current reaction of the American middle class to trends in the USA. Both believe themselves to have made major historical sacrifices on behalf of marginal ethnosocial groups. The American middle class has traditionally taxed itself very heavily to raise money to be invested in the solution of social problems - more often than not the social problems posed by ethnic marginals - once the tenement slums of Jewish and Catholic white ethnic immigrants, then Black and Hispanic ghettos, Okie, Chicano, and wetback migrants and itinerants, and so on. Indeed, the elite has educated the American middle class to approach all such social problem with a sense of guilt, assuaged, however, by the promise that these problems can be solved by throwing enough money at them. The conventional term for this dual strategy is "the politics of compassion." The Russians, too, have persuaded themselves that they have been extraordinarily generous to, and borne great sacrifices for, other ethnic groups: witness the elaborate school systems in native languages, the substantial publication activities, health and technological investments, and the like, that have been bestowed upon supposedly retarded ethnic groups. Thus, the Russian analogy to the American "politics of compassion" might be termed the "politics of elder brotherhood."

Suddenly, in this decade of the 1970s, all this has changed. If a Marxist term may be used here, the American middle class and the Russian ethnic group have each decided to become "a class [or category] in and for itself" bringing an end to guilt; an end to compassion; an end to elder brotherhood. Moreover, the resultant backlash - which is more pervasive and profound than simply a white ethnic hardhat backlash (as it is conventionally mislabeled and dismissed) - does not take the form of a defense of normative institutions and established elites. Rather, the ruling elites and their institutions are accused of having betrayed the hard-working, self-taxing, self-sacrificing, altruistic middle class (here) and Russian people (there) - betrayed them to the ethnic and social marginals to save their own skins. Indeed, the middle class and the Russians claim that they are the ones who have been reduced to political marginality by the unholy collusion between central elites and alleged ethnic free-loaders. And, in reaction, they are rediscovering and honing their own ethnic militancy. This is the root of the general complaint in both societies that nothing works properly anymore, that institutions do not perform instrumentally, that elites cannot be trusted. Herein lies the current crisis in both countries: the grievances of the demographic pillars of the two societies no longer sustain the claims for support by the elites and their supposedly normative institutions; the social fabric is suffused with ethnic antagonism and competition.

NOTE

(1) Ivan Dzyuba, <u>Internationalism or Russification?</u> (London: Weidenfeld and Nicholson, 1968), p. 189.

V

RSFSR or USSR: Confusing a Part with the Whole

Proposition 5: Russians lack some of the crucial official recognition (for example, a branch of the Communist Party of the Soviet Union designated for the RSFSR, a separate union republic capital for "Russia," or a specific arm of the Academy of Sciences of the USSR) which supports the group awareness of many other Soviet ethnic groups. This deprivation may continue to deny significant support to Russian ethnic identity.

19 The Russia-Wide Soviet Federated Socialist Republic (RSFSR): Privileged or Underprivileged?

Michael Rywkin

Russians in the USSR lack some of the essential symbols of official Soviet recognition. They have no separate RSFSR Communist Party Central Committee, no Russian (as opposed to USSR) Academy of Sciences, no separate capital (Moscow is the capital of both USSR and the RSFSR). Certain union republican ministries usually found in the individual union republics, wherever the latters' industrial activity warrants their presence, are also absent. Missing from the RSFSR is a Minister of Heavy Industry, Non-Ferrous Metallurgy, Coal Mining, Chemicals, Oil Industry (both extraction and processing), and for Timber and Paper Industries. Their functions at both RSFSR and Union-wide levels are directly assumed by the corresponding USSR ministries. Similarly, television and radio broadcasting in the RSFSR is directly managed by the State Committee for TV and Radio of the USSR Council of Ministers.(1)

Are the Russians, as a result of all such limitations affecting the RSFSR, but sparing the non-Russian union republics, deprived of some valuable functions of their self-government and required to exercise greater ethnic self-restraint than the others, who possess all such attributes of autonomy? Or, on the contrary, is the RSFSR synonymous with a USSR to which other republics are just appendages? Does the RSFSR use Union-wide and Union republican institutions interchangeably, and is it thus privileged in comparison to its 14 junior partners, the non-Russian eponymous Soviet Socialist Republics (SSRs)?

To start with, there is a general confusion both in the Soviet Union and in the West about the terms USSR and Russia. Most people view Moscow as the historical center of "Mother" Russia rather than as the Soviet Union-wide, ethnically neutral capital. Few visualize the Academy of

179

Sciences of the USSR as anything but a Russian academy.(2) And, finally, most people see in the Politburo of the Central Committee of the Communist Party of the Soviet Union (CPSU) a Russian rather than a Union-wide institution.

There was a period between the Twentieth and the Twenty-Third Congresses of the CPSU, (Feb. 27, 1956 to Apr. 8, 1966) when a Bureau of the Central Committee of the CPSU for the RSFSR (a substitute SFSR Central Commitee--Tsk) was in existence.(3) Prior to that date, three separate units were in existence within the Central Committee: the above-mentioned RSFSR Bureau, the Administrative Affairs Bureau in charge of other Union republican parties, and a Secretariat in charge of Foreign and Bloc parties as well as of the Army and Navy.

Speaking at the Twenty-Third Party Congress, CPSU General Secretary Leonid I. Brezhnev demanded the abolition of this "purposeless" creation of Nikita S. Khrushchev: "Practice has shown that even in the presence of the Bureau of the CC of the CPSU for the RSFSR, the most important questions concerning activities of krai and oblast' party organizations of the Russian Federation are being considered by the Presidium and Secretariat of the CC of the CPSU."(4) Thus fusion (or confusion?) between parallel Union-wide (USSR) and Russian (RSFSR) authority and jurisdiction is commonplace at the highest levels of government in the Soviet Union.

Almost all the theoretical discussions about the rapprochement and fusion of ethnic groups are based on the assumption that the Russian group acts as the magnetic centerpiece of the process. Only on one occasion has a hypothesis published in the USSR been seen dealing with the possibility of such future fusion taking place around another ethnic group. That was the fusion of Muslim ethnic groups of Soviet Central Asia around the area's predominant and most vital component, the Uzbek groups.(5) The reality of Russian privileges and limitations within the USSR will be examined in six selected fields: language and education, law, administration, army, church, and historiography and terminology.

In the domain of languages, Russian functions not only as a convenient common language in the USSR but, in practice, as the official language of the entire country. Some Union republican constitutions mention other languages as official languages within their borders. Georgians and Armenians were faced in 1978 with the threat of having such an article deleted from their new constitutions, but Moscow backed down.(6) But Russian is the language of all three branches of the USSR's Union-wide agencies (party, government, and Soviet), of the army, diplomacy, federal law, post office, filing cabinet, accounting, and so on. No important career can be pursued, no technical breakthrough recorded, no important decision implemented in another language. All other languages play only limited political and social roles and approximate the importance of Russian only in cultural and social fields, and this within the borders of their respective Union republics and never throughout the USSR as a whole.

In the field of education, the Russian language is obligatory for all pupils in schools of non-Russian eponymous republics. But reciprocity does not exist, and Russian pupils attending Soviet schools outside the RSFSR are no longer required to learn local languages. This is a return to the practice followed in Stalin's time.

Every imperial structure of the past had a master language. Russian was the master language of the Romanov Empire in a more predominant form than it is today in the USSR. But one cannot attribute the dominant position of a master tongue solely or even mainly to forceful imposition, especially in our age of technology, mass media, fast travel, and ever present bureaucracy. The dominance of Russian in the USSR, like that of English in the United States, results mostly from voluntary and/or natural reasons such as the obvious attraction of a widely spoken and internationally accepted idiom. In addition, one must consider the convenience of mastering a language which gives its speakers professional, geographic, and social mobility within the borders of the multiethnic country they inhabit.

Nevertheless, neither mastering Russian as the second language nor linguistic Russification (Russian replacing the mother tongue) results in a loss of the feeling of ethnic identity by the individual (notice the Jewish example) or in lessening resentment against Russian dominance (the Baltic example).

In the judicial field, not only is Russian the language of Soviet federal law, but the laws of the RSFSR often apply outside its borders, something unthinkable in the United States, where state laws never apply outside state borders. Until February 1957, the Criminal Code of the RSFSR covered not only Russia, but Kazakhstan, Kirgizia, Latvia, Lithuania, and Estonia. Its Civil Code reached the same union republics plus Turkmenistan and Tajikistan.(7)

Soviet journals specializing in public administration (such as Sovetskoe gosudarstvo i pravo) tend to discuss Union-wide and RSFSR laws interchangeably. Except for the lowest courts in non-Russian areas, the Russian language is also commonly used in Soviet court proceedings held outside the RSFSR.

The possibility of at least some local differences in interpreting and applying the law cannot be denied. There is better opportunity for private legal or illegal economic initiative in Tbilisi (Georgian SSR) than in Tula or Riazan (RSFSR). And this could not be the case if the almost identical laws in effect throughout the USSR had been uniformly interpreted, applied, and enforced in all places.

A permanent feature of administrative and party arrangements in non-Russian constituent Soviet republics is the staffing of key power positions by Russians. Second party secretaries, heads of special sections, chiefs of the Committee for State Security (KGB), and of communications, of deputy ministries with the task of "assisting" non-Russian ministries locally, heads of enterprises of Union-wide importance and of "post office box" (secret) factories involved in military production are all predominantly Russian. The Slavic Ukraine and Belorussia alone have been mostly exempted from this pattern. Georgia and Armenia were also spared for many years, but this is no longer the case.

The total number of key security positions is quite small and may encompass less than one percent of all the jobs. A much larger category of Soviet jobs outside the RSFSR is subject to "reverse discrimination," with non-Russians enjoying preference over Russians (a subject of numerous complaints by individual Russian residents). Such are the positions of first party secretaries at all levels, most ministerial and governmental positions in general, all public relations jobs, and a number of directorships in local industry and trade. It is more or less certain that, given equal qualifications, a Georgian or Uzbek will not be granted preferential treatment in the RSFSR or in Estonia, but he will suffer no special discrimination either, except on Union-wide levels.

There is a growing tendency to increase the number of Union-republican ministries which function both in Moscow and at the union republic's level, while reducing the number of purely republican ministries which function without Moscow's counterparts. This has been partially compensated for by a reduction in the number of exclusive Union-wide ministries as well. But the administrative tendency toward centralization, so well known to Americans from the federal vs. state power conflicts, is taking place in the USSR. It obviously increases the importance of Moscow-based Russian bureaucrats at the expense of their mostly non-Russian republic homologues. Furthermore, union republics, unlike the states of the United States, have no tax levy power, but are given back a part of turnover tax moneys collected in their territory according to a centrally established, but variable, formula. The formula often tends to favor the non-Russian Union republics, who get back a larger part (or sometimes the totality) of their money.(8) Central Asia and Kazakhstan were allowed to keep 100 percent of the turnover tax that originated in their republics as against 25 percent for the RSFSR. This is something Russians view as another proof of their benevolence toward smaller ethnic groups. Other union republics, however, tend to produce less tax money for each person than the RSFSR, resulting in smaller per person sums available for their budgets, a fact some analysts view as discriminatory.

So far as the Soviet army is concerned, its tradition is totally Russian, despite the growing proportion of non-Russian draftees from a population whose younger generations are becoming increasingly non-Russian. The military command, training, codes, and all other aspects of military life are drawn from Russian prerevolutionary tradition with no allowance for the military past of other component ethnic groups of the USSR. The language of command is Russian; military schools and academies function in Russian. Ranks and uniforms are patterned after the old czarist Russian army. This return to Russian tradition was accomplished during World War II, when most of the international "Soviet" characteristics of military life and behavior were dropped and replaced by pre-1917 Russian ones. Soviet elite regiments follow the same tradition: Guards, Cossacks, and soon "national units," temporarily created in the image of famous Latvian Revolutionary sharp shooters, were soon dissolved.(9) The decree of March 7, 1938, ended "national units." Some were revived during World War II. Molotov's 1945 speech mentions Lithuanian, Estonian, Georgian, Armenian, Azeri and Kazakh formations. The "Military Commissars" of the union republics, a surprising creation of Stalin after World War II, were immediately relegated to mere formal functions, then to oblivion. Furthermore, in non-Russian areas, heads of military districts are usually Russians, Russified Ukrainians, or Belorussians.

Among the higher army personnel, non-Russians are generally not represented in proportion to their population. The figures of Jewish, Latvian, or Georgian revolutionary commanders and commissars such as Yona Yakir and Sergo Ordjonikidze, are memories of the past as are those of Stalin and Leon Trotsky themselves.

Among all the religions in the officially atheist USSR, the Russian Orthodox Church has been the least exposed to discrimination since World War II. It is also the only one (except for some public relations missions abroad by Soviet Muslim clergy) consistently used to further Soviet state interests on the foreign international scene. This policy included such varied initiatives as the reconversion of the Uniates to Russian Orthodoxy in the 1940s, the haggling over the possession of some holy places in Jerusalem, or continuous meddling in Orthodox church affairs abroad.

There is an obvious degree of self-imposed restraint in the exercise of every kind of ethnocentrism in a multiethnic community such as the USSR. Remember Vladimir Il'ich Lenin's invectives against Russian chauvinism and local ethnocentrism. But presently, against Lenin's advice, Russian chauvinism is allowed to flourish more freely. Thus, contrary to the situation in the 1920s and 1930s, outbreaks of Russian chauvinism are less punishable than similar actions by other ethnic groups. In one instance, in 1973, the head of the USSR's Central Committee propaganda agency lost his job merely for his overzealous attempts at silencing the so-called extreme Russian ethnocentrists who published articles directly glorifying czarist generals involved a century earlier in the colonial conquest of Central Asia.(10)

Suppressed now is only Aleksandr I. Solzhenitsyn's style of Russian ethnocentrism advocating, among other things, a physical and spiritual return to old Muscovy and the abandonment of imperial ambitions, in line with the ideas of the Old Believers of past times. St. Petersburg's imperial ethnocentrism becomes the source of Soviet Russian patriotism, with practical distinctions between "Soviet" and "Russian" being blurred. It is considered an inherent Russian right to be patriotic, a right always, at least in part, denied to other Soviet ethnic groups, whose history is respected until the moment it conflicts with Russia's, but never beyond.

A present-day Russian political pamphleteer felt proud of Russia's "burden" and declared:

> There is no, there was no, and there
> will probably be no other nation [ethnic group] in
> the world, that like the Russian people,
> labored and labors for all the people
> of the USSR, and not only of the USSR.(11)

At the same time, the First Secretary of the Central Committee of the Communist Party of Armenia felt compelled to admit his ethnic group's subordinate position as the recipient of Russia's benevolence: "May the sacred hour be blessed when the/foot of a Russian stepped on Armenian soil."(12)

Among the ethnic groups of the Soviet Union, the Russian group is the only one officially entitled to be called great (velikii), an adjective also reserved for powerful foreign nations such as the United States and China and is the only one so labeled in the Soviet anthem. On the occasion of the fiftieth anniversary of the formation of the USSR, Brezhnev called the RSFSR first among equals,(13) a translation of primus inter pares, among other constituent Soviet republics. Thus, he openly stressed if not its privileged status, at least its special position, within the USSR.

Yet, some union republican party secretaries, like Ivan G. Kebin of Estonia and Ivan I. Bodiul of Moldavia, speaking at the Twenty-fifth CPSU Congress in 1976, abstained from using the "older brother" terminology. And only three non-Slavic party secretaries (of Turkmenistan, Azerbaijan and Kazakhstan) obediently repeated Brezhnev's code-word "full unity," a term which recently replaced the even less acceptable "merging" in the lingo of Soviet ethnic politics.(14)

But while the Twenty-fifth CPSU Congress showed significant variations in the degree of conformity to Brezhnev's line in ethnic politics, nobody expects the representatives of non-Russian groups to compete for top positions within the Moscow leadership. Unlike the situation during the 1917 revolution and the 1920s, when many non-Russian leaders did emerge in Moscow, such a possibility is now widely discounted. Few non-Russians rise to high positions in Union-wide organizations, especially within the Central Committee. Nobody expects a Georgian, a Jew, or even a Ukrainian to inherit Brezhnev's chair. A Russified Belorussian is the only possible non-Russian contender. At the Moscow-USSR level it is the Soviet equivalent of an American WASP who has the best chance to reach the top of the career ladder. A non-Russian has hardly any hope outside his own constituent republic.

The recently renewed emphasis on the "new community of peoples, the Soviet People," does not affect the usual Russian ethnic identification with the entire USSR. The formula covers Russian-led and Russian-controlled subordinate ethnic groups in analogy to the relation between the USSR and the non-Russian, ethnic Union republics led by the RSFSR and controlled by Moscow. The term "Soviet People" may be resented by the non-Russians, for whom terms "Soviet" and "Russian" tend to be synonymous, or by those Russian ethnocentrists who prefer to see the Russians' dominant position stressed more openly. But to the average Russian, the term "Soviet" refers only to the social regime of his country, a regime he may either like or dislike, but which carries no threat to his own ethnicity.

Finally, control by Russia exercised through Union-wide agencies and on the spot through specially-selected Russian bureaucrats is the rule of the game. But this does not involve special privileges for individual Russians in non-Russian Union republics nor any personal discrimination against local ethnic groups, except for security considerations.

Thus, the extent of privileges enjoyed by Russians, individually and by their eponymous republic in general, is rather mixed. As a republic, the RSFSR enjoys a privileged position; its citizens, however, enjoy neither superior living standards nor personal privileges. The Russians are the dominant group. Their past, their traditions, and their institutions mark the Soviet way of life. The Russians occupy top Union-wide positions and provide personnel for security-sensitive jobs within other Union republics. But Russians also suffer from a degree of reverse discrimination in those Union republics. Unlike the British and the French empires, the Soviet/Russian system seems to have devised means of securing political domination without socioeconomic privileges for the dominant ethnic group. This might be one of the reasons for its continuous survival, despite growing resentment and unfulfilled expectations of its non-Russian components.

NOTES

(1)   Mikhail G. Kirichenko, Vysshie organy gosudarstvennoi vlasti v RSFSR (Moscow: Izdatel'stvo "Sovetskaia Rossiia," 1968), p. 175; V. I. Shabailov, Upravlenie sotsial'nokul'turnym stroitel'stvom v soiuznoi respublike (Minsk: Nauka i tekhnika, 1974), p. 70.

(2)   Istoriia Akademii Nauk SSSR Vol. I (Moscow-Leningrad: Izdatel'stvo Akademii Nauk SSSR, 1958), starts with vol. I, covering the period between 1724 and 1803.

(3)   "Postanovlenie XII s"ezda kommunisticheskoi partii sovetskogo soiuza o chastichnykh izmeneniakh v ustave KPSS," Izvestiia (April 9, 1966), p. 4.

(4)   "Doklad tov. L. I. Brezhneva 29 marta 1966, XXIII s"ezd kommunisticheskoi partii sovetskogo soiuza," Izvestiia (March 30, 1966), p. 7.

(5)   Klara Khalik, "Rol' kul'turnykh sviazi v ukreplenii druzhby sovetskikh luidei," Kommunist Estonii, no. 9, (1969), p. 35.

(6)   Ann Sheehy, "National Languages and the New Constitutions of the Transcaucasian Republics," Radio Liberty Research Bulletin 97-78 (May 13, 1978).

(7)   Mark A. Shafir, Kompetentsiia SSSR i soiuznoi respubliki (Moscow: Nauka, 1968), pp. 99-100.

(8)   According to The Soviet Economy in Regional Perspectives, edited by N. Bandera and Z. L. Melnik (New York: Praeger, 1973), pp. 99 and 272ff.

(9)   Theofil K. Kis, Le federalisme sovetique. Ses particularites typologiques (Ottawa: U. of Ottawa, 1973), p. 92; V. F. Samoilenko, Druzhba narodov - istochnik mogushchestva sovetskikh vooruzhennykh sil (Moscow: Voenizdat, 1972), p. 54.

(10) Aleksandr Iakovlev, "Protiv antiistorizma," Literaturnaia Gazeta (Nov. 15, 1972), pp. 4-5; Hedrick Smith, "Soviet Said to Punish Party Aide for His Attacks on Nationalism," New York Times (May 7, 1973), p. 8.

(11) Samoilenko, p. 26.

(12) "XXV s"ezd kommunisticheskoi Partii sovetskogo soiuza....Rech' tovarishcha K. S. Demirchiana," [K. S. Demirchian], Pravda (Feb. 29, 1976), p. 5.

(13) L. I. Brezhnev, O piatidesiatiletii Soiuza sovetskikh sotsialisticheskikh Respublik. Doklad. 21 dek. 1972g. (Moscow: Politizdat, 1972), p. 35.

(14) "XXV s"ezd kommunisticheskogo Partii sovetskogo soiuza....Rech' tovarishcha D. A. Kunaeva," Pravda

(Feb. 26, 1976), p. 3; "...Rech' tovarishcha G. A. Alieva," Pravda (Feb. 27, 1976), p. 4; "...Rech' tovarishcha I. I. Bodiula," Pravda (Feb. 28, 1976), p. 5; "...Rech' tovarishcha I. G. Kebina," Pravda (Feb. 28, 1976), p. 6; "...Rech' tovarishcha M. G. Gapurova," Pravda (Feb. 28, 1976), p. 7.

20 Special Status of the RSFSR

Vadim Medish

The Russia-wide Soviet Federated Socialist Republic (RSFSR) lacks some of the official trappings - such as a separate branch of the Communist Party of the Soviet Union (CPSU) and a separate union republic capital - possessed by other component republics of the Soviet Union. This fact symbolizes the failure of Soviet leaders to find an equitable solution to the basic conflict inherent in Russia's history. It is the conflict between a dominating ethnic Russia and the subjugated ethnic groups.

Far from being a case of "reverse discrimination," the absence of the official recognition tokens has always signified a special privileged status of the RSFSR within the "union of equals" - as Soviet spokesmen like to call the USSR. By omission, this anomaly is supposed to convey the same message that the Soviet Union's anthem puts across much more bluntly in its opening lines: "The unbreakable union / Of the free republics / Has been forever bound together / By great Rus'...." Here, Rus' - historic Russia, not merely the RSFSR - is the only ethnic entity mentioned, making its "more-equal-than-others" status quite explicit.(1)

It is a question here not of a historic accident, but of a deliberately conceived and preserved difference. Since the founding of the Soviet Union in 1922, there have been many opportunities to adjust the official status of the RSFSR. The most logical of these opportunities presented themselves in 1924, 1936, and 1977 when three successive Soviet constitutions made their appearance. Indeed, more than 100 different changes in the ethno-administrative structure of the country were implemented, or retroactively approved, on those occasions. The majority of them directly affected the RSFSR, but did not attempt to correct its official image. Only once - immediately after the "second death" of Joseph V. Stalin (in

Nikita S. Khrushchev's secret speech denouncing him in 1956) - was an abortive effort launched to treat the RSFSR on an equal basis. As will be seen, it was a short-lived attempt.

The symbolic meaning of the message has remained the same; the RSFSR - because it serves as a surrogate for Russia - is the central core and the metropolis of the Soviet Union, rather than just one of its component republics. But the practical ramifications of this message have undergone important changes reflecting shifts in Soviet ethnic policy, from a promise of unconditional ethnic independence contained in the 1917 "Declaration of Rights of the Peoples of Russia" to the current emphasis on the creation of a single "Soviet people."

At the beginning, the name "RSFSR" (Rossiiskaia rather than Russkaia in which "Russia-wide" has a geographic rather than ethnic connotation) was used during Vladimir Ilyich Lenin's time for the entire territory under the regime's control. Officially founded in January 1918, the "Russia-wide Federation," as it was usually called, soon became engulfed in a four-year civil war which included separatist efforts of several ethnic groups to break away from traditional Russian domination. By the early 1920s, the Red Army had recaptured the homelands of most of these groups: the Ukraine, Belorussia, Armenia, Georgia, Azerbaijan, and much of Central Asia. At the same time, still quite weak militarily, the Moscow regime was compelled to recognize the independence of some other former Russian-controlled domains: Finland, Poland, and the Baltic groups.

Next, a loose union was formed between the RSFSR and recaptured ethnic lands which had been renamed "Soviet republics." Called contractual agreements, the legal ties between the central administration in Moscow and the recaptured ethnic groups were of an improvised and temporary nature, pending a more permanent solution. That was expected to reconcile the theoretical principles of Marxist internationalism with the interests of the entire Soviet state.

During the last twenty years, much has been written in the Soviet Union about the dispute between Lenin and Stalin on the eve of the founding of the USSR. Stalin, who at that time was officially in charge of ethnic policies, favored outright incorporation of the Ukraine, Belorussia, Armenia, Azerbaijan, and his native Georgia into the RSFSR. Under his plan, called "autonomization," all subordinate ethnic groups presumably were to have the status of autonomous units within the RSFSR.(2) Lenin objected to this scheme, saying that it looked too much like a return to the old Russian Empire. Instead, he proposed the creation of a higher level of administration presiding over a "free union of equal Soviet republics."

Lenin's view prevailed and a new political entity, the Union of Soviet Socialist Republics (USSR) was established late in December 1922. Lenin called the occasion a "declaration of a life-or-death fight against Russian chauvinism."(3) Present Soviet historians see this event as an important victory for proletarian internationalism. But, in reality, Lenin's idea of a new union - or at least its implication - differed merely in semantics from Stalin's notion of an expanded RSFSR. As initially formed, the USSR was comprised of only four components: the RSFSR, which was not cut in size or dismembered; the Ukrainian SSR; the Belorussian SSR; and the newly formed Transcaucasian SFSR, made up of Armenia, Azerbaijan, and Georgia.

No effort was made to break up the RSFSR and admit the various ethnic groups like Tatars and Bashkirs which it encompassed directly into the newly established Soviet Union.(4) Thus, the RSFSR was ensured an overwhelmingly dominating role in the USSR from the very start. Many times larger than other components of the USSR, and possessing almost 80 percent of its population and area, the RSFSR benefited from the official myth that all member republics were equal.

It would be idle to speculate about what could have happened if Lenin had stayed in power longer than he did. It is a matter of record that the creation of both union-wide governmental (1923) and party (1924) agencies was accomplished by simply renaming and elevating the RSFSR's existing offices. But only the first of these transformations was accompanied by the establishment of a new republic-level bureaucracy for the RSFSR. No separate party bureaucracy - central committee, politburo, secretariat, and the like - was even considered at that time for the RSFSR. The apparent inconsistency may have had to do with Lenin's death, which occurred in January 1924, between the time of the two changes. The question of separate capitals for the USSR and the RSFSR was never officially raised before nor after Lenin's death.

The first USSR constitution, closely modeled after the 1918 RSFSR constitution, was published late in 1924. It described the Soviet Union as a federation of "free, sovereign republics," implying that it was "open-ended" and that its membership would grow. However, during the next decade only three new union republics in Central Asia came into existence: the Turkmen SSR and Uzbek SSR (1924), and the Tajik SSR (1919).

In 1936, on the occasion of the publication of the second ("Stalin") USSR constitution, the areas of two more Central Asian ethnic groups were promoted to the rank of union republics: that of the Kazakhs and of the Kirgiz. Rather than follow the precedent of the Transcaucasian Federation, the five

Central Asian Union republics, that shared much more than
mere geography, were not allowed to form a similar federation.
The concept of regional coalition was no longer in favor, and
the Transcaucasian SFSR was disbanded. The new Soviet
constitution listed all ten non-Russian union republics,
including Armenia, Azerbaijan, and Georgia, as separate
components of the USSR, without distinguishing between those
that did or did not have recognized ethnic subentities within
their borders. In 1936, eponymous union republics with a
federated structure were: Azerbaijan, Georgia, Tajikistan,
Ukraine, Uzbekistan; the Ukraine lost this status in 1940.

The RSFSR, however, retained its special status as a
federation encompassing homelands of the Russians and several
other ethnic groups with territories ranked as autonomous
republics, autonomous oblasts, or "nationality okrugs" (ten of
the last, all in the RSFSR, were renamed "autonomous okrugs"
in 1977). Now inequality of ethnic groups became codified and
written into the supreme law (constitution) of the country.
What the 1917 Declaration had called unlimited rights of
ethnic groups to self-determination, including secession, was
reduced by the 1936 Soviet constitution to a limited cultural
autonomy granted on the basis of the official rank of a given
group and under the formula: "National in form, socialist in
content." The union republics alone were promised the right
to secede, but no legal procedure was provided for its
implementation.

The next decade witnessed many and frequent changes in
the ethnic map of the country involving not just administrative
division and semantic nomenclature, but also forced deportation
and resettlement of entire ethnic groups. With the annexation
of three Baltic republics and elevation of Karelia and Moldavia
to SSRs, the number of union republics rose to sixteen - a
result of territorial expansion and purely political moves
designed to intimidate neighboring countries. (In 1956, the
Karelo-Finnish SSR was demoted to Karelian ASSR, reducing
the number of union republics to the present 15).

But by far the most important change in Soviet ethnic
policy of that period involved the official attitude toward
ethnic Russia, past and present. It occurred almost overnight
as a direct result of the mortal danger that Stalin's regime
faced during the initial phase of the German invasion.
Assuming that Lenin had been sincere in his pledge to fight
Russian chauvinism, this was one war that his heirs lost.
Ever since that time, Russian ethnocentrism has been an
integral part of Soviet ideology. During World War II, Soviet
mass media, literature, and arts depicted Russia as the natural
leader of all other Soviet ethnic groups. Russia's imperial
past was completely rehabilitated and Russian war efforts were
singled out for special praise. In official speeches of the
Soviet leaders, as well, references to Russia and to the USSR
began to be used interchangeably.

In a curious way, the openly unequal status of the Soviet ethnic groups, including those whose names labeled union republics, was reflected in international politics of the mid-1940s. On Stalin's insistence, in addition to the USSR as a whole, two Soviet union republics - the Ukraine and Belorussia - became full members of the United Nations. Stalin, who initially had demanded membership for all 16 Soviet union republics and none for the USSR, accepted this compromise calling for three Soviet representatives, including one from the USSR as a whole. The reason for omitting the RSFSR from the formula was crystal clear: the USSR was in Stalin's eyes synonymous with the RSFSR and, hence, with Russia.

In the wake of Khrushchev's de-Stalinization campaign ten years later, a half-hearted effort was made to liberalize ethnic policy. Most, but not all, deported ethnic groups were restored to their historic homelands and non-Russian officials were appointed to top positions in ethnic territories. In 1957, a separate Bureau was established for the RSFSR's portion of the Communist Party of the Soviet Union (CPSU), as if to put the Russian federated republic on the same footing with other union republics. And four years later, Khrushchev created a special commission as well to prepare a new, presumably more liberal and rational, constitution.(5) It is not known whether any of these changes in ethnic policy contributed to Khrushchev's political demise in 1964. But it is significant that one of the first actions of his successor was to abolish the RSFSR's party Bureau and to slow down the work on a new Soviet constitution. Since then, nothing further has been done to standardize the special status of the RSFSR.

The new ("Brezhnev") Soviet constitution, adopted only in 1977, is a mixed bag of old and new notions concerning the ethnic question. It shows little evidence of more rational and equal treatment of ethnic problems. The special status of the RSFSR has been preserved fully. Under the new constitution, the RSFSR continues to dwarf the other 14 ethnic union republics.(6) The new Soviet constitution also continues to list the component republics of the Soviet Union in a seemingly irrational order that defies explanation. Of course, the RSFSR heads this list, which establishes protocol for all official functions and occasions.

The 1977 constitution contains the promise of continuing ethnic autonomy under the formula: "national in form, socialist in content." And it retains the old allegation concerning the right of union republics to secede (Article 72) solely to justify the lower status of autonomous republics given to homelands of several large ethnic groups. In this way, one fiction supports another fiction: to be able to secede, a union republic must have outside borders or access to an open sea; conversely, ethnic territories deep inside the RSFSR or USSR that cannot meet this requirement must be content with the status of autonomous republics.

The meaning of all of this is clear; the USSR is not moving toward a more equitable ethnic policy. On the contrary, the slogan "the all-out building of Communism" means that ethnic pluralism must be eventually replaced by countrywide unification. From an ideological point of view, quite limited ethnic diversity is tolerable only during the lower phase of "socialism," but not under "communism."

The official schema for this new phase of sociopolitical development envisages the creation of one, homogeneous, Soviet ethnic group by gradually consolidating and blending all present ethnic groups. In theory, this means "de-ethnization" of the entire population including Russians, through the accumulation of new communistic traits expected to submerge completely and supersede ethnic differences and peculiarities.

Given the realities of Soviet ethnic policy, the net result of the new emphasis on creating a single "Soviet People" will be further Russification of ethnic groups. The future Soviet People is expected to be "communist in content, but Russian in form." To this extent, the advent of communism in the USSR yet holds special promise for Russian ethnocentrism. At the same time, it condemns subordinate Soviet ethnic groups to de-ethnization and assimilation. All members of the future Soviet classless society are expected to be Russian communists.

In the meantime, during the transition to communism, the difference between first-class and second-class Soviet citizens is likely to depend progressively on the degree of conformity to both aspects of this ideal model, which is Russian communist. This gives the ethnic Russians a natural advantage, while encouraging non-Russians to assimilate faster. The centripetal forces that promote assimilation now include ideology, in addition to economic, educational, and social factors. These methods of demographic engineering are turning Russia's traditional melting pot into a much more efficient pressure cooker.

Ethnic Russians and completely Russified members of subordinate groups, such as the Belorussian Andrey A. Gromyko and Ukrainian Andrey P. Kirilenko, dominate all major policy-making bodies in the USSR. The percentage of Russians in the Communist Party of the Soviet Union (CPSU) as a whole, and especially in its ruling councils - the central committee, politburo, and secretariat - is greater than one-half. The same imbalance is seen in the USSR council of ministers and other top government agencies. In terms of positions of power and prestige, native and naturalized Russians are doing much better today than at any other time since 1917.

It is the ethnic Russians who can most readily identify themselves with the USSR's global posture of superpower.

And, while there are obviously different perceptions of ethnocentristic pride, many Russians feel that Soviet economic and technological achievements are both rooted in Russia's historic past and serve Russia's future ethnic interests. This is a view evidently shared by the "neo-Slavophile" author, Vladimir Soloukhin, and contributors to such official Soviet publications of Russian ethnocentristic bent as Nash sovremennik and Molodaia gvardiia.

Many members of the growing Soviet "new class," regardless of their ethnic origin, see the Russian language and culture as symbols of their ethnic origin, their privileged status, and behave accordingly. This is especially true of the party-government bureaucracy, but also frequently applies to the formally non-Russian professional intelligentsia. This tendency enriches ethnic Russia at the expense of the subordinate groups and, in the long run, threatens to undermine such group resistance to further assimilation by attrition.

Today, Russification already is a phenomenon of unprecedented proportions in one important area: the question of linguistic preference. A comparison of the 1959 and 1970 USSR censuses shows that a growing number of non-Russians claims Russian as its mother tongue. The number of such linguistic converts is estimated at between 15 and 20 million, including several million of those who no longer speak their native language. In addition, at least 45 million other members of subordinate ethnic groups consider Russian to be their second language.(7) Within the context of Soviet ethnic policy, the expressed preference for the Russian language, bilingualism, and the loss of one's ethnic tongue are supposed to represent stages of irreversible assimilation.

Most vulnerable to Russification are members of ethnic groups who live outside their territories or belong to groups who do not possess eponymous territories within the USSR. The first category includes more than 10 million Ukrainians and Belorussians, as well as members of many smaller groups. The second category consists mainly of Germans, Jews, and Poles. These displaced ethnic groups, regardless of where they live, are pressed into using Russian as a means of communication and education. For their cultural needs they must depend on Russian culture, because only Russian culture is exportable within the Soviet Union.

The process of Russification is aided by a large contingent of Russians who permanently live in non-Russian territories. This contingent is estimated at 40 to 45 million and it is steadily growing. Russians already outnumber the eponymous ethnic groups in a majority of the fourteen ASSR's, six autonomous oblasts, and ten autonomous okrugs of the RSFSR (see Appendix A). In one of the non-Russian Union republics, Kazakhstan, their proportion is as high as 42 percent.(8)   The Russian influx into urban centers in Asian parts of the USSR is especially heavy.

Such current demographic trends as urbanization and migration from the European to Asian parts of the country break up traditional non-Russian communities and contribute to a sharp increase in mixed marriages.   The number of interethnic marriages rose from fewer than 5.5 million in 1959, to almost 8 million in 1970, and to an estimated 10 million today.(9)   In an overwhelming majority of such unions, one of the partners is Russian, and, as a rule, their children are brought up as Russians (see Chapter 37).   This contributes further to the process of Russification.   Of considerable significance is the fact that a disproportionately large number of mixed marriages involves the Soviet elite.

Not all ethnocentristic Russians would react positively to indiscriminate Soviet assimilation.   But in official and semiofficial Soviet publications of ethnocentric bent, the word "Pan-Russians" is being used with increasing frequency and with reference to all assimilated and assimilating members of other ethnic groups living in the USSR.   Faced with a declining rate of natural growth, the Russians may find assimilation the only alternative to the threat of losing their dominant position.

How many members of other ethnic groups, how easily, and how fast the Russian group can assimilate them without becoming completely diluted are moot questions.   The historic record credits the Russians with an unusual capacity to absorb large numbers from other ethnic groups.   Playing the role of "big brothers" and making converts to their culture has been practiced with considerable success for many centuries by both Moscow rulers and frontier Cossacks.   Ethnic Russia always has been expansionist, "color-blind," and open to converts from another culture.   Names of converts to Russian culture can be found in every chapter of its history and in every field of endeavor, including the highest levels of political power and artistic achievement.   Perhaps not too surprisingly, many of these converts have been "more Russian" than native Russians themselves.   This, however, does not mean that the newcomers to ethnic Russia have not, in turn, contributed certain durable qualities to Russian group character.   The same, undoubtedly, will be true in the future; assimilation of large numbers of non-Russians is bound to produce lasting effects of an unpredictable nature in the Russians as a group.

It is unlikely that sporadic manifestations of ethnocentrism among non-Russians can, in the long run, stop Russification. Although statistically the subordinate Soviet ethnic groups are rapidly approaching the half-way mark in the USSR's population, as a whole they continue to be much less than the sum total of the parts.   The regime makes sure that the non-Russians have no means for collaboration or joint action.

In fact, Moscow often manages to play the subordinate groups against each other. Thus, for example, the direct cause for a manifestation of Georgian ethnocentrism in 1978 was not the threat of immediate Russification, but an attempt to raise other ethnic-group tongues spoken in the Georgian union republic to the level enjoyed by the Georgian language.(10) By the same token, the first waves of migrants to new localities in Central Asia are often not Russian, but Ukrainian and Belorussian, who play the role of Russian "Kulturträgers."

In terms of Marxist dialectic, the continuing anomaly that distinguishes the RSFSR from the rest of the USSR's component republics is progressive, because it symbolizes an advance from ethnic diversity and a trend toward consolidation and eventual blending into a single ethnic group. In terms of Soviet ethnic policy, the special status of the RSFSR stands for a Russian solution of the inherited problem of multi-ethnicity.   As Russification of subordinate groups gains momentum, the RSFSR (Russia), is likely to become more and more synonymous with the entire USSR. In this way, political symbols, including such silent symbols as the RSFSR's lack of certain official attributes parallel to those in other Union republics, will catch up with changing Soviet reality.

NOTES

(1)   "Lyrics for Soviet Anthem Revised, so People no Longer Have to Hum," New York Times (Sept. 1, 1977), p. A2.
(2)   P. N. Pospelov, Istoriia kommunisticheskoi partii sovetskogo soiuza (Moscow: Politizdat, 1970), Vol. 4, Book 1, p. 199.
(3)   V. I. Lenin, Sobranie sochinenii (Moscow: Politizdat, 1961, 5th ed.), Vol. 45, pp. 350–62.
(4)   P. N. Pospelov, ed., Vol. 4, Book 1, pp. 199 and 282.
(5)   Leonid Ilyich Brezhnev, (in English), (Moscow: "Moscow News," 1976), p. 30.
(6)   "Constitution (Basic Law) of the Union of Soviet Socialist Republics," Pravda and Izvestiia (Oct. 8, 1977), pp. 3–6, in The Current Digest of the Soviet Press XXIX, no. 41 (Nov. 9, 1977), Articles 71, 85, 87, pp. 7–8.
(7)   Naselenie SSSR, edited by A. Ia. Boiarskii (Moscow: Politizdat, 1974), pp. 99–104.
(8)   A. Ia. Boiarskii, pp. 90–95.
(9)   V. A. Boldyrev, Itogi perepisi naseleniia SSSR (Moscow: "Statistika," 1974), pp. 36–38.
(10) Ann Sheehy, "The National Languages and the New Constitutions of the Transcaucasian Republics," Radio Liberty Research Bulletin no. 19 (May 12, 1978), p. 12.

21 Comment — The Impact of Common RSFSR/USSR Institutions

Seweryn Bialer

The proposition that the lack (in the RSFSR) of certain union republic institutions is detrimental to Russian ethnic identity sounded interesting at first reading because one never thought about it (see Introduction). After thinking about it, it is easy to agree with Professor Vadim Medish (Chap. 20) that the proposition is a misstated concern about a real case of reverse discrimination. There is no merit in it as it was advanced. The proposition is overstated, for there is some separate political identity with regard to the Russians and the Russian institutions in the Soviet Union, in newspapers for example, a very important entity. Although there is no separate bureau or there is no separate branch of the party, this does not mean that within the leadership there is no division of labor, that there are no large groups who are concentrating exactly on the RSFSR or on the Russian regions, just as there are those who concentrate on other regions. So, it is somewhat overstated to say that the constitutional reality does not completely reflect the political reality. The chapters by Professor Michael Rywkin (Chapter 10) and Professor Medish make a strong argument against the proposition. Generally, it is possible to agree with them. There is little to add to what they say.

Agreeing, though, with the general argument against the proposition does not imply specific agreement with the chapters. All of the disagreements point in one direction: to an overestimation of the degree of Russian control and Russification in the USSR. It is easier to agree with what Professor Rywkin has written here than with some of his earlier statements. To strengthen the tenor and the general direction of his argument there are a number, not all, but a number of remarks which are simply overstatements about the question of Russian domination within the USSR. There is no doubt about the domination, without even going into it. This is an obvious fact that anybody who studies the Soviet Union knows. If the degree of domination, assimilation, and everything else were as high as Professor Medish, for example, asserted, there would have been no political problem for the Russians. But there is a major political problem, a long range political problem. The Russian leaders find themselves in the long range in a difficult situation. In the medium range, everything is soluble, but in the long range, probably it is not soluble in its present form. So, in this sense, the overstatement of the problem removes the political aspect, the political problem, from the arena of concern.

The statement in Professor Rywkin's article, which he has modified now, about the degree of domination of the Russian bureaucracts over the non-Russian republics seems to be a tremendous overstatement. One must take the non-Russian elites very seriously. In Georgia or Armenia it is no longer the case that there is no domination by the local elites. There is an overwhelming domination by local elites in Georgia and Armenia. Forget about union republics in general and go ahead republic by republic. There are differences, but there are some union republics where the domination by local elites is very great, and in all such republics the trend in the last twenty years has led with zigzags toward a greater role for local elites, but this has not been achieved. If it had been, there woud be no major elite problem in the ethnic question.

Professor Rywkin's position with regard to assimilation is correct. To make a statement, like the one Professor Medish is making, that bilingualism means irreversible assimilation, is unacceptable. Bilingualism hardly proves anything; it not only does not prove assimilation, it proves nothing. If one lists the Russian language as one's mother tongue it proves something, but bilingualism does not. The problem is that there are two points that should be made about the Soviet ethnic question and the relations between Russians and non-Russians from the point of view we are now discussing, questions that are politically important. First, the duality of Soviet ethnic policies, despite all the zigzags, remains that they are policies that on the one hand are providing a dominant role for the Russians, and on the other hand providing a formal expression, formal administrative divisions, which make the growth of dissent against Russian domination possible. And secondly, and more important, is the question about the influence of economic development, and development in general, on the ethnic question. And here the hopes of the Soviet leadership, the hopes expressed from the 1920s onward, are not fulfilled. The whole idea that Union-wide development leads to a melting pot is not true. Union-wide development has produced contradictory results. It leads, in some respects, to greater assimilation and, in others, it provides a growth of local elites or local intelligentsia. Thus, it supplies a basis for the increase of separateness and autonomous desires by the non-Russian elites in their search for power, anti-Soviet power sometimes and but not always necessarily.

Finally, a last remark addressed directly to the proposition: Does it mean that the question of the lack of Russian separateness in political institutions is unimportant? No, it is important, but from a different perspective, from the reverse perspective of the one that was posed. From the point of view of ethnic identity, there is no problem, but from the point of view of political implications of ethnic separateness, there is a lot of difference in whether or not there are separate political institutions. The lack of separate institutions is a form of domination as it is expressed now. But the lack of separate Russian political entities as pronounced as those for other ethnic groups in the Soviet Union makes more difficult or even impossible the solution of the ethnic question on the political plane in the Soviet Union. It works in the same way as, for example, it functioned in the Yugoslavian case. Therefore, in the short and medium run, the present arrangements point to the strength of the Russians and to their ability to delay a political solution to the multiethnic character of the Soviet state in the political arena. In the long run, this kind of an arrangement precludes a political solution, because without the separateness of Russians and without the separateness of Russian institutions, a real federation of equals cannot be created.

22 Comment — What Russia Lacks: Symbolism or Legitimacy?

Leopold Labedz

The conception that the Russian ethnic group suffers debilitating "deprivation" through the absence of some institutions labeled "Russian" in the USSR is probably formulated in a way to provoke some answers which possibly are not even being considered here, except by Professor Michael Rywkin (Chapter 19). One scholar after another has been laboriously rejecting the proposition, but the proposition is an obvious non-problem (see Introduction). To talk about deprivation, for instance, in the context of the institutional arrangements of the Soviet Union, as some do, is simply to misunderstand the situation. Ask a simple question: Why, then, was there no change in this arrangement when there was, for over 55 years, an opportunity to do so? Or, even more, pushing the contention to its logical conclusion: What would happen if, as a matter of fact, this "deprivation" could be rejected now and changed? It would be quite obvious to a political infant that such an arrangement would not mean the strengthening of the Soviet position, strictly speaking. On the contrary, it would mean in one way or another a weakening of potential Russian ethnocentrism.

This raises, of course, the question that Professor Ladis Kristof mentioned in his article (Chap. 24), that is, that the focus on the problems now arising in the Soviet Union to a greater point of intensity are truly not to be seen entirely through the spectacles of ethnicity. The proposition is a misleading formulation, which intends to be neutral. Through this linguistic neutrality, it really contributes to confusion, because problems of ethnicity are not the same as problems of "nationalism" or potential "nationalism." The intensification of ethnicity is a polite way of saying that there is a possibility of the rise of ethnocentrism, whether Russian ethnocentrism or that of subordinate ethnic groups. The real problem is not, obviously, whether there is some kind of a situation in which the Russians are undergoing an identity crisis which puts them on the verge of losing their ethnic identity. If a visitor from Mars read this exchange, he could not really tell that we are discussing whether the Russians face problems that anybody conversant with Russian history would recognize as non-problems. The Russians are not facing any such danger, and, indeed, if some 60 years of Soviet history testify to anything, it is only to the durability of this ethnic identity as it has persisted throughout Russian history. But, as a matter of fact, there is a rise, to a certain extent, of Russian ethnocentrism, just as there is a rise in other ethnic groups' feelings and possibly the rise of their ethnocentrism. Now, that is why the real analysis of the genuine problems as they exist now should start with bypassing the focus on ethnicity proper and ask the question: Where does one go from ethnicity to potential "nationalism," and what are the social, political, and other conditions which, in fact, may mark such a passage? Obviously, it would not be something which could be answered in a sort of inclusive way for all Soviet ethnic groups. Dr. Seweryn Bialer (Chap. 21) is quite right to note that the problems look different in various union republics, but that these problems existed from the very beginning. The duality of the Soviet state and duality of Soviet ethnic policies all along had to face this question and try to diffuse it somehow in different ways throughout these 60 years. This does not mean that analyzing the question now does not require some kind of greater sharpness.

This leads to the last point to be made: It does not deal simply with either the matter of ethnicity alone or the problems of a "nation state" which may eventually, through some kind of assimilation, acculturation, or integration - these three things are, of course, different - bring about a Russification of the Soviet Union and the re-creation of the Russian Empire without the need for any form of legitimation other than Russian ethnocentrism. This is precluded by the very nature of the Soviet Union. There is a question here which has to be faced by the Soviet leadership. This dilemma cannot be resolved in the long run simply through Russification. Obviously, releasing the genie of Russian ethnocentrism from the bottle also releases the genies of subordinate groups' ethnocentrists in various union republics and among different non-Russian groups. The problem of ethnocentrism is not a matter of economics. You can have higher or lower levels of economic development. You have got Georgian ethnocentrism in Soviet Georgia, for instance. This is not a difficulty, as Professor Rywkin mentioned, of linguistics. You have the rise of Irish ethnocentrism when the native language has been lost. You have got a numerically small group dominating the British Empire. The English ruled over a vast area in the nineteenth century while being a minority of the population. So, it is not a question of 49 percent or 51 percent of the Russians, as Professor Robert A. Lewis (Chap. 26) rightly noted. This is a question which has something to do with the nature of the state and the long-term process of legitimation of that state. And that, of course, is, as the English author would have said, quite a different story.

VI

Locating the
Ethnic Frontier

Proposition 6: Neither the present RSFSR
nor USSR as such provides the Russians,
staunch adherents of the idea of homeland,
with a symbolic territory which offers an
emotional attachment precise enough for their
ethnic needs today.

23 Economic Development of the Russian Homeland: Regional Growth in the Soviet Union
Ralph S. Clem

economic growth

Since the time of Vladimir Il'ich Lenin, the Soviet government has advocated policies designed to promote economic growth in non-Russian areas of the USSR, principally for the purpose of reducing disparities in the level of developments among the various ethnic territories of the country.(1) Through pursuing such policies, it assumed that economic development in formerly disadvantaged regions would lead to the integration of the indigenous, non-Russian population into the emerging modernized society. The country was expected to arrive via this route at an approximate socioeconomic leveling along ethnic lines. These policies are based conceptually on the Leninist notion that ethnic discontent would be exacerbated by the perpetuation of socioeconomic inequalities among ethnic groups inherited from the czarist regime, and particularly from the disparities between Russians and non-Russians.(2) Thus, in the new scheme of things, it was felt necessary to insure that "...special attention [be given] to the peoples trampled on by the ... Russians of the Tsarist Regime."(3) By implication, therefore, regional economic growth in the Soviet Union was to take place in such a way as to favor non-Russian over Russian areas. At least in theory, the Soviet government has had the ability, through the medium of state control over economic planning and capital investment, to achieve this goal of interregional equalization by directing resources toward underdeveloped areas of the country.

The purpose of this analysis is to determine to what extent Soviet regional economic development practice has conformed to the policy of promoting greater relative growth in non-Russian areas. Beyond the scope of this inquiry is a systematic treatment of the extent to which economic development in non-Russian areas has led to the socioeconomic advancement of the non-Russians themselves. It is well documented that Russians have established favored positions in many non-Russian areas, particularly in cities, and mainly in those of Kazakhstan and Central Asia.(4) The focus here will be placed on ethnoterritorial rather than ethnic group development. The latter does not necessarily follow from the former. Has the Russian homeland (and, indirectly, the Russian) benefited disproportionately from membership in the Soviet "federation": compared to the non-Russian homelands (and, indirectly, non-Russians)? The relative or comparative aspect of this question, that is, the Russian versus non-Russian side, is important. In the absolute, material sense, all regions and ethnic groups of the USSR have experienced advances in many respects. But that is not now, nor has it ever been, the point addressed conceptually or explicitly by Soviet policy. Rather, the success or failure of policies and programs of the Soviet government in this critical regard must be judged according to the degree to which the development gap between the Russian homeland and non-Russian regions has been closed.

What is meant by "Russian" homeland and "non-Russian" regions? The use of the Russia-wide Soviet Federated Socialist Republic (RSFSR) as a surrogate for Russian homeland is inappropriate, because its vast territory is subdivided further into 16 major and 15 minor non-Russian units. As "Russian" will be considered, hereafter, all units of the RSFSR not constituted as Autonomous Soviet Socialist Republics (ASSRs). The non-Russian Autonomous Oblasts (AObs) and Autonomous Okrugs (AOks) of the RSFSR are treated here as Russian areas, inasmuch as the population of these units is small and predominantly Russian, and the areas themselves peripheral and administratively subordinate to Russian units (see Appendix A).

The population of this Russian homeland amounted to some 111 million persons in 1970, with about 89 percent of that figure accounted for by ethnic Russians - over 75 percent of all Russians in the Soviet Union. By comparison, no union republic (SSR) eponymous ethnic group comprises a higher percentage of the population of its respective unit than do the Russians (89.4 percent) in the RSFSR outside the ASSRs (although the Armenians, at 88.6 percent, come close). At the ASSR level, only the Azerbaijanians in Nakhichevan account for a larger share of the population than the Russians in their homeland as here defined.(5) Thus, the Russians are concentrated in and dominate this area numerically, lending credence to this consideration of the RSFSR, without its ASSRs, as the "unofficial" Russian homeland. For these purposes, "non-Russian" areas are defined as the 14 non-Russian constituent union republics of the USSR and the 16 non-Russian ASSRs of the RSFSR.

Given this division between Russian and non-Russian units, next comes the task of adducing data representing the phenomenon of comparative socioeconomic advancement. To satisfy this requirement, from Soviet and other census materials, a set of socioeconomic data has been derived. It permits tracing regional development trends on a relatively refined geographical scale from the early period of Soviet dominance to the present. Until recently, problems of consistent definition and of comparing territories have severely limited longitudinal geographical analysis of socioeconomic phenomena in the Soviet Union. For example, radical changes have occurred in both the state's territory and the internal political-administrative units in which census data are presented. That renders impossible making meaningful, direct, regional comparisons between different times. To solve these problems, data from the 1926 Soviet census were reordered into administrative units used in the later (1959 and 1970) censuses of the USSR. These estimates form the empirical base for this study.(6)

Utilizing these data, two measures based upon the growth and redistribution of the urban population of the USSR will be employed as indicators of the extent of regional development. The first measure is the level of urbanization of each geographic unit, the variable being defined as the percentage of the population of each unit living in urban centers at some specified time. Because the census definition of "urban" changes from time to time (and in some cases among units of the same census), operationally "urban" was defined as any place with a population of 15,000 persons or more. Urbanization is not the perfect surrogate for development; for one thing, the relationship in coordinate space between development and urbanization is not linear, but rather describes an S-shaped curve. However, levels of urbanization related to levels of development tend to be more nearly linear in the intermediate stage of modernization, which is the phase that the USSR has been in during the period covered here.(7) Urbanization is linked both conceptually and empirically to other commonly used measures of development such as nonagricultural employment and per capita income. For example, in the Soviet case, the level-of-urbanization variable for 142 political-administrative units correlated highly with a variable representing the share of the work force engaged in nonagricultural pursuits for three recent census years: $r = .945$ for 1926, $.890$ for 1959, and $.853$ for 1970.(8) Assume that the level of urbanization variable is related closely and positively to socioeconomic development and is a good surrogate for that broader process. Higher levels of urbanization will be regarded as evidence of higher levels of socioeconomic development, and vice versa.

The major shortcoming of the level-of-urbanization variable is the extent to which it can be influenced longitudinally by differential change in the denominator among regions. Thus, a region with a low rate of rural population growth may experience significant urbanization as economic development takes place, whereas a region characterized by a high rate of population growth in rural areas might show only a small change in the level of urbanization despite substantial economic development. This kind of demographic situation has characterized the Soviet Union. Since about the time of World War II, marked differentials have emerged in the rate of rural population growth among regions of the USSR. To take an extreme case, between 1959 and 1970 the rural population of southern Central Asia (the Uzbek, Tajik, Kirgiz, and Turkmen republics) grew by 37 percent, while, during the same period, the rural population of the three Baltic republics (Estonia, Latvia, and Lithuania) declined by six percent. Such disparities in growth will influence comparisons of change in the level of urbanization among regions. In the case of Central Asia, rural growth reduces the "visibility" of urban growth, whereas in the Baltic republics, urbanization is arithmetically enhanced by rural population decline. Such dramatic differences in rural population growth obscure analysis of interregional shifts in development which could presage equalization.

To meet this difficulty here, a second measure is utilized. It is based on the geographic distribution of the urban population and is defined as the share of the Union-wide urban population accounted for by each unit. This variable will be termed urban distribution. The assumption here is that the Union-wide urban population will "redistribute itself" toward regions of development as time passes. One objection to this measure is that interregional shifts in the distribution of the urban population may be influenced by differential urban natural increase. In fact, there are substantial differences in urban natural increase among regions of the contemporary USSR. For example, in 1970, the ratio of children age 0-9 for every 1,000 women aged 20-49 (a census measure of fertility) in urban areas ranged from a high of 1,444 in the Turkmen SSR to a low of 524 in the Latvian SSR.(9) To control for this factor, the urban distribution measure was refined to include only those in the age group 20-39. That procedure reduces the impact of differential natural increase (which particularly affects the youngest age groups). Utilizing this particular measure, an increase in the share of the Union-wide urban population accounted for by a unit or aggregation of units will be considered to indicate higher than average change in socioeconomic development. A decrease will be considered a decline relative to the Union-wide trend. Taken together with the level-of-urbanization variable, the urban-distribution measure should provide at least an approximate answer to the question about relative ethnoterritorial development.

Trends in the level-of-urbanization index indicate that,(10) according to this measure, the Russian homeland has experienced substantially greater socioeconomic development than non-Russian areas of the USSR. In 1926, the percentage-point gap between Russian and non-Russian territorial units was 2.2; whereas by 1959, the margin had increased to 13.7; and by 1970 to 16.3 percentage points. Viewed another way, during the period from 1926 to 1970, the level of urbanization in the Russian homeland increased by 41.4 percentage points, but the comparable figure for non-Russian areas was 27.3. In no case did any non-Russian union republic exceed the change in the level of urbanization for all Russian units during the entire study period (1926-1970), although the Armenian and Kazakh constituent republics were not far behind. Yet, four non-Russian union republics did outstrip the Russian homeland during the intercensal period (1959-1970). In large measure, this was because of absolute declines in the rural population in these units (the three Baltic republics and Belorussia). By 1970, the Russian homeland (the RSFSR exclusive of ASSRs) was the most urbanized ethnoterritory in the USSR. This makes a sharp contrast with the situation in the early Soviet period (as illustrated by figures for 1926), when the Russian homeland ranked fifth.

The urban distribution index provides another perspective on the question, one not biased by differential rural growth.(11) Data here indicate that the Russian homeland increased its share of the urban population during the first decades of the Soviet regime. But recently this trend has been reversed. The urban population of the country became relatively more concentrated in Russian units between 1926 and 1959, but between 1959 and 1970 the urban population of non-Russian units grew at a faster rate than in the Russian homeland. On a regional basis, the recent above-average, non-Russian, urban growth was almost totally restricted to Kazakhstan and the ASSRs of the RSFSR. If the spatial redistribution of the urban population is an indicator of regional economic growth trends, then from these figures it would be inferred that the Russian homeland developed economically at a greater pace than the remainder of the country during the earlier period. In later years, the impetus shifted geographically toward certain non-Russian areas. Over the entire time span, a small positive balance remains for Russian areas with regard to urban redistribution.

The two gross categories of Russian and non-Russian regions disguise significant internal variation. In terms of both urbanization and urban distribution, there have been marked regional differentials within the Russian homeland and within the non-Russian territories of the USSR. Prominent among areas of development in Russian units have been the Urals, Volga, and Siberian regions, whereas older Russian territories to the west have, for the most part, languished economically. In the non-Russian realm, major development has occurred in the eastern Ukraine, in Kazakhstan, and in some of the ASSRs of the RSFSR (mainly those in the Volga and Urals areas).

Summarizing the quantitative evidence: Disaggregating the Soviet Union into Russian and non-Russian areas discloses a marked divergence in terms of the level of urbanization. This indicates that little progress has been made in effecting equalization in this measure along the critical ethnoterritorial dimension. The urban distribution variable points to some recent absolute equalization. The difference between the level of urbanization and urban distribution patterns is largely a reflection of high rates of population growth in rural areas of most non-Russian units. Those rates offset the shift of urban population toward these units in terms of a relative measure.

The combination of these measures suggests an actual increase in interregional (ethnoterritorial) inequality during the first three decades of Soviet dominance. It is reflected by the redistribution of the urban population toward Russian units and the divergence of the level of urbanization between Russian and non-Russian areas. Those areas of the country undergoing rapid development, measured both by changes in the level of urbanization and urban-distribution variables, were mostly Russian units. In the period 1959-1970, movement occurred toward interregional equalization, measured by a shift of urban population toward non-Russian areas. Only the level-of-urbanization variable, split between Russian and non-Russian units, continues to reflect growing inequality, owing mostly to the effects of differential, rural population growth.

Specific patterns of regional development shed some light on the spatial nature of economic growth in the USSR. They suggest answers to the questions, posed earlier, regarding ethnoterritorial equalization of development. The Soviet government has yet, after more than six decades of rule, to effect closure in the level-of-development gap between Russian and non-Russian regions. Probably, the principal reason for this lack of success is that the non-Russian territorial development policy was not the only concern of economic planners and decision makers, particularly in the prewar period. In addition to the policy of promoting growth in non-Russian areas, it was also necessary to give simultaneous consideration to maximizing aggregate economic growth and the building up of heavy manufacturing, and to take into account strategic military factors in the spatial allocation of scarce investment funds. Regarding location, these goals often proved to be mutually exclusive. Thus, the well-known emphasis put on heavy industry in the Soviet economy in the early five-year plans favored those regions already possessing natural resources for such industries as iron and steel. The need for resources close by to operate heavy industry, therefore, constrained planners and limited choices of location to the Urals, the eastern Ukraine, Siberia, and later, to Kazakhstan.(12) Likewise, strategies designed to raise aggregate economic output in the shortest possible time discouraged investment in underdeveloped regions where incremental capital-output ratios were high. This gave an advantage to established industrial zones such as the Leningrad and Moscow regions.(13) Finally, threats of invasion and aerial bombardment apparently did much to limit investment in western border areas before World War II.(14)

Altogether, these conflicting pressures on the process of decision making about locations favor areas of the country within the Russian homeland. However, as the Soviet economy increasingly moves into sectors other than heavy manufacturing (such as chemicals, electronics, and machine production), the location of industry becomes less constrained. Such flexibility facilitates the geographic dispersal of economic activity. This is evidenced by the most recent changes in urban distribution. Also, economies of scale will eventually be lost with increasing agglomeration in older regions of development. Concentration of industry in interior zones makes less sense than it did before the age of mutually-assured destruction through intercontinental nuclear-armed missiles. To be expected, therefore, might be a continuation of the trend toward economic growth in some relatively underdeveloped non-Russian areas.

The overt, political-administrative manifestation of Russian territory may be less clear than in the case of many other ethnic groups. The Russians have, nevertheless, benefited from the economic progress achieved by the USSR to a greater degree than others making up the Soviet Union. Principally, but not exclusively, this has come about through the development of the Russian homeland. Although the reasons for this situation must be inferred, they appear to result from economic, strategic, military, and geographic influences, not out of some conscious design to better the lot of Russians at the expense of non-Russians. In the Soviet situation, "urban-industrial" translates into higher incomes and generally higher standards of living than "rural-agricultural." Typically, industrial wages are higher than those in other sectors. Services, which constitute a large share of real wages in the Soviet Union, are in much greater supply in urban than in rural areas. Thus, in general the higher levels of industrialization and urbanization which characterize the Russian homeland mean socioeconomic advantages for the

Russians relative to most non-Russians. The material well-being of the Russians offsets, to a great extent, whatever insecurities they might feel from the pressures of dominant majority status. It is also clear that socioeconomic considerations alone would not necessarily suffice to qualify a region or territory as an entirely adequate ethnic homeland.

It has been demonstrated elsewhere that significant interregional leveling of economic development has taken place in the USSR.(15)   True in the purely statistical sense, this point overlooks the ethnoterritorial basis of the Soviet Union. It fails to note that much of the interregional economic equalization has taken place within the Russian homeland, leaving most non-Russian areas relatively behind. In a multiethnic state such as the Soviet Union, where ethnicity is defined mainly in territorial terms, the fortunes of the ethnic groups become inextricably linked with the development of their respective homelands. Lenin recognized with considerable insight that disparities in development among different ethnic groups could result in conflict. He insisted on devising policies designed to raise the level of development in peripheral areas of the USSR inhabited by non-Russians. To date, such policies have not resulted in accomplishing this goal. The position of the Russian ethnic group remains relatively better than the situation of other Soviet groups in the development of an ethnoterritorial homeland.

NOTES

(1)   Vsevolod Holubnychy, "Some Economic Aspects of Relations Among Soviet Republics," Ethnic Minorities in the Soviet Union, edited by Erich Goldhagen (New York: Praeger, 1968), pp. 50-120; Iu. V. Arutiunian, "Izmenenie sotsial'noi struktury sovetskikh nastii," Istoriia SSSR, no. 4 (1972), pp. 3-4.

(2)   V. Rutgaizer, "Torzhestvo leninskoi natsional'noi politiki v ekonomicheskom stroitel'stve," Kommunist, no. 18 (1968), pp. 24-35.

(3)   Holland Hunter, Soviet Transportation Policy (Cambridge: Harvard University Press, 1957), p. 22.

(4)   Ralph Scott Clem, "The Impact of Demographic and Socioeconomic Forces Upon the Nationality Question in Central Asia," in The Nationality Question in Soviet Central Asia, eidted by Edward Allworth (New York: Praeger, 1973), pp. 35-44; Robert A. Lewis and Richard H. Rowland, "East Is West Is East...Population Redistribution in the USSR And Its Impact On Society," International Migration Review, XI, no. 1 (1977): 3-29; Robert A. Lewis, Richard H. Rowland, and Ralph S.

Clem, Nationality and Population Change in Russia and the USSR (New York: Praeger, 1976), Chapter 10.

(5) Itogi vsesoiuznoi perepisi naseleniia 1970 goda. Natsional'yi sostav naseleniia SSSR (Moscow: Statistika, 1973), IV: 12-19.

(6) R. S. Clem, "Estimating Regional Populations for the 1926 Soviet Census," Soviet Studies, XXIX, no. 4 (1977): 559-602.

(7) Chauncy D. Harris, Cities of the Soviet Union (Chicago: Rand-McNally, 1970), Chapters VII and VIII; Robert A. Lewis and Richard H. Rowland, "Urbanization in Russia and the USSR: 1897-1966," Annals of the Association of American Geographers, LIX, no. 4 (1969): 776-96.

(8) Ralph Scott Clem, "The Changing Geography of Soviet Nationalities and Its Socioeconomic Correlates: 1926-1970," Unpublished Ph.D. Dissertation, Columbia University, New York, 1975, Chapter IV; Allan Rodgers, "The Locational Dynamics of Soviet Industry," Annals of the Association of American Geographers, LXIV, no. 2 (1974): 229.

(9) V. I. Kozlov, Natsional'nosti SSSR (Moscow: Statistika, 1975), p. 171, Table 25.

(10) Ralph Scott Clem, "The Changing Geography...," Ch. IV, appendices I and II.

(11) Ibid.

(12) Theodore Shabad, Basic Industrial Resources of the U.S.S.R. (New York: Columbia University Press, 1969), pp. 35-44.

(13) Holland Hunter, Soviet Transport Experience (Washington: Brookings Institution, 1968), pp. 18-30.

(14) I. S. Koropeckyj, Location Problems in Soviet Industry Before World War II (Chapel Hill: University of North Carolina Press, 1965), Chapter 5.

(15) I. S. Koropeckyj, "Equalization of Regional Development in Socialist Countries: An Empirical Study," Economic Development and Cultural Change, XXI, no. 1 (1972): 68-86.

24 The Concept of Homeland
Ladis K.D. Kristof

The Soviet Union's policy toward the culture (in the broadest sense) of the multitude of its ethnic groups is based on the principle "national in form and socialist in content." The "national in form" is permissible, the "socialist in content" is imperative.

The "national" form is considered to be a heritage from history, more exactly: a survival of the past. The socialist content on the other hand, is the present that is being forged: the future in the process of superseding the past. The past cannot be shaped, but the present and future can (whether in the mold of the past or in contrast to it). Consequently, our (as distinct from that of our ancestors') consciousness and will are irrelevant to the objective existence of the accomplished fact of our historical heritage, though they are, of course, highly relevant to our subjective acceptance of it. Our consciousness and will mold the present and future largely on the basis of how and what we have subjectively accepted from the past. This is why non Marxists, as well as the Marxists, speak of historical continuity but why the latter strive for a discontinuous continuity. The socialist content parading in a "national" form is always tormented by irreconcilable contradictions and is at best incongruous. Only within an international form can the full development of the socialist synthesis be truly consummated. A "scientific" acceptance of the objective historical past permits a dialectical trascendence of the continuity-discontinuity, "national-international" contradictions.

To sum up, the Soviet formula satisfies, or at least is tolerant toward, those cultural needs related to the past. It is intransigent in its insistence on defining the needs related to the culture of the present and future. It follows that certain distinctions must be drawn, in order to consider the questions raised by the proposition that neither the present RSFSR nor the USSR gives the Soviet Russians a homeland precise enough to be adequate for their ethnic needs today.

The most important such distinction is that between ethnic and "national" needs. Ethnic (folk) groups are the product of history primarily in a passive way; an individual simply happens to be a member of an ethnic group and a carrier of its material and spiritual culture (language, customs, dress, art, and the like). The needs of the ethnic group are an outgrowth of down-to-earth practical requirements related to its basically undynamic, conservative nature. The group is essentially a commune, and in order to survive as a whole (and facilitate the material and psychological survival of its individual members) it requires primarily the cultivation of continuity with the past, not a vision of the future. Hence, the laws of the polity must not suddenly alter the customs and cohesiveness of the group and should tolerate a considerable degree of customary values and behavior. What the group needs is respect for its customs as of old, not an autonomy vesting it with the right to legislate new rules of behavior. Things new come from without, not from within, and are accepted as the doings of an outside force to which, as to forces of nature, a person must bend.

"Nations (nationalities)," on the other hand, are the product of history and self-determination. They have an active attitude toward both the past and the future. The historical heritage is not something that simply is (and weighs upon the present) for it is selectively accepted and rejected. In other words, "national" history is not what is but what ought to be in terms of a conscious vision of the future. Thus, a "nation" is a society, more exactly, a political society, and membership in it is the result of a self-conscious act of will - of a political decision. "National" culture is ultimately political, too, for to be "national" it must express and reflect, even if only very indirectly, not merely the "nation's" static self-image molded by past experiences but also its future-oriented image tied to a sense of dynamic purpose and mission. A Quebec poet, Gaston Miron, recently said: "Any culture that does not have a political expression is destined sooner or later to retreat and become simply ethnic or folkloric."(1)

Ethnic group membership is something largely external, that is, visible and objectively observable. An outside observer can determine to what group somebody belongs by noting what language, customs, dress, furniture, architectural style, and other artifacts he favors. "National" membership, on the other hand, is rather an internal decision. The use of English (or at least the accent) may tell us that somebody feels Irish or English, American or Australian, but not necessarily. Jawaharlal Nehru spoke Oxford English to fight

Englishmen. By all cultural externalities he was an assimilated
Englishman until he made the conscious decision to light a
bonfire of Western clothes, books, and other paraphernalia on
the front lawn, don Indian grab, and become an Indian
"nationalist." Taras Shevchenko preferred to use Russian
when writing his private diary, yet, at the same time,
deliberately stirred the Ukrainian soul with fiery patriotic
poetry.

One of the major issues in the dispute between Slovenes
and Germans in Carinthia is the question of objective versus
subjective criteria of "nationality." "The Slovene
organization . . . insist that the way to tell a Slovene is by
his ancestry, language, and other 'objective criteria' and not
as the Heimatdienst would have it, by his voluntary and
democratic 'confession' that he wants to be one."(2)

A further important distinction needs to be made between
homeland and "national" homeland. Homeland is the land of
one's home, where one personally feels at home. It may be
the land of one's ancestors. It is not necessarily one's
fatherland (motherland) in the political sense, for it may be
located in someone else's "national" fatherland. In other
words, to love one's homeland may mean to love a foreign
fatherland, or at least a part of it. To display attachment to
one's homeland often involves localistic patriotism scorned by,
or even treasonable in the eyes of, "nationalists." In every
"multinational" area there always is tension between the
impulsive feeling of closeness to and trust in all of one's
coinhabitants and the consciously "national" duty to
discriminate, to separate in one's heart the mere coinhabitants
(whose presence possibly should be deplored) from the
legitimate coinhabitants, the "conationals" whom alone ought to
be loved and trusted.

The "national" homeland is not possessed by individuals
but by a "national" group. Neither the sons nor their fathers
may have been born in, or even ever have seen, that which
they choose to call "fatherland." While the ties to a personal
homeland are always direct and concrete, they often operate
chiefly spontaneously and on a subconscious level. The ties to
a "national" fatherland, on the other hand, may be abstract,
but are always consciously willed or at least consciously
accepted. Because the strongest ties are those that are the
product both of consciousness and of subconsciousness, of
spontaneous inclination and of willed dedication, the state
builder's ideal is found where the personal homeland merges
and overlaps with the "national" homeland, and vice versa.
Hence, the ideal of "nation-state": a compact state rooted in
individual and collective experience, in a lived in past and a
hoped for future, where the land of the fathers is also the
political fatherland.

Can a large state be at the same time an adequate homeland and fatherland? Can a "multinational" state generate feelings that are proper for both homeland patriotism and "national" patriotism? The official ideals of Soviet man and Soviet patriotism attempt to transcend homeland patriotism as well as "national" patriotism. From a Marxist point of view both are obsolete and the second is, in addition, off course. But it does not mean that either of them is, in fact, dead. There are signs that both attempt to reassert themselves with a vengeance. Condemned and frustrated, they may never succeed in reasserting themselves, only in frustrating the realization of the offical ideology. And so, the Soviet Union, including the RSFSR, may continue to sail like a flagship without a genuine flag.

NOTES

(1) Henry Giniger, "Gaston Miron, Poetic Voice of Quebec Nationalism," The New York Times (April 2, 1978), p. 52.
(2) Dennison I. Rusinow, "Nationalism Today: Carinthia's Slovenes, Part II: The Story of Article Seven," Fieldstaff Reports, American Universities Field Staff, Southeast Europe Series, XXII, no. 5 (Oct. 1977): 3.

25 Ethnic Significance of the Non-Black Earth Renovation Project
Daniel Vanderheide

When Leonid I. Brezhnev announced the opening of a massive developmental plan for the non-black earth region of the RSFSR in 1974, Soviet Russian officials were openly ecstatic.(1) For too long, the authorities contended, Russia's ethnic center had been neglected. With the creation of this special zone, the Russian ethnic group was provided with a symbolic territorial unit suited to its increasing ethnic needs as a federated member of the Soviet Union. Discussions concerning the general and particular problems that Russians face could now be treated within the context of problems confronting the non-black earth region. The creation of this unit also helped assuage fears about greater Russification among the outlying ethnic groups, for it appeared that interest in Russian ethnic difficulties would be concentrated on this region. And, more important, the living conditions of Russian rural inhabitants would finally be given the attention that conservative guardians of Russian culture had been demanding.

It can be hypothesized that the creation of this territorial unit serves a wide range of ethnic and economic needs confronting contemporary Russia, and that these needs may not necessarily be contradictory but are, in fact, complementary. The rural economic conditions of the non-black earth area are severely depressed and have needed attention for years. Yet the desire to improve the economic plight of the historic Russian countryside was championed not only by demographers and economists, but by those in many other sectors of Soviet Russian society. They saw the economic renovation of the region as only one part of a larger process - creation of a symbolic homeland for the Russian people. It would be within the framework of discussion concerning that symbolic homeland that issues such as ethnic

Russia's place within an increasingly complex society could be raised, the new interest in earlier Russian artifacts could be focused and directed, and conservative guardians, anxious over the erosion of Russian traditions, could have a forum.

Many sectors of Soviet Russian society have taken part, and continue to do so, in the discussions concerning the total character of the non-black earth project, yet it is noteworthy that a prominent economic planner would describe the region this way: "The predominant part of the non-black earth region consists of the territory which represented the historic nucleus of the Russian state."(2) And a distinguished Soviet demographer would feel compelled to remind his readers that: "The basic political and economic nucleus of the Russian state was formed in the non-black earth region. This zone by right became the fundamental base for the development of a national economy, culture and the country's resources."(3) To Russians living within the region, within the RSFSR or in the USSR, the Union-wide attention focused on the agricultural development of the historic Russian plain means the symbolic renovation of the ancient Russian homeland.

As early as General Secretary Brezhnev's first speech before the Central Committee in 1965,(4) he declared that the party would devote more attention to this central Russian region. This became part of the general "Brezhnev line" for agriculture, a policy which included the establishment of guaranteed wages and higher incentives designed to slow the rapid flight of trained youths from the countryside.(5) With the announcement in 1974 of the developmental plan, General Secretary Brezhnev proceeded to adhere to the logic of his overall agricultural line. By doing so, he certainly won the support of conservative Russian party officials in the region, but at the expense of considerably slowing down rural investment in other Union republics of the Soviet Union. The Union-wide growth in agricultural spending during the tenth Five-Year Plan (1976-1980) is considerably slower than it was under the ninth Five-Year Plan (1971-1975). But the growth of investment in the non-black earth region during the present Five-Year Plan is conservatively estimated to be over twice the USSR standard.(6) Whether such a vast shift of capital to the non-black earth region can be fully exploited is by no means certain, yet the party seems prepared to take the risks involved.

Despite all the material incentives the earlier reforms of 1965 had offered, the strength of various demographic currents had not waned by 1970, as had been hoped, but had increased. As recently as 1974, it was apparent that the rate of outmigration from the non-black earth countryside and from the entire non-black earth zone had increased. Census statistics for 1970 showed three basic demographic trends:

1)   the massive concentration of population in the cities of Moscow and Leningrad and the newer cities of the southern Urals;
2)   the flight of trained youths from the countryside to urban areas, leaving an unusually aged rural population; and
3)   the general outflow from the non-black earth region as a whole.(7)

The actual territorial unit, the non-black earth, includes 29 oblasts and ASSRs concentrated within the westernmost part of the RSFSR, and is home to 44 percent of the population of that entire constituent republic. It is, as one Soviet planner described, "the territory which had represented the historic nucleus of the Russian state."(8)

These demographic phenomena are a direct reflection of the region's position, geographically and historically, in Soviet Russia. In this century, the area's population has been battered by two world wars, a famine, a civil war, and, more recently, the administration's desire to invest heavily in industrial potential outside the region. These have produced a staggering decline in the area's living conditions. Farm lands under cultivation before World War II still lie dormant today. The agricultural goods produced under arduous and often unprofitable conditions in the region have only recently been adequately subsidized.(9) In short, life in the non-black earth countryside meant a poor standard of living and small, dying villages with few cultural or educational facilities. And, until recently, it signified a severe rural numerical imbalance of sexes.(10)

The demographic developments described above are a reflection of the general worldwide trend, but in the non-black earth area they are distorted by the region's recent history. The younger Soviet generation is undergoing a complex set of basic changes in attitude. Contemporary young Russians are escaping from the backwardness of their countryside and viewing it scornfully, as a place suitable only for those who are unfit. This has been accompanied by a general indifference to their ethnic heritage, and substituting for that heritage, material standards. Television and urban conveniences became the contemporary icons of Russian society, and serving as goals popular among the young, alarmed considerably older Soviet administrators. Anxious to maintain their self-confidence in their position as the glue which holds all Soviet society together, Russian administrators wished to pass on their ethnic heritage to a young generation of Russians, but felt largely frustrated in their efforts.

A number of official agencies, pressured for action to confront the situation throughout the 1960s, became openly active after Brezhnev's 1965 Central Committee speech. Many party officials dismissed by Khrushchev, during his last years, returned to the Central Committee with their restored positions. Among them were seven party chairmen from the non-black earth region. All attacked Khrushchev's agricultural policy, particularly in relation to the non-black earth land, described by an official of Kirov oblast, as "our vast, immemorably Russian lands."(11) But he went on in his praise for the new attention to the non-black earth and singled out one group that was especially responsible for this change: "This includes writers also . . . .They love and know the countryside. They can see the changes occurring in it and share with their readers their valuable, artistically-based observations."(12) His observations were correct. Throughout the early 1960s, members of the writers' union had been engaged in debating the relationship of the countryside and the Russian people, a debate that still continues. Numerous village prose writers detailed the precarious living conditions in the countryside, and warned that fundamental, irreversible changes were taking place in the attitudes of rural inhabitants, particularly the young.(13)

Even more dire prophesies of ethnic doom were being heard from one group publishing its view in samizdat writings, the "Veche group." In an article entitled "Russian demographic problems,"(14) a samizdat author, in 1975, vigorously argued for a conservative Russian ethnocentrism quite unlike anything Western eyes expect to see in a samizdat source. Basing most of his evidence upon demographic phenomena from the non-black earth area, the samizdat author sees as the truly striking and important aspect of the most recent census reports, the "catastrophic fall of the birth rate in many regions of the RSFSR."(15) He cites Pskov oblast as an example where the natural rate of increase had fallen to 0.6 per thousand, which is also characteristic of Kalinin, Smolensk, Kostroma, Novgorod and many other regions of Russia. (This compares with a natural increase of 9.2 per thousand throughout the USSR and 5.9 per thousand in the RSFSR. The rate of natural increase in Union republics ranges from 3.3 per thousand in the Latvian SSR to 28.6 in the Turkmen SSR.)(16) The samizdat author concludes that the indexes of Pskov oblast "can be viewed as a small model of all Russia. Yesterday's demographic conditions in Pskov are being repeated today in many regions of the RSFSR."(17) After considering data analyzing the rate of population growth throughout the USSR, he concludes that the very "ethnic health"(18) of the Slavic people is subject to concern.

In an effort to explain this ethnic crisis, the same author reviews developments in the Russian countryside. The wage level and weather conditions, he says, have adversely affected the economic conditions of the rural worker in northern Russia, especially in comparison to the rural worker of Central

Asia. Russian farmers, he felt, bore the highest costs of Soviet history, from World War I through the Russian Civil War and World War II - all "blows which inflicted a heavy toll on the psychological and physical health of the Russian nation."(19) These many setbacks could have been overcome had not the demographers and administrators been fundamentally mistaken in their classification of the farming populace as a "backward and reactionary part of the ethnic group."(20) The author clearly implies that the Soviet administration's failure to understand the vital importance of farmers to the society's ethnic health had led to a general feeling that official policy has drifted for a period and still remains confused. He reminds the planners that Karl Marx himself regarded the countryside as "the reserve fund for the revival of ethnic strength,"(21) an opinion a leadig Soviet sociologist has been said to have rephrased in these terms: "The nation shares the fate of the peasantry." The process of rapid urbanization and rural flight threatens Russian ethnicity because it drastically affects the rate of natural reproduction.(22) The very survival of the Russian people seems at stake when the observer says, "the cause of the degeneration of the Russian nation is the dying out of the countryside."(23)

> On the enormous spaces of the greater Russian oblasts, one village after another dies silently . . . . Many homes are forgotten, in others only one elderly person lives. One rural school after another closes . . . . Not one mother, not one father calculates that the children will become kolkhozniks.(24)

Whether other Russians felt as threatened as this author did is uncertain. During a 1975 conference of economists and demographers held in Moscow State University, the most widely accepted view was that the demographic situation in the non-black earth region and in the Soviet Union as a whole was beyond purely legal countrols. One economist stated that "the natural population decline is related not only to a decline in the birth rate, but to a large-scale migration of the rural population, particularly the young, to cities or other parts of the country."(25) He added that "measures are being undertaken to bring order into the population's migration within the Nechernozem."(26)

Another legal expert asserted that a change was necessary in the present legislation: "The entire system of legal and economic measures should be directed toward encouraging families with two and three children."(27) That the benefits of such legal measures would greatly aid the Russian population and, indeed, all of the western USSR as opposed to Central Asia, where family sizes are so much larger than in the Soviet west, was not mentioned by the speaker, but would certainly be the effect of such a policy. What the official Soviet legal authority is calling for would hardly be inconsistent with the sentiments of the samizdat author quoted above, that is, a legal and economic incentive to raise the birth rates within Russia and other western, predominantly Slavic, sections of the Soviet Union.

A major role in the developmental plan was officially assigned to the Young Communist League (Komsomol). Although their involvement in the region, and, indeed, in the revival of interest in the Russian rural worker as a whole, had been less than enthusiastic through the late 1960s and the early 1970s. With the official announcement of the campaign, the Komsomol openly moved to the fore in championing it. All of the large construction projects were to be assisted by local and visiting Komsomol "brigades." Local "brigades" were instructed to sponsor festivals and rural excursions to acquaint the local young people and their visitors with ethnic treasures of the region. Announcements in Komsomol journals detailed various job opportunities in the region, and young readers were assured that, "there, they could work the land their fathers had worked."(28) Journals directed toward Russians in their early teens stressed the beneficial aspect of rural work and family ties with articles such as "The father's land is protected by the son."(29)

As discussions concerning the project developed, undercurrents of Russian ethnic self-assertion began to appear regularly. In one 1975 article, entitled "Kaluga land," the author lamented that he "had been to the Pamirs, but never to Riazan, he had been to Samarkand but never to Ivanovo, to Kamchatka but not to Kostroma."(30) He proceeded to describe the role of Kaluga and the non-black earth region as a whole in the development of Russian history, art, and music. As a source of inspiration, he pointed to "the beauty of the Russian land, covered (in Kaluga) by mixed Russian forests" and he asked, "what is more beautiful on earth?"(31)

The series of articles devoted to the non-black earth region continued to appear throughout 1976 with similar descriptions and interviews from Smolensk, Novgorod, Tula, Orel, Vladimir and Briansk, among other areas. This constant presentation of places and objects immediately recognizable to Russians as symbols of their cultural and ethnic identity characterizes the Komsomol literature about the region. This makes such literature similar to the expressions of attitudes of the Russian Society for the Preservation of Ancient Landmarks. The tone of one Komsomol article about the non-black earth region clearly displays affinities between the official party youth agency and the semi-official Russia-wide Society for the Preservation of Historical and Cultural Landmarks:

> The non-black earth region - the native land of white-trunked birches. And together with this symbol of Russia - maples, spruces, pines, willows with ash trees, a dozen other arboreal types and bushes, all make up our mixed forests and our uniquely beautiful landscape. . . .(32)

The Komsomols' enthusiasm with the project surely stems, at least in part, from a growing fear that demographic conditions in the non-black earth countryside went out of control and that Russian youths had to be convinced of their duty to the state to work in those rural areas. But the constant presentation of the region in maps, medals, songs, and literature, using obvious ethnic symbols, seems to indicate that the fealty the Komsomol leaders are appealing to is devotion to "age-old Russian loyalties" more than economic needs of the state. What is more remarkable about these appeals to ethnic Russian loyalty is that they come from a journal whose editorial board is composed of the highest Komsomol officials, including former Komsomol First Secretary Evgeniy M. Tiazhelnikov, now head of the CPSU Central Committee's Department of Propaganda.

Soviet propangandists are unquestionably using ethnic Russian symbols to promote economic goals of the state. What is important is that 60 years after the "internationalist" revolution, the Soviet leadership would use ethnic Russian symbols and still find them effective.

While the Young Communist Leaguers were busy preparing work detachments to be sent into the countryside, the state publishing houses were developing a series of publications aimed at the young concerning the region's history. In an interview, a minister of the RSFSR state committee for publications described the emphasis in the printed material: "Our great contemporary deeds rest on the deepest stratum of ancient ethnic traditions, founded and nurtured in the great cradle of central and northern Russia."(33) In the non-black earth region were the forests, lakes, and rivers that "perfected the ideals of the ethnic group (narod) and gave birth to its ethnic treasures."(34) The official follows the course of Russian literary history and demonstrates how inextricably linked it is to this region, from "Song of Igor's Host" through Aleksandr S. Pushkin, N.A. Nekrasov, Leo Tolstoy, and Fedor M. Dostoevsky. Out of this great ethnic tradition, he suggests, have come the strongest social and moral elements:

> On the native Russian land arose the first breeding ground of native industries, and the renowned strength of Russian science was acquired. . . .
> The central non-black earth was the cradle of three

revolutions,   most   important,   Great   October
(1917).(35)

By the state's actions, he feels, it has rightfully pledged to
preserve these qualities. He concludes: "The vanguard of
the Russian people has long dreamed of transforming the
non-black earth region."(36)
        Various state publishing houses have responded to the
reclamation project in different ways. The publishing house,
Soviet Russia (Sovetskaia Rossiia), in order to encourage the
preservation of ethnic treasures in the region, has begun
publishing a new series, "Writings from the countryside," and
has sponsored a number of continuing competitions for the best
poetry and prose about the non-black earth region.
        Probably most significant is the attention that literature
for juveniles has achieved. In addition to the daily Komsomol
newspapers, a bi-monthly Komsomol publication targeted at
young readers has featured regular articles describing the
responsibilities and opportunities for young people in the
non-black earth region. In that journal, party officials have
chided teachers for not stressing the "morally-uplifting"
features of farm labor, and stressed repeatedly that rural
librarians must display writings concerning the non-black earth
more prominently and recommend them to young readers. At
least one state publishing house has declared that it is the
obligation of Soviet writers to strengthen contacts between
young people and the countryside and to develop among the
young a sense of love for the land. The countryside,
according to one official, is of "fundamental importance in the
moral formation of young people."(37) It is, therefore, the
duty of literature to acquaint the young and particularly the
very young "with the nature of the non-black earth
countryside."(38) To meet this critical need, publishing houses
had already distributed 300 million copies of children's literary
books and magazines devoted to this region during 1975.(39)
        The non-black earth developmental plan, by focusing
Soviet-wide attention on the traditionally Russian plain, serves
to provide Russians with both a specific and symbolic
territorial unit that can offer a focused emotional attachment
for their contemporary ethnic needs. The non-black earth
region may not be an actual microcosm of the demographic,
economic, and social developments that contemporary Russia is
undergoing, but to form an effective symbol of Russia, its
heritage and future, the region does not need to be an
absolute replica or microcosm of contemporary Russia or
Russians within the Soviet Union. Symbols involve manners of
perception which have extraordinary power to overlook
objective reality.
        The Russian farmer is reassured by the non-black
earth campaign that he, too, is taking part in historic projects

directed toward developing a new Soviet society. He can be
confident that the labor he devotes to his soil is as worthy as
the construction of great railroad lines through Siberia or the
development of millions of acres of virgin soil. The Soviet
press, in fact, continuously repeats that the non-black earth
is the second Virgin Lands Project. And, in a uniquely Soviet
way, the developmental plan is truly a second Virgin Lands
Project. Throughout Soviet history this central and northern
sector of the RSFSR has borne the highest human and physical
costs. Some sixty years after the establishment of the Soviet
Union, attention and capital are returning to the lands which
formed the basis of Imperial and Soviet Russia - the traditional
Russian plain. This comes at a time when, among Russians
(particularly the young), interest in their ethnic history is
rising. One Komsomol official remarked: "Indeed, it seems
unwarranted to call this region virgin territory. It long was
the historic center of Russia, not an abandoned place, but a
livable region. . . ."(40)

Perhaps the best summation of the party's attitude toward
the relationship between the project and Russian ethnic
identity was given at the recent Eighteenth Union-Wide
Komsomol Congress by its First Secretary, B. N. Pastukhov:

> The development of the non-black earth is not simply
> construction, but developing a zealous relationship to
> the land, cultivating higher yields on it. All the
> development of agriculture in this zone is the vital
> responsibility of the Komsomols, as it was in the
> Virgin Lands. . . . The non-black earth will become
> the joyous home of the working man, augmenting the
> wealth and beauty of this immemorial Russian area,
> which is figuratively known as the heart of Russia
> (serdtse Rossii).(41)

The upswing of Russian ethnocentrism during the late
1960s and early 1970s, particularly one so conservative and
obsessed with rural, ancient Russian, was an expression of
anti-modernism and anti-Marxism. It was also an expression of
a need felt by Russians to possess a symbolic continuity
between ancient Russia and the contemporary Soviet state.
The symbol that best expresses that continuity is the
non-black earth zone - the homeland of ethnic Russia.

NOTES

(1) "O merakh po dalneishemu razvitiiu sel'skogo khoziaistva
     nechernozemnoi zony RSFSR," Pravda, April 3, 1974), p.
     1.

(2) A. N. Gladishev, Proizvoditel'nye sily nechernozemnoe zony RSFSR (Moscow: Mysl', 1977), p. 238.
(3) Vladimir I. Staroverov, Sotsialno-demograficheskie problemy derevni (Moscow: Nauka, 1975), p. 246.
(4) Leonid I. Brezhnev, "Miting na krasnoi ploshchadi. Rech' tovarishcha L. I. Brezhneva," Pravda (March 24, 1965), pp. 1-4.
(5) Alec Nove, "Soviet Agriculture Under Brezhnev," Slavic Review, (Sept., 1970), pp. 1-24.
(6) Calculated from David W. Carey, "Soviet Agriculture: Recent Performances and Future Plans" in Soviet Economy in a New Perspective (Washington, D.C.: U. S. Government Printing Office, 1976), pp. 575-600. These figures indicate increased investment in the non-black earth region will be 79.5 percent greater than during the ninth Five-Year Plan, while overall USSR investment will grow by only 32.7 percent during that same period.
(7) Itogi vsesoiuznoi perepisi naseleniia 1970 godu. Natsional'nyi sostav naseleniia SSSR Vol. IV (Moscow: Statistika, 1974).
(8) A. N. Gladishev, p. 238.
(9) Ibid.
(10) Anatolii V. Topilin, Territorial'noe pererapredelenie trudovykh resursov v SSSR (Moscow: Ekonomika, 1975), p. 76.
(11) B. Petukhov, "Urozhainyi marsh," Literaturnaia gazeta (March 30, 1965), pp. 6-12.
(12) Ibid.
(13) Fedor Abramov, "Vystuplenie uchastnikov s"ezda. . . Fedor Abramov (Leningrad)," Literaturnaia gazeta (June 30, 1976), p. 11.
(14) K. Voronov (pseudonym), "Demograficheskie problemy Rossii," Arkhiv samizdata, no. 2040 (1975), p. 126.
(15) Ibid, p. 116
(16) Murray Feshbach and Steven Rapawy, "Soviet Population and Manpower Trends and Policies," in Soviet Economy in a New Perspective, p. 123.
(17) Vonorov, p. 117.
(18) Ibid, p. 120.
(19) Ibid, p. 124.
(20) Ibid, p. 124.
(21) Ibid, p. 126.
(22) Ibid, p. 128.
(23) Ibid, p. 129.
(24) Ibid.
(25) A. F. Shebanov, "Pravovye aspekty demograficheskoi politiki," Sovetskoe gosudarstvo i pravo no. 1, (Jan. 1975), pp. 28-29.
(26) Ibid.

(27) G. I. Litvinova, "Pravovye aspekty demograficheskoi politiki," Sovetskoe gosudarstvo i pravo no. 1, (Jan. 1975), pp. 33-34.

(28) "Fomiruem eshelon dobrovol'tsev. Pamiatka dobrovol'tsa," Komsomol'skaia pravda (Dec. 17, 1975), pp. 1-2.

(29) I. Norkina, "Ottsovskoe pole berech' synoviam," Komsomol'skaia zhizn', no. 2, (Jan. 1978), pp. 18-19.

(30) Ia. Golovanov, "Zemlia kalyzhskaia," Komsomol'skaia pravda (Dec. 17, 1975), p. 2.

(31) Ibid.

(32) Viacheslav Pal'man, "V dobryi put', Nechernozem'e," Znamia (March, 1975), p. 164.

(33) N. V. Sviridov, "Nechernozem'e: problemy i knigi," Molodaia gvardiia no. 4, (1976), pp. 10-31.

(34) Ibid, p. 12.

(35) Ibid, p. 11.

(36) Ibid, p. 12.

(37) Ibid, p. 22.

(38) Ibid, p. 25.

(39) Ibid, p. 13.

(40) V. Iaroshevets, "Nechernozem'e: tvoia tselina," Iunost', no. 2, (Feb. 1976), pp. 3-5.

(41) "Otchet TsK VLKSM i zadachi Komsomola po formirovanie u molodezhi kommunisticheskoi soznatel'nosti, gotovnosti, voli i umeniia stroit' kommunizm; Doklad pervogo sekretaria TsK VLKSM B. I. Postukhova," Pravda (April 26, 1978), p. 3.

26 Comment — Factors Overriding Ethnicity in the Non-Black Earth Zone
Robert A. Lewis

Implicit in the proposition that neither the present RSFSR nor USSR offers the Russians a sufficiently precise ethnic attachment today is the contention that a homeland is vital as an objective factor in defining ethnicity. The best way to determine this is through comparative research, which has generally demonstrated that such objective factors as religion, homeland, and language do not adequately define ethnicity. Others maintain that subjective factors which contribute to an intuitive sense of group identity are the most important. Professor Walker Connor (in a private communication) has pointed out that, although subjective factors are more important, both schools have overly dichotomized the issue and objective factors contribute to the sense of the vital uniqueness of ethnic identity. Ethnicity can survive and intensify without a homeland. Immigrant countries such as the United States of America and Australia demonstrate this. Without considerably more evidence to the contrary, it is not reasonable to assume that the Russian homeland is not geographically precise enough to fulfill their ethnic needs, or that the existence of non-Russian ethnic enclaves within the RSFSR is a disturbing factor, or that the homeland must be precisely delimited to exclude all other ethnic groups. This is not to deny, of course, that homelands are viewed with intense emotion.

The purpose here, however, is not to investigate this issue, but to put the development of the non-black earth zone in a broader perspective. Nevertheless, over 80 percent of the population of the RSFSR is Russian, and most of them live in predominantly Russian areas. This is particularly true of the rural population. There is also a tendency for the dominant groups in a multiethnic state to view the whole country as its homeland. A Frenchman thinking of France would probably not exclude Brittany as a part of his homeland.

The reason for the increased rural investment in the non-black earth zone is primarily economic, with its demographic consequences, even though there may have been some ethnic considerations. Although agricultural investment has greatly increased in the past two decades in the USSR, the non-black earth zone has been neglected to the extent that the cultivated acreage and, particularly, the rural population have declined, and this zone is one of the poorest agricultural areas in the USSR. Since 1970, the rate of decline of the rural population has accelerated. There are severe labor shortages throughout the area, and most young people are leaving rural areas for the cities. The Soviet government is primarily attempting to diminish this exodus and raise labor productivity in agricultural regions in order to increase production. Thus, the primary purpose of this program is not to create a Russian homeland, even though they may use ethnicity for political purposes.

This paper tends to be polemical in that the ethnic significance and consequences of this agricultural program have been overemphasized. A stronger argument can be made for the economic and demographic rationale of the program. In any event, the ethnic significance of the program can best be isolated by a more thorough and balanced investigation of the project. Moreover, there are a number of overstatements that require documentation and definition. For example, who are the ecstatic Soviet Russian officials, the conservative guardians of Russian culture, and the Russian administrators who wish to pass on their ethnic heritage? Is ethnicity or concern for cultural heritage incompatible with material standards and urban life? Elsewhere in the world it has not been so. Has there been a "staggering decline in the area's living conditions?" Or are they higher than before the 1917 revolution, but low relative to urban areas and most other agricultural areas in the USSR? A historical perspective is required in the analysis of conditions in the non-black earth zone. This zone has traditionally been characterized by a relatively poor rural economy and, as a result, for at least the past 400 years these rural areas have been the major sources of out-migration in Russia and the USSR. "The massive concentration of population in the cities of Moscow and Leningrad" is not a basic demographic trend and, even if it were, it could not be documented from the nationality volume of the 1970 census that was cited. Between 1959 and 1970, the population of these two cities grew at about half the rate of the Soviet urban population as whole. Nor can "the flight of the trained youth from the countryside" be documented in the census, even though it can be from survey data.

As to the future of the non-black earth zone, many governments have viewed rapid rural depopulation and the exodus of the young from the land with alarm. The idea of the superiority of bucolic rural life over evil urban life is not unique to the Soviet Union. Yet, with economic development, governments have generally been unable to stem the exodus from the land, because it relates to socioeconomic factors that are difficult to control. Currently, rural depopulation in the RSFSR and the non-black earth zone is intensifying. The crude birth rate in rural areas continues to decline as the young leave, and the crude death rate continues to rise because of an aging population. As a result, some oblasts are experiencing natural decrease, particularly in their rural sectors. With continued out-migration of the young, this phenomenon should become more widespread, resulting in even slower rural natural increase, more severe rural labor shortages, and a continued rapid decline in the rural population.

By the year 2000, the rural agricultural population of the non-black earth zone should be greatly depleted if current trends persist. The rural agricultural population will probably constitute not more than 10 or 15 percent of the total USSR population. The Soviet government will have to invest increasing amounts of money in order to raise labor productivity and to change the system of agriculture. This should, by necessity, entail a further concentration of the farm population into agricultural settlements (a program that is currently well-established), and the continued abandonment of many rural villages. In short, rural life in the area will, by necessity, be radically and fundamentally changed, as it has been elsewhere in the world, to a quasi-urban way of life that could hardly be viewed as a locus of traditional ethnic identity.

27 Comment — Russians as "World Citizens"

Wesley Andrew Fisher

Professor Ladis Kristof (chap. 24) basically restated, in a more sophisticated form, the proposition that the RSFSR is inadequate for Russian identity. Daniel Vanderheide (chap. 25) claims that smaller regions of the RSFSR may still be a significant "homeland" for those inhabiting a given territory. Professor Ralph Clem (chap. 23) essentially argues that the proposition is irrelevant. Russians are "bought off," he says, by the advantages of living in a multiethnic state in which they get the lion's share of economic investment. That offsets any inadequacy the political unit they inhabit may have as a source of emotional attachment.

The proposition itself is of some interest, however. Ideally, it would be desirable to survey the attitudes of ethnic Russians in the USSR to ask them questions that would get at the extent to which they view the terms "USSR," "Soviet Union," and "RSFSR" as synonymous with "Russia" and the adjective "Soviet" as synonymous with "Russian." Whether or not Soviet political authorities would permit such questions to be asked of the population, notwithstanding the recent growth in Soviet public opinion surveys concerning ethnic attitudes (particularly the work of the Sociology Section of the Institute of Ethnography, USSR Academy of Sciences, under Iu. V. Arutiunian), no such opinion poll is available. In the absence of such a survey, it is necessary to resort to a number of observations which, taken together, argue rather persuasively against the proposition.

Historically, Russians have never lived in a political entity called "Russia" that included only ethnic Russians. Only in the twentieth century has the term "Russian" come to refer to ethnic Russians. Before 1917, the term referred rather to the three East Slavic groups. It included the "Little Russians" (Ukrainians) and "White Russians" (Belorussians) as

well as the "(Great) Russians." The Russian Empire was
commonly referred to as "Russia" but never consisted of only
those territories to which ethnic Russians were native. Thus,
insofar as a historical homeland is the source of the kind of
symbolic attachment described in the proposition, it would seem
that Russians have never really had such a political territory.
Russian ethnocentrists have not generally advocated a separate
political territory for Russia proper. Aleksandr I.
Solzhenitsyn is the only major proponent of such an entity.(1)

Historically, Russians' attachment has not been to the
land on which they were living but rather to the social group
to which they belonged. The periodic divisions by the commune of peasant landholdings underscored the importance of
being a member of the group in order to participate in any
redivision of the land. Such a system did not, however,
create the kind of attachment to the land itself characteristic
of the primogeniture systems of northwestern Europe. A
contemporary manifestation of the importance of the social
group rather than the specific territory to Russians may be
found in the longing, among the so-called "third emigration,"
for social contact with the circles of friends they left behind
in the USSR to a far greater extent than for birch trees and
the Russian earth itself. Thus, it can be argued that
Russians differ from most Soviet ethnic groups, because
"territory" is not as salient to them as to others.

Except for a brief period in the 1920s, the word "Soviet"
has been a rough equivalent for "Russian." This practice is
not unlike the use of the word "Zionist" to mean "Jew." The
Soviet regime has generally been identified with ethnic
Russians and with Russian history. That this is so in the
perception of foreigners is obvious. A journalist's title for his
book, The Russians, may have evoked some protest from
members of some Soviet ethnic groups,(2) but ethnic Russians
and most foreigners have made no objection. It seems likely
that the achievements of the USSR, even when called Soviet
accomplishments, are a source of specifically Russian pride.
As a topical song puts it: "Oh, how fine that Iu. Gagar(in) /
is neither Tungus nor Tatar(in)...." (See Professor Oleh
Fedyshyn, chapter 16).

It is likely that calling the RSFSR and the USSR by terms
more directly appealing to ethnic Russian group sentiment
might "serve their ethnic needs" better than the current
appellations do. But there would still be a problem, for
another important ethnic need or trait of Russians would
definitely not be served by such a change. It has often been
noted that one of the characteristics of Russians is their
identification of themselves as "world citizens" and their
ambivalence toward the outside world. Russians, historically,
have seen themselves as having a mission that goes beyond
their own borders and have been obsessed with foreigners'

opinions of them. It may be argued that a political territory called "Russia" that included only ethnic Russians would be bothersome to some members of that ethnic group on the grounds that it would not permit this "international" aspect of their character to flourish.(3)

NOTES

(1)   Aleksandr I. Solzhenitsyn, Letter to Soviet Leaders, trans. by Hilary Steinberg (New York: Harper & Row, 1974).
(2)   Hendrick Smith, The Russians (New York: Quadrangle/The New York Times Book Co., 1976).
(3)   Ronald Hingley, The Russian Mind (New York: Scribner, 1977), pp. 136-55.

VII

Shared Language/
Jargonized Language:
The Risk to
Ethnic Identity

Proposition 7: Alien usages introduced into
the tongue by the widespread adoption of
Russian among nonnative speakers, and by
the officially encouraged use of Russian as
an intergroup language among all Soviet
ethnic groups, have undermined the important role of the language as an exclusive
attribute of Russian identity and, thus,
removed another pillar heretofore bolstering
Russian group unity.

28 Whose Russian Language? Problems in the Definition of Linguistic Identity

Jonathan Pool

A curious thing happened to a group of linguists from the United States during a visit to Peking in 1974. They were listening to a professor at the Central Institute for Nationalities explain that it was the immediate goal of Chinese linguistics to teach everyone in China standard Chinese. What, he asked his visitors, was the immediate goal of American linguistics?(1) The question made the Americans aware that their profession differed from one country to another not only in what its goals were but, more basically, in whether it was a single effort directed toward a single goal.

The Soviet way of talking about languages can create the same kind of awareness. It would not be a caricature for a Soviet observer of linguistic life to describe Russian as "the national language of the Russian people, the second native language and the voluntarily selected language of interethnic communication and cooperation of the peoples of the USSR, the language of a historically new human community, the Soviet people, and one of the five world languages." In fact, Soviet discussions of language policy often contain similar passages.(2)

This kind of description attributes an identity to a language. Like linguistics and its "immediate goal," the languages of the world differ not only in their identities, but also in the extent to which they have identities at all. To make this clear, the identity of a language and its characteristics should be distinguished from one another. The characteristics of a language are properties that it objectively possesses and that can be interpersonally verified. Every language has them. Some of them are linguistic (the properties of its lexicon, morphology, and syntax; the changes that these properties have undergone; and so on), and others are sociolinguistic (who speaks it under what conditions, what proportion of its speakers are native, does it have a written form, how standardized is it, and the like).

In contrast, the identity of a language is neither true nor false; rather, it is believed or rejected. There is no way for those who differ to reconcile their differences. Just as the ethnic identities that people adopt, or that others attribute to them, are not fully determined by or predictable from their ethnic characteristics (skin color, heredity, residence), likewise, the identities that people invest in languages cannot be seen as mere offshoots of the latter's objective characteristics. The fact that languages of small minorities or of colonial domination have assumed the identity of "national language" (for instance, Bahasa Indonesia, Papua-New Guinea Pidgin) illustrates this relative autonomy of linguistic identity.

One way to view the identities of languages is to separate them into different aspects. Soviet statements about linguistic identities suggest four such aspects, which we may call: the ontological aspect, or what kind of language it is; the associative aspect, or to whom the language is linked; the historical aspect, or what social and political roles the language has played, plays now, and is destined to play in the future; and the moral aspect, or how the language ought to be treated.

Wherever there is identity, an identity crisis may also be found. Languages can, indeed, have identity conflicts, and if the problems encountered in the definition of their identities become serious enough, it is reasonable to speak of languages as suffering identity crises.

Identity conflicts can arise for a language in at least four ways: 1) One aspect of its identity may be incompatible with another aspect; 2) an incompatibility may exist within one of the aspects; 3) leading language identifiers might disagree about a certain aspect of the identity of a certain language; or 4) the identity of one language might be incompatible with the identity of another language.

It has been observed that different languages are not competitive when they are used by different people for the same things, or by the same people for different things. Conflict arises when two or more languages are defined as appropriate for use in the same situation by the same people.(3) This explanation of language conflict relies on colliding identities of different languages: Type 4 above. On the other hand, language conflict was once attributed to relative status inconsistency - one language could dominate another in (among other things) number of speakers; frequency with which speakers of other languages learn it; or use for official purposes. It was hypothesized that conflict arises from inconsistency among these kinds of dominance, such as when the official language is one that is spoken by a numerical minority.(4) This explanation combines identity conflicts of Types 1 and 4.

The Soviet Union is a country in which much attention is paid to language, for obvious reasons. Soviet specialists have sought to discover and to change the characteristics of languages. At the same time, they have devoted great effort to defining linguistic identities. There is good reason for this effort. One of the most effective and least expensive ways to influence how people behave toward languages (for example, which languages they use, or how well they learn a language) is by manipulating their linguistic attitudes.(5) And in a multiethnic state with historical ethnic antagonism, whose leadership is striving toward higher levels of education, cooperation, and economic integration for the entire population, how the citizenry behaves linguistically is one of the most important things that one might want to shape.

Of all Soviet languages, Russian has been the object of by far the most effort at identity-building. The range of different identities that have been given to Russian has been wide; the impact of Russians' identity on the daily life of Soviet citizens has been great; hence, the basis for conflict over, or conflict among, the aspects of Russian's identity has been clearly present. Every aspect of its identity, in fact, as defined by Soviet scholars and political leaders, either is in some doubt or is composed of elements whose compatibility is questionable.

Ontologically, Russian is identified as a highly developed standard language, but also as a collection of nonstandard varieties or dialects. In addition, it is the language of one particular ethnic group; a domestic <u>lingua franca</u> (medium of communication among people with different native tongues); and an international language. For different people it has the identity of a native language, a "second native language," a non-native but not foreign language, or a foreign language.

Associatively, Russian belongs to the Russian people, but it is also the "language of Lenin" and of the whole Soviet population, as well as of the people of the world who use it internationally, especially in the countries that are politically allied with the Soviet Union.

Historically, Russian serves to express the Russian culture; to transmit cultural values from the rest of the world to the Russians and to the other Soviet people; to bring branches of Soviet culture closer together, increase tolerance and interethnic friendship, and promote a unique supraethnic Soviet culture; and to aid economic mobility and growth in the USSR. The historical identity of Russian has also been affected by the deep controversies over the nature of language in society that raged in the 1920s, 1930s, and 1950s in particular. These colloquies related to whether language is autonomous or is a product of socioeconomic forces, and, hence, whether economic and political mobilization and integration produce linguistic homogenization and, if so, what kind of homogenization.(6) The principal impact these disputes had on the identity of Russian was on whether Russian or a conglomerate of Russian and other Soviet languages was destined to become the Soviet-wide language of the future. A similar implication was discussed regarding the future language of the world.

Russian also has a multiple moral identity. It is urged that Russian be taught to everyone in the USSR and millions outside, but also that it be meticulously standardized on the basis of the accepted native variety. No one should be coerced into learning it, yet no one can be a fully qualified member of the skilled Soviet labor force without knowing it.(7) Russian should be treated equally, yet be elevated to a unique, supreme status among Soviet languages.

These intraaspectual conflicts are products and reflections of conflicts between different aspects of Russian's identity, and of conflicts between the identity of Russian and the identities of other languages. Thus, ontologically, Russian is clearly an ethnic language; yet associatively, historically, and morally, it extends far beyond the Russian ethnic group. One way to resolve this contradiction is to create a new, wider ontological identity: "second native language" is one embodiment of that strategy. Similarly, the historical aspect of the identity of Russian includes continual progress toward more use by more people for more purposes. Yet, several other Soviet languages, spoken by millions of these same people, have this same content in their own identities. Can Uzbeks, for example, use both Russian and Uzbek for an ever-expanding repertoire of purposes? Most Soviet language identifiers say yes, by postulating that in a socialist society languages are symbiotic. The wider use of Russian causes the use of Uzbek to widen also, because the crucial question is not which language is used, but whether people are rendered capable of new linguistic activities, in which case both languages can assume new roles.

Linguistic identities are carefully defined, then, with the effect of changing the meaning that might otherwise be attributed to language policies and language behavior. If Russian is the specific language of one ethnic group, then its adoption for intergroup communication can be seen as a kind of domination. If it is the language of communication among various ethnic groups, then its adoption as such is hardly an act at all, for this role is inherent in the very identity of the language.

Some of the attempts to resolve conflicts over language by defining or redefining linguistic identities may not fully succeed, particularly if the options are perceived to affect interests differently, and the stakes are high. Let us look more closely at three conflicts which may someday become apparent and severe enough to yield crises. If they do, the reason will not be that they have survived long and strenuous efforts at resolution. On the contrary, these conflicts are serious ones that are basically ignored by Soviet language identifiers, just as they have generally been neglected by the apologists of language policies elsewhere.

First, there is a conflict between the ontological and the associative identities of Russian, that is between what Russian is and to whom it belongs. A major thrust in the efforts to redefine Russian's associative identity has been to widen it. Russian belongs not just to Russians, but to all Soviet citizens, and even to millions of foreigners. Universal fluency in Russian among the Soviet population is predicted for the near future, and the increasing use of Russian internationally is also projected. Yet the mainstream of Soviet thinking also calls for the increasing standardization of the language according to native-speaker norms.(8) Consequently, as more and more nonnative speakers learn Russian, it should also become harder and harder to learn correctly, and nonnative speech should become easier and easier to detect. In a recent volume about Russian in the Ukraine, x-rays and fine acoustic measurements were used to document the minutest differences in tongue, jaw, and lip positioning, length of vowels in milliseconds, and other features of Russian speech behavior between native Russian speakers and native Ukrainians speaking Russian. The book's purpose is not merely to make it clear why nonnative speech is different; the analysis is followed by recommendations about how the schools should use this knowledge to teach Ukrainian children to speak Russian with more perfect (more native-like) pronunciation and intonation, well past the point where the differences would have caused any misunderstanding.(9)

Were the Soviet Union to implement a rigid policy identifying Russian as belonging to a large fraction of the human race but as being defined by the speech of the native-speaking subset of its "owners" alone, one could predict serious tension. Such a policy would satisfy some ethnic aspirations among the Russian half of the Soviet population, but would create a permanently inferior outgroup that could never fully master the language that in theory belongs equally to it. Besides creating friction between Russians and non-Russians, this policy would create antagonism within the non-Russian Soviet nationalities by elevating their linguistically most versatile (but otherwise not necessarily most qualified) members to the highest positions, and by encouraging parents to enroll their children in Russian-medium schools as the only realistic means by which they could acquire fluency in "correct" Russian. If the demands of Russian purists for the exclusion of "unnecessary" (almost all) foreign loan words were satisfied, then resentment against Russian would increase, because it would be less of a window on the world than before for the other Soviet ethnic groups.

    The opposite policy would create different problems.
Control over the features of Russian would be thrown open to
all its speakers, second as well as native. Regional dialects of
Russian emerging from the cultural and linguistic differences
between groups of its learners would be tolerated,
legitimatized, and even romanticized, as is now beginning to
happen - after years of stubborn elite opposition - to regional
varieties of English in India, Africa, and elsewhere.(10)
Nonnative speakers of Russian within the USSR might adopt
strategies of deliberate differentiation from native-like Russian
while, in general, still preserving intelligibility, so as to
communicate their ethnic identity along with the content of
their message.(11) While these consequences would enhance
the loyalty of non-Russians to the regime, the Russian
language would lose much of its potency as a focus of Russian
ethnic pride. Russians would be able to consider themselves
the only Soviet ethnic group that had lost control of its own
language. The counter-argument would certainly be heard
that Russian puts its stamp on every other Soviet language, so
the proliferation of nonnative Russian dialects makes for
genuine mutuality. To the extent that this diversification
became extreme, however, Russian would cease being a usable
medium of communication among those who learned it, except
for those who already shared another language.
    Soviet policy has not clung steadily to either of these
models. Fears of disidentification through the excessive
borrowing of words from other languages have often been
expressed in the Soviet press. The main sources of worry
have been foreign languages rather than other Soviet ones.
The last two decades, however, have seen some linguistic
dogmatisms, including purism, fall into disrepute.(12) Some
moderation of the demand for native-like pronunciation among
learners of Russian can be found in recent writings,(13) along
with the advice that a native-like command of Russian is
destined to remain a rarity.(14) This argument has been
strengthened by sociolinguistic research on Russian, showing
that native Russian itself naturally varies across time, space,
and social position.(15) Praise for the borrowing of words
from the languages of the world and from other Soviet
languages by Russian can also be found.(16) Whereas
Russian's irregularity was once praised for its positive
aesthetic effect,(17) now its regularity is cited as a feature
that enhances its learnability by nonnative speakers.(18)
    This shift toward a more tolerant policy has not gone far
yet, however. The native Russian-speaking population is not
being educated to accept nonnative varieties of Russian as
equally legitimate with the standard variety. And hardly
anyone ever argues that the further standardization of Russian
should be carried out with a view to reducing its difficulty
for nonnative learners, as a Soviet scholar did many years

ago.(19)   Thus, a potentially serious gap remains between
what Russian is identified as being and to whom it is identified
as belonging.

A   second   serious,   but   unacknowledged,   conflict   is
between the historical identity of Russian as the only language
for communication among Soviet ethnic groups and the ideal of
equality that enters into the moral identity of Russian and
every other Soviet language.   Only about three percent of the
Russians in the Soviet Union claim to be fluent in any other
Soviet language, whereas about half of the non-Russians claim
to be fluent in Russian.   The response to this situation by
nearly all Soviet commentators is not indignation or a call for
new effort at rectifying the imbalance; it is to treat the
phenomenon as natural, desirable, and deserving of further
encouragement.   Thus, analysts of bilingualism in the Soviet
Union   only   occasionally(20)   describe   bilingualism   among
Russians, and only rarely(21) is the learning of other Soviet
languages by Russians advocated (even though this is a
feature of Russian-medium schools outside the RSFSR).   The
most commonly expressed attitude is that non-Russians should
do the learning, and this belief is expressed to foreign as well
as domestic audiences:

> While a knowledge of any two languages and their
> utilization in daily communication can be regarded as
> bilingualism, the specific type of bilingualism that is
> needed in the Soviet multinational state is the one in
> which a person knows both his native tongue and
> Russian.   While other forms of bilingualism may also
> be   developing...their   importance   is   of   a   local
> character.(22)

The crucial justification for this point of view is the
argument that all Soviet languages and all Soviet language
groups are equal.   Instead of seeing the selection of Russian
for the role of lingua franca as a sign of inequality, Soviet
commentators see it as a sign of equality.   If the Soviet
language groups were not equal, they would never tolerate the
selection of one (dominant) language as their means of
intercommunication.   Since they have voluntarily embraced one
such language, the language groups must, therefore, be
equal, and that language must, therefore, not be dominant.   It
would follow, then, that the efforts being made in some other
countries, like Canada or Yugoslavia, to achieve behavioral
symmetry among language groups are necessary because of,
and are evidence for the existence of, inequality among the
languages and their speakers.   In other words, the more
unequally the languages of a country are treated, the more
equal they must actually be.

This is a fragile edifice on which to build the justification for selecting a lingua franca, because the acceptance of one language among many as the common medium of transethnic communication not only reflects a situation of equality or inequality, but also affects it. On its face, native speakers of the selected language are differentially benefited. The group whose members must acquire that language anew in each generation or be denied the benefits of speaking it affords are relatively worse off. This principal is supported by much evidence, is easily understood, and is widely believed, as language conflicts in many countries show.

What is interesting is that this problem has been left untouched by those who have made both equality and universality components of Russian's identity. They have not argued that the unequal learning burden is compensated for by the Russians' loss of control over their own language; that monolingualism is more of a liability than an asset; nor that Russians have subsidized other ethnic groups economically to counterbalance their own linguistic advantage; though all of these are potentially plausible claims. Instead, they have simply ignored the issue, suggesting that Russian's predominance does not impair equality because the adoption of Russian as the lingua franca either is objectively or technically inevitable (something which Professor Rywkin's article in this volume, chap. 19, claims but which has never been shown to be true), or, more often, is completely voluntary. Evidence supporting the claim that it is voluntary is almost never provided, and the evidence that is offered(23) really shows only that language shift is taking place and says nothing about how voluntary it is. Even if unidirectional linguistic accommodation is voluntary, its consequences require analysis. Subordination is no less subordination merely because it is voluntary.(24) Are Soviet claims to an egalitarian language policy true in practice? Some theorists claim that different languages are in principle incapable of being treated equally, regardless of intention.(25)

Third and last, there is an identity conflict between the domestic and the international aspects of the Russian language's historical and moral identity. Domestically, as already indicated, the future role of Russian as the common tongue has been decided. It is treated like an accomplished fact and the major issues raised by this decision are not treated as issues. Internationally, however, the eventual position of Russian is by no means certain, and the authoritative sources of Soviet language policy are arguing for two alternatives at once. One is the growing world role of Russian, seen as a by-product of the progress of socialism and of Soviet policy in the global arena. Promoting Russian as a world language, however, brings with it at least three dangers. Two of them are those already discussed: that

Russian will cease to be defined by the speech norms of the Russians themselves; and that international dominance by Russian, if achieved, will cause unequal burdens and resentment against the USSR. The third danger inherent in identifying Russian as a world language is that doing so requires also admitting English, French, German, and perhaps some other languages into the same identity class. The result is to legitimize a competition among these languages for world hegemony, and, if Russian loses to another language, the outcome would be a total defeat, from the Soviet point of view.

The second line of argumentation in the international arena avoids this risk by denying the possibility of a single international language, at least in the foreseeable future. Russian is identified as at least a "zonal" international language, and a synthetic auxiliary language, generally Esperanto, is promoted for a supplementary role (not yet specified in any detail) among the world's various zonal international, nonsynthetic languages.

In advocating that the auxiliary world language be a synthetic one, some Soviet specialists in interlinguistics make, cite, or imply three powerful arguments: first, that it would be fundamentally inegalitarian for the world to adopt the language of any one ethnic group as the general means of international communication; second, that a synthetic language, if properly designed, can be learned much less expensively that a nonsynthetic one;(26) and third, that the supporters of a neutral, constructed language will become a mass movement only where (as in socialist countries) the government promotes intergroup communication and friendship and is willing to invest in radical good ideas long before they are expected to be profitable.(27) It is precisely these kinds of arguments, however, that are missing on the domestic level, in spite of the fact that at first view, they are just as applicable there as internationally. The more effectively Soviet interlinguists put the case for a synthetic international auxiliary language, the greater the protection they will be affording Russian against the risk of a disastrous loss at that level. At the same time, they will be calling attention to the parallelism between the multiethnic USSR and the multinational world and, hence, to the following question: Even if the language which is best for the Soviet Union is not best for the world, why is the language that is best for the world not best for the Soviet Union?

The strategy that Soviet language identifiers generally follow, in order to cope with conflicts between the identities of languages, is conflict denial rather than conflict resolution. On the domestic level, Russian's identity as the lingua franca is argued not to be at the expense of the other Soviet languages, but actually to help promote their enrichment and flourishment. It was said that those who learn Russian are not suffering a loss in comparison with the Russians; they, and their native languages, are, rather, making an absolute gain. At the international level, a synthetic international language does not interfere with the regional and even global aspirations for Russian; it is auxiliary, so it has no effect on ethnic group languages either domestically or in international use.(28)

Conflict, however, cannot be avoided so easily. Such rhetoric renders preferences among alternative language policies purely a matter of opinion, providing no basis for using evidence and reasoning to reach agreement. A Soviet sociolinguist has recognized this, implicitly, by saying that, once trust among the ethnic groups of a state has been established, "the problem of choosing a common language comes down to choosing the one that is most convenient and least demanding in terms of time and effort." He, thereupon, departs from the identity-defining style and describes nine characteristics of Russian that contribute to making it the language that satisfies this criterion in the USSR.(29)

The next step in the argument should be that, if time, effort, costs, and benefits are the basis for language policy, then how those costs and benefits are distributed among the affected people is a relevant consideration as well. Most language policies appear to impose enormous costs on some, while conferring considerable benefits on others. Perhaps this is why language policies not only in the Soviet Union but everywhere have for centuries been justified by the manipulation of identities rather than by analysis of the consequences that flow from them.

NOTES

(1) Language and Linguistics in the People's Republic of China edited by Winfred P. Lehmann (Austin: University of Texas Press, 1975), p. 21.

(2) V. G. Kostomarov and P. N. Denisov, "Mirovoe znachenie russkogo iazyka v XX v. i ego polozhenie sredi drugikh mirovykh iazykov," Part I, in Russkii iazyk v sovremennom mire, edited by F. P. Filin (Moscow: Izdatel'stvo "Nauka," 1974), pp. 58-59; Iu. D. Desheriev and I. F. Protchenko, "Rol' russkogo iazyka v sodruzhestve sotsialisticheskikh natsii SSSR," Part I, in Russkii iazyk ..., p. 85.

(3) William A. Stewart, "A Sociolinguistic Typology for Describing National Multilingualism," in Readings in the Sociology of Language, edited by Joshua A. Fishman (The Hague: Mouton, 1968), p. 541.

(4)   Charles A. Ferguson, "The Language Factor in National Development," in Study of the Role of Second Languages in Asia, Africa, and Latin America, edited by Frank A. Rice (Washington: Center for Applied Linguistics of the Modern Language Association of America, 1962), pp. 11-12.

(5)   Jonathan Pool, "Language Planning and Identity Planning," International Journal of the Sociology of Language, no. 20 (1979).

(6)   George P. Springer, Early Soviet Theories in Communication (Cambridge: Massachusetts Institute of Technology, Center for International Studies, 1956), pp. 19-37.

(7)   "Uluchshit' kachestvo obucheniia russkomu iazyku v natsional'noi shkole," Russkii iazyk v natsional'noi shkole, no. 1 (1976), p. 3.

(8)   V. G. Kostomarov, Kul'tura rechi i stil' (Moscow: Izdatel'stvo VPSh i AON pri TsK KPSS, 1960), pp. 4-5, 14, 20-24; S. I. Ozhegov, Leksikologiia, leksikografiia, kul'tura rechi (Moscow: "Vysshaia Shkola," 1974), pp. 255, 277, 287,

(9)   Kul'tura russkoi rechi na Ukraine, edited by G.P. Izhakevich (Kiev: Isdatel'stvo "Naukova Dumka," 1976).

(10) Papers delivered at panels, "Regional Standards of English, I" and "Regional Standards of English, II", Sociolinguistics Program, 9th World Congress of Sociology, Uppsala, Sweden, August 14-19, 1978.

(11) Rodolfo Jacobson, "Interlanguage as a Means of Ethno-Cultural Identification," paper presented in the Sociolinguistics Program, 9th World Congress of Sociology, 1978.

(12) Margarete Obermann, Beitrage zur Entwicklung der russischen Sprache seit 1917 (Meisenheim am Glan, Federal Republic of Germany: Verlag Anton Hain, 1969), p. 34.

(13) R. I. Avanesov, Russkoe literaturnoe proiznoshenie (Moscow: "Prosveshchenie," 1972), pp. 4-5.

(14) A. I. Kholmogorov, "Konkretno-sotsiologicheskie issledovaniia dvuiazychiia," in Problemy dvuiazychiia i mnogoiazychiia, edited by P. A. Azimov, Iu. D. Desheriev, and F. P. Filin (Moscow: Izdatel'stvo "Nauka", 1972), p. 161; Russkii iazyk po dannym massovogo obsledovaniia edited by L. P. Krysin (Moscow: Izdatel'stvo "Nauka," 1974), p. 17.

(15) Krysin, ed., Russkii iazyk...

(16) L. I. Skvortsov, "Terminologiia i kul'tura rechi (zametki iazykoveda)," in Issledovaniia po russkoi terminologii, edited by V. P. Danilenko (Moscow: Izdatel'stvo "Nauka," 1971), p. 225; E. M. Vereshchagin and V. G. Kostomarov, "Lingvostranovedenie v prepodavanii

russkogo iazyka," in Russkii iazyk..., edited by Filin, pp. 286-87; A. V. Kalinin, "Russkaia leksika s tochki zreniia proiskhozhdeniia," in Sovremennyi russkii iazyk, edited by D. E. Rozental' (Moscow: Izdatel'stvo Moskovskogo Universiteta, 1971), pp. 40-41.

(17) S. P. Obnorskii, Kul'tura russkogo iazyka (Moscow: Izdatel'stvo Akademii nauk SSSR, 1948), p. 5.

(18) M. I. Isayev, National Languages in the USSR: Problems and Solutions (Moscow: Progress Publishers, 1977), pp. 342-43.

(19) L. V. Shcherba, "Literaturnyi iazyk i puti ego razvitiia (Primenitel'no k russkomy iazyku)," 1942, repr. in L. V. Shcherba, Izbrannye raboty po russkomy iazyku (Moscow: Gosudarstvennoe Uchebnopedagogicheskoe Izdatel'stvo Ministerstva Prosveshcheniia RSFSR, 1957), pp. 139-40.

(20) Kholmogorov, pp. 164-65.

(21) M. N. Guboglo, "Etnolingvisticheskie kontakty i dvuiazychie," in Sotsial'noe i natsional'noe, edited by Iu. V. Arutiunian (Moscow: Izdatel'stvo "Nauka," 1973), p. 268; A. Zemliakov, "Dvuiazychie - moguchee sredstvo vzaimosviazi i splocheniia sovetskikh narodov," Russkii iazyk v natsional'noi shkole, no. 3 (1976), p. 11.

(22) Isayev, p. 350.

(23) M. N. Guboglo, "Leninskaia natsional'naia politika i problemy iazyka mezhnatsional'nogo obshcheniia," in Torzhestvo leninskoi natsional'noi politiki (Cheboksary: Nauchno-issledovatel'skii Institut pri Sovete Ministrov Chuvashskoi ASSR, 1972)), pp. 372-75.

(24) Cf. V. I. Lenin, "Chto delat,'" Sochineniia, vol. 5 (n.p.: OGIZ, Gosudarstvennoe Izdatel'stvo Politicheskoi Literatury, 1964), 4th ed., pp. 345-368.

(25) Vernon Van Dyke, "Human Rights Without Distinction as to Language," International Studies Quarterly, no. 20 (1976), pp. 8, 22.

(26) Isayev, pp. 395-97; E. A. Bokarev, "O mezhdunarodnom iazyke nauki," in Problemy interlingvistiki (Moscow: Izdatel'stvo "Nauka," 1976), p. 22.

(27) S. Podkaminer, "Socialismo kaj internacia lingvo," Der Esperantist, 13, no. 3 (1977): 6-8.

(28) M. I. Isaev, "Problema iskusstvennogo iazyka mezhdunarodnogo obshcheniia," in Problemy interlingvistiki (Moscow: Izdatel'stvo "Nauka," 1976), p. 34.

(29) Isayev, pp. 337-46.

29 Two Russian Sub-Languages and Russian Ethnic Identity

Tomas Venclova

A few years ago, in the Soviet bimonthly journal Voprosy iazykoznaniia, appeared an editorial dividing all languages of the USSR into three groups: those having a future, those having a limited future, and others without any future.(1) To the first group belonged Georgian, Armenian, Lithuanian, Latvian, and Estonian; to the second group - mainly languages of the 20 ASSRs; to the third group - languages of small tribes. Languages of the first group are widely used in the media and in the universities and each has a significant branch of literature. Languages of the second group are permitted in high school and in the press, but their main use is in daily life. Languages of the third group are restricted to the sphere of daily life. It is significant that Ukrainian and Belorussian were not included in this typology at all, which, of course, stirred strong protests in Ukrainian samizdat. Russian, also, was somehow left unclassified, for probably no one had any doubts concerning its future. Nevertheless, Russian has a serious handicap when we compare it with languages of non-Russian groups: it loses, to a significant degree, one of its main functions - that of guaranteeing Russian ethnic identity.

This chapter is based to a degree on personal observations and hypotheses and should be considered a reference point for further study. Inevitably, such a study has to be of an interdisciplinary nature; the linguistic data in it should be treated as essential indicators of psychological states.

Russian is compulsory in all non-Russian Soviet union republics. It is taught in schools and preferred in the courts. Administrative and scientific activities are performed mainly in Russian. Besides this, Russian is the sole language of the Soviet Army. Russian is often given preference on signboards and in other ways. Soviet constituent republics, in this respect, are characterized by a relative variety of approaches. For instance, local languages are much more often used in all spheres of social life in the Baltic union republics than in many other areas. The choice of using Russian instead of a local language is considered positive by the authorities and generally helps to promote the social status of a person. The realm of the local languages is gradually diminishing and sometimes is reduced by administrative measures. That is why the 1970 census has shown about 13 million non-Russians to be using primarily Russian and not their native languages. The reverse process is considered negative by the authorities and is hampered by them, although, to a certain degree it also takes place, especially in the Baltic union republics. For example, mixed Lithuanian-Russian families, to my knowledge, more often use Lithuanian than Russian in family life, and their children more often choose Lithuanian identity than Russian.(2)

Expansion of Russian is supported by a significant administrative circumstance. Not one Soviet ethnic group except the Russian has extensive cultural institutions in its language outside its eponymous territorial boundaries. Russians in this aspect enjoy some kind of extraterritoriality and are "more equal than others," in Orwellian terms.

Nevertheless, Russian to a growing degree is seen not as Russian, but as "Soviet," and large groups of Russians themselves perceive it in just this way. The fact is that Russian is more connected with the official ideology than non-Russian languages of the Soviet Union. It serves as the channel of transmission and vehicle for official Soviet myths, and this function of Russian is becoming predominant. At the same time, other languages of the Soviet Union have preserved their connection with the traditional values of corresponding ethnic groups to a larger extent and have not lost their role of stimulating ethnic self-consciousness.

Certain secondary systems of signs are always built on the basis of the primary semiotic system, and they determine the model of the world for a given collectivity.(3) Here a model of the world may be defined as "a certain articulation and classification of the semantic universe." The secondary systems use natural language as their material, as signifier of their signs, and, therefore, exert essential influence on natural language. The concept of secondary semiotic systems was introduced in 1962 and was widely used by the Tartu school of semiotics. In totalitarian states, a tendency can be observed to turn an official ideological system into the sole secondary semiotic system. In this way, natural language also fuses entirely with the secondary system of the ideology. Of course, it is possible only theoretically, in extreme cases. (A literary presentation of such an extreme case is the Orwellian "newspeak"). But the systems of art, of science, and so on, in totalitarian states are treated as second-rate and generally are dominated by the ideological system.

Analysis of the Soviet ideological system in semiotic terms cannot be the purpose of this inquiry. We should only note some of its characteristic traits.(4) Soviet ideology explicitly divides the world into "white" and "black," into "our" world where certain social rituals are performed, and "their" world where these rituals are uncommon or unknown. Behavior is ritualized to a large degree, and ceremonial forms of behavior are rather complex. The differences between the members of the collectivity are erased, for language always refers to "us," not to "me." Nevertheless, the world is classified according to principles of bureaucratic hierarchy. Also, the differences between description and evaluation are erased. All descriptions are evaluations. Mythical schemes of history, of our times and of the future, are presented to society, and everything that does not conform with these schemes is declared nonexistent. Sharp reversions of unlike signs are always possible. There is no appeal to the meta-language or another system which is outside or above "our" system. Theoretically, all such systems must be expelled from one's mind.

Ideology is oriented to monolingualism; "another", (foreign) language is always conceived of as incorrect. There also exists a belief that the "foreign," "non-our" word has a magic and dangerous power. Therefore, it must be repressed by censorship. Languages of other totalitarian systems - Nazi or Maoist - are, so to speak, doubly incorrect. One must not notice their striking resemblance to one's own language. This resemblance is devilish fraudulence. Changing of the existing state of affairs must appear to the member of the totalitarian society as irrational and even absurd. Russian, being the language of politics, press administration, military complex, court, punitive organs, official science and pedagogy, to a large extent has experienced the retroactive and destructive influence of that secondary semiotic system. The Russian language now gravitates to the opposite poles - to the pole of official bureaucratic jargon and to the pole of slang.(5) These opposites exist in other languages also, but in modern Russia that tendency is pushed to the extreme. Often there is almost nothing left between the poles and almost every member of the society very easily passes from one "sub-language" to the other. In the languages of non-Russian ethnic groups, the field of bureaucratic jargon and the field of slang are narrower, and the "neutral" field is much more significant than in modern Russian usage.

Bureaucratic jargon has permeated the schools, daily lives, and relations. This phenomenon is noticed by many Russian writers from Mikhail Zoshchenko and Aleksandr T.

Tvardovsky to Aleksandr A. Galich and Aleksandr A. Zinov'ev. We can say - perhaps slightly exaggerating - that two separate sub-languages of home and institution in modern Russia exist no more. The whole world, including the intimate world, is conceived of as a totalitarian institution. Bureaucratic cliches pervade even love letters. Galich shows us very strikingly how absurd the ideas of common Soviet citizens are about geography, history, biology, and so on. Those ideas are obtruded primarily by the official language.

The Russian language of the USSR is impoverished by the liquidation of numerous social strata, with their linguistic habits, and also by the material poverty of life in general. The daily vocabulary is restricted to some simple and necessary words, with the addition of some ideological and technical terms. Many words belonging to "foreign" ideologies or religion are proscribed or semantically "purified." For example, "holy" (sviatoi) is applied primarily to the actions and duties of Soviet people; "independence" (nezavisimost') usually is applied only to Third World states and must not be applied to the former situation of certain Soviet constituent republics, and so on. Very often an interesting semantic shift can be observed, when meaning changes into its opposite: "prosperity" (blagosostoianie) means lack of goods, "improvement" (pod"em) means stagnation. Not only certain words, but often metaphors are compulsory; "clear sky" (chistoe nebo) denotes desired military superiority of the Soviets. Avoiding such metaphors can entail serious trouble for the person concerned.

Bureaucratic jargon includes numerous abbreviations. Joseph Brodsky has noticed that "evil likes to be abbreviated - for in this way it obtains a certain domesticated air, something like one's initials."(6) Bypassing the well-known abbreviations for governmental, and especially punitive, institutions, observe, for example, that the official club was named BOV (budem otdykhat' veselo - "let us rest joyfully."(7) Such phenomena occur also in the West, but they are much more widespread in Russia. On the other hand, abbreviations are compensated for, in a way, by redundant constructions.(8) Tautologies, contradictory expressions, and numerous superlatives are characteristic in the jargon. Also, the percentage of international words is sharply increasing. Between 1950 and 1970 about 3,500 new words have enriched the Russian vocabulary, including many English words and certain words of non-Russian Soviet ethnic groups. Native words form only 21 percent of this number.(9) A Western scholar has observed that "the most striking feature of the Russian language today is its complete lack of any trace of lexical xenophobia."(10) Naturally, this does not mean lack of ideological xenophobia. The proliferation of foreign words in modern Russian has stirred opposition and even outrage on the part of certain Russian writers, among them Aleksandr I. Solzhenitsyn and so-called Neo-Slavophiles; however, it does not appear probable that this tendency will slow down.

In everyday life, bureaucratic forms of speech receive additional semantic value - they signify social prestige, higher social status, also loyalty of the individual, and his conformity to the rituals. The Soviet world is "overcoded" and tends toward the disappearance of interpersonal communication. Only social roles communicate, using abstract schemes and concealing unpleasant facts.

When members of non-Russian ethnic groups are Russianized, they almost invariably adopt just this bureaucratic jargon, connected with the Soviet, and not the traditional Russian system of values. Russianization is felt by them and by others to be Sovietization. Jews are an interesting exception. Usually having difficulties in obtaining higher social status in the USSR, an assimilated Jew often accepts traditional values of the Russian culture and literature - probably more often than Russians themselves. (Of course, the reason mentioned is not the only one, but it is rather significant.) Russian words which enter or are forced upon the languages of non-Russian groups are almost exclusively taken from the official Soviet vocabulary. In the same manner, when attempts are made to eliminate old customs, the suggested replacements do not come from Russian ethnic tradition; new Soviet customs are being forced upon all Soviet citizens, Russians and non-Russians alike. Persons adopting Russian bureaucratic jargon often preserve in their daily life certain traditional semiotic systems of their ethnic groups. This applies mainly to the Caucasus and Central Asian people. On the other hand, when a native Russian adopts a non-Russian language, he usually also adopts a traditional and non-Russian system of values. An interesting asymmetry can be observed here.

Other languages of the Soviet Union also experience the destructuring influence of Soviet ideology, but to a lesser extent. Their political and administrative role is much less important, and their role in the army and in the punitive agencies is nonexistent. For instance, Lithuanians - and, perhaps, other non-Russians - rarely use abbreviations. Such abbreviations as KGB (Committee for Security of the State), ZAGS (Registry of Civil Records), partly also kolkhoz (collective farm), are used in their Russian form, although Lithuanian forms exist, with special reference to the fact that they are alien (Soviet). In Russia, an unofficial poetical movement, too, has been named SMOG (the Youngest Association of Genius), but in Lithuania such a phenomenon would be nearly impossible. Puristic attitudes, especially in onomastics, are also much more common in Lithuania. Although Lithuanians have retained their Catholic tradition to a significant extent, the common Christian names are relatively rare in present-day Lithuania. Names that are also used in similar form by Russians (Sergius, Andrius, Marija) are generally avoided. Ethnic names surviving from the pagan past, and more or less successful imitations of such names, absolutely predominate. Bureaucratic forms of language in everyday life appear less often than in Russia. Well-educated strata, and sometimes the common people, consciously try to use only traditionally Lithuanian words and constructions. Linguistic discussions with an evident puristic tinge evoke more interest among Lithuanians than among Russians. They are conducted in the press, although restricted to a certain extent, and very frequently are further developed in informal circles. A similar situation also seems to prevail in many other non-Russian constituent republics. The linguistic strategy of Solzhenitsyn, and of his character, the puristically-oriented Sologdin as well,(11) is shared by extensive social groups in these Soviet union republics.

At the opposite pole stands Russian slang. If bureaucratic jargon functions primarily inside the formal groups, connoting loyalty and conformity, slang is the language of informal groups with a certain amount of nonconformity. Slang is perceived as a "truthful," "honest" language compared to the "false," official language. It expresses a latent anarchy of the disciplined Soviet society.(12) It names things directly. It is not hypocritical, and if the official language gives a person a static model of the world, slang, by its very nature, presents itself as changeable and dynamic. Multiform Russian slang is based primarily on prison camp speech produced and used by speakers of every ethnic origin - Slavs, Jews, Gypsies, Balts, and Turks.(13) Slang is known, to a degree, to almost all Soviet citizens, and is sporadically used by most of them. But it is perceived also as Soviet, not Russian, language - the reverse, the parody, and the twin brother of official jargon. Slang reflects the social condition of a Soviet citizen and helps to reconcile the person to this rather tragic condition. Being truthful, frank, and dynamic, slang essentially also teaches one to accept existing reality as everlasting, based on the instincts and on permanent deceit. From its point of view, attempts to change the present state of affairs are also absurd.

Those are the mechanisms washing out Russian ethnic identity by linguistic means. At the same time, the feeling of ethnic identity in other groups is often strengthened. That, in turn, gives to the Russians a sort of secondary ethnic feeling by placing them against the non-Russian background.

NOTES

(1) "XXII s"ezd KPSS i zadachi izucheniia zakonomernostei razvitiia sovremennykh natsional'nykh iazykov sovetskogo soiuza," Voprosy iazykoznaniia, no. 1 (1962), p. 5.

(2) L. N. Terent'eva, "Opredelenie svoie natsional'noi prinadlezhnosti podrostkami v natsional'no-smeshannykh sem'iakh," Sovetskaia etnografiia, no. 3 (1969), pp. 25-27; V. I. Kozlov, Natsional'nosti SSSR: ethnodemograficheskii obzor (Moscow: "Statistika," 1975), p. 240.

(3) A. A. Zalizniak, V. V. Ivanov, V. N. Toporov, "O vozmozhnosti strukturno-tipologicheskogo izucheniia nekotorykh modeliruiushchikh semioticheskikh sistem," in Strukturno-tipologicheskie issledovaniia: Sbornik statei (Moscow: Izdatel'stvo Akademii Nauk SSSR, 1962), pp. 134-43.

(4) Adam Michnik, Kosciol, lewica, dialog (Paris: Instytut Literacki, 1977), pp. 116-17.

(5) Unfortunately a book about Soviet language that is analogous to Victor Klemperer's "LTI" does not exist. Some useful studies are: Afanasii M. Selishchev, Iazyk revoliutsionnoi epokhi: iz nabliudenii nad russkim iazykom poslednikh let (1917-1926) (Moscow: Rabotnik Prosveshcheniia, 1928, 2d ed.); L. Rzhevskii, Iazyk i totalitarizm (Munich: Institut po Izucheniiu Istorii i Kul'tury SSSR, 1951); Andrei and Tat'iana Fesenko, Russkii iazyk pri Sovetakh (New York: Rauson Brothers, 1955); Kornei Chukovskii, Zhivoi kak zhizn': O russkom iazyke (Moscow: Molodaia Gvardiia, 1962).

(6) Joseph Brodsky, "Fate of a Poet," The New York Review of Books no. 5 (April 1, 1976), p. 39.

(7) D. I. Alekseev, "Graficheskie sokrashcheniia i slovaabbreviatury," in Rasvitie sovremennogo russkogo iazyka (Moscow: Izdatel'stvo Akademii Nauk SSSR, 1963), p. 145.

(8) Chukovskii, pp. 128-32.

(9) Novye slova i znacheniia: Slovar'-spravochnik po materialam pressy i literatury 60-kh gg. edited by N. Z. Kotelova and Iu. S. Sorokin (Moscow: Sovetskaia Entsiklopediia, 1971); Vera Karpovich, "Issledovanie novoobrazovanii i dalevskikh solv u Solzhenitsyna," Grani, no. 94 (1974), p. 243.

(10) Valentin Kiparsky, "On the Stratification of the Russian Vocabulary," Oxford Slavonic Papers: New Series, IV (1971): 11.

(11) Boris O. Unbegaun, "The 'Language of Ultimate Clarity,'" in Aleksandr Solzhenitsyn: Critical Essays and Documentary Materials edited by John B. Dunlop, Richard

Haugh, and Alexis Klimof (New York: Collier Books, 1973), pp. 195-98.

(12) Hedrick Smith, The Russians (New York: Quandrangle/ The New York Times Book Co., 1976), p. 9.

(13) Meyer Galler and Harlan E. Marquess, comps., Soviet Prison Camp Speech: A Survivor's Glossary   (Madison: The University of Wisconsin Press, 1972).

30 Comment — Analyzing Language Policies: Pitfalls and Perspective

Robert Austerlitz

Professor Jonathan Pool's contribution (chap. 28) is elegantly couched in philosophical terms and, thus, provides an abstract insight into the entire complex of problems associated with language in the Soviet Union. The USSR is unique among multiethnic states in that it has more languages which have official status of one sort or another than any country one can think of. Furthermore, although it is only some 60 years old, it inherited an entire set of tensions from the empire which preceded it. Thus, the crises which Professor Pool mentions are historically embedded in a way different from those in, say, Belgium or Switzerland; they are also different from the crises faced by such emerging ethnic entities as Nigeria or Malaysia. A philosophical approach is, therefore, called for, precisely to allow us to focus on such concepts as identity, crisis, identity crisis, the equality of Russian, and its efficiency. A slightly more expanded ontological discussion: what does it mean "to be in a state of crisis?" would have been desirable.

However, since by well-established tradition philosophy poses questions without being obliged to answer them, we are confronted with the contrast between the political philosopher and the political scientist who uses sociological methods which require some sort of value judgment. The political philosopher poses the questions and the political scientist teases out the answers from the structure of society by means of all the tools at his disposal. Because these are always imperfect and can never promise to be exhaustive, the political scientist is at a disadvantage. Professor Pool has done us a service by restricting his discussion to a purely philosophical framework, thus avoiding the pitfalls of the social scientist.

These pitfalls are evident in Professor Tomas Venclova's essay (Chap. 29). Most glaring is the one in which he speaks of "vocabularies of small Northern tribes [which] are half-Russian percentage-wise, but almost all the Russian words in them are Soviet." If Professor Venclova had only said <u>and</u> instead of <u>but</u> he would have stumbled on an explanation for the puzzlingly large number of "Soviet" words in a Siberian language. He is probably thinking of one of the early Nenets dictionaries.(1) These are indeed dictionaries of the small Northern tribe called Nenets or Yurak-Samoyed, spoken by some 20,000 persons in the Nenets Autonomous Okrug, Dolgan-Nenets Autonomous Okrug, Yamal Nenets Autonomous Okrug, and the Komi (Zyrian) ASSR. The Nenets were, and to a significant extent still are, a nomadic group whose economy is based on reindeer herding and fishing. They were introduced into the twentieth century only after 1917. During the idealistic Soviet period of the 1920s, they were given an alphabet, schools, hygiene, technology of some sort - in short, all the amenities which the USSR could or wished to provide at that time.

What kinds of words are likely to be found in a practical dictionary aimed at easing the transition of a group such as the Nenets from a reindeer-breeding, nomadic society to a potentially Stakhanovite (crash effort) kolkhoz-society? Technical words. And where are these words likely to come from? Russian. And are these Russian words to be old, cultural words or recent neologisms and acronyms? Recent neologisms and acronyms, because Soviet society and its economy favor neologisms and acronyms. (Whether some like or dislike them is irrelevant at this point). It is, therefore, not surprising that such practical dictionaries are "half-Russian" and that all (really <u>all</u>?) the "Russian words...are Soviet." The "percentage" would look quite different in an anthropologists' word list aimed at cataloguing Nenets culture, or in a linguist's etymological dictionary aimed at identifying cognates from related languages or, for that matter, in a frequency list of vocabulary items used in a traditional setting.

This is an instance of the somewhat exaggerated and unreflecting social science-quantifying approach from which Professor Pool remained aloof and exempt; Professor Venclova counts words in a dictionary. There is lexical frequency ("How many Persian words in a well-specified Turkish dictionary?") and there is textual frequency ("How many Persian words in a well-defined Turkish text?"). The results of such word-counts then depend on the ability to identify and select the source desired for a specific purpose.

Professor Venclova undoubtedly knows all this. If he does, the role of critic is rendered all the more painful, because the rancor which is discernible throughout the article (otherwise probably justified) also guided the choice of examples.

There are two things missing in both articles: comparative breadth and historical perspective. It is true that the role of Russian within the Soviet Union today is unique, but that is no reason not to look at other countries and other models. One of the benefits of this broader approach may be a more informed, cosmopolitan and, therefore, tolerant view of the "crisis" of Russian in the USSR. Such a view - think of all the emerging "nations" at the present time, of the Danish-Norwegian-Swedish complex, of Brazil and Yugoslavia, of diglossia in Norway, Greece, and the countries in which a colloquial variety of Arabic is spoken - would discourage pomposities and encourage a finer weighing of the evidence. Historical perspective needs no explicit justification; it is good for anyone who thinks. But it is essential for the political scientist who wishes to understand the present and predict things to come. Thucydides said so; people should listen.

NOTES

(1)   Peter   Hajdu,   *Chrestomathia samoiedica*   (Budapest: Tankonyvkiado, 1968); Peter Hajdu *The Samoyed Peoples and Languages* (Bloomington: Indiana University Publications. Uralic and Altaic Series, Vol. 14 1963); A. P. Pyrerka and N. M. Tereshchenko, *Russko-nenetskii slovar'* (Moscow: Ogiz. Gosudarstvennoe Izdatel'stvo Inostrannykh i Natsional'nykh Slovarei, 1948); N. M. Tereshchenko, *Nenetsko-russkii slovar'* (Leningrad: Gosudarstvennoe Uchebno-Pedagogicheskoe Izdatel'stvo Ministerstva Prosveshchanie RSFSR, Leningradskoe Otdelenie, 1955); N. M. Tereshchenko, *Nenetsko-russkii slovar' . S prilozheniem kratkogo grammaticheskogo ocherka nenetskogo iazyka*   (Moscow: Sovetskaia Entsiklopediia, 1965).

31 Russification versus De-Russification: Some Linguistic Thoughts
William W. Derbyshire

During the more than 60 years of the Soviet regime, the Russian language, through a combination of cultural and political forces, has become the <u>lingua franca</u> of the well over 100 ethnic groups of the USSR. Leaving aside questions of internationalism and linguistic parity versus the domination of Russian over all other major languages of the Soviet Union, let us focus attention here on the possible effects of that situation on the language which is, in reality, the first language of the USSR. Fears have been expressed that Russian has become subject to an invasion of alien usages, a condition which may implicitly lead to the ultimate bastardization, if not, indeed, to the total decay of the language. Furthermore, there is concern that the conglomeration of multiethnic Soviet union republics comprising the Soviet Union, by having as its capital Moscow, historically a Russian city, effectively deprives Russians of a definable and separate group unity, of a homeland for the Russian language.

The title of this article employs a pair of antonyms, one of which is a standard, well-known, Russian vocabulary item, and the second of which does not find an entry in any general or dialectal dictionary of the Russian language. The term Russification (<u>obrusenie</u>) underlies among other things questions of language policy. The concept of Russification has been a matter of considerable concern for centuries among the Ukrainian and Belorussian ethnic groups, who see in it the potential for the loss of those cultural characteristics which are uniquely theirs. In terms of language, the fear lies in an influx of Russian words, and in the worst extreme, in a drastic reworking of their entire linguistic systems which might lead to the total obliteration of those languages as separate entities. Belorussian, with a shorter history as a separate literary language, is in a more precarious position than is

Ukrainian, despite the latter's significantly different dialectal differences (the eastern dialect displaying more affinities with Russian). With the formation of the Soviet state in the twentieth century, concern was raised for the non-Slavic ethnic groups as well. Events in spring 1978 in Soviet Georgia and Armenia involving the potential removal of their respective languages as the official languages of those republics underscore the fear of Russification by non-Russians.(1) Carried out to its fullest, an aggressive policy of Russification could, indeed, reduce many subordinate groups of the USSR to the status of "ethnics." Although there is certainly some justification for that fear, the actual potential for the obliteration of Armenian, Georgian, the various Baltic or Asiatic languages of the USSR, or even the numerous Siberian languages, has probably been overstated. Tenacity in attachment to one's mother tongue is not easily destroyed by political decree. There are numerous examples in both Europe and the Americas of politically or numerically subordinate groups refusing to relinquish language rights. Think of French Canadians or South American Indians. But the linguistic integration of old German settlers or Italians in the twentieth century in the United States revolves around more complicated problems of the "melting pot" concept in this country and may find few parallels in the building of the Soviet state. Furthermore, repressive policies exercised during czarist times, and under Joseph V. Stalin as well, have failed to destroy any of the major languages of the Russian/Soviet empire.

Linguistic thought in this century has been dominated in great part by the theory of binary oppositions. In its most simplistic reduction, the theory holds that linguistic features must necessarily stand in opposition to one another. Thus, if Russian verbs occur as perfective, imperfective must exist; if X be cold, then there must exist the potential for X, Y or Z being warm or hot. If something is Slavic, then something else must be non-Slavic. If, then, there can be Russification (obrusenie), the possibility of de-Russification (razrusenie) must likewise exist. If this were not the case, the original hypothesis and rationale of the first proposition would be meaningless. De-Russification may be interpreted as a mere purging of Russian elements from a given language, or the term may be extended and have a homonym implying the total reworking of Russian as it is now known. Thus an antonym of Russification could suggest the reshaping of Russian by someone else's language, and de-Russification, a reworking of the Russian language from external non-Russian influences. This is the old who-whom opposition. The coined term de-Russification (razrusenie) may sound particularly distasteful to a Russian who will draw an obvious analogy to the word "destruction," "havoc" (razrushenie). There was, indeed, a brief period in Stalinist times when lip service was paid to the probability that under a new world order (of socialism), a language would emerge combining the elements of many languages through mutual enrichment. This language could not and would not be any previously existing language. Ethnic languages, after all, were thought to be bourgeois manifestations doomed to die out with time, and their death would be a major achievement of the Soviet state. No doubt, memories of such naive statements continue to cause some anxiety among Russians and to lend support to a fear of the razrusenie or razrushenie axis. Remnants of this concern, combined with an emphasis on the leading role of the Russian language in the USSR, may be found in the pages of numerous articles by Soviet linguists in journals such as The Russian Language in School.(2)

The term lingua franca has been defined in the following way: "In such areas, where groups desire social or commercial communication, one language is often used by common agreement. Such a language is called a lingua franca."(3) History has known a number of such languages. The term itself originated from the name of the language which was used in medieval times as the trade language of the Mediterranean area. It consisted of a mixture of French, Spanish, Greek, and Arabic superimposed upon an Italian base. Swahili serves that function in vast areas of Africa. Malay over the centuries served as the lingua franca of the East Indies to the point where it has become the native language of some 80 million people and an official language of Indonesia and Malaysia. It is often claimed that English is the lingua franca of our twentieth century world. It is spoken as a native language on several continents by hundreds of millions of speakers, and at the peak of the expansion of the British Empire, it became the lingua franca of the Indian subcontinent and huge areas of Africa. This situation remains in force in great part today.

Smaller versions of lingua franca, more restricted geographically, are known as pidgin tongues. These are languages which emerge combining the elements of two or more languages, originally to enable rapid communication between traders, missionaries, and the like. A number of English pidgins exist, and we find a Russian-Chinese pidgin along the border of those countries. The obvious should not escape us here: a lingua franca may, as in the case of English, leave the language intact. In other cases, the original lingua franca may be an admixture of many elements built into one specific language. But both Italian of the medieval period and English today remained as separate entities, each continuing to develop throughout history, each with its own native speakers in the "homeland," each language evolving through a series of natural internal processes and changes. Is there a fear that Russian will perform differently in this respect?

An axiom of the discipline of linguistics is that language is in constant flux and evolution. Morphology, phonology, and syntax change slowly throughout time so that, for example, Russian or English of the twentieth century hardly differs from that of the nineteenth, a bit more from its state in the eighteenth century, and so on. Thus, the several-centuries old language of <u>Beowulf</u> has become remote and difficult for us to comprehend. The same may be said about "Song of Igor's Host" for a Russian. Only the most traumatic political and social upheaval brings about substantial changes in the three areas of language structure noted above in relatively short periods of time. There are, of course, sufficient instances of this in linguistic history for example, when those changes were brought about by the invasion of hordes from the East which forever altered the structure of Bulgarian. Likewise, under heavy French influence, English witnessed the great influx of new words and the reshaping of the grammar of what had once been a Germanic dialect. Russian itself, over a period of several centuries, was very heavily influenced by Church Slavic. The extent of that influence is still a matter of considerable debate among linguists.

Identifying specific changes in morphology, phonology, and syntax is a complicated chore, but the one area of language change in which empirical data are most easily retrieved is lexical borrowing. That process takes place for several reasons: place names are borrowed; the names of products available in a more technically advanced society are taken over; abstract words enter languages to express concepts lacking in the receiving language; and so on. These may be reduced to a single common denominator, cultural/political prestige. Analyzing the degree of pressure applied in the borrowing or lending of lexical items is better left to political historians. It is the dominant culture, nevertheless, not numerically, but rather in terms of cultural and/or political prestige, which lends words, and this tends to be an almost exclusively unilateral process. If, in a given pair of languages, borrowing turned out to be a bilateral process, this most likely would indicate a shifting of influences. Only recently, the Academie Francaise has raised a vigorous protest concerning the Anglicization of French, the complete reversal of the process which took place a few hundred years ago. When loan words flow in only one direction, fears of these alien influences arise. Like the French, the Russians have begun to express grave concern at the invasion of "barbarisms" into their language in the twentieth century. Hundreds, if not thousands, of new lexical items have entered the language. A cursory glance at the dictionary <u>New Words and Meanings</u> (1973), reveals 3,500 new vocabulary items used in the Soviet press in the 1960s alone.(4) A large percentage of these are of non-Russian origin, and many of them are from English.

The contemporary Russian language has had its own history of existence for nearly a thousand years, during which time it has undergone significant changes and modifications and developed a rich literature. Russian is one of the world's major languages, with not fewer than 150 million native speakers and well over 100 million people who use it with varying degrees of fluency as a second language within and without the Soviet Union. The Russian language has been subject to enormous external pressures during the course of its history. No aspect of its structure has emerged unscathed as the result of hundreds of years of Church Slavic influence. New phonemes entered the language, grammar and syntax structure was altered, and the vocabulary was enriched. Church Slavic provided the language with numerous lexical doublets, calques, and neologisms which aided in expanding Russian vocabulary. Church Slavic was, of course, a sister Slavic tongue. How has Russian fared with respect to other languages? The successive domination of Russian lands by Scandinavians, Mongols, French (at least in a cultural sense), is historical fact. It might be presumed that the Russian language would have gone through a series of irreversible modifications, bringing the language system into closer alignment with that of each new dominator. That happened in the case of English. But for Russian, not at all. True, thousands of new words entered the language from Dutch, German, French, Latin, and now, English. Many of these have remained, others have been purged or replaced with time. The once ubiquitous merci ultimately yielded to the native spasibo, as did numerous other gallicisms introduced in the eighteenth and nineteenth centuries. The language as a system, however, has changed relatively little and at a normal rate in the past few centuries, Church Slavonicisms aside.

The modern Russian language of the twentieth century is guarded, as it were, by a very high number of native speakers. Can the more than 100 million nonnative speakers of Russian destroy the "great and beautiful Russian language" so eloquently evoked by Ivan Turgenev in the nineteenth century? Can the admittedly large numbers of nonnative speakers speaking, to greater or lesser degree, imperfect Russian really affect the total language system? Probably not. It is unlikely that a series of subordinate ethnic languages found in the USSR, often with radically different linguistic structures, could collectively bring about a reworking of the linguistic system of the major language of the Soviet Union. Russian as a lingua franca for commercial, political, or scientific purposes can hardly be expected to undergo modification in its basic form, as a language of oral communication.

Further, the lack of a "pillar of group unity," a homeland and identifiable native speakers providing "Russian identity" should be of no grave concern. Political boundaries throughout history have never coincided completely with linguistic boundaries, yet languages survive. English is English despite its various and often distant large clusterings of native speakers. Nor has the widespread and sometimes incorrect use of the language in India and Africa modified it. This occurs in the absence of a guiding Academy to help "protect" the language and prescribe usage. With greater contact and more direct exposure across the Soviet Union, coupled with an Academy which addresses itself to language problems, can Russian be expected to behave differently? It possesses an incredibly strong cohesiveness, stronger than, for example, English. Russian dialectically differs less than English. A distinct and larger group unity exists which will contribute to Russian identity, regardless of future political borders and alien people speaking their language. That unity, though its center, Moscow, is cosmopolitan and international in naturel, is hardly likely to see its linguistic aspect modified in the USSR by outside forces, by speakers of other languages, all of whom put together hardly outnumber the Russians. It is they who must find a way to guard and preserve their languages. Collectively or individually, subordinate Soviet ethnic groups, by their very presence, neither effectuate changes in the Russian language, nor can they destroy Russian group unity.

If the hypothesis is acceptable that a series of non-Russian groups cannot introduce substantial, permanent changes into Russian and that a lingua franca will remain intact despite misuse by those who employ it, consider briefly one final area of possible "danger" to that language. This concerns internal, partially extra-linguistic factors, mainly the bureaucratization of Russian as it has been foisted into the role of political and ideological communication. Voices of objection have been raised against the introduction of endless neologisms, acronyms, the development of political jargon, and the like. Some emigrant authors believe these changes to be a process of uglifying language.(5) Soviet linguists have found it necessary to remind native speakers, through articles in various pedagogical journals, that words are frequently subject to misuse. That seems to be a relatively trivial objection. Words acquire new meanings, and new words (including acronyms) are always being invented. A greater problem concerns the creation and subsequent mixing of several distinct levels of language - the literary, the spoken, and the language to be used for political purposes. Not only is the political medium replete with overly clumsy syntax and phraseology, but users of that language are forced to apply a different model of interpretation to the text in order to understand its message. Though politicization of the language requires a new approach to its comprehension, and the creation of a new level of expressions gives rise to the use of malapropisms by its speakers, Russian retains its special identity. Changes will be generated primarily by its own speakers, perhaps aided by extra-linguistic forces. The likelihood is minimal that other languages of the USSR will alter the external structure of Russian.

NOTES

(1) Yaroslav Bilinsky, "Education of the non-Russian Peoples in the USSR, 1917-1967: An Essay," Slavic Review, XXVII, no. 3 (Sept. 1968): 411-37; John Kolasky, Education in the Soviet Ukraine: A Study in Discrimination and Russification (Toronto: Peter Martin Associates, 1968); V. Stanley Vardys, "Soviet Nationality Policy Since the XXII Party Congress," Russian Review, no. 4 (Oct. 1965), pp. 323-40.

(2) M. I. Isaev, "Vzaimodeistvie i vzaimoobogashchenie natsional'nykh iazykov," Russkii iazyk v shkole, no. 6 (1972), pp. 6-11, or V. G. Kostomarov, "Russkii iazyk v sovetskom obshchestve i sovremennom mire," Russkii iazyk v shkole, no. 3, (1977), pp. 3-9.

(3) Victoria Fromkin and Robert Rodman, An Introduction to Language (New York: Holt, Rinehart and Winston, 1974), p. 266.

(4) Novye slova i znacheniia: slovar'-spravochnik po materialam pressy i literatury 60-kh gg. edited by N. Z. Kotelova and Iu. S. Sorokin (Moscow: Sovetskaia Entsiklopediia, 1971).

(5) Andrei V. and Tatiana S. Fesenko, Russkii iazyk pri sovetakh (New York: Rauson Brothers, 1955).

32 Language Purity and Russian Ethnic Identity*

Kenneth E. Nyirady

Russian is not only the native language of the Russian ethnic group but also the intraethnic language of the Soviet Union. The 1970 Soviet census showed that nearly half of the non-Russians in the Soviet Union claimed Russian either as a first or a second language.(1) The Soviet government promotes this spread of Russian within the USSR as a means of welding the ethnic groups into what is called "The Soviet People."(2) Russian also serves as a lexical fund or as a source of loan words for the non-Russian languages of the USSR. The Soviet government has insisted on the standardization of certain political and economic vocabulary of the non-Russian languages through borrowings from Russian. This has included those groups for whom equivalent terms existed already or could have been created from internal linguistic resources.(3)

Yet this "internationalization" of Russian within the USSR stands in sharp contrast with its historically being closely associated with Russian ethnic identity. Since the eighteenth century, many well-known Russian writers have glorified their native tongue for its supposed unique characteristics. This trend has been continued in the twentieth century by Soviet

---

*The main Russian source utilized for this study was the periodical Russkaia rech', a bimonthly publication of the USSR Academy of Science's Russian Language Institute. This journal was systematically surveyed from 1967 through 1976. Describing itself as a "scientific-popular" journal, it is published for a fairly wide readership. Voprosy iazykoznaniia, a highly specialized periodical for linguistics, was surveyed for the same period.

Russian writers. How widespread this sentiment is among Russians in general is hard to say, but it is noteworthy that in the 1970s an American newspaper reporter came across a doorman in Murmansk who lectured him about the beauty and mystical origins of the Russian language.(4)

Both the information just mentioned and the general argument - that the role of Russian is the recognized interethnic language in the USSR and the alien usages thus introduced have undermined its exclusiveness as an attribute of Russian group identity - suggest the following. Because certain forces in Soviet society are attempting to revitalize the Russian ethnic group with a regenerated sense of ethnic identity, and given the publicly-voiced concerns of many Russians about threats to the "purity" of their language, the Russian language issue again becomes crucially important in any study concerning Russian ethnic consciousness in the 1970s. Russian language "purists" can be considered part of the larger body of forces in Soviet society who wish to instill a strong sense of ethnic distinctiveness in the Russian group. Russian language purists are aware of and are attempting to deal with and counter the related problems of adopting foreign loan words in Russian and the incidence of dialectization and pidginization attributable to nonnative speakers. The tension, muted or open, which exists between the purists and party language-planners promoting Russian as the USSR's "internationalist" medium plus lexical fund for non-Russian vocabularies in the Soviet Union, reflects disagreements concerning the aims of Soviet ethnic policies in general and especially the role of the Russian language.

Therefore, it seems proper to argue that Russians concerned with the purity of their language evidently attempt to limit its adoption by non-Russians or at least make Russian more exclusive through the introduction of older Russian word forms (Church Slavonic not necessarily implied here), through the creation of new words from the native Slavic and Russian lexical stock, and by the utilization of native Russian dialect forms. This would serve to "refresh" the Russian language and restrict its use to the Russians, or a select group of them perhaps along with coopted elites from the other ethnic groups. This attempt to purify the language, and in that way make its use more exclusive, conflicts with Soviet designs to broaden it as the common language of the USSR and thus generalize Russian for a single Soviet People.

Before analyzing the reaction of the present-day purists to the language problems they perceive, the nature of these problems should be made clear. First, there is a tendency in Russian, as in any language spread over a large geographical area, toward dialectization. Non-Russian languages also affect Russian within and adjacent to their areas of use. Although dialectization can occur without contact with other languages, it is more likely to take place in the speech of Russians living near or among other ethnic groups. In the southern part of the RSFSR near Volgograd, the Ukrainian language has left "an appreciable imprint" on Russian speech of the region in grammar, phonetics, and especially vocabulary.(5) Azerbaijanian borrowings into Russian (presumably in the Transcaucasius region) have been known to take the form of word doublets. A foreign word has been incorporated into Russian that has a Russian counterpart, but the borrowing receives a nuance and is used only in certain situations.(6) Certain dialects spoken by Russians living in Voronezh on the Don, in the Ashkhabad region, in the Bashkir Autonomous Soviet Socialist Republic, and the Komi-Permiak Autonomous Okrug have also been investigated.(7) However, such dialectization does not appear to be of such a magnitude that it hinders communication between native Russian speakers.(8)

Alterations occur in Russian spoken by other ethnic groups who learn it as a second language. Such modifications include the inability to distinguish between nuances in Russian words, introducing non-Russian words into Russian speech, and pidginization. This sort of influence of the ethnic group languages on the Russian speech of non-Russians has been studied in many areas of the Soviet Union. One study of bilingualism in Azerbaijan clearly describes the difficulties of the Azeri population in mastering Russian. Phonetic difficulties included the inability to articulate sounds or combinations of sounds not present in the native language. The Russian for "verb" (glagol) becomes, as in some other Turkic tongues, (galagol), for example. Because Russian possesses gender but Azeri does not, disagreement of gender of nouns and adjectives occurs, as well as between subject and verb. Syntactically, there are problems with word order. According to the author of the study, only a small percentage of those bilingual Azeri attending higher educational institutions in the USSR have perfected their Russian to an extent where interference by the native language is fully absent.(9)

Because Soviet statistics showing bilingualism are quantitative and not qualitative, there are grounds for suspicion that knowledge of Russian is shallow at best among a good portion of the non-Russian population.(10) One scholar, comparing the situation of Russian among the non-Russians in the USSR to English in India on the eve of Indian independence, sees "wide diffusion and considerable acquaintance with the language among the intelligentsia, but few and parched roots for the language among the vast majority of the population, even among school children who were instructed in it."(11) The potential for occurrence of pidginization and similar phenomena is, therefore, quite high.

Nevertheless, the earnest Russian language purists do not concern themselves with effects upon Russian of imperfect command by others in the Soviet Union; rather, they worry most about what they regard as the problem of foreign loan words whose origins lie beyond the western borders of the USSR. It appears that such Russian purists believe English, for example, to be more of a threat to their language than the hundred-some languages within the borders of the Soviet Union. One writer has protested, in fact, that the damaging influx has encompassed not merely English words, but especially "those with American pronunciation."(12)

Russian has always been receptive to foreign borrowings, and there are various estimates of the percentage of such words in its literary language.(13) Such loan words constitute 10-25 percent of the Russian literary language; estimates such as these, however, can be misleading because they usually reflect word counts from dictionaries and not usage. More foreign words had been borrowed before the reign of Peter the Great than is usually assumed - primarily administrative, scientific, and military terms.(14) Anglicisms first appeared in the eighteenth century. The initial borrowings were mostly nautical terms, which, along with similiar terms borrowed from the Dutch, still comprise a sizable portion of the contemporary Russian marine vocabulary.(15) The late eighteenth and nineteenth centuries saw an influx of French and German terms,(16) and the borrowings of the twentieth century have been primarily but not exclusively political, economic, and technological words. English penetration into Russian is second to French and equal to German in the number of words in the contemporary Russian lexicon.(17) These borrowings reflect the influence of Western culture on its Russian counterpart. Presently, such borrowings may represent the individual choice of various writers, perhaps trying to imply familiarity with Western languages and cultures (in some cases a status symbol?), or, as some have suggested, may truly represent their ignorance of equivalent Russian terms.(18)

A distinction must be made between two types of words borrowed: the item or idea that is imported from the West for which there is no Russian word, and a Western word used instead of an already-existing, genuinely Russian one. In general, Russian language purists oppose the second form of borrowing more than the first, although some favor the creation of the new lexicon from native Russian linguistic resources. This distinction is important, for it shows that opinions about the problems of foreign words in Russia are far from united.

For nearly two centuries, various Russians have spoken out against the incorporation of foreign words into their language.(19) Prominent among the contemporary segment of this group is Solzhenitsyn. Although his exile abroad has removed

him from the immediate Soviet Russian literary scene,
his role in the attempt to revitalize the Russian language
makes him too significant to disregard here. His ideas about
the subject, in exaggerated form, received wide readership
through his novel The First Circle (V kruge pervom) (1964).
It is a major eccentricity embodied in one of Solzhenitsyn's
literary personages, Dmitri Sologdin, that he avoids using
words of foreign origin and replaces them with words rooted in
Church Slavonic.(20) Incidentally, Solzhenitsyn does not view
this as the main source for the lexical enrichment of
Russian.(21) His works incorporate many dialectisms from
Central Russia, archaism, regionalism, peasant speech, and
words created from Russian word roots. He does not shun
Russified foreign words, if useful, but avoids those that have
suitable Russian equivalents.(22) Solzhenitsyn earlier gave a
detailed prescription for lexically enriching the Russian
language in the principal Soviet literary tabloid in 1965. This
article represents his most comprehensive views, published so
far, about language purity. Entitled "You Don't Season Soup
with Tar, Sour Cream is Better," it dealt directly with the
causes of and remedy for what he considered the
impoverishment of Russian. His plans for restoring and
enriching the language included extensive use of prefixing
and compounding to create new lexical items and a search to
discover genuine Russian words instead of borrowing foreign
ones.(23)

Solzhenitsyn's has not been the only voice expressing
concern about the Russian language. In a book entitled Fate
of the Mother Tongue (1962), its author decried the "spoiling"
of the language through "unneeded foreign words."(24)
Nearly ten years later, people were warned against allowing
Russian to lose its "clarity, freshness, expressiveness, and
ethnic (narodnaia) basis."(25) A more forceful polemic against
foreign loan words was a 1974 article "Can't It Be Translated
into Russian?". Insisting that he was not referring to foreign
words "which historically flowed into the Russian language,"
nor proposing "the erection of a Chinese wall around new
terminology," its author called for moderation and "a sense of
measure" in the adoption of foreign nomenclature. Quoting
both isolated words ("eskalatsiia," "transplantatsiia,"
"interpersonalizatsiia," "konformizm," "isteblishment,"
"kheppening," "bestseller," and others and phrases
("metodologicheskaia konseptsiia esteticheskogo progressa,"
"real'nye potentsii analiticheskogo metoda," and the like), he
pleaded:

Really, isn't translation to the Russian language
what is being suggested here? This regrettable
carelessness toward the mother tongue is explained
by insufficient scrupulousness in the selection and

weighing of each word or term of foreign origin
[and] a readiness to find in foreign terminology a
panacea and 'philosophers stone'. . . . (26)

A month after this article appeared, three replies were
published in the same magazine. The first, by a librarian,
noted that "many had waited for those words a long time" and
thanked the author for publishing his article. Although
bringing up the necessity to rename cracker (kreker) table
biscuit (stolovoe pechen'e), she insisted that "the struggle for
a 'clean' language by no means supposes a maniacal
suppression of foreign words."(27)

In the second reply, an assistant professor in the Minsk
state teachers' institute of foreign languages noted that most
of the examples of borrowings in Literaturnaia gazeta were not
actually "foreign" but "international" words. The author of
this reply found 42 words of Greek origin and 62 of Latin
extraction, with 50 of the latter present in the Russian
language for a long time. Drawing an analogy to the Russian
usage of the word transplantatsiia, he pointed out that an
English speaker had the option of choosing between the Latin
root plant and the German root set. In addition, the word
planta was found in eighteenth century Russian in the place of
growth (rastenie). Although he voiced his opposition to the
"piling up of a borrowed lexicon," the language professor
maintained that this whole question of foreign words was really
a matter of the "stylistic flair and taste" of the individual
writer.(28)

The third reply came from a graduate degree candidate in
technical science. His argument can be summed up by means
of an example that he offers concerning the word komp'iuter.
He claimed that the Latin form 'komputer' was a more
acceptable form to him than the Anglicized komp'iuter because
the Latin form was the base of the English. Better yet, he
suggested, would be the word samochet (self-calculation). Of
the three replies to the original article, this was the least
passionate.(29)

Because Literaturnaia gazeta published only these three
replies, the full reaction to "Can't It be Translated into
Russian?" cannot be judged. The three letters chosen for
publication appear to be balanced - one basically agreed with
the original article, one disagreed, and the last fell somewhere
between the other two. It appears, too, that the editors of
Literaturnaia gazeta were more interested in presenting a
balanced debate than pushing one point.

Still, the struggle for the "purity" of Russian continued.
In 1976 the book How We Spoil the Russian Language devoted
at least nine of its sixteen chapters to the problem of
foreign loan words. The writer bitterly attacked those "most
zealous worshippers of the West" who oppose the replacement

of foreign words by Russian and who "attempt to tightly close off the popular nurturing sources (narodnye, rodnikovye istoki)" of the Russian language. He also denounced the book of Korney Chukovsky's Lively as Life (Zhivoi kak zhizn') (1962), for its defense of foreign synonyms in Russian. He claimed that Chukovsky's opinions about the subject as well as his subsequent appearance on radio and television promoted the spreading of the idea that "if you want to be acquainted with culture, be acquainted with foreign words."(30) Yet Chukovsky himself, while defending the use of such words in Russian, did concede that they "can evoke an annoying feeling where they are used for no purpose, incoherently, [and] without any kind of basis."(31)

More up-to-date is an article in Komsomol'skaia pravda. Like others concerned with this problem, its author did not attack the use of foreign loan words in general but rather opposed their "unthinking borrowing, . . .many of which do not enrich us spiritually but rather clutter the mother tongue, depriving it of its clean lines and internal strength." Most interesting is the comparison of the number of words in the latest, 17 volume dictionary of the Russian literary language (120,000) with the latest edition of Webster's English dictionary (450,000). The disparity, we are told, results from the "fencing in" of common Russian with all sorts of limitations - popular, dialect, and antiquated forms are omitted. However, foreign words are free to enter. He implied that the compilers of this Russian dictionary were to blame.(32) This charge suggests that the question of language standardization may be the main focus of a clash between the "official language planners" and "purists."

There are many Soviet Russian-language experts who desire standardization, because adopting a norm regularizes Russian usage. By stabilizing the teaching and learning of the language, acquisition of it by another ethnic group is facilitated. This enhances the role of Russian as the main interethnic medium for the USSR. By itself, standardization is not necessarily harmful to Russian, but it could be if the language were standardized, for example, on the basis of the present, jargon- and foreign loan word-filled journalistic or bureaucratic medium. The Komsomol'skaia pravda article just cited suggests existence of an antipathy between the "standardizers" and the "purists," because foreign loans seem to be preferred by Soviet lexicography over the dialect or popular forms sought by the purists. The following brief polemic illustrates.

In 1974 appeared the book Man and His Languages (Chelovek i ego iazyk) which attacked the book Fate of the Mother Tongue, mentioned previously. The 1974 volume took issue with the earlier one's claim made in 1962 that "the whole of the language [for example, all dialects] of the Russian people" was literary and, for that reason, "impossible to regulate." (33)   The author of the 1974 publication attacked his target's anti-standardization stance, its opposition to foreign loans, as well as the concept of the "Russianness" of the Russian language.(34)   Fate of the Mother Tongue, however, was not without friends.   One writer praised its author as a passionate defender of popular terms in the literary language and an opponent of both those who wish to prevent popular speech from becoming literary and the introduction of unnecessary foreign loan words.(35)

Thus, there is evidence that those concerned with the purity of Russian would oppose its standardization on the basis of the present-day literary language, which contains more foreign but fewer popular forms than they would like. However, it appears that the Soviet government, through the appropriate institutes of the Academy of Sciences, supports standardization on the contemporary foundation, for this is the actual common language of the USSR.   The "internationalist" loan words incorporated into the other ethnic-group languages through Russian is a step toward homogenizing the Soviet languages.   It is not hard to see that the "internationalist" political expediency and necessity dictating such a policy automatically clash with ethnic aspirations which manifest themselves in a concern for language purity.

Nevertheless, one cannot view this dispute in terms of Marxists versus Russian language purists.   The purist Aleksey Iugov, for example, protests the present-day literary standards of the Russian language as "class norms."(36) Others appeal to Vladimir Il'ich Lenin's statements against unnecessary foreign loan words in Russian.(37)   On the other hand, Marxist language theoreticians who favor the growing role of Russian in the USSR do not necessarily favor the wholesale adoption of foreign words.   One book, devoted to the respective roles of Russian and the other ethnic languages in the USSR, notes that

> ...international terminology necessary for the development of a modern language should not be confused with the unnecessary use of foreign words that often encumber the speech of certain individuals....As for borrowed international terms, these have been totally assimilated by the Russian language and are no longer perceived as foreign.(38)

Such Soviet Marxist opposition to some foreign words arises not because these words are non-Russian but because they are Western or English (American) and represent the culture of the ideological enemy.

So, while the language purists may find some common ground with the ideologists concerning foreign loan words, each group has very different views regarding both the role of Russian in the USSR and the quantity of permissible foreign words in it.

The present-day lack of standardization, combined with the successful "enrichment methods" described previously by Solzhenitsyn, might almost ensure the sharp setting off of native Russian speakers from other Russian-speaking people of the USSR. The distinct Russian flavor of such a protected language, achieved through utilizing Russian linguistic resources, should enhance its role as a defining characteristic of Russian ethnicity. The lack of rigid codification would serve further to decrease the likelihood that non-Russians would learn Russian like a "native," thereby enhancing its character as the exclusive possession of the real (ethnic) Russians. Also, the replacement of many borrowed socio-economic, scientific, and political terms by native Russian expressions could isolate the foreign terms already incorporated into the non-Russian languages. Thus, it appears that while Russian language purists are not primarily concerned with the influence of the other ethnic groups' languages on Russian, their remedy for the foreign loan word problem would, in fact, affect the interrelation between Russian and the non-Russian languages.

Such an attempt to revitalize and, by implication, limit the use of a clean Russian language represents a conflict with Soviet designs to expand the adoption of it as the common language of the USSR. Now, rather than discovering in all of this a resolution of the identity dilemma, one can more easily envisage the Soviet government's taking another course. It might continue to laud the "glorious Russian language" and push for its standardization, using it as the Soviet interethnic medium, and provide the means to unify the terminology and, possibly, vocabularies of non-Russian languages. In effect, this amounts to praising the "Russianness" of the language in name, but disqualifying it simultaneously for purposes of uniquely identifying one ethnic group.

Thus, the Russian language is losing its ethnic specificity. The reason for this is not so much a matter of who is using the language, but rather, how the language is being used. That some 50 million non-Russian Soviet citizens also use the language does not seem as important to some Russians as the changes the nonnative speakers effect in the language. Still, these changes do not seem to be as considerable, in the eyes of language purists, as those wrought by the constant inundation of Russian with Western (particularly American) loan words. To the Russian who identifies his language closely with his ethnic group, here lies the danger.

NOTES

(1) Itogi vsesoiuznoi perepisi naseleniia 1970 goda: Natsio-
     nal'nyi sostav naseleniia SSSR, Vol. 4 (Moscow: Statistika,
     1973), p. 20.
(2) M. Sheliatin, "Aktual'nye problemy prepodavaniia
     russkogo iazyka," Kommunist Estonii, no. 10 (1976), p.
     87.
(3) A. S. Sidorov, "Soveshchanie po voprosam izucheniia
     komi iazyka," Voprosy iazykoznaniia, no. 4 (1953), p.
     144; Iuri D. Desheriev and I. F. Protchenko, "Soiuz
     ravnopravnykh narodoy i russkii iazyk," Russkaia rech',
     no. 5 (September-October 1972), pp. 8-9.
(4) Hedrick Smith, The Russians, (New York: Quadrangle,
     1976), p. 430.
(5) Aleksandra F. Manaenkova, Leksika russkikh govorov
     Belorussii, (Minsk: BGU, 1973), p. 6.
(6) Ibid.
(7) E. Glyn Lewis, Multilingualism in the Soviet Union, (The
     Hague: Mouton, 1972), p. 200.
(8) Kuchkar Khanazarov, Reshenie natsional'no-iazykovoi
     problemy v SSSR, (Moscow: Politizdat, 1977), p. 103.
(9) A. N. Baskakov, "Tipologicheskie osobennosti
     azerbaidzhanskogo i russkogo iazykov," in Raxvitie
     natsional'no-russkogo dvuiazychiia, edited by A. N.
     Baskakov (Moscow: Nauka, 1976), pp. 105-27, 191-98,
     238-43, 279-84, 319-27. Also in this volume are analyses
     of bilingualism in Estonia, Lithuania, and the Buriat
     eponymous units.
(10) F. Chernyshev, "Tolstogo chitat' po-russki!",
     Uchitel'skaia gazeta (July 29, 1972), p. 2; Lewis, p. 202.
(11) Lewis, pp. 16, 203.
(12) Konstantin Iakovlev, Kak my portim russkii iazyk
     (Moscow: Molodaia Gvardiia, 1976), p. 44.
(13) Gerta Huttl Worth, "Foreign Borrowings in Russian," The
     Slavic and East European Journal, 17, no. 1 (Spring
     1959): 47; M. I. Isaev, National Languages in the USSR:
     Problems and Solutions, (Moscow: Progress Publishers,
     1977), p. 354.
(14) Worth, p. 50.
(15) Morton Benson, "English Loan Words in Russian," The
     Slavic and East European Journal, 17, no. 3 (Fall 1959):
     249.
(16) Valentin Kiparsky, "On the Stratification of the Russian
     Vocabulary," Oxford Slavonic Papers, 4 (1971): 9.
(17) Benson, p. 249.
(18) Nikolai Fedorenko, "Ne perevesti li na russkii?,"
     Literaturnaia gazeta, (January 30, 1974), p. 6; V.
     Vasil'ev, "Monolog o slove," Komosomol'skaia Pravda,
     (September 23, 1977), p. 4.

(19) Nikolai M. Karamzin, "On Love for the Fatherland and National Pride," in The Literature of Eighteenth Century Russia, edited by Harold B. Segel, Vol. 1 (New York: Dutton, 1967), pp. 447-48; Aleksandr P. Sumarokov, "'Two Epistles," the First Treating of the Russian Language, the Second of Poetry," in Segel, pp. 224-25.

(20) Alexander I. Solzhenitsyn, The First Circle (New York: Bantam Books, 1969), pp. 155-56; Boris O. Unbegaun, "The 'Language of Ultimate Clarity,'" in Alexander Solzhenitsyn: Critical Essays and Documentary Materials, edited by John Dunlop, Richard Haugh, and Alexis Klimoff (New York: Collier, 1975), p. 198.

(21) Vera Carpovich, "Lexical Peculiarities of Solzhenitsyn's Language," in Dunlop, Haugh, and Klimoff, p. 192.

(22) Ibid., pp. 191-92.

(23) Aleksandr Solzhenitsyn, "Ne obychai degtem shchi belit', na to smetana," Literaturnaia gazeta (November 4, 1965), p. 3.

(24) Aleksei Iugov, Sud'by rodnogo slova (Moscow: Molodaia gvardiia, 1962), p. 125. This publication was enlarged and re-released as Dumy o russkom slove (Moscow: Sovremennik, 1972).

(25) Vil' Lipatov, "Slovo v opasnosti," Literaturnaia gazeta, (August 18, 1971), p. 5.

(26) Fedorenko, p. 6.

(27) I. Ignat'eva, "Nauka dlia nemnogikh," Literaturnaia gazeta, (February 27, 1974), p. 6.

(28) Ia. I. Poretskii, "Chuvstvo mery," Literaturnaia gazeta, (February 27, 1974), p. 6.

(29) B. Andrianov, "Chto takoe displei," Literaturnaia gazeta, (February 27, 1974), p. 6.

(30) Iakovlev, pp. 42, 48, 75.

(31) Kornei I. Chukovskii, Zhivoi kak zhizn': razgovor o russkom iazyke, (Moscow: Molodaia gvardiia, 1962), p. 43.

(32) Vasil'ev, p. 4.

(33) Iugov, p. 62.

(34) Ruben A. Budagov, Chelovek i ego iazyk (Moscow: Moskovskii Universitet, 1974), pp. 184-86.

(35) Iakovlev, p. 42.

(36) Iugov, p. 66.

(37) Iakovlev, p. 61; Iugov, p. 45; Vasil'ev, p. 4.

(38) Isaev, p. 356.

33 Russian Language and Ethnocentrism in the Soviet Union

Nicholas Ozerov

All our authors have disagreed with the proposition that the increasing use of Russian by non-Russian ethnic groups in the Soviet Union poses a real threat to the purity of Russian and serves to undermine the sense of Russian ethnic identity. It has also been noted that the attacks of Russian purists are usually directed against something entirely different, the influence of Western European languages. The phenomenon of purism is not specifically Russian and need not be discussed here. The only sensible attitude seems to be that of Korney Chukovsky, holding that the choice of words should be determined not by their origin, but by their adequacy to thought and appropriateness to the context. Chukovsky has also made a very interesting observation that certain words may strike one as offensive not so much because they are foreign but because they, so to speak, "smell" of an office. For Chukovsky the real danger consisted in what may be termed "bureaucratization" of language, and he coined a term for this language disease - office talk (kantseliarit). Bureaucratization of language is one of the problems of the twentieth century and, as such, not a specifically Russian problem; however, the situation in the Soviet Union has its unique aspects which have a direct bearing on our discussion. And here we come to the problem of ideology.

The role of ideology in the Soviet Union has been evaluated in different ways. Some would consider it the dominant factor in Soviet life, others would pronounce it dead and dismiss it as a real force. The correct answer is, rather, the following. The ideology is dead and may be compared to a corpse, but the crucial fact is that this corpse has not been buried and continues to poison everything it comes in contact with. The realm where ideology is fully "alive" is precisely the bureaucracy which permeates the whole fabric of life in the

278

Soviet Union. The distinction between public and official realms so important in the United States is nonexistent in the Soviet Union. There, everything that is public is, by that very fact, official - whether a store, a school, a factory, or a kolkhoz. The bureaucratization of language involves, at the same time, its "ideologization." This truth is reflected in the choice of the topic, in what one says about it, and in the way one says it.

What this ideologization may mean could be illustrated with a humorous sketch by Arkadiy Raikin. The sketch requires some background information. In standard school textbooks of Russian literature, the names of individual authors occur, as a rule, in standardized statements such as: "so and so portrayed (izobrazil) . . . ," "so and so reflected (otrazil) . . . ," "so and so unmasked (razoblachil). . . ;" the object of the verbs is, of course, the socioeconomic conditions of the authors' time. The sketch goes as follows: Students applying to a literary faculty are interviewed by an old professor who is assisted by his secretary. The students explain their reason for applying and mention their favorite authors. They are naive, sentimental, and full of youthful enthusiasm. After they depart, the secretary asks the professor, "Well, what do you think?" The professor answers, "They are all right, but they lack any kind of system." The secretary assures him "We will certainly give them that." Later, the course of studies is completed and the students are taking their final examination. They all speak in a chorus in a most assured tone of voice: "So and so portrayed, so and so reflected," and so on. The authors they mentioned when applying for admission to the course are no longer mentioned at all.

This little sketch is, of course, humorous, but situations can easily be imagined in which the humor may become grim and where a public statement not couched in the official language would be considered high treason. It is generally known that, according to the Soviet press, the movement of Soviet troops into Czechoslovakia in 1968 was, in fact, "an act of brotherly help"; that the recent raising of prices was done "in response to popular demand"; that Idi Amin is a "progressive leader of black Africa." What makes the situation particularly distasteful is the official intonation one hears on the radio or in a movie in a scene where a party official is talking to an erring (but well intentioned) subordinate. This intonation can be best described as both intimate (the party is one's best friend, it really cares) and didactic (the party knows all).

In the history of mankind there have always been liars; some would lie in order to obtain what they desired, others would do so to avoid an unpleasant situation, still others could not resist the temptation to add a picturesque detail. An entirely new phenomenon has developed in the Soviet Union.

When a speaker addresses an audience, it very often happens that he knows that he is lying, that his audience knows that he is lying, and that he knows that his audience knows that he is lying, and everybody has a deep sense of satisfaction of fulfilling his highest civic duty. Under such conditions, language often ceases to be a means of communication and acquires an entirely new function - that of approved behavior. In the process of "ideologization" of language, Russian, being the central government language of the Soviet Union, has suffered more than the other languages.

It may be objected that the picture presented above is an exaggeration. Such an objection is perfectly valid. Soviet reality is certainly more complicated, and exceptions can easily be found to the above "rules." Nevertheless, these few random examples catch something very essential and can convey a very real sense of Soviet reality. Exceptions do exist, but they are rather minor and are very well kept in check by the party bureaucracy. The best proof comes in recent Soviet cultural policies.

Now to the problem of Russian ethnic identity, or to put it in other words, to the problem of Russian ethnocentrism (this term is used in a neutral sense). Throughout this volume, many references are made to the "institutionalization" of Russian ethnocentrism by the Soviet government. Everything Russian - history, language, literature, art - is proclaimed "great" and "glorious." After a long period of desecration and destruction, old churches are restored and proclaimed "national" treasures, almost all of the Russian past is rehabilitated and proclaimed "great." It could be expected that, under such conditions, the matter of Russian ethnic identity would cease to be a problem and, yet, this is not the case. There are people who accept and support the official policy of institutionalizing Russian ethnocentrism, but there are also people who deplore these policies precisely because they are Russians. To put it very simply, for many Russians the great Russian traditions and values proclaimed by the government are not their traditions and not their values. What the official policies may mean in the realm of language and literature was already mentioned. Another example may be added. The official attitude toward Andrey Rublev (d.ca.1430) may be summarized as follows: This great Russian painter expressed in his works the most cherished ideals and aspirations of his people, and these ideals and aspirations, have, of course, been fully realized in the Soviet Union.

One is fully justified in objecting that we are dealing here not with rehabilitation of the past but with its distortion. In the Soviet context, however, such a statement would necessarily become political and be considered almost an act of treason. To choose a more pointed example, a person speaking of Soviet military intervention in Czechoslovakia would certainly not be considered a Russian but an enemy of the Russian people, a traitor and a paid agent of capitalism. To sum it all up, there are sufficient reasons not to equate being a Russian with being a "new Soviet man," and not to consider the official language of the Soviet Union the highest point in the "progressive development" of the Russian language.

It should not be assumed that the two types of grass roots ethnocentrism outlined above must exist in a pure form; all kinds of combinations are, of course, possible. A person radically opposed to official Soviet ideology, nevertheless, may welcome the fact that some of the old churches are being restored (even though not as functioning churches) and that Fedor M. Dostoevsky's works have again become available in print. It is impossible to predict which type of ethnocentrism will ultimately prevail, and one can only hope that it will not be the ugly type.

To summarize, the real danger facing the Russian language is the official ideology which has deprived the language of its primary function, that of real communication. In the course of these discussions, numerous references have been made to the relatively recent group of Russian ruralists (derevenshchiki). The reason for popularity of these writers has been explained by reference to the Russians' sentimental attachment to their native soil. This explanation may very well be correct, but only partially. What attracts readers to these writers is that they "ring true," that they communicate some "truth" for which one would vainly look in Pravda ("The Truth"), the main press outlet for the Communist Party of the Soviet Union.

VIII

Blurring the Russian Demographic Profile

Proposition 8: As the Russian population urbanizes, grows in number but slips closer to plurality status among the people of the state, and further disperses throughout the USSR, the Russian group's basic physical outline seems to become ever less distinct. These demographic developments put pressure upon those concerned with guarding Russian values and identity to counteract or compensate for this diffusion of the ethnic group.

34 Spatial Diffusion of Russians in the USSR

William Boris Kory

Spatial diffusion of Russians in the Soviet Union has been a continuous process.(1)   As the largest and the dominant group in the country, the Russians have migrated and settled in every corner of the USSR.   In 1970, they accounted for nearly 20 percent of the population living outside the RSFSR, and over 30 million Russians now reside in the traditionally non-Russian areas of the country.

The migratory flows of Russians have been channeled primarily to the urban centers of the various Union republics. Because Russian migrants possess the skills required in the industrialized urban centers, their relocation to these areas comes naturally, not as a result of coercive governmental policy.   But incentives provided for these migrants played a major role in their decisions to move.

As a result of this migration, ethnic Russians today make up substantial minorities in many cities of the non-Russian Soviet republics.   The interaction of Russians with the non-Russian majority residing in these cities had, and continues to have, an effect on the ability of the Russian population to maintain its ethnic identity.   This study briefly examines the question of whether spatial diffusion of the Russians throughout the Soviet Union strengthens or weakens their ethnic identity, and tests the proposition that demographic developments in the USSR put pressure upon the guardians of Russian identity to compensate for such diffusion.

Data from the 1970 census of the Soviet Union showed that the country was home for 241.7 million people.   Of that total, 129 million Soviet citizens identified themselves as ethnically Russian, making up 53.4 percent of the total population of the USSR.   Since the population census of 1959, Russians had gained some 15 million people, although their percentage in the total population declined slightly (Appendix A).

The decline in percentage of Russians between 1959 and 1970, along with the fact that they have one of the lowest birth rates in the country, had led to a supposition among some Westerners and USSR citizens that the Russians will constitute only a plurality in the Soviet population by the census year of 1979.(2)   Moreover, owing to the increasing numbers of Russian intermarriages with persons from other ethnic groups, the dispersion of Russians throughout the country, and the internal emphasis on the concept of the Soviet People ("Sovetskii narod"), there is an assumption that the Russian population will not only lose its majority status but is in danger of losing its ethnic identity.   This expression, "Soviet People," has been increasingly used both in the speeches of political leaders and in the media.   It has also been used in many literary works, especially those dealing with World War II.(3)

Given the demographic parameters of the country, it is safe to predict that Russians will again constitute a majority of the Soviet population in the census year of 1979.(4)   The maintenance of this majority status by the Russian population is important for psychological effect if for no other reasons. The difference between comprising 51 percent of the total population versus 49 percent is obviously more significant than the difference, say, between 46 and 44 percent.   To maintain their majority status, assuming a high population projection of 267 million people in the USSR by 1979,(5) the Russians would need an increase of 4.5 million in the decade of the 1970s. Notwithstanding a low fertility rate, the Russians should reach that number.(6)

If natural increase will not produce the 4.5 million Russians needed for the majority status, the total should be augmented by a "natural unification process."   The above phraseology, along with terms like consolidation, integration, assimilation, convergence, and merging, has been widely used by Soviet geographers and ethnographers.(7)   One of them points out that the unification process, which leads toward forming larger ethnic groups, is "historically natural and progressive," and that evidence of such processes is seen in the reduction by nearly 50 percent of the number of ethnic group names between the 1926 and 1959 censuses.(8)

Many small ethnic groups have thus been merged with larger ones.   Groups like the Pomors, Kerzhaks, and certain groups of Cossacks have merged with the Russians, and it is almost impossible today to single them out as separate ethnic groups.(9)   They now form an integral part of the Russian group.   The process of consolidation has brought over two million Soviet citizens into the "Russian" ethnic classification between 1959 and 1970.(10)   This merging was due, in part, to the spatial mobility and intermarriage of the Russians with other ethnic groups.

The numerical decline among the entire Slavic population within the USSR, unlike the Russian population alone, will continue in the future. The proportion of Slavs decreased from 76.3 percent in 1959 to 74 percent in 1970. That 1970 figure may prove difficult to increase or even to maintain. The Slavs, as a group, have a much lower birth rate than the Soviet Asian population, and the assimilation process will not increase the proportion of the Slavs in the total population. The reason is that a great bulk of assimilation in the Soviet Union in the past absorbed Ukrainians and Belorussians into the RSFSR. One scholar suggests, however, that the demographic picture in the Soviet Union may drastically change, thus affecting the population's composition in the country.(11) He goes on to say that the government may institute a dual population policy, although that prospect is highly unlikely.(12)

With continuing migration in the USSR outside their own union republic, assimilation with other ethnic groups, and a steady decline in their birth rates, are the Russians in the process of losing their ethnic identity? Before answering that question it is important to look at the spatial distribution of Russians resulting from their migration, and at their intermarriages and assimilation with other ethnic groups throughout the country. The Russians are the most mobile group within the Soviet Union, and, as a result, constitute sizeable minorities in 14 of the union republics (Appendix A). In only four of the constituent republics do they make up 10 percent or less of the total population. In the Kazakh SSR, Russians comprise nearly half (42.4 percent, 1970), of all residents.

The migration of Russians has been particularly heavy to the urban centers of the country. Not only have they moved to the cities within the RSFSR, they have also migrated to urban centers in other union republics. One of the reasons for Russian migration is the fact that Russians provide many needed skills which the indigenous people do not as yet possess. In fact, the more underdeveloped the indigenous group, the greater the need for skilled, educated Russians coming to their cities.(13) Because the majority of these Russian migrants are moving to urban centers, they have become the second most urbanized group in the Soviet Union. Only the Jews, 98 percent of whom are urban dwellers, lead the Russians, who are nearly 70 percent urbanized.(14)

Russians constitute a majority in most cities within the RSFSR. In other union republics, Russians gravitate toward larger cities. Thus, the proportion of the Russian population tends to be higher in larger cities than in smaller ones outside the RSFSR.(15) Because each capital city is also the largest city of that union republic, it was a substantial percentage of ethnic Russians. Between the census years of 1959 and 1970, the migration of Russians to larger urban centers resulted in a higher rate of growth for cities with over 100,000 people.(16) Of the 36 million increase in the Soviet urban population between 1959 and 1970, about 17 million, or nearly half of the total increase, resulted from migration.(17)

Outside of Erevan and Tbilisi, Russians make up well over 20 percent of the population in the capital cities of the union republics. One of the reasons for a relatively low percentage of Russians in Erevan and Tbilisi is the fact that Armenians and Georgians are highly educated groups in the USSR. They can, therefore, provide skilled labor for their capitals and not depend on ethnic Russian migrants. In Frunze and in Alma Ata, capitals of the least developed republics, Russians make up the majority of the population. The larger cities continue to grow in the USSR. In 1970 there were ten cities with over one million people.(18) In 1977, 14 cities had reached that plateau, and by 1979 there may be 20 cities in the country with over one million people.(19)

It seems clear that urbanization will continue in the Soviet Union,(20) and that many cities outside the RSFSR will house Russian ethnic minorities. Yet, in spite of being a minority group and despite great distances from the Russian heartland, the ethnic Russian migrants retain their language and ethnic identity. In fact, the influx of Russians to cities of non-Russian areas has enhanced linguistic Russification of non-Russian groups and, in some instances, resulted in complete assimilation of non-Russian urban dwellers.(21) It is not unusual to hear Russian spoken in Riga, Kishinev, Frunze, and other cities outside the RSFSR. A similar conclusion has been reached by an American political scientist who showed that both urbanization and spatial diffusion of Russians in the various non-Russian union republics subjected other ethnic groups to substantial linguistic Russification.(22) A Soviet author went even further in analyzing the effect of Russian migration on the various non-Russian groups residing in the urban centers. He states that "the higher the percentage of Russians in the urban population, the greater the proportion of the indigenous population that regards Russian as its native tongue,"(23) and "the more intensive the change in the proportion of the Russian population, the faster is the change in the popularity of the Russian language."(24)

Thus, the spatial distribution of Russians within the USSR resulting from their migration shows them to be a highly urbanized group. As other ethnic groups become more urbanized, they will be coming to the cities which have already experienced substantial Russian influence. It is doubtful that non-Russian migrants to these urban centers will exhibit the cultural ascendancy which Russians brought to the cities. Non-Russian migrants will, therefore, be compelled to adopt the language and some culture of the dominant group in order to compete and function in the urban environment.

The language brought by Russian migrants and adopted by some non-Russian urban dwellers should not be viewed negatively. In an industrialized society like the Soviet Union, there is a case to be made for a wider usage of the Russian language. In 1970, over 129 million ethnic Russians and 13 million non-Russians identified Russian as their native tongue, and another 42 million non-Russians declared Russian to be their second language. Thus, 76 percent of all Soviet citizens know Russian very well, and that number is growing.(25) The non-Slavic population would benefit the most from a knowledge of Russian for it would enable them to be more competitive with native speakers of Russian. Linguistic Russification is quite different from total assimilation, although it is the first and probably the most important step in the assimilation process.

The spatial diffusion of Russians in the Soviet Union has led, inevitably, to their intermarriage with other groups. Families in which members belong to different ethnic groups numbered nearly 8 million and accounted for 13.5 percent of all families in the country in 1970.(26) In both rural and urban areas the tendency is toward the greater use of the Russian language among members of mixed families.(27) Some urban residents have not only adopted the Russian language but have gone one step further and now consider themselves to be Russian, adding to the Russian urban population.(28) However, a non-Russian living in an urban area outside the RSFSR has a much greater chance of being linguistically Russified than a rural non-Russian, because most Russian migration goes to urban centers.

Intermarriages in urban areas are much more prevalent than in the rural areas, and reflect the basic migration trends of the population. There are, obviously, significant differences among the various constituent republics in the percentage of families whose members come from different ethnic groups. It is not entirely clear why some groups in the Soviet Union exhibit a higher degree of exogamy than others.(29) What is clear, however, is that intermarriages are mounting in the country as the result of the growth of urban population, migration of ethnic groups, rising educational standards, and increasing usage of the Russian language (see chap. 37). The leaders of the USSR also have a positive attitude regarding exogamy, thus assuring the continuation of the process. Because most Soviet intermarriages occur in urban areas where the Russian presence and influence is strong, maintenance of the Russian language and, to a lesser degree, of Russian culture is assured. In the urban environment, if either of the marriage partners is Russian, in a great many cases, Russian becomes the language of the family. There may be a period of functional bilingualism, but this stage is quickly passed and the family becomes rapidly Russianized.(30)

In intermarriages between non-Russian people residing in urban areas, the use of Russian is also increasing. There is a story of a Korean teacher who married his Kirgiz pupil.(31) The man spoke both Korean and Kirgiz and was also fluent in Russian. The man's mother, who lived with them, spoke Korean and a little Russian. His wife spoke no Korean and a little Russian. Thus, Russian became their language of communication. The children of such families would become linguistically Russianized very quickly.

To conclude, spatial diffusion of Russians throughout the Soviet Union has resulted in increased urbanization and intermarriage between persons of Russian and other ethnic groups in the country. The processes of both urbanization and intermarriage have been positive factors in preserving and maintaining the ethnic identity of the Russian population.

As Russians migrate in the USSR outside the RSFSR and marry spouses of other ethnic groups, the usage of the Russian language and, to a smaller degree, the adoption of Russian culture continue to grow. The ethnic identity of the Russian population does not seem to diminish with the increased distance from the Russian heartland. In many cities outside the RSFSR the presence of Russian migrants promotes the usage of the Russian language by the local population. Some non-Russians have not only adopted the Russian language but have been completely assimilated and consider themselves to be Russian.

Because migration plays a major role in increasing the urban population, and all indications point to continuing migration in the Soviet Union, the merging of the population should continue.(32) As the rural population in the various union republics outside the RSFSR becomes more educated, it will migrate not only to the cities within the eponymous union republics but to other cities of the USSR. It is difficult to predict what effect this migration, along with the migration of Russians to areas outside the RSFSR, will have on the future of Soviet society. Because urbanization, in most cases, is associated with economic development and modernization, and because the Soviet Union is a pluralistic state, there are predictions by Professor Robert A. Lewis (see chaps. 26 and 36) that ethnic animosities within the country will lead to "... heightened tensions and ultimately to conflict."(33) In this view, the ethnic problems in the country are "...almost certainly intensifying and collectively becoming a dominant force shaping the future Soviet society."(34) Such ethnic conflict may represent too gloomy a picture of future relations among ethnic groups residing within the Soviet Union. The author of that view went on to suggest that those conflicts were not beyond control. Whatever Soviet ethnic relations may be in the future, it seems certain the migration will continue, and the use of the Russian language will grow. It may be that, as a Soviet analyst suggests, "the spread of fluency in Russian to wider sections of the Soviet population and the growth of ethnic intermarriage may bring certain benefits, including perhaps greater cultural tolerance and stability, to the Soviet Union."(35)

NOTES

(1) Peter R. Gould, Commission on College Geography, Spatial Diffusion, Resource paper #4, Association of American Geographers (Washington, D.C.: 1969).

(2) G. A. Bondarskaia, Rozhdaemost' v SSSR (Etnodemo-graficheskii aspetk) (Moscow: "Statistika," 1977).

(3) Andrei A. Grechko, Gody voiny (Moscow: Voennoe Izdatel'stvo, 1976).

(4) Nas 250 Millionov edited by N. S. Shubina (Moscow: "Statistika," 1974); Naselenie SSSR edited by A. J. Boiarskii (Moscow: Politicheskoe Izdatel'stvo, 1974); V. A. Boldyrev, Itogi perepisi naseleniia SSSR (Moscow: Izdatel'stvo "Statistika," 1974); Godfrey Baldwin, Estimates and Projections of the Population of the USSR, by Age and Sex: 1950-2000, (Washington, D. C.: U. S. Department of Commerce, Series P-91, #23, Dec. 1972); Boris Urlanis, Statistika naseleniia (Moscow: Izdatel'stvo "Statistika," 1971).

(5) "The Soviet Peoples: Population Growth and Policy," Population Bulletin, 28, no. 5 (1972): 18; James W. Brackett, Projections of the Population of the USSR, by Age and Sex: 1964-1985, International Population Reports, Series P-91, No. 13, (Washington, D.C.: U.S. Government Printing Office, 1964).

(6) D. Peter Mazur, "Constructing Fertility Tables for Soviet Population," Demography, 13, no. 1 (Feb. 1976): 19-35.

(7) V. I. Kozlov, "Ethnic Processes in the USSR," Geoforum, no. 9 (1972), p. 48-49; V. V. Pokshishevsky, Geography of the Soviet Union, (Moscow: Progress Publishers, 1974), p. 62; V. I. Perevedentsev, "Ob upravlenii migratsii Naselenia," in Migratsiia naseleniia RSFSR, edited by A. Z. Maikov (Moscow: Izdatel'stvo "Statistika," 1973), p. 155; S. I. Bruk, "Changes in Population Structure," Geoforum, no. 9 (1972), p. 16.

(8) Kozlov, p. 48.

(9) S. I. Bruk, "Endothermic Processes in the USSR," Soviet Review, 13, (Fall 1972): 221.

(10) Rein Taagepera, "The 1970 Soviet Census: Fusion or Crystallization of Nationalities," Soviet Studies, XXIII, no. 2, (October 1971): 217.

(11) J. F. Besemeres, "Population Politics in the USSR," Soviet Union, 11, part I (1975): 64-65.

(12) Ibid., p. 77.
(13) Robert A. Lewis, Richard H. Rowland and Ralph S. Clem, Nationality and Population Change in Russia and the USSR (New York: Praeger Publishers, 1976), chs. 5, 6.
(14) Narodnoe khoziaistvo SSSR, 1922-1972, (Moscow: "Statistika," 1972), pp. 13, 16-18; Itogi vsesoiuznoi perepisi naseleniia 1970 goda. Natsional'nyi sostav naseleniia SSSR IV (Moscow: "Statistika," 1973), pp. 20, 27.
(15) V. V. Pokshishevsky, "Etnicheskie protsessy v gorodakh SSSR: nekotorye problemy ikh izucheniia," Sovetskaia etnografiia, no. 5, (1969).
(16) Chauncy D. Harris, "Urbanization and Population Growth in the Soviet Union, 1959-1970," Geographical Review, 61, no. 1, (January 1971): 102-24.
(17) Itogi...1970 goda... Vol. IV (1973).
(18) Kenneth A. Erickson, "A Map of Urban Places, USSR, 1970," The Journal of Geography (Dec. 1971), pp. 555-60.
(19) The Statesman's Year Book: 1977-1978, edited by John Paxton (New York: St. Martin's Press, 1977), lists 14 cities (p. 1401) with over one million people. It also lists five cities with over 950,000 people. These may well reach one million by the census year of 1979.
(20) Chauncy D. Harris, Cities of the Soviet Union (Chicago: Rand McNally, 1970); B. S. Khorev, Gorodskie poseleniia SSSR (Moscow: Izdatel'stvo "Mysl'", 1968); B. S. Khorev, Problemy gorodov (Moscow: Izdatel'stvo "Mysl'", 1971); O. A. Konstantinov, "Geographical Study of Urban Places in the USSR," Geografiia naseleniia v SSSR: Osnovnye problemy edited by E. N. Pavlovskii (Moscow-Leningrad: "Nauka," 1964); Robert A. Lewis and Richard H. Rowland, "Urbanization in Russia and the USSR: 1897-1966," Annals of the Association of American Geographers, (December 1969), pp. 776-96.
(21) Robert A. Lewis et al., p. 132.
(22) Brian Silver, "The Impact of Urbanization and Geographic Dispersion on Linguistic Russification of Soviet Nationalities," Demography, 11, no. 1 (February 1974).
(23) A. A. Susokolov, "The Influence on Interethnic Relations of Differences in the Educational Levels and the Number of Ethnic Groups in Contact," Soviet Sociology, XV, no. 2 (Fall 1976): 38.
(24) Ibid., p. 52.
(25) Itogi . . .1970 goda. . . Vol. IV (1973).
(26) Itogi vsesoiuznoi perepisi naseleniia 1970 goda. Migratsiia naseleniia, chislo i sostav semei v SSSR, Vol. VII (Moscow: "Statistika," 1974), pp. 273-303.

(27)   E. Glyn Lewis, "Migration and Language in the USSR," International Migration Review, Vol. 5, (Summer 1971), p. 172.

(28)   Robert A. Lewis and Richard H. Rowland, "East is West and West is East...Population Redistribution in USSR and its Impact on Society," International Migration Review, 11, no. 1, (Spring 1977): 3-29.

(29)   Wesley A. Fisher, "Ethnic Consciousness and Inter-marriage: Correlates of Endogamy Among the Major Soviet Nationalities," Soviet Studies, XXIX, no. 3 (July 1977): 395-408. See also a rebuttal by Brian Silver, "Ethnic Intermarriage and Ethnic Consciousness among Soviet Nationalities," Soviet Studies, XXX, no. 1 (January 1978): 107-16.

(30)   E. Glyn Lewis, p. 175.

(31)   J. A. Newth, "Inter-Racial Marriages in Soviet Turkestan," Soviet Studies, XV, no. 4 (April 1964): 220.

(32)   V. A. Shpiliuk, Mezhrespublikanskaia migratsiia i sblizhenie natsii v SSSR, (L'vov: L'vovskii Gosu-darstvennyi Universitet, 1975).

(33)   Robert A. Lewis et al. p. 350.

(34)   Ibid., p. 381.

(35)   J. F. Besemeres, p. 80.

35 Ethnic Impact of Russian Dispersion in and Beyond the RSFSR

Matthews Pavlovich

Ethnic Russians are moving in a great and lasting migratory pattern in and from the RSFSR. This entails wide demographic dispersion from the traditional core of Russia to the other Soviet union republics, as well as to fringe areas of the RSFSR.(1) This dispersion has created two distinct Russian groups: the core and the periphery - a condition which will ultimately weaken Russian ethnic cohesion and probably alter the future of both groups.

The Soviet Russian population outside the RSFSR, in both relative and absolute numbers, has been increasing in response to the lure of better economic opportunities in agriculture and industry elsewhere, and as a by-product of tight ideological and bureaucratic strictures in the RSFSR. Relatively and absolutely, Soviet Russians migrate more than any other ethnic group in the Soviet Union.(2) Although Russians still (1970) represented 82.8 percent of the total RSFSR population(3) (a declining figure, but one that places them second in concentration only to Armenians in the Armenian SSR)(4) (see Appendix A), examination of census figures for three key years demonstrates that the rate of migration is increasing.(5) 1926 census data indicate that over 10 million Russians then lived in the administrative territories of other eponymous groups in the Soviet union republics. Those numbers had increased by 1959 to over 16 million; not considering the span of time, a striking increase.(6) However, by 1970, over 21 million Soviet Russians lived in 14 non-Russian Soviet union republics, or 16.3 percent of the entire Russian population.(7) These numbers do not include those Russians who reside in non-Russian territories in the RSFSR: Autonomous Soviet Socialist Republics (ASSRs), Autonomous Oblasts (AObs), and Autonomous Okrugs (AOks), where 31 different national-ities live(8) (Bashkir, Buriat, Chechen-Ingush, Chuvash,

Dagestan, Kabardin-Balkar, Kalmyk, Karelian, Komi, Mari, Mordvin, North Osset, Tatar, Tuvin, Udmurt and Yakut ASSRs; Aga Buryat AOk, Adygey AOb, Chukchi AOk, Evenk AOk, Jewish AOb, Gorno-Altay AOb, Karachay-Cherkess AOb, Khakass AOb, Khant-Mansi AOk, Komi Permiak AOk, Koriak AOk, Nenets AOk, Taimyr Dolgan-Nenets AOk, Ust Orda Buriat AOk, Yamal Nenets AOk). There was also an increase in the number of Russians living on the fringes of the RSFSR (along the Seas of Japan and Okhotsk and China's borders) from more than 8 million in 1959 to over 9 million in 1970. Russians who had migrated from, or were born outside, the heart of the RSFSR, surpassed 30.5 million by 1970, or 23.5 percent of all Soviet Russians.(9)

Moreover, the pattern of migration from northern Russia has changed; most Russians are now migrating not to the Soviet western Slavic union republics (Ukraine and Belorussia), as they once did, but to the more distant eastern territories, notably Northern Kazakhstan, Western Siberia, and Central Asia in the Soviet Union.(10)

The Russians' traditional core settlements are focused mainly in these oblasts of the RSFSR: Archangel, Bryansk, Gorky, Ivanovo, Kaliningrad, Kaluga, Kirov, Kostroma, Leningrad, Moscow, Murmansk, Novgorod, Orel, Perm, Pskov, Ryazan, Smolensk, Sverdlovsk, Tula, Vladimir, Vologda and Yaroslave. This section of the RSFSR has long been a poor area for agriculture.(11) The hostile surroundings and poor farming conditions have driven Russians to seek better opportunities in other Soviet Union republics. This is reflected in the fact that the non-black earth region had 62.3 percent of the total Soviet Russian population in 1959 whereas that proportion had declined to 59.8 percent by 1970.(12)

The core area has subsequently provided the bulk of Russian migration to the Kazakh SSR,(13) a region with natural conditions better suited to productive agriculture. From 1959 to 1970, the Kazakh SSR has seen a constant increase in the movement of Russians, Belorussians, Ukrainians, and Asians(14) to its large and accommodating urban centers, where urbanized Russians mainly settle.(15)

Another factor has made the Kazakh SSR attractive to Russian settlers. During the 1950s and 1960s the Soviet government infused enormous amounts of capital into the economy to develop the virgin lands of the northern section of the Kazakh SSR.(16) This action offered great opportunities for the Russian group to satisfy the Kazakh Union republic's need for a technically skilled labor force to develop the lands.(17) According to the Soviet census for 1959, there were already 3.5 million Russian settlers in the Kazakh SSR. As agricultural capital investment increased for the development of the area, so did the Russian migration.(18) Eleven years later the Russian group there had increased to

over five million.(19)   Concentration of Russian settlers in the
Kazakh SSR was highest in the following northerly oblasts:
Karaganda,   Kokchetav,   Kustanay,   Pavlodar,   Semipalatinsk,
Severo-Kazakhstan and Tselinograd.   In 1959, these oblasts
contained a total population of 4,290,020, with the Russians
comprising 1,960,085 or 45.7 percent of this total.   Eleven
years later, the absolute numbers of Russian settlers had
increased to 2,735,858, or 48.03 percent of the total population
of the northern Kazakh oblasts (5,695,040).(20)   Russian
settlers in Northern Kazakhstan have established permanent
settlements mainly in the oblasts of Karaganda, Kokchetav,
Kustanay, Pavlodar, and Tselinograd.(21)
    Economically motivated outmigration from the non-black
earth region to Siberia and northern Kazakhstan add to the
developing labor forces of these distant regions in the Soviet
Union,(22) so that these regions of northern Kazakhstan,
western Siberia and Siberia have absorbed a substantial
number of Russians in urban centers.(23)   Urbanized
Russians,   though   migrating   for   better   economic
opportunities,(24) do not migrate to the Far East and eastern
Siberia in great numbers.(25)   In spite of the privileges and
rewards, such as housing and higher pay offered for
permanent settlers to go to the Far East and eastern Siberia,
their harsh climate and few urban centers make these regions
unattractive for the Russians.   According to 1970 census
figures, only 3.1 percent of the Russian group living outside
the central RSFSR moved to the Far East and 2.6 percent to
eastern Siberia.(26)   Migration is mainly to existing cities,(27)
though western Siberia (which encompasses Tiumen, Omsk,
Novosibirsk, Kemerovo, and Kurgan oblasts, including the
Altai Krai and Gorno-Altai Krai) in 1959 reported 10,570,464
Russians and in 1970, 11,596,037.(28)
    Those Russians who had migrated and who migrate to
non-Slavic areas among various ASSRs, AObs, and AOks in
the RSFSR numbered 10 million in 1970.(29)   Added to the 21
million Soviet Russians outside the RSFSR the same year, 23.8
percent of all Soviet Russians – those who live outside their
main ethnic concentration(30) – are, strictly defined, a
potential loss to the core group at home.
    Further examination shows that Russians living outside
the RSFSR in other Soviet union republics were dispersed, to
begin with, throughout the Baltic republics: the Estonian SSR
in 1959 had 240,227 or 21.1 percent of the total Estonian SSR
population, and in 1970 Russians made up 334,620 or 24.7
percent of the SSR total.   The Latvian SSR in 1959 had
556,448 Russians or 26.8 percent, and in 1970, 704,599 or 29.8
percent; the Lithuanian SSR had 231,014 Russians or 8.5
percent in 1959 and in 1970, 267,989 or 8.6 percent.(31)   Most
of those Russians settling in these Baltic republics are highly
skilled technicians and professionals.(32)

In the Belorussian SSR, Russians are concentrated mainly in the western oblasts or Brest, Gomel, Mogilev and Vitebsk. In 1970, Russians in these oblasts represented 62 percent of the total population of the oblasts.(33) In the Ukrainian SSR the Russian population increased from 7,090,813 (16.9 percent) in 1959 to 9,126,331 (19.4 percent) in 1970, an increase of 2,035,518 during the period.(34) In the Central Asian SSRs, such as the Uzbek, Tajik, and Kirgiz, the Russian population declined in some of the oblasts of the SSRs in relative numbers, due to the increase of the neighboring central Asian groups within the area, but to the west, in the Moldavian SSR, it increased from 292,930 (10.2 percent) in 1959 to 414,444 (11.6 percent) in 1970.(35)

Moreover, the Russian outmigration from the non-black earth region flows not only to other Soviet union republics, but also to urban centers of ASSRs, AObs, and AOks within the RSFSR, often to the Chuvash, Udmurt, Karelian, Komi, Mari, and Mordvin ASSRs, and others whose eponymous population differs from the Russian group.   Finno-Ugric groups combine with Turkic ones like the population of the Tatar and the Chuvash ASSRs along the upper Volga basin.(36)   A look at Russian migration into the ASSRs during the period from 1959 to 1970 shows that in the Chuvash ASSR in 1959 there were 263,692 Russian settlers (24.0 percent) and in 1970 299,241 (24.5 percent); the Udmurt ASSR in 1959 had 760,002 (56.8 percent) and in 1970 809,563 (57.1 percent); the Karelian ASSR in 1959 had 412,773 Russians (63.4 percent), and 486,200 (68.1 percent) in 1970; the Komi ASSR saw a much higher increase, from 395,975 (48.6 percent) in 1959 to 512,203 (53.1 percent) in 1970; Mari ASSR had 309,514 (47.8 percent) in 1959 and 321,800 (46.9 percent) in 1970; and the Mordvin ASSR in 1959 had 592,355 Russians (59.1 percent), and in 1970, 606,817 (58.9 percent of the total population of the unit.)(37)

Besides ethnic depletion through outmigration from the RSFSR, dilution creates some losses for the core group owing to the geographical dispersion of Russians in other Soviet union republics.   One relatively minor form of dilution is that of intermarriage between Russians and non-Russians. Intermarriages in northern Kazakhstan are more frequently among Slavic groups, such as Russians, Ukrainians, Belorussians, and to a lesser degree, the Poles.(38)   Studies by a Soviet sociologist show not only that intermarriages occur mainly among the Slavic groups, but much less between Russians and the eponymous group (Kazakhs) in the area.(39) Another demographic factor more important than intermarriage is the birth rate among the Russian group in the USSR.   The Russian natural birth rate falls among the lowest in the Soviet Union, (40) far below some of the Asiatics in the Central Asian SSRs.   The recorded birth rate during the period from 1959 to

1970 among Ukrainians was 15.8 per 1000, among Russians 19.0, among Georgians 24.0, but among Kazakhs 41.2.(41) However, another study by a Soviet sociologist made comparisons of natural increases in population per 1000 and showed 14.0 for 1963 in the USSR and 11.3 in the RSFSR.(42) The indication is that the higher degree of industrialization which produces better living conditions, along with urbanization,(43) is related to the lower birth rate among the Russian group.

The lower birth rate among Russians will influence both relative and absolute aspects of the Russian group's dominant status in the Soviet Union. The least effective dilution affecting the Russian group is that of the official promotion of the "Soviet People" with its unitary stress. It carries the smallest degree of influence affecting the group's ethnocentrism.(44) In fact, the assertion of some Soviet writers is that the "Soviet People" does not pose a problem for the Russian group, nor for that matter any ethnic group in the USSR. The "Soviet People," they say, is a common denominator for all Soviet people with emphasis on existing ethnic differences in linguistic and group characteristics, with rights and freedom for all.(45)

Traditional ways of life are ended and, to some extent, family bonds are loosened by the migration, industrialization, and urbanization of the Russian group. Furthermore, new environments created by the demographic movement create discontinuity between the core group and the peripheral group. For example, the Kazakh people are Asians possessing traditions and language strikingly different from those of the Russian settlers.(46) This ultimately forces the peripheral Russian group to adapt to the new surroundings and traditions, including linguistic assimilation, which further separates them from the core group. One observer has remarked: ". . . in mixed Yakut-Russian communities [of the Soviet Far East and Siberia], the Yakut language often proved the dominant one, and the Russian inhabitants even in some cases forgot their own language."(47) In fact, history has shown that major migrations of an ethnic group have, at times, produced certain shields that the core group uses to protect itself from the intrusion of alien traditions that the peripheral group may have assimilated. The Russian group may not be an exception.(48) Even within the RSFSR, especially the fringe areas far from the center, notable variations exist in Russian life style like those evident among the "Sibiryaks," whose past has been associated with exiles to Siberia.(49) The core group's reaction may, in fact, be unfavorable toward the Russians of the periphery because of its fear that the peripheral "frontier" group will develop independently, and may have been influenced by the new surroundings, tradition, and culture of alien eponymous groups.(50) Records indicate that long-term Russian settlers and their descendants remaining away from the heartland are rarely used in the service of the central government administration. They are conspicuously absent from the positions of First and Second Communist Party secretaries for non-Russian Soviet union republics. Also, these peripheral Russian settlers in the RSFSR areas are far from the center. The reason seems to be that central authorities believe Russian settlers may develop too close an identification with another eponymous group's interests or its area, even though such Russian settlers might prove useful administrators precisely because, from residence there, they have certain practical experience with the local ethnic group by living among it.(51) Actual realization of the notions of socialist equality, especially of integration among different ethnic groups, or elevation of "socialist consciousness,"(52) is a rarity in the Soviet Union. Even those Soviet writers initially convinced of the "merging and converging among nationalities of diverse origin"(53) find that it appears primarily on paper. "Merging and converging" among different ethnic groups (Russians and other Slavic people, Ukrainians, and Belorussians with Central Asians, Kazakhs and Tajiks) is not very common in the status-conscious Soviet Union, including, of course, Soviet Russia (where in particular data are to be found on the subject).(54)

Some Western specialists, observing Soviet demographic movements, conclude that industrialization could have stabilizing effects upon all ethnic groups' social and economic life.(55) Soviet writers see the interrepublic migration and industrialization not on the level of the capitalist competition creating a social conflict, for they see socialist industrialization as a democracy having an interethnic character.(56) First, in the eyes of Western specialists, the demographic dispersion of the Russians is good for the Russian group and will have little or no effect upon the group's future cohesion. As far as Soviet authorities are concerned, migration is an offspring of industrialization; therefore, it is good for multiethnic socialism.(57) However, if any ethnic group's wide demographic dispersion is regarded as good for the group's ethnic cohesion, it must be felt that sooner or later all ethnic groups are going to merge into this economic group. Though economic stabilization, or equalization, may work positively among non-Russian ethnic groups, for the Russian group it represents a psychological danger, if not a real threat, to keeping the group cohesive, that is, at home in their ancestral land and not widely dispersed over such geographic and often alien distances.

In the Soviet Union, where pressures for group conformity are great, the effects of cultural and sociohistorical differences between ethnic groups cannot be lightly dismissed.

These same problems face the peripheral Russian group in non-Russian areas.(58) Yet, industrialization, with its attributes such as mass urbanization - including rural migration to many industrialized centers throughout the Soviet Union - carries large social and political implications for the future of the Russian group. Migrational intensity largely depends on the economic development of a region;(59) therefore, the industrialization of those distant regions in the non-Russian Soviet Union republics and fringe areas of the RSFSR where Russians settle will emphasize more and more the basic economic inequalities among ethnic groups across the USSR's geographic regions.(60) Those geographically dispersed Soviet Russians throughout the Soviet Union will bring about changes in their own group's ethnic makeup, both at home within the core group and within the peripheral group.

Continuing Russian demographic dispersion evidently has finally stirred the central government into initiating a major effort for developing that quintessentially Russian zone, the non-black earth region. This resulted in injecting major capital investment for agricultural development. On March 20, 1974, the Central Committee of the Communist Party of the Soviet Union (CPSU) discussed the importance of agricultural development in the non-black earth region.(61) It was decided that the region needed an investment of capital over a ten-year period for development of the area. According to Soviet writers, the real cause for outmigration from there is the economic situation and the lack of natural resources of the region.(62) Thus, it could be deduced that one reason behind development projects for the non-black earth region is ethnic preservation. This represented significant recognition by the central government of the symbolic importance of the non-black earth region for the Russian group. The non-black earth region encompasses 23 Russians oblasts and six ASSRs of non-Russian ethnic groups which have been economically and culturally neglected in the past.(63) Among those 23, the Archangel Oblast takes in the large Nenets Autonomous Okrug along the Pechora Sea. Also, Perm Oblast includes the Komi Permiak Autonomous Okrug.

Necessary capital investment in agriculture in the non-black earth region should help bring better socioeconomic conditions to the people, both to the Russian group and the non-Russians in the ASSRs, AObs, and AOks; however, the development is seen as a vehicle designed mainly to prevent further Russian outmigration from the zone.(64) The regime would argue that what is good for Russians is good for the entire USSR. But, according to Soviet writings, a "difference in migrational intensity is relative to the economic development of a region."(65) Moreover, money spent on the non-black earth region's agricultural development over the next decade could well have developed other, more suitable areas, where the climate is milder and the already-existing agricultural conditions could be improved, areas such as Ukraine or Kazakhstan. If the region's development was to help primarily Russians, it would be fairly obvious that the central regime's main concern was for this ethnic group.

There are no clear-cut definitions of economic development in the RSFSR today; the only exceptions are the future projections for the development of the non-black earth region where five-year plans and billions of rubles have been set aside for its agricultural development. In the past ten years this region has absorbed over 40 billion rubles, and the same amount is set aside for the next five-year plans to develop agriculture.(66) Western observers state that there is a growing conflict between ethnic groups in competition for future economic betterment, particularly between the dominant Russian group and other ethnic groups in the Soviet Union.(67) The fight for equal distribution among the ethnic groups will produce more of a gap between the core group and the peripheral Russian group for, in other eponymous Soviet union republics, the peripheral Russian groups constitute a serious minority.(68)

In essence, the question may arise: How are the peripheral Russians to maintain their identity outside the Russian core area and RSFSR boundaries, regardless of the core group's feelings? One answer lies in the prevention of further outmigration from the core area. That would minimize, to some extent, the significance of widening dissimilarities between the core and the peripheral group. Also, the real problem for the core group, at present, is how to keep its youth on a collective or state farm (kolkhoz or sovkhoz).(69) An analysis of Russian group movement will not reveal significant changes in the patterns of the present demographic migration in the foreseeable future, unless there is a new, far-reaching change in Soviet economic development. The already prolonged separation of the core group from the peripheral group can change the core's outlook toward the periphery. This separation of the two groups mandates more artificial or planned contacts to prevent further erosion of the group's ethnic cohesion. Effort will be required to reinforce the closeness that an ethnic group exhibits beyond sharing the same ethnic traits such as language, cultural patterns, ancestral home, and other things. One helpful factor, for example, could be the mass media, placed at the disposal of an ethnic group, but this is not possible, because such communication is controlled by the supra-ethnic Soviet central government. The mass media is used entirely for communist state propaganda purposes, advancing slogans of international socialism.(70) Television and phototelegraphy reach exceptionally distant regions of the Soviet Union from Moscow and Leningrad, but always to elevate a consciousness of

internationalism and socialism.(71) Emphasis is invariably put
on the central government information media reaching the far
corners, into Kiev, Minsk, Kuibyshev, Kharkov, Lvov,
Sverdlovsk, Tashkent and other cities.(72) Media would need
to be more specifically ethnic oriented if it were to keep the
Russian periphery in close touch with the core group. The
centrally controlled communications media in this case have less
effect upon such an ethnic group than Western media might
with their regional programming.

Identification of the Russian core group as the right arm
of the central government, and in the sociopolitical life of the
Soviet Union as the group favored by the Soviet regime,(73)
does not necessarily strengthen Russian group identity. The
Russians' possession of most-favored-nation status in the
multiethnic Soviet Union may, in fact, be damaging to the
central Russian group in the future. Also, most of the second
secretaries of the CPSU serving throughout the Soviet Union
in non-Russian SSRs come from the Russian core group. They
are used in administration as a buffer between the SSR's first
secretary and interests of the eponymous population at
large.(74)

Most settlements of Russians in non-Russian Soviet union
republics are permanent ones, well established among the
eponymous populations of the SSRs.(75) It is inconceivable
that large proportions of these peripheral Russians would
return to the RSFSR now or in the distant future. That is
why the development of demographic dispersion and
urbanization have, to some extent, put pressure on concerned
guardians of Russian values, to counteract and to compensate
for the diffusion of the ethnic group at home. This diffusion,
especially migration from the home area to other Soviet union
republics, may serve as a catalyst acting to strengthen the
group sentiment of the Russian core. Thus, in the not too
distant future, the gulf between the core group and the
periphery will widen irreparably.

If there is a substantial increase in numbers among the
Russians in the future, though they slip into plurality status
among all people of the state, the Russian group's basic
physical outline, and above all the peripheral Russian group,
will become less and less distinct. It is not impossible that
the peripheral Russians may, in some distant future, largely
integrate, if not assimilate, with the other ethnic groups of
the borderlands. This possibility is strongly expected by
informed persons from Eastern Europe. Also, in this author's
conversation with Soviet Russians in 1977, they volunteered
the observation that there is sure to be a sharper contrast
developing among Russians of the Soviet periphery within the
fringe areas of present RSFSR's present borders. Thus, the
ethnic Russian diaspora within the USSR may have become
separated forever from the core group at home, regardless of

the present dominant sociopolitical status of the Russians
under the Soviet regime.

NOTES

(1) Galina Alekseevna Bondarskaia, Rozhdaemost' v
     SSSR: etnodemograficheskii aspekt (Moscow: Izdatel'stvo
     "Statistika," 1977), pp. 28-51.
(2) A. V. Topilin, Territorial'noe pereraspredelenie
     trudovykh resursov v SSSR   (Moscow: Izdatel'stvo
     "Ekonomika," 1975), pp. 44-89.
(3) Itogi vsesoiuznoi perepisi naseleniia 1970 goda. Natsio-
     nal'nyi sostav naseleniia SSSR   (Moscow: "Statistika,"
     1973), Vol. IV, p. 12.
(4) Ibid., p. 15.
(5) Ibid., pp. 12-15.
(6) Vsesoiuznaia perepis' naseleniia 1926 goda   (Moscow:
     Tscentral'noe statisticheskoe upravleniie SSSR, otdel
     "perepisi," 1928), Vol. V, p. 5; Vol. X, p. 9; Vol. XI,
     p. 8; Vol. XIV, pp. 6-28 ff; Vol. XVIII, p. 474; Vol.
     XXI, Sect. II, p. 437; Vol. XXII, pp. 25, 152-57, 481;
     Vol. XXIII, pp. V, 124, 145, 235, 384; Vol. XXIV and
     XXVI, Sect. II. pp. 18-37. Also, Itogi . . .1970
     goda . . ., Vol. IV, p. 12.
(7) Itogi . . .1970 goda . . ., pp. 12-15.
(8) Ibid., pp. 61-129.
(9) Ibid.
(10) A. V. Topilin, pp. 44-89.
(11) Robert A Lewis, Richard H. Rowland, Ralph S. Clem,
     Nationality and Population Change in Russia and the
     USSR: An Evaluation of Census Data, 1897-1970 (New
     York: Praeger Publishers, 1976), p. 17; Nechernozem'e:
     demograficheskii ezhegodnik   (Moscow: Izdatel'stvo
     "Statistika," 1977), p. 15.
(12) Narodnoe khoziaistvo SSSR v 1975 godu: Statisticheskii
     ezhegodnik (Moscow: Izdatel'stvo "Statistika," 1976), p.
     11; Lewis el al., p. 206; Nechernozem'e . . ., pp. 37-58.
(13) Topilin, pp. 44-90; Nechernozem'e . . ., pp. 26-36.
(14) Topilin, pp. 40-90; Iu. A. Evestigneev, "Interethnic
     Marriages in Some Cities of Northern Kazakhstan,"
     (Vestnik Moskovskogo universiteta, Istoriia, 1972. #6),
     Soviet Sociology, XIII, no. 3, (Winter 1974-1975): 3-17;
     also, V. A. Shpiliuk, Mezhrespublikanskaia migratsiia
     i sblizhenie natsii v SSSR   (Lvov: Isdatel'stvo
     Ob"edinenie "Vysshaia Shkola," 1975), pp. 59-61.
(15) Evestigneev, pp. 3-17.
(16) Ibid.

(17) Topilin, pp. 44-80. Also Shpiliuk, pp. 73-75.
(18) Topilin, pp. 44-80.
(19) Itogi . . . 1970 goda . . ., Vol. IV, pp. 242-50.
(20) Itogi vsesoiuznoi perepisi naseleniia 1959 goda, Kazakhstan SSR (Moscow: Gosstatizdat, 1963, "Kraus Reprint: A Division of Kraus Thomson Organization Limited, Nendeln, Liechtenstein, 1975), pp. 168-72; also Itogi . . . 1970 goda . . ., Vol. IV, pp. 232-51.
(21) Evestigneev, pp. 3-17.
(22) Topilin, pp. 40-90.
(23) Viktor Ivanovich Perevedentsev, "Population Movement and Labor Supply in Siberia. Part III," (Novosibirsk: "Nauka" Publishing House, 1966), Soviet Sociology, VIII, no. 1 (Summer 1969): pp. 24-68; also, Shpiliuk, pp. 41-44.
(24) L. L. Rybakovskii, Regional'nyi analiz migratsii (Moscow: Izdatel'stvo "Statistika," 1973), pp. 109-12.
(25) E. D. Malinin and A. K. Ushavov, Naselenii Sibiri (Moscow: "Statistika," 1976), pp. 44-62.
(26) Lewis et al., p. 213.
(27) Malinin and Ushavov, pp. 44-62.
(28) Itogi . . . 1970 goda . . ., Vol. IV, pp. 61-130.
(29) Ibid., pp. 16-18, 62-130.
(30) Ibid.
(31) Ibid., pp. 14-15.
(32) Topilin, p. 86.
(33) Itogi . . . 1970 goda . . ., Vol. IV, pp. 196-201.
(34) Ibid, p. 12.
(35) Ibid., pp. 13-15.
(36) Nechernozemie . . ., pp. 9-19.
(37) Itogi . . . 1970 goda . . ., Vol. IV, pp. 17-18.
(38) Evestigneev, pp. 3-17.
(39) Ibid.
(40) Bondarskaia, pp. 21-40.
(41) Ibid., pp. 28-29.
(42) Perevedentsev, p. 10.
(43) Evestigneev, pp. 3-17.
(44) Maxim Kim, The Soviet People-A New Historical Community (Moscow: Progress Publishers, 1972); Roy A Medvedev, On Socialist Democracy (New York: Alfred Knopf, 1975), pp. 70-80.
(45) Shpiliuk, pp. 54-58.
(46) Bondarskaia, pp. 40-41.
(47) Ibid., p. 40. Also, Terence Armstrong, "The Administration of Northern Peoples: The USSR," in The Arctic Frontier, edited by Ronald St. John Macdonald (Toronto: University of Toronto Press, 1966), p. 63.
(48) Bondarskaia, p. 40.
(49) Rybakovskii, pp. 109-12.

(50) John H. Miller, "Cadres Policy in Nationality Areas: Recruitment of CPSU First and Second Secretaries in non-Russian Republics of the USSR," Soviet Studies, XXIX, no. 1, (January 1977), 26; A. A. Susokolov, "The Influence of Interethnic Relations or Differences in the Educational Levels and the Number of Ethnic Groups in Contact," Soviet Sociology, Vol. XV, no. 2, (Fall 1976): 39.
(51) Miller, pp. 22-23.
(52) Shpiliuk, pp. 54-58.
(53) Evestigneev, pp. 3-17.
(54) Ibid.
(55) Lewis et al., p. 87.
(56) Shpiliuk, p. 67.
(57) Ibid.
(58) Bondarskaia, p. 40.
(59) Shpiliuk, pp. 41-54.
(60) Ibid.
(61) Nechernozem'e . . ., p. 18.
(62) Shpiliuk, p. 73.
(63) Nechernozem'e . . ., pp. 9-19.
(64) Ibid.
(65) Shpiliuk, p. 41.
(66) FBIS-Sov-78-15. (Monday, January 23, 1978), Vol. III, No. 15, p. T1.
(67) Miller, pp. 3-36.
(68) Ibid., p. 10.
(69) Topilin, pp. 40-90.
(70) FBIS-Sov-77-250. (Thursday, Dec. 29, 1977), Vol. II, No. 250, p. R5.
(71) Shpiliuk, pp. 54-58.
(72) Ibid.
(73) Miller, pp. 19-30.
(74) Ibid., pp. 3-36.
(75) Evestigneev, pp. 3-17.

36 Comment—
Intensifying Russian
Ethnic Identity by
Dispersion
Robert A. Lewis

The proposition contends that the urbanization, dispersal, basic physical outline, and relative decline to plurality status of the Russian ethnic group are important factors that may have contributed or will contribute to a lessening of Russian ethnicity. However, if one assumes that there is a universality in ethnic processes in the USSR, it can be argued that these factors either are not important to, or intensify, Russian ethnic identity.

Basic to an understanding of ethnicity is the concept of the us-them dichotomy, which essentially maintains that it is the existence of another ethnic group that is the necessary precondition for ethnic identity. Ethnic groups are characterized by a "prenational" stage, when interaction among groups is limited and ethnic identity is either weakly developed or absent. The processes of modernization appear to intensify ethnicity through such forces as transportation, communication, and migration. As groups come into contact and competition with one another, ethnic differences are perceived. That heightens the feeling of ethnic identity of all the groups involved, and generally results in animosities and tensions. Dominant groups tend to impose sanctions on other groups and to benefit disproportionately from the economic development that is occurring. Migration is a crucial factor in this process, because economic development ultimately results in a massive redistribution of the population, and in multiethnic states this results in much geographical mixing of the various ethnic groups and heightened ethnic awareness. So economic development has resulted in social and cultural change and an intensification of ethnicity.

Professor Kory correctly notes (chap. 34) that urbanization and dispersal of the Russians have not led to a loss of Russian ethnic identity, because of such factors as

Russianization and intermarriage, and that the urban population in non-Russian areas is frequently very heterogeneous. It is precisely in these urban areas, however, that geographical intermixing of the Russians with other ethnic groups promotes a rise in ethnic awareness of all groups involved. Moreover, because the USSR is divided into a series of homelands based on its political administrative structure, much of the migration that occurs results in intrusion into another homeland, something not appreciated the world over. Another consideration important to Russian ethnicity is that the Russians are the only major ethnic group that can attend primary and secondary school in their own language outside of their republic.

With respect to the changing physical outline of the Russian people, this factor would appear to be of little significance with respect to Russian ethnic identity because of the above considerations. Moreover, there are many examples of groups in multiethnic, modernizing states that have experienced considerable redistribution, and yet have experienced an appreciable intensification of ethnic identity. American Blacks and Scots in the United Kingdom are notable examples. Clearly, one does not need to perceive a compact physical outline of his group to have a sense of ethnicity. The U.S. experience is instructive in this regard.

As to the plurality issue, Professor Kory correctly maintains that at least by 1980 the Russians should still constitute a majority of the Russian population. His emphasis on Russification with regard to the growth of the Russian population is well placed. However, even if there were no Russification during the decade of the 1970s and the natural increase of the Russians averaged five per thousand, which is slightly below the 5.9 per thousand registered in the RSFSR in 1970 and 1975, their natural increase would be some 6.5 million, well over the 4.5 million that was estimated to be required to maintain majority status.

However, a more pertinent issue with regard to the dominance of the Russians is, so what if they were only a plurality and not a majority of the Soviet population? Clearly, 50 percent or more is no magic number that would have a psychological or political impact on the Russians, particularly since voting is not a very serious exercise in the USSR. The Russians are and have been the dominant political group in the USSR and in the Russian Empire, despite their varying relative share of the population. Furthermore, there is no indication that their dominance has varied with their relative share of the population. Their dominance relates primarily to political, historical, economic, and ideological factors, and not just to sheer numbers. In fact, a dominant group need not be in the majority; witness South Africa. In terms of the present-day boundaries, it has only been since 1926 that the

Russians have comprised a majority of the Soviet population, and no appreciable change in their influence can be related to this relative increase. Within the boundaries of the Russian Empire in 1897, their share was 44.3 percent; it rose to about 53 percent within the 1926 boundaries, and to 58.1 percent in the 1939 boundaries. With the territory and population acquired during World War II, the Russians declined relatively. Russians enumerated in the census as a percent of the 1939 population (in present-day boundaries) comprised 51.3 percent of the population.(1) Thus, Russians have not always been in the majority in the Russian Empire and the USSR, and their proportion of the total population has varied considerably, apparently much more than their dominance has varied.

NOTES

(1)   Frank Lorimer, The Population of the Soviet Union (Geneva: League of Nations, 1946), pp. 55, 138; Robert A. Lewis, Richard H. Rowland, Ralph S. Clem, Nationality and Population Change in Russia and the USSR. An Evaluation of Census Data, 1897-1970   (New   York: Praeger Publishers, 1976), pp. 278-79.

37 Comment —
The Extent of Intermarriage in the Russian Group
Wesley Andrew Fisher

Both Matthews Pavlovich (Chap. 35) and Professor William B. Kory (Chap. 34) discuss intermarriage as a consequence of the spatial diffusion of Russians throughout the Soviet Union, but they do not provide data about the intermarriage of Russians. To what extent are Russians in the USSR intermarrying with other ethnic groups? No Soviet data directly concerning the intermarriage of Russians exist for the USSR as a whole. It is possible, nonetheless, to estimate fairly closely, from available census figures, the proportions of Russians currently intermarried.

The number of Russians living in families containing only Russians is calculable from the 1970 census.(1) Unfortunately, the number of Russians living in families of all kinds or the number of families composed of husband-wife pairs containing a Russian is unknown. Assume, however, that the tendency of Russians to live in families does not differ very much from the tendency of the Soviet population as a whole to live in families. In other words, assume that 89.96 percent of Russians in the USSR lived in families at the time of the 1970 census. It is then possible to calculate the expected number of Russians living in families of all sorts in a given region, had the tendency of Russians to live in families been the same as that of the entire Soviet population.

This technique shows that the proportion of Russians living in families, who lived in all-Russian families in 1970 in the USSR as a whole, was 776 per thousand standardized population. This means that if the tendency for Russians to live in families is assumed to be the same as for the USSR population as a whole, 77.6 percent of Russians who were living in families were living exclusively with other Russians. While these figures are not the same as the actual percentages of homogamous marriages, they indicate quite accurately the extent to which Russians experience and have contact with ethnic intermarriage in their immediate families.

The proportion of Russians in the RSFSR who live in homogeneous families is quite high (81.6 percent). This is lower than the proportions of all other major ethnic groups living in homogeneous families within their respective republics with the exception of Belorussians, Estonians, Latvians, and Ukrainians.(2) The opportunity to meet members of other ethnic groups clearly plays a great role in the extent to which Russians are likely to intermarry. Presumably, the proportion of Russians intermarrying within the predominantly Russian center is even lower than for the RSFSR as a whole.

In terms of the impact of spatial diffusion on Russians, as Professor Kory discusses, Russians are more likely to be found in mixed families outside the boundaries of the RSFSR where, obviously, the chances of meeting members of other ethnic groups are greater. For the same reason, Russians are also more likely to be present in mixed families in urban areas than in rural areas both within the RSFSR and outside it. Note, however, that Russians tend to intermarry considerably more in some parts of the USSR than in others. Thus, a minority of families including Russians was homogeneous in 1970 in Armenia, Belorussia, Moldavia, and the Ukraine; in fact, only 33.9 percent of families in Belorussia, including Russians, were unmixed. In contrast, 73.0 percent of Russians living in families in Kirgizia lived only with other Russians. Similarly, high proportions of homogeneous Russian families were to be found in the other Central Asian union republics.

Moreover, when Russians do intermarry, they tend to marry into Slavic much more than other ethnic groups. Mr. Pavlovich properly points out that Russians intermarrying in Central Asia are primarily marrying Ukrainians and into other Soviet Western ethnic groups, not the indigenous Asian populations. There is evidence suggesting that the numbers of Russian-Ukrainian marriages and, to a smaller extent, Russian-Belorussian marriages in the USSR are about equal to their theoretical probability, that is, to what they would be if ethnicity were not a factor in the choice of a mate.(3) Such is clearly not the case regarding Russian marriages with most of the non-Slavic ethnic groups, however. It makes no sense to talk about the impact of spatial diffusion and intermarriage on the Russian group as if it were the same everywhere in the USSR.

To the extent that these proportions of Russians living in homogeneous families represent rates of Russian intermarriage, there does not seem to be much erosion of the Russian group through mixed marriage. Even if the estimated 77.6 percent endogamy rate is seen to represent a significant amount of intermarriage, whatever intermarriage of Russians takes place is occurring mostly among only the Slavic groups.

NOTES

(1) Itogi vsesoiuznoi perepisi naseleniia 1970 goda. Migratsiia
     naseleniia, chislo i sostav semei v SSSR, soiuznykh i
     autonomnykh respublikakh, kraiakh i oblastiakh, Vol. VII
     (Moscow: "Statistika," 1974), pp. 274-303.
(2) For a full discussion of ethnic intermarriage in the
     USSR, see Wesley A. Fisher, The Soviet Marriage Market:
     Mate Selection in Russia and the USSR   (New   York:
     Praeger, forthcoming).
(3) O. A. Gantskaia and L. N. Terent'eva, "Sem'ia -
     mikrosreda etnicheskikh protsessov," Sovremennye
     etnicheskie protssey v SSSR edited by Iu. V. Bromlei et
     al. (Moscow: Nauka, 1975), pp. 466-67.

IX

Leadership Quandaries in a Multiethnic State

Proposition 9: Reconciliation of the opposing Soviet drives for ethnic integration vs. self-determination in the Russian case will probably entail including one drive in the other. The second will likely camouflage the inner drive. This will produce a Russianism thinly covered by Sovietism - barely differing from the past - until the Russian group finally becomes uncontrollably apprehensive for its survival and turns actively ethnocentric once more, destroying all pretense of "internationalism" in the RSFSR and USSR.

38 Dilemma of the Dominant Ethnic Group

Bogdan Denis Denitch

In discussing the problems of multiethnic polities, it is usual to focus on the problems of subordinate ethnic groups. Since the development of modern "nationalism," particularly its Jacobin "nation-building" forms, the paradigm of a "nation state" was that of one dominated by a single people which would, in a properly arranged, legal-minded society, provide for a minimum of subordinate-group rights. Subordinate ethnic groups were seen as a problem which would be alleviated by the proper extension of general rights to citizens, combined with more or less attention to their attempts to maintain cultural identity. The underlying presupposition of much of Western political thought since the nineteenth century was that these residual ethnic groups would at some point or other integrate into the mainstream of the entire state, maintaining, perhaps, some colorful, particular traditions of folk art, poetry, and ethnic costumes for the rare festive occasions where ethnic identity was to be asserted.

The assumption was that it was naturally desirable for the general social good to integrate the subordinate groups into a general, individual citizenship of the "nation state." Even in the heyday of liberal "nationalism," however, a number of multiethnic states existed, posing a special problem particularly for subordinate ethnic groups. Before the 1917 Bolshevik revolution the pattern in multiethnic states - with the exception of Switzerland - was that of a dominant ethnic group ruling with more or less tolerance over the subject groups. In some of the liberal states, subordinate ethnic group rights were expressly not accepted; France comes to mind, as does Italy.

Multiethnic states in the Western world were always far more significant and normal than the common wisdom allowed for. Czarist Russia (the well-known prison of ethnic groups),

the Austro-Hungarian Empire, the Ottoman Empire in Europe, Belgium with its dominant Walloons, and Switzerland are examples. To these could be added Canada, Spain, Great Britain and, to a minor extent, France. If one also considers the situations in which religion acts as an ethnic divider, the Netherlands would have to be added and, of course, Ireland. The United States, whether one focuses on the racial divider or on the masses of more or less integrated immigrants, certainly would represent a multiethnic state. The majority, or dominant ethnic group in all but the Swiss case, took for granted its role as the political leader whose role was to integrate the other fragments into a political whole. This was most explicit, legally and in practice, in the case of the Hungarian section of the Austro-Hungarian Empire, where the non-Magyar majority of Hungary was systematically deprived of rights in an attempt to develop a liberal, political Hungary which would not recognize particularist rights.

The relations between the dominant and other ethnic groups within European "nation states" were affected by three sets of considerations: Traditional ethnocentrism, where the dominant ethnic group asserted its rights by conquest over others, as in the case of Russia, Austro-Hungary, Great Britain, and the German Empire; Jacobin and Mazzinian liberal democratic "nationalism," where ethnicity focused not on legitimate territorial divisions but on the living populations or, to be more specific, majority populations in defining the boundaries of the "nation state," as in the case of France and Italy; and Neo-Darwinism, expressing itself in terms of cultural superiority of the dominant group, making it self-evident that the historically necessary and progressive thing was for the less-developed groups to integrate or subordinate to the culturally more advanced center.

In the first case, dominant/subordinate relations led to separatist ethnic movements which asserted their identity, sometimes in legitimist historical terms, sometimes in the language of romantic modern ethnocentrism, challenging the right of the dominant ethnic group to rule over subordinated territories which were compact. In the second case, the more common pattern was that of marginal ethnic groups whose rights were deprived as a group in a framework where individual rights were usually extended to members of the subordinate ethnic group. In the third case, the claims of cultural superiority, when successfully pressed, often involved the cooptation of significant sections of the subordinate ethnic group's middle and intellectual classes into the mainstream culture. The United States and the German section of the Austrian Empire provide historically useful examples.

The most poisonous intraethnic relations occur in the rare cases where the dominant political ethnic group is seen as culturally more backward than the subject groups. This was

clearly the case in the latter days of the Ottoman Empire, where Christian ethnic groups, either in the Balkans or in Armenia, saw themselves as heirs to a higher culture and as potentially more modern or "European" than the dominant Muslim Ottoman establishment.   In that case, neither is the dominant ethnic group accorded grudging tolerance because of its modernizing role nor can it assert its cultural hegemony over the subordinate groups.   And ultimately, maintenance of the ployglot state rests on repressions.

Czarist Russia/USSR is a peculiar case in that it historically combines a number of problems common to other multiethnic states and because it shows different relations in terms of cultural dominance to differing subject ethnic groups. During the days of the czarist empire, its Western ethnic groups saw themselves as culturally more advanced than the dominant group, and were basically accepted as such by the ruling establishment.   The Asian empire provided a case where Russian culture, even in its relative backwardness with respect to the rest of Europe, was seen as more advanced and modern.   In the case of the larger Asian groups, religious and linguistic barriers against integration were very high indeed and, so long as the dominant ethnic group also expressed its identity partially in religious terms, cultural penetration was very limited.

The rules of the game in multiethnic states changed after the 1917 Bolshevik revolution, and Leninist policy toward subordinate ethnic groups, attenuated though it was over the years, has created a new, complex model in two cases of communist-ruled multiethnic states - the Soviet Union and Yugoslavia.   For the rest of the East European states, the ethnic question really amounts to no more than a policy toward subordinate ethnic groups numerically incapable of posing a major problem of legitimacy.   Thus, Poland, East Germany, and Bulgaria are highly homogeneous states, whereas Hungary has marginal ethnic subject groups.   Czechoslovakia, once the problem of Slovak autonomy was resolved, has minor ethnic problems.   Romania has substantial, historically-rooted ethnic groups in Transylvania, but its policy is not notably affected by Leninist ideology.   On the contrary, in the Romanian case, there is a typical integrative ethnocentrism which reluctantly yields minor cultural rights to its subordinate groups.

Yugoslavia and the USSR, however, are states which explicitly accept their own multiethnic character and provide for the expression of that multiethnic reality through the formation of politically autonomous, more or less homogeneous, federal subdivisions which are supposed to assert their roles as the eponymous homes of the given ethnic groups.   Thus, for example, in the Yugoslav case, a legal distinction is made among ethnic groups - between "nations" and "nationalities" -

with the "nations" having autonomous republics which normally
and legitimately assert their ethnic selfhood and where any
attempt at developing a composite Yugoslav ethnicity is
explicitly denied. The so-called "nationalities" are what are
normally termed subordinate ethnic groups and, even in that
case, although territorial autonomy is not given, extensive
cultural autonomy, in the form of independent cultural
institutions of the given language group, is maintained,
sometimes at considerable cost. While variants of the Serbian
and Croatian languages are mutually fully comprehensible and
are spoken by close to 80 percent of the population of
Yugoslavia with reasonable fluency (a figure similar to the
number of Russian speakers in the Soviet Union), the separate
languages of the two non-Serbo-Croat speaking republics –
Slovenia and Macedonia – are firmly protected, as is the
linguistic autonomy of Albanians and Hungarians.

The problem in the multiethnic federation of Yugoslavia
most often focused on by outside observers following the
Soviet example is that of the real or potential discontent of
the smaller ethnic groups, primarily the problem of the Croats
and Albanians. However, a number of Yugoslav scholars,
myself included, have always maintained that potentially the
most dangerous ethnocentrism is Serbian. Examining why this
should be so can provide insight into the general problem of
the dominant ethnic group in any multiethnic federation.

To manage a multiethnic polity successfully, at all times,
the restraint or self-restraint of the dominant ethnic group is
required above all else. It is this group that can threaten the
entire edifice of multiethnicity by asserting even those rights
which it, as a matter of policy, extends to the subordinate
groups. Other than separatism, the subordinate groups pose
no unmanageable problem to the survival of the state itself.
Their self-assertion can rarely threaten the dominant group's
feeling of ethnicity or security within the state. Whether the
demands of the lesser, or rather smaller, groups are seen as
reasonable or unreasonable is a secondary question. If the
major ethnic group, the one which has the plurality within the
state, begins to assert its ethnic identity and separate
tradition, it immediately awakens not-so-dormant fears among
subordinate groups about their very existence. This is
because (to take a hypothetical example), while it is
conceivable that Serbs could culturally swamp and dominate the
Macedonian republic, it is hardly possible that the Macedonians
could threaten Serbian ethnic identity. The majority ethnic
group has a double problem: it must restrain its assertiveness
within those geographic boundaries which are given to it, and
it must not appear to be the guardian of members of its ethnic
group within the other constituent republics. Thus, Serbs in
Croatia, Bosnia, and Vojvodina must not appear to be in
alliance with or dependent on the Serb republic in matters

which pertain to those republics or in intrarepublic negotiations. That requires extreme delicacy in managing the limits of ethnic group self-assertion. The consequence is something that more traditionalist Serbs never tire of positing: only a minority of Serbs lives within the boundaries of Serbia, the remainder of the Serbian population is forced to repress its natural assertion of ethnic group identity in order not to tread on the ethnic group egos of the other republics.

The fact of multiethnicity is rarely seen as anything but a problem by traditional ethnocentrists. And here, of course, two competing visions of what legitimate ethnic boundaries are, clash. One can either stress historical, legitimate frontiers, which, unfortunately, provide no solution for there are conflicting historical claims as each ethnic group puts forward its maximum demands based on that historical period which was most expansionist in its history; or, there can be an attempt to base proper frontiers on plebiscitary considerations. That opens up several perilous options. One is that of repeatedly redrawing the frontiers as populations shift, another is to attempt to limit internal migration to prevent a local ethnic group from being swamped. An example of this problem can be seen in the Soviet case with Estonia and Ukraine, where large Russian populations exist; or, in the case of Yugoslavia, where the fertility of the Albanian majority in the province of Kosova, if extrapolated over the next two decades, may well make them the second most numerous ethnic group in the federation. Therefore, in both the Soviet and Yugoslav cases, an uneasy compromise has to be maintained, one which sustains quasi-historical frontiers and, in practice, freezes them into perpetuity. The hope of the central authorities is that an amalgam, political but not ethnic identity, Soviet or Yugoslav, will develop sufficient links of loyalty to act as an additional prop for the values necessary to maintain the federation.

The game of multiethnicity is most successfully played when there are more than two partners, and no single partner is overwhelmingly more powerful than the other. Under those circumstances, there are reasons of state which continue to limit the self-assertiveness of the dominant group and there are possibilities of numerous alternate coalitions over different questions, rather than a polarization which always lines up the dominant group versus all others. In Yugoslavia, this is provided for by the north-south divide, which cuts across some of the republics and which does not coincide with ethnic frontiers.

The Soviet Union would appear to have a more difficult future in maintaining cohesion without continual repression. The relations of power between the union republics are grossly asymmetrical. The larger western union republic of Ukraine is increasingly less homogeneous and, therefore, threatened, while the Asian republics are too historically and ethnically

separate from the main Soviet population to make for easy
integration combined with maintenance of local cultural
standards.   Therefore, such stability as exists in the relations
within the Soviet Union ultimately rests both on the systematic
spread of Russian immigrants, culture, and language into the
historically less-developed areas, and upon the thin hope that
the differences with the western constituent republics can be
attenuated over time.   Sufficient counterbalances to Russian
dominance are lacking to give the Soviet federation reality.
On the other hand, in order to avoid exacerbating the
situation, romantic traditional and religious symbols of Russian
ethnocentrism will continue to have to be repressed, because
they increase the "alienness" of Russian culture for the
non-Russian ethnic groups of the Soviet Union.   Ironically, it
would seem, the multiethnic makeup of the Soviet Union
remains a major barrier against the liberalization of Soviet
society.   The former "prison of nationalities" also becomes a
prison for the ethnic Russians themselves (see Fig. 38.1).

Fig. 38.1.   Large coat of arms of the USSR, alludes to fifteen
key Soviet ethnic groups by language, with Russian at center.
This resembles the seal of Ivan the Terrible (Fig. 1.1) and
that of the Later Russian Empire (Fig. 1.2) in design and
substance.

Source: Izvestiia, Oct. 8. 1977, p. 3.

Scholarship in the nineteenth century in Eastern Europe had a contradictory dual function. It could and did act as a link with the universal world of intellectual discourse and technology, linking the hitherto isolated Eastern European areas to the world at large or, rather, to Western Europe. On the other hand, a second tradition which developed quite early and deeply influenced the revivals among the Slavic ethnic groups in Eastern Europe was a romanticist, historical attempt to reconstruct one's "nation." In this second tradition occurred the development of what was then a revisionist historiography. It stressed the contributions of Czechs, Serbs, Croats, Bulgars, Ukrainians, and other submerged ethnic groups to European history and dwelt on their moments of glory and empire. It created the necessary group myth for the revival of a new ethnocentrism. The second strand in this tradition was an equally utilitarian development of ethnography and ethnology. The first would be used for endless arguments about what were the appropriate borders of a given ethnic group, and the second would stress the uniqueness, the distinctness, and the specificity of one's own group.

The second tradition, and particularly its ethnographic aspects, tended to envenom debates between the emerging groups in the nineteenth century. Both historically and ethnographically, these emerging, previously-suppressed ethnic entities ended up pressing claims that were mutually exclusive and that led to entirely new sets of conflicts. A good example of this can be found in the relationship between the developing Serbian and Bulgarian ethnic revivals, and in their rivalry over Macedonia. It can be seen, too, in the fact that these two very similar Balkan ethnic groups had the advantage of a common history of oppression under the Ottomans, a common linkage with pan-Slavism in the struggles for group liberation, and a common religious tradition - not only was it .Orthodox but it required that the group's church be freed from Greek domination. With even a common tradition of a joint church language and a mutually comprehensible modern language, these two minor countries managed to fight no less than three wars in a 50-year period, and crippled each other's possibilities for development by an almost pathological preoccupation with preventing the neighboring country from getting any advantage whatsoever. Similar relations can be found between Poles and Ukrainians, between Romanians and Bulgarians, between Croats and Serbs, between Ukrainians and Russians, and so on. Proximity not only breeds contempt but often wars and conquest.

The major intellectual point to press, however, is that it was the new ethnocentric intelligentsia that created a popular basis for the new ethnic chauvinism that began to permeate Eastern Europe in the period before World War I. This rise of ethnicity and ethnic chauvinism was the dynamite that blasted

apart the three multiethnic states which covered most of
Eastern Europe - Turkey, Austro-Hungary, and the Russian
Empire. But what made absolutely sure that they would be
ripped apart was not only a rise of separatist, intolerant,
narrow, provincial ethnocentrism, but the fact that the
dominant ethnic group in each case reacted in a manner which
guaranteed the destruction of the multiethnic state. It is
curious, almost pathetic, to read today the nostalgic histories
of the Austro-Hungarian Empire - mostly written by Magyar or
German-speaking, Jewish historians - deploring the destruction
of the polyglot empire and the rise of the intolerant, new,
ethnically more-or-less homogeneous "nation-states." Why was
Austro-Hungary so attractive? It was attractive to the socially
mobile because it offered entry into the middle administrative
layers of a bureaucracy, and even to higher military and
administrative ranks, sometimes to all those who would drop
their ethnic baggage behind. For the Jews in Eastern Europe
this was an enormously liberating feature. More precisely, for
the unreligious, non-Yiddish speaking, deculturated Jews, it
was an enormously liberating fact. But for the Croat, Serb,
Czech and Romanian intellectuals, it was an intolerable policy,
demanding the submergence of their ethnic groups into the
Magyar and German "state-nation."

Ethnic groups without a homogeneous territorial base or a
substantial prospect of separate political existence could well
see themselves as benefiting from participation in a multiethnic
empire. If one is to be a subordinate group, presumably it is
better to be one in a large, powerful empire than in a small
ethnically-homogeneous "nation-state." Thus, the Jews without
a geographic center, and the smaller ethnic groupings without
much of a prospect of an independent political existence (for
example, the Slovenes or the Ruthenians), might actually have
found the multiethnic empire to be an asset. The more
obscure, smaller ethnic groups in Siberia, and the Jews before
the development of a new Soviet anti-Semitism, could have
found the Soviet Union to be that. The assertion of ethnic
identity by these micro-groups is not a threat, and the
multiethnic state can afford to be tolerant. It can take some
pride in creating what amounts to a living ethnographic
museum, with its stress on custom, folkways, and languages.
But an ethnic group sufficiently numerous and homogeneous to
constitute a "nation-state," particularly when imbued with
romantic ethnocentrism carried by new intelligentsia,
represents an entirely different problem. The Ottoman Empire
could tolerate the gypsies, the Jews, and even a homogeneous
ethnic group like the Albanians, because the latter, until 1912,
seemed incapable of seriously seeking independence. But the
development of Greek, Serbian, or Bulgarian ethnocentrism was
fatal. The fate of the Armenians and the massacres which
followed the outbreak of World War I probably represent the

shift in the way the dominant Turkish groups looked at the Armenian <u>millet</u> (community). It had first classified them in the category of a group similar to the Jews and the gypsies, and when it began to confront the possibility that they were more like the Serbs or Bulgarians, it proceeded to try to carry out what was the first, modern genocidal policy.

The reasons why Turks reacted pathologically lie in the fact that Islam prescribed a relationship between the dominant and subordinate ethnic groups quite precisely. Whereas the Ottomans could be relatively tolerant of cultural diversity and religious differences, the notion of sharing power was utterly alien. This factor was made more complicated by the fact that subject Christian ethnic groups of the Ottoman Empire invariably regarded themselves as the cultural and political superiors of their rulers. Room for compromise, therefore, was nonexistent.

For the Ottomans to have accepted a federal solution would have made eminent sense economically, both for the dominant and the subordinate ethnic groups. The obstacles were historical, religious, and ideological. But modern ethnocentrism has also created a set of values which make rational compromises unlikely. There are really, it seems, only two solutions for the problem facing a multiethnic polity, two solutions other than an attempt to impose a melting pot or undergoing secession. One is a very traditional attempt to create a federal state composed of historic geographic units which collectively create a state entity. Under those circumstances, it may well happen that the dominant ethnic group ends up with less than its "fair" share of power, less than the power which its numbers would imply. Such federal solutions require that the notion of one-man-one-vote be rejected. The second approach would be to create a multiethnic state which explicitly recognizes that the social contract is between ethnic groups and not between the individuals in the state.

Both of these solutions require a most elaborate structure of checks and balances, distribution of leading posts in the government, wholesale application of the principle of quotas throughout the federal civil service, and the most difficult of all, a sharing of a single state by several ethnic groups. Sharing a state is very distinct from granting rights to subordinate ethnic groups. The whole concept of granting rights assumes that the state "belongs" to the dominant group, and that it, as an obligation of high rank, chooses to respect the rights of the lesser groups. That is, after all, the most common pattern of dominant/subordinant ethnic relations in modern, democratic polities.

The alternate conception, present today perhaps only in Switzerland and Yugoslavia, is that there is no such thing as a dominant group, that ethnic differences are not a problem to be settled over time, but a permanent feature of the conditions of the state. The smaller ethnic groups (for example, the Romansch speakers in Switzerland or the Macedonians in Yugoslavia) have rights equal with those of the more numerous groups. That option can be grotesquely expensive in practice. It costs an estimated thirty times as much for taxpayers in Switzerland to educate a child speaking Romansch as to educate a child speaking German, French, or Italian. In the Yugoslav case, the elaborate minuet required to distribute the same number of ambassadorships and under-secretaryships to each of the constituent republics must appear absurd to outsiders. But both of those are costs which undoubtedly are lower than the cost of maintaining an artificial set of universalist standards which are, in reality, rejected by most of the subordinate groups within a multiethnic state.

Stressing the Swiss and Yugoslav examples can be profoundly discouraging to students of the Soviet Union or, for that matter, Canada, because other than those two examples, attempts to deal with the fact of multiethnicity prove to be at best compromises and at worst more subtle and systematic ways of maintaining the dominance of the leading ethnic group. But in Canada and the Soviet Union, the dominant ethnic group does not, as it did in the case of Hungary in Austro-Hungary, assert the right to rule for the dominant ethnic group alone. On the contrary, it states its claims in universalist terms, in melting-pot terms. The English-speakers in Canada presumably include second-generation Jews, Ukrainians, Russians, Slavs, and others. English becomes the language of the state, not merely of the Anglo-Saxons, and there is, at least formally, an attempt to create a common culture. In the Soviet case, it is clear that Russian ethnocentrists are not the force behind the spread of Russification. It is, rather, that willy-nilly the Soviet state has adopted Russian as the state language. Russian thus becomes the passport to success for non-Russian Soviet citizens, if they want to succeed outside of their own region and union republic.

READINGS

Barron, Milton L. Minorities in a Changing World, New York: Alfred Knopf, 1967.

Denitch, Bogdan Denis. The Legitimation of a Revolution: The Yugoslav Case, New Haven: Yale University Press, 1976.

Rose, Richard. Governing Without Consensus: An Irish Perspective, Boston: Beacon Press, 1971.

39 Spirit of Empire or Minority Complex? A Closing Statement

Robert L. Belknap

Columbia University's Program dealing with Soviet "minorities" was established in 1970. For the first time the Russians have qualified for discussion under that Program. In symmetry with the old definition of a language as a dialect with an army, this historical development suggests a nonstatistical definition of a "minority," as a cultural entity without an army. Our authors have discussed the shift of populations within the army and the efforts to provide administrative and even military power to some of the other ethnic groups. Yet, as the investigation ranged from demography to sociology to literature, it has become plain that minority status depends more on perceived impotence than on impotence residing in statistical fact or political structure.

This inquiry has reminded everyone that the great majority of mankind has lived, in recent history, not in tidy Greek or Italian city states, not even in culturally coherent "nation states" of the kind often seen today, but rather in multiethnic empires. This reminder is needed because of American geographical and chronological provincialism. The nucleus of our own "nation" of Americans seceded from such an empire, which had been created, it is said, in a moment of inadvertence by an insular people. Like this country, these times lack the usual imperial experience. World War I destroyed the great contiguous empires, the Turkish and the Austrian, and World War II assured the dissolution of the overseas empires of England, France, Belgium, and the Netherlands. As the only survivor of an otherwise extinct species, the Soviet Union has lost its place in Western consciousness and in the consciousness of its own people as the heir to the 5,000-year old tradition of the multiethnic empire.

These empires share certain tendencies. They often fear civil war to the point of tolerating political activity only within a small group. Cultural tolerance, on the other hand, often reaches the level of cultural indifference. If a member of a "minority" pays perfunctory obeisance to some deity, emperor, or ideology, and makes a limited number of other basic gestures, he has satisfied the cultural demands of a multiethnic empire. In return, the empire does something which has been described in this volume as giving "special attention to the peoples trampled upon." Rudyard Kipling called that attention the white man's burden, and Virgil summoned Romans to the government of peoples, sparing subjugated ones and battling down the proud. Beyond this sense of obligation, this cultural tolerance, and this antipathy to any widespread political activity, the imperial stance has that optimistic, expansionist, risk-taking spirit associated with the real or legendary founders and restorers - Gilgamesh, Cyrus, Alexander, Caesar, Constantine, Heraclius, Napoleon, or the Elizabethans.

The colloquies here are really centered on the clash between this exciting spirit of empire and the cautious, narrow, ethnic spirit which Shakespeare's John of Gaunt expressed better than any political theorist:

> This royal throne of kings, this scepter'd isle,
> This earth of majesty, this seat of Mars,
> . . . .
> This happy breed of men, this little world,
> This precious stone set in the silver sea,
> Which serves it in the office of a wall,
> Or as a moat defensive to a house,
> Against the envy of less happier lands....
>
> (King Richard II, II,i,40.)

John's preoccupation with defense, with a discrete landscape, with ancient virtue, and with a sense of hereditary identity reaching far into the past prefigures the cluster of characteristics which enables us to group Aleksandr I, Aleksandr I. Solzhenitsyn, Vladimir Soloukhin, Fedor Abramov, and many others as members of a school which thinks and writes with the passion of an oppressed minority. And yet Professor Robert A. Lewis (chap. 26) was right when he simplified the Russians' history into their expulsion from the black soil beginning in the thirteenth century and an ongoing reconquest of that soil that has given Russia the dominion over its other inhabitants. Paradoxically, these current rural writers glory in the land least fit for agriculture, and members of the dominant ethnic group call desperately for a return to better times.

The patterns should, however, be familiar. Pastoral poetry has always flourished in imperial capitals. Augustus struggled to restore the oldest Roman cults. The prophets of Israel reacted to its imperial moment under David and Solomon as Solzhenitsyn reacts to the Russian empire, with a call for a return to the old morality, the old faith, and the old geography. In England, at the turn of this century, the malaise of empire came at the same time as a fascination with the rural scene. Is the Soviet Union entering a crisis as Russians become a statistical minority? No one here has emphasized any sign of such a Russian crisis. After all, the General Secretary of the Communist Party of the Soviet Union relies on an elective majority or ethnic solidarity about as much as the Empress of India did. Rather, these studies have found the doubts and the turning inward that Kipling shows when he writes: "...Lo, all our pomp of yesterday / Is one with Nineveh and Tyre. / Judge of the nations spare us yet, / Lest we forget, lest we forget" ("Recessional"). Kipling was consciously comparing England with the antique empires, thinking not of any current crisis, but reminding his contemporaries that nothing lasts forever. The thought of mortal empires produces the call not to forget, and the absence of a direct object for the verb "forget" leads back to the old ethnic ideals which may preserve but must survive the imperial stage as Kipling or Thomas Hardy understood it.

This book has brought together the events in the physical worlds of geography and economics, the social worlds of sociology and political change, and the mental worlds of religion and literature. Such visions of these worlds converge upon the picture of a sad, vast, clumsy empire accommodating itself, as empires do, to the shifts of doctrine and the stabilities of ethnic identities that survive while empires come and go.

Appendix — Where the USSR's Russians Were and Are: 1959-70 Statistical Tables

The Soviet Union in 1970 was, and remains, comprised of 15 Soviet Socialist Republics (SSRs), many of which, in turn, are made up of nonethnic administrative units (oblasts, krais) and/or eponymous administrative units (Autonomous Soviet Socialist Republics [ASSRs], autonomous oblasts [AObs], and autonomous okrugs [AOks]. The designation "nationality okrug" (NO) was superseded by the term "autonomous okrug" in 1977. Autonomous oblasts and okrugs are usually subordinated to a higher administrative unit (an oblast or krai) within a union republic, but, in some cases, can be found directly under the control of a union republic like the Georgian SSR. In order to provide greater detail about Russian distribution, the areas and population statistics given for the autonomous oblasts and autonomous okrugs are not included in the statistics for the ordinary oblasts and krais. The ordinary oblasts and krais so affected are marked with an asterisk (*).

RUSSIANS IN SOVIET TERRITORIAL ADMINISTRATIVE UNITS
CHANGES IN DISTRIBUTION (1959, 1970)

I:A   Soviet Russians in RSFSR outside Non-Russian Units

Unit (Oblasts)	Area (1,000s of km²)		Unit Population All Ethnic Groups (1,000s)		Russians in Unit Population (1,000s)		(Russian % in unit)	
	1959	1970	1959	1970	1959	1970	1959	1970
Amur	363.7	363.7	717.5	793.4	630.1	721.4	87.8	90.9
Arkhangel*	410.6	410.7	1230.3	1362.2	1135.5	1265.0	92.3	92.9
Astrakhan	44.1	44.1	702.0	867.5	544.1	654.9	77.5	75.5
Belgorod	27.1	27.1	1226.3	1261.1	1151.5	1198.0	93.9	95.0
Briansk	34.9	34.9	1549.9	1582.0	1505.1	1533.8	97.1	97.0
Cheliabinsk	87.9	87.9	2976.6	3288.8	2372.2	2653.2	79.7	80.7
Chita*	410.9	412.5	987.3	1079.2	916.3	997.2	92.8	92.4
Gorkii	73.2	74.8	3590.8	3682.5	3382.0	3477.3	94.2	94.4
Iaroslav	36.3	36.4	1395.6	1400.2	1362.8	1366.0	97.6	97.6
Irkutsk*	746.5	745.9	1843.4	2167.0	1586.7	1932.9	86.1	89.2
Ivanovo	24.0	23.9	1322.2	1339.1	1291.4	1295.1	97.7	96.7
Kaliningrad	15.1	15.1	610.9	731.9	473.9	564.5	77.6	77.1
Kalinin	84.3	84.1	1806.8	1717.2	1706.5	1627.5	94.4	94.8
Kaluga	29.8	29.9	935.9	994.9	906.0	949.8	96.8	95.5
Kamchatka*	170.8	170.8	193.2	256.7	159.5	219.1	82.5	85.4
Kemerovo	95.5	95.5	2785.9	2918.4	2386.5	2596.5	85.7	89.0
Kirov	122.5	120.8	1916.5	1727.3	1761.0	1572.2	91.9	91.0
Kostroma	60.3	60.1	920.0	870.6	898.3	841.7	97.6	96.7
Kuibyshev	53.7	53.6	2258.4	2750.9	1848.5	2276.6	81.8	82.8
Kurgan	71.0	71.0	999.2	1085.6	925.5	995.9	92.6	91.7
Kursk	29.8	29.8	1483.3	1473.9	1456.4	1445.3	98.2	98.1
Leningrad	85.9	85.9	1245.0	1435.7	1140.2	1315.9	91.6	91.7
Leningrad (city)	-	-	3321.2	3949.5	2951.3	3514.3	88.9	89.0
Lipetsk	24.1	24.1	1141.5	1224.3	1124.4	1202.3	98.5	98.2
Magadan*	461.4	461.4	188.9	251.3	138.5	196.8	73.3	78.3

(continued)

I: A   (continued)

Unit	Area (1,000s of km^2)		Unit Population All Ethnic Groups (1,000s)		Russians in Unit Population (1,000s)		(Russian % in unit)	
(Oblasts)	1959	1970	1959	1970	1959	1970	1959	1970
Moscow	47.0	47.0	5863.0	5774.5	5519.4	5430.0	94.1	94.0
Moscow (city)	-	-	5085.9	7061.0	4507.9	6301.2	88.6	89.2
Murmansk	144.9	144.9	567.7	799.5	484.2	676.3	85.3	84.6
Novgorod	55.3	55.3	736.5	721.5	715.9	699.3	97.2	96.9
Novosibirsk	178.2	178.2	2298.5	2505.2	2056.9	2286.6	89.5	91.3
Omsk	139.6	139.7	1645.0	1823.8	1273.7	1458.5	77.4	80.0
Orel	24.7	24.7	929.0	931.0	915.7	916.2	98.6	98.4
Orenburg	123.9	124.0	1829.5	2050.0	1296.5	1472.3	70.9	71.8
Penza	43.3	43.2	1509.6	1536.0	1311.9	1323.5	86.9	86.2
Perm*	130.8	127.7	2775.8	2811.3	2348.8	2413.8	84.6	85.9
Pskov	55.2	55.3	951.9	875.3	920.8	845.4	96.7	96.6
Riazan	39.6	39.6	1444.8	1411.6	1419.7	1382.6	98.3	97.9
Rostov	100.8	100.8	3311.7	3831.3	3023.7	3493.3	91.3	91.2
Sakhalin	87.1	87.1	649.4	615.7	504.7	495.2	77.7	80.4
Saratov	100.2	100.2	2162.8	2454.1	1899.7	2151.1	87.8	87.7
Smolensk	49.9	49.8	1143.0	1106.1	1113.6	1070.4	97.4	96.8
Sverdlovsk	192.8	194.8	4044.4	4319.7	3560.1	3838.4	88.0	88.9
Tambov	34.3	34.3	1549.0	1511.9	1529.4	1487.7	98.7	98.4
Tomsk	316.9	316.9	746.8	785.7	643.7	702.6	86.2	89.4
Tula	25.7	25.7	1920.3	1952.5	1822.0	1869.3	94.9	95.7
Tiumen*	134.2	161.8	905.8	1055.0	776.4	895.0	85.7	84.8
Ulianov	37.3	37.3	1117.4	1224.7	868.6	930.9	77.7	76.0
Vladimir	28.9	29.0	1402.4	1510.9	1367.2	1465.8	97.5	97.0
Volgograd	114.1	114.1	1853.9	2322.9	1691.2	2104.1	91.2	90.6
Vologda	145.5	145.7	1307.5	1295.9	1280.4	1264.2	97.9	97.6
Voronezh	52.4	52.4	2368.7	2526.9	2172.5	2355.9	91.7	93.2

(continued)

I:A   (continued)

Unit	Area (1,000s of km^2)		Unit Population All Ethnic Groups (1,000s)		Russians in Unit Population (1,000s)		(Russian % in unit)	
(Krais)	1959	1970	1959	1970	1959	1970	1959	1970
Altai*	169.1	169.1	2526.1	2502.0	2192.3	2225.0	86.8	88.9
Khabarovsk*	788.6	788.6	979.7	1173.5	805.0	1005.7	82.2	85.7
Krasnodar*	79.2	76.0	3477.8	4124.2	3163.2	3705.4	91.0	89.8
Krasnoiarsk*	734.6	710.0	2160.3	2465.4	1863.2	2177.7	86.2	88.3
Primore	165.9	165.9	1381.0	1721.3	1120.7	1472.3	81.2	85.5
Stavropol*	66.4	66.5	1605.0	1961.1	1465.4	1759.8	91.3	89.7

Sources: Itogi vsesoiuznoi perepisi naseleniia 1959 goda. RSFSR (Moscow: Gosstatizdat, 1963, repr. 1975), pp. 12-17, 300, 312-87; Itogi vsesoiuznoi perepisi naseleniia 1970 goda, Natsional'nyi sostav naseleniia SSSR, Vol. IV (Moscow: "Statistika," 1973), pp. 12, 61-151, RSFSR: Administrativno-territorial'noe delenie (Moscow: Izvestiia Sovetov Deputatov Trudiashchikhsia, 1972), pp. 11-339; Narodnoe khoziaistvo SSSR v 1970 g. (Moscow: "Statistika," 1971), pp. 27-29.

RUSSIANS IN SOVIET TERRITORIAL ADMINISTRATIVE UNITS
CHANGES IN DISTRIBUTION (1959, 1970)

I:B. Soviet Russians in Non-Russian Territorial Administrative Units

Unit (ASSRs)	Area (1,000s of km^2) 1959	1970	Unit Population All Ethnic Groups (1,000s) 1959	1970	Russians in Unit Population (1,000s) 1959	1970	(Russian % in unit) 1959	1970
Bashkir	143.6	143.6	3341.6	3818.1	1418.1	1546.3	42.4	40.5
Buriat	351.3	351.3	673.3	812.3	502.6	597.0	74.6	73.5
Chechen-Ingush	19.3	19.3	710.4	1064.5	348.3	367.0	49.0	34.5
Chuvash	18.3	18.3	1097.9	1223.7	263.7	299.2	24.0	24.5
Dagestan	50.3	50.3	1062.5	1428.5	213.8	209.6	20.1	14.7
Iakut	3103.2	3103.2	487.3	664.1	215.3	314.3	44.2	47.3
Kabardin-Balkar	12.5	12.5	420.1	588.2	162.6	218.6	38.7	37.2
Kalmyk	75.9	75.9	184.9	268.0	103.3	122.8	55.9	45.8
Karelian	172.4	172.4	651.3	713.5	412.8	486.2	63.4	68.1
Komi	411.1	415.9	806.2	964.8	390.0	512.2	48.4	53.1
Mari	23.2	23.2	647.7	684.7	309.5	320.8	47.8	46.9
Mordvin	26.1	26.2	1000.2	1029.6	590.6	606.8	59.0	58.9
North Osset	8.0	8.0	450.6	552.6	178.7	202.4	39.6	36.6
Tatar	68.0	68.0	2850.4	3131.2	1252.4	1328.7	43.9	42.4
Tuva	170.5	170.5	171.9	230.9	68.9	88.4	40.1	38.3
Udmurt	42.1	42.1	1336.9	1417.7	758.8	809.6	56.8	57.1

I:B (continued)

Unit	Area (1,000s of km^2)		Unit Population All Ethnic Groups (1,000s)		Russians in Unit Population (1,000s)		(Russian % in unit)	
	1959	1970	1959	1970	1959	1970	1959	1970
(Autonomous Oblasts)								
Adygei	4.5	7.6	284.7	385.6	200.5	276.5	70.4	71.7
Evrei	36.0	36.0	162.9	172.4	127.3	144.3	78.2	83.7
Gorno-Altai	92.6	92.6	157.2	168.3	109.7	110.4	69.8	65.6
Karachai-Cherkess	14.1	14.1	278.0	344.7	141.8	162.4	51.0	47.1
Khakass	61.8	61.9	411.0	445.8	314.5	349.4	76.5	78.4
(Autonomous Okrugs)								
Aga Buriat	20.6	19.0	49.1	65.8	23.9	29.0	48.6	44.0
Chukchi	737.7	737.7	46.7	101.2	28.3	70.5	60.7	69.7
Evenk	745.0	767.6	10.3	12.7	6.0	7.7	57.9	61.1
Iamal Nenets	750.3	750.3	62.3	80.0	27.8	37.5	44.6	46.9
Khant-Mansi	550.8	523.1	123.9	271.2	89.8	208.5	72.5	76.9
Komi Permiak	31.8	32.9	217.0	212.1	71.4	76.3	32.9	36.0
Koriak	301.5	301.5	27.5	30.9	16.7	19.5	60.6	63.1
Nenets	181.5	176.7	45.5	39.1	31.3	25.2	68.8	64.4
Taimyr (Dolgan-Nenets)	860.2	862.1	33.4	38.1	21.8	25.5	65.3	66.9
Ust Orda Buriat	21.4	22.0	133.1	146.4	75.1	86.0	56.4	58.8
RSFSR TOTAL	17075.4	17075.4	117534.3	130079.2	97863.6	107747.6	83.3	82.8

Note: Very minor variations occur between column totals shown for population here taken directly from the published Soviet sources and column totals reached by adding the detailed unit figures shown. These small discrepancies can be accounted for by vagaries in Soviet statistics and differences between their way of rounding off for thousands and the methods used in preparing these tables. Such variations sometimes occur in Soviet data for a single administrative unit for which 1959 figures are given in both the 1959 and 1970 published reports. Information for 1959 reproduced in this Appendix has come from the 1959 census. The same comment applies to the tables that follow. Note also that published data for the 1959 census give main city areas (square km.) as separate figures, whereas those for 1970 incorporate cities' areas into the immediately larger parent administrative units. In order to adjust for this, 1959 city areas have been added to figures either for the oblast with the same name, to the raion under union republic supervision, or to "union republic minus city," depending upon the administrative-territorial arrangements of the particular union republic.

Sources: Itogi vsesoiuznoi perepisi naseleniia 1959 goda. RSFSR (Moscow: Gosstatizdat, 1963, repr. 1975), pp. 12-17, 312-87; Itogi vsesoiuznoi perepisi naseleniia 1970 goda. Natsional'nyi sostav naseleniia SSSR, Vol. IV (Moscow: "Statistika," 1973), pp. 61-150; Narodnoe khoziaistvo SSSR v 1970 g. (Moscow: "Statistika," 1971), pp. 27-29.

RUSSIANS IN SOVIET TERRITORIAL ADMINISTRATIVE UNITS
CHANGES IN DISTRIBUTION (1959, 1970)

I:C RUSSIANS OUTSIDE RSFSR IN NON-RUSSIAN SOVIET UNITS

Unit	Area (1,000s of km^2) 1959	1970	Unit Population All Ethnic Groups (1,000s) 1959	1970	Russians in Unit Population (1,000s) 1959	1970	(Russian % in unit) 1959	1970
Armenia								
Erevan	-	-	509.3	766.7	22.6	21.5	4.4	2.8
Armenia less Erevan	29.8	29.8	1253.7	1725.2	33.9	44.6	2.7	2.6
SSR Total	29.8	29.8	1763.0	2491.9	56.5	66.1	3.2	2.7
Azerbaijan								
Baku	-	-	987.2	1265.5	337.8	351.1	34.2	27.7
(Raions)	76.7	76.7	2438.7	3499.1	158.5	153.7	6.5	4.4
Nakhichevan ASSR	5.5	5.5	141.4	202.2	3.2	3.9	2.2	1.9
Nagorno-Karabakh AOb	4.4	4.4	130.4	150.3	1.8	1.3	1.4	0.9
SSR Total	86.6	86.6	3697.7	5117.1	501.3	510.0	13.6	10.0
Belorussia (Oblasts)								
Brest	32.6	32.3	1190.7	1294.6	87.9	106.0	7.4	8.2
Gomel	40.2	40.4	1361.8	1533.3	89.7	137.4	6.6	9.0
Grodno	25.0	25.0	1077.4	1120.4	72.3	86.1	6.7	7.7
Minsk	41.0	40.8	1473.0	1540.1	84.8	106.2	5.8	6.9
Minsk (City)	-	-	509.5	916.9	116.3	214.2	22.8	23.4
Mogilev	28.7	29.0	1166.1	1227.0	89.2	120.5	7.6	9.8
Vitebsk	40.1	40.1	1276.1	1370.0	118.8	167.7	9.3	12.2
SSR Total	207.6	207.6	8054.6	9002.3	659.1	938.2	8.2	10.4

(continued)

I:C (continued)

Unit	Area (1,000s of km^2) 1959	Area (1,000s of km^2) 1970	Unit Population All Ethnic Groups (1,000s) 1959	Unit Population All Ethnic Groups (1,000s) 1970	Russians in Unit Population (1,000s) 1959	Russians in Unit Population (1,000s) 1970	Russians in Unit Population (Russian % in unit) 1959	Russians in Unit Population (Russian % in unit) 1970
Estonia								
Tallinn	-	-	281.7	362.7	90.6	127.1	32.2	35.0
Estonia less Tallinn	45.1	45.1	915.1	993.4	149.6	207.5	16.3	20.9
SSR Total	45.1	45.1	1196.8	1356.1	240.2	334.6	20.1	24.7
Georgia								
Tbilisi	-	-	775.5	889.0	135.3	124.3	17.5	14.0
(Raions)	54.2	54.2	2521.7	2898.3	150.7	142.1	6.0	4.9
Abkhaz ASSR	8.6	8.6	404.7	487.0	86.7	92.9	21.4	19.1
Ajar ASSR	3.0	3.0	245.3	309.8	32.8	35.8	13.4	11.5
Iugo Ossetian AOb	3.9	3.9	96.8	99.4	2.4	1.6	2.5	1.6
SSR Total	69.7	69.7	4044.0	4686.4	407.9	396.7	10.1	8.5
Kazakhstan (Oblasts)								
Aktiubinsk	299.8	299.8	401.0	550.6	105.2	145.2	26.2	26.4
Alma Ata	227.6	104.7	946.1	712.1	400.9	251.2	42.4	35.3
Alma Ata (City)	-	-	456.5	729.6	333.5	512.9	73.1	70.3
Chimkent	150.0	114.1	921.4	1287.4	209.2	282.6	22.7	22.0
Gurev	278.6	278.6	287.8	499.6	59.7	136.3	20.7	27.3
Jambul	145.2	144.6	561.5	794.3	176.2	257.4	31.4	32.4
Karaganda	394.7	398.8	1018.7	1552.1	482.7	785.6	47.4	50.6
Kokchetav	79.0	78.1	493.3	589.2	205.7	238.0	41.7	40.4
Kustanai	197.0	114.6	710.7	889.6	291.1	408.1	41.0	45.9
Kzyl Orda	232.0	227.0	327.3	491.8	50.2	91.7	15.3	18.6

(continued)

I:C   (continued)

Unit	Area (1,000s of km^2) 1959	1970	Unit Population All Ethnic Groups (1,000s) 1959	1970	Russians in Unit Population (1,000s) 1959	1970	(Russian % in unit) 1959	1970
Pavlodar	127.8	127.5	455.0	697.9	178.8	310.0	39.3	44.4
Semipalatinsk	179.6	179.6	520.2	713.8	235.0	292.0	45.2	40.9
Severo Kazakhstan	41.4	44.3	457.0	555.8	294.9	352.7	64.5	63.5
Taldy Kurgan	-	118.5	-	610.0	-	249.5	-	40.9
Tselinograd	155.1	124.6	637.1	755.0	271.9	349.2	42.7	46.3
Turgai	-	111.8	-	221.4	-	74.6	-	33.7
Uralsk	151.2	151.2	381.2	513.1	158.2	197.2	41.5	38.4
Vostochno Kazakhstan	97.3	97.3	734.9	845.3	521.1	587.5	70.9	69.5
SSR Total	2756.0	2715.1	9309.8	13008.7	3974.2	5521.9	42.7	42.4
Kirgiziia (Oblasts)								
Frunze City	-	-	219.7	430.6	150.7	284.7	68.6	66.1
Issyk Kul	-	43.2	-	312.0	-	100.1	-	32.1
Naryn	-	50.6	-	186.4	-	6.7	-	3.6
Osh	73.9	73.9	869.4	1232.9	120.1	144.8	13.8	11.7
Tien Shan	50.6	-	136.0	-	12.5	-	9.2	-
(Raions)	74.0	30.8	840.7	771.0	340.3	319.6	40.5	41.5
SSR Total	198.5	198.5	2065.8	2932.8	623.6	855.9	30.2	29.2
Latvia								
Riga City	-	-	604.7	731.8	238.6	312.9	39.5	42.7
Latvia less Riga	63.7	63.7	1488.8	1632.3	317.9	391.7	21.4	24.0
SSR Total	63.7	63.7	2093.5	2364.1	556.4	704.6	26.6	29.8
Lithuania								
Vilnius City	-	-	236.1	372.1	69.4	91.0	29.4	24.5
Lithuania less Vilnius	65.2	65.2	2745.4	2756.1	161.6	177.0	6.5	6.4
SSR Total	65.2	65.2	2711.4	3128.2	231.0	268.0	8.5	8.6

(continued)

I:C   (continued)

Unit	Area (1,000s of km^2) 1959	1970	Unit Population All Ethnic Groups (1,000s) 1959	1970	Russians in Unit Population (1,000s) 1959	1970	(Russian % in unit) 1959	1970
Moldavia								
Kishinev City	-	-	216.0	356.4	69.6	109.3	32.2	30.7
Moldavia less Kishinev	33.7	33.7	2668.5	3212.5	223.3	305.1	8.4	9.5
SSR Total	33.7	33.7	2884.5	3568.9	292.9	414.4	10.2	11.6
Tajikistan (Oblasts)								
Dushanbe City	-	-	227.1	373.9	108.2	157.1	47.7	42.0
Leninabad	-	26.1	-	937.7	-	99.8	-	10.6
(Raions)	78.8	53.3	1679.7	1488.3	153.0	86.0	9.1	5.8
Gorno - Badakhshan AOb	63.7	63.7	73.0	97.8	1.4	0.8	1.9	0.8
SSR Total	142.5	143.1	1979.9	2899.6	262.6	344.1	13.3	11.9
Turkmenistan (Oblasts)								
Ashkhabad City	-	-	169.9	253.1	85.5	108.1	50.3	42.7
Charjou	93.5	93.6	320.8	457.0	49.9	57.1	15.6	12.5
Mary	118.6	133.0	417.6	622.3	54.0	57.6	12.9	9.2
Tashauz	75.4	75.4	294.8	410.9	9.2	9.6	3.1	2.3
(Raions)	200.5	186.1	313.2	412.4	64.1	79.8	20.5	19.3
SSR Total	488.0	488.1	1516.4	2158.9	262.7	313.1	17.3	14.5
Ukraine (Oblasts)								
Cherkassy	21.1	20.9	1503.3	1535.0	66.9	87.7	4.5	5.7
Chernigov	31.5	31.9	1553.8	1559.9	61.1	73.5	3.9	4.7
Chernovitsy	8.0	8.1	774.1	844.9	51.3	53.4	6.6	10.0
Dnepropetrovsk	32.0	31.9	2704.8	3343.0	466.0	697.2	17.2	20.9

(continued)

I:C   (continued)

Unit	Area (1,000s of km^2)		Unit Population All Ethnic Groups (1,000s)		Russians in Unit Population (1,000s)		(Russian % in unit)	
	1959	1970	1959	1970	1959	1970	1959	1970
Donets	26.5	26.5	4262.0	4892.0	1601.3	1987.2	37.6	40.6
Ivano-Frankovsk	13.9	13.9	1094.6	1249.3	37.9	46.5	3.5	3.7
Kharkov	31.6	31.4	2520.1	2826.1	665.5	829.4	26.4	29.3
Kherson	27.1	28.3	824.2	1030.0	128.2	186.6	15.6	18.1
Khmelnitskiy	20.8	20.6	1611.4	1615.4	61.6	69.1	3.8	4.3
Kiev	28.9	29.0	1719.1	1834.0	82.4	111.5	4.8	6.1
Kiev City	-	-	1104.3	1631.9	254.3	373.6	23.0	22.9
Kirovograd	23.8	24.6	1217.9	1259.4	102.2	115.8	8.4	9.2
Krym	25.6	27.0	1201.5	1813.5	858.3	1220.5	71.4	67.3
Lvov	21.7	21.8	2107.9	2428.9	181.1	199.8	8.6	8.2
Nikolaevsk	24.9	24.7	1013.8	1148.1	139.2	184.9	13.7	16.1
Odessa	33.1	33.3	2026.6	2389.0	440.4	578.2	21.7	24.2
Poltava	29.0	28.8	1631.7	1706.2	83.3	123.2	5.1	7.2
Rovno	20.3	20.1	926.2	1047.6	39.1	44.6	4.2	4.3
Sumy	24.2	23.8	1513.7	1504.7	167.6	176.6	11.1	11.7
Ternopol	13.9	13.8	1085.6	1152.7	26.9	26.3	2.5	2.3
Vinnitsa	26.8	26.5	2142.0	2131.9	93.5	102.8	4.4	4.8
Volyn	20.0	20.2	890.5	974.5	37.1	39.8	4.2	4.1
Voroshilovgrad	26.7	26.7	2452.2	2750.6	950.0	1148.3	38.7	41.7
Zakarpate	12.8	12.8	920.2	1056.8	29.6	35.2	3.2	3.3.
Zaporozhe	27.0	27.2	1463.8	1774.7	379.1	514.0	25.9	29.0
Zhitomir	29.8	29.9	1603.6	1626.6	87.0	100.6	5.4	6.2
SSR Total	601.0	603.7	41869.0	47126.5	7090.8	9126.3	16.9	19.4

(continued)

I:C   (continued)

	Area (1,000s of km^2)		Unit Population All Ethnic Groups (1,000s)		Russians in Unit Population (1,000s)		(Russian % in unit)	
Unit	1959	1970	1959	1970	1959	1970	1959	1970
Uzbekistan (Oblasts)								
Andijan	6.4	4.3	1163.0	1059.2	69.8	50.7	6.0	4.8
Bukhara	127.0	143.2	584.8	933.7	43.2	103.3	7.4	11.1
Fergana	11.9	7.1	1138.8	1332.0	107.7	125.1	9.5	9.4
Kashkadaria	-	28.4	-	801.5	-	28.5	-	3.6
Khorezm	4.5	4.5	380.6	553.7	10.8	13.3	2.8	2.4
Namangan	-	7.8	-	847.5	-	29.5	-	3.5
Samarkand	37.5	29.2	1148.2	1468.9	115.7	114.4	10.1	7.8
Surkhandaria	45.2	20.8	919.3	662.0	54.5	44.3	5.9	6.7
Syrdaria	-	23.1	-	575.5	-	81.8	-	14.2
Tashkent	20.6	15.6	1349.0	1478.8	265.5	292.6	19.7	19.8
Tashkent City	-	-	911.9	1384.5	400.6	564.6	43.9	40.8
Karakalpak ASSR	156.1	165.6	510.1	702.3	23.0	25.2	4.5	3.6
SSR Total	409.4	449.6	8105.7	11799.4	1090.7	1473.4	13.5	12.5
USSR Total Less RSFSR	5326.8	5326.8	91292.3	111640.9	16250.6	21267.5	17.8	19.0
RSFSR	17075.4	17075.4	117534.3	130079.2	97863.0	107747.6	83.3	82.8
USSR Total	22402.2	22402.2	208826.7	241720.1	114113.6	129015.1	54.6	53.4

Sources: Itogi vsesoiuznoi perepisi naseleniia 1959 goda. (Moscow: Gosstatizdat, 1962-1963,
repr. 1975), Vol. II, pp. 12, 168, 174-79; III, pp. 11, 124-27; IV, pp. 11, 138, 144-
147, V, pp. 12, 162, 168-73; VI, pp. 12, 134, 138-41; VII, pp. 11, 134, 140-41; VIII,
pp. 17, 160-63; IX, pp. 11, 90-93; X, pp. 11, 92-95; XI, pp. 11, 128, 132-33; XII,
pp. 11, 116, 122-23; XIII, pp. 11, 102-03; XIV, pp. 11, 128, 132-133; XV, pp. 11,
94-97;   Itogi vsesoiuznoi perepisi naseleniia 1970 goda. Natsional'nyi sostav naseleniia
SSSR, Vol. IV (Moscow: "Statistika," 1973), pp. 12-15, 152-359; Narodnoe khoziaistvo
SSSR v 1970 g. (Moscow: "Statistika," 1971), pp. 30-32. Data have been compiled by
Kenneth E. Nyirady and Ruslan O. Rasiak and prepared for this appendix by Mr.
Nyirady.

Index

About the Contributors

EDWARD ALLWORTH - Columbia University, Professor of Turco-Soviet Studies.

ROBERT AUSTERLITZ - Columbia University, Professor of Linguistics and Uralic Studies.

FREDERICK C. BARGHOORN - Yale University, Professor of Political Science.

ROBERT L. BELKNAP - Columbia University, Professor of Russian Language and Literature.

SEWERYN BIALER - Columbia University, Lecturer in Political Science.

RALPH S. CLEM - Florida International University, Associate Professor of International Relations.

BOGDAN DENIS DENITCH - Queens College and Graduate Center, City University of New York, Professor of Sociology.

WILLIAM W. DERBYSHIRE - Rutgers University, Professor of Russian.

JOHN B. DUNLOP - Oberlin College, Associate Professor of Russian.

OLEH S. FEDYSHYN - College of Staten Island, City University of New York, Professor of Politics.

WESLEY ANDREW FISHER - Columbia University, Assistant Professor of Sociology.

SHEILA FITZPATRICK - Columbia University, Associate Professor of History.

GEORGE GIBIAN - Cornell University, Professor of Russian Literature.

JACK V. HANEY - University of Washington, Associate Professor of Slavic Languages and Literature and Russian and East European Studies.

EDWARD KEENAN - Harvard University, Professor of History.

GEORGE L. KLINE - Bryn Mawr College, Professor of Philosophy.

WILLIAM BORIS KORY - University of Pittsburgh at Johnstown, Assistant Professor of Geography and Social Sciences.

LADIS K.D. KRISTOF - Portland State University, Professor of Political Science.

LEOPOLD LABEDZ - Editor of Survey magazine, England.

MARINA LEDKOVSKY - Barnard/Columbia University, Associate Professor of Russian.

ROBERT A. LEWIS - Columbia University, Professor of Geography.

ROBERT A. MAGUIRE - Columbia University, Professor of Russian Language and Literature.

VADIM MEDISH - The American University, Professor of Russian Studies.

MICHAEL AKSENOV MEERSON - Associate Rector, Christ the Savior Orthodox Church (Orthodox Church in America), New York City.

CATHARINE THEIMER NEPOMNYASHCHY - Columbia University, graduate student in Russian Literature.

KENNETH E. NYIRADY - Columbia University, graduate student in Uralic Studies.

NICHOLAS OZEROV, Columbia University - Assistant Professor of Russian.

MATTHEWS PAVLOVICH - Columbia University, graduate student in political science.

JONATHAN POOL - University of Washington, Assistant Professor of Political Science.

DIMITRY V. POSPIELOVSKY - University of Western Ontario, Professor of History.

RUSLAN O. RASIAK - Columbia University, graduate student in political science.

JOSEPH ROTHSCHILD - Columbia University, Professor of Political Science.

MICHAEL RYWKIN - City College of New York, Professor of Germanic and Slavic Studies.

ROMAN SZPORLUK - University of Michigan, Professor of History.

PAUL R. VALLIERE - Columbia University, Assistant Professor of Religion.

DANIEL VANDERHEIDE - New York University, graduate student in business administration.

TOMAS VENCLOVA - University of California at Los Angeles, Visiting Professor of Slavic Languages.